ROMAN
BRITAIN
through its
OBJECTS

IAIN FERRIS

AMBERLEY

To my two friends John Boden and Julian Parker
who I really should have seen more of over the past few years.

First published 2012

Amberley Publishing
The Hill, Stroud
Gloucestershire, GL5 4EP

www.amberleybooks.com

Copyright © Iain Ferris 2012

British Library Cataloguing in Publication Data.
A catalogue record for this book is available from the British Library.

ISBN 978 1 4456 0130 4

Typeset in 10pt on 12pt Sabon.
Typesetting and Origination by Amberley Publishing.
Printed in the UK.

CONTENTS

ACKNOWLEDGEMENTS

I have been writing about different aspects of the study of finds from Roman Britain on and off for over twenty-five years and in that time I particularly have been influenced by, and inspired by, the specialist work of Nina Crummy, Lindsay Allason-Jones, Jenny Price, Bill Manning, and Hilary Cool. Collectively their various published small finds catalogues and typologies of objects from the province form the foundation of the academic study of non-ceramic artefacts from Roman Britain.

In putting this volume together I have received help from a large number of individuals and organisations and I would like to take the opportunity to thank them all here. Firstly, for help in obtaining photographs and drawings for reproduction in the book I would like to thank: Dr Ralph Jackson and Dr Richard Hobbs of the British Museum; Sally Worrell of the Portable Antiquities Scheme; Richard Brewer of the National Museums of Wales, Cardiff; Penny Icke of the Royal Commission on the Ancient and Historical Monuments of Wales; Marina de Alarcon, Cathleen Wright, and Malcolm Osman of the Pitt Rivers Museum, Oxford; Professor David Breeze; Paul Bidwell and Alex Croom of Tyne and Wear Archives and Museums; Roy Friendship-Taylor; Jude Plouviez of Suffolk County Council; Dr Alison Taylor; Emma-Kate Lanyon of Shropshire County Council; Dr Nick Wickenden of Chelmsford Museum; Angela Wardle and Sarah Williams of the Museum of London; Dr Pete Wilson and Eddie Lyons of English Heritage; Ruth Fillery-Travis; Dr Edith Evans of the Glamorgan Gwent Archaeological Trust; Dr Fiona Haarer of the Society for the Promotion of Roman Studies; Dr Lynne Bevan; the Civic Archaeological Museum of Valle Sabbia, Gavardo; the *Soprintendenza per i Beni Archeologici delle Marche*; and Dr Fraser Hunter of the National Museums of Scotland, Edinburgh. I am also indebted to Julian Parker for scanning and cleaning up a dozen or so discrepant, sometimes poor, images provided by me and turning them into digital prints suitable for reproduction here.

Copies of articles ahead of publication or of difficult-to-obtain articles, and information on various topics has been kindly provided by Dr Nicholas Cahill, Alex Croom, Ruth Fillery-Travis, Dr Emma-Jayne Graham, Professor Richard Hingley, Professor Jenny Price, William Southwell-Wright, and Felicity Wild.

The staff of the Institute of Classical Studies Library, London, the Institute of Archaeology (UCL) Library, London University, the British Library, London, and the library of University of Wales Trinity St David's, Lampeter were unfailingly helpful in obtaining books and journals for my reference while researching this book.

As always, my colleague and wife Dr Lynne Bevan read and commented on a number of draft chapters of the book, much to the benefit of the finished work. At Amberley Publishing I would like to thank Alan Sutton and Peter Kemmis Betty, for commissioning this book in the first place, and Nicola Gale and Tom Furby for their editorial advice.

I was very tempted to 'name and shame' here a number of local authority museums whom I approached while gathering images to use in this book and who now presume to charge not only astronomical fees for the provision of photographs of objects in museums in their care but also further high fees for reproduction rights for those photos in books such as this. When this occurred unfortunately I was forced to change my mind about including these images in the book on cost grounds alone. These organisations are foolishly using, or rather misusing, copyright law as a way to more or less prevent the wider dissemination of information about items in their collections and, in so doing, stymieing their academic study.

Image Credits

Figures (see bibliography for full details of works cited here): 1 Drawn by Sandy Morris. From Ferris 2010, Fig. 63 No. 27; 2 Drawn by Ruth Fillery-Travis. From Fillery-Travis Forthcoming, Fig. 2; 3 From Woodward and Leach 1993, Fig. 225; 4 Drawn by Joanna Richards. From Woodward and Leach 1993, Fig. 76; 5 Drawn by Mark Breedon. From Ferris et al. 2000, Fig. 4; 6 Drawn by Mark Breedon. From Ferris et al. 2000, Fig. 34; 7 Drawn by Sandy Morris. From Ferris In Press; 8 From Woodward and Leach 1993, Fig. 88; 9 From Frere 1972, Fig. 49; 10 Drawn by Mark Breedon, John Halstead et al. In Ferris 2010, Fig. 86; 11 Compiled from RIB II 2503.100, RIB II 2417.4, and Ferris 2010, Fig. 71 No. 14; 12 From Evans 2000, Fig. 72; 13 Drawn by Donna Wreathall. From Plouviez 2005, Fig. 1; 14 Drawn by Eddie Lyons. From Wilson 2002, Fig. 260; and 15 Drawn by I. Bell. Essex County Council and Portable Antiquities Scheme.

Plates: 19, 23, 27, 29, 38, 39, 50, 51, 52, 57, 61, and 69 Author; 5, 7, 11, 15, 16, 17, 18, 22, 33, 36, 45, and 76 Graham Norrie; 1, 8, 14, 40, 49, 55, 59, 60, 74, and 75 the former Birmingham University School of Continuing Studies archive slide collection; 3, 4, 6, 9, 12, 20, 28, 30, 31, 42, 47, 48, 62, 67, and 72 copyright the British Museum; 10, 13, 25, 26, 43, 56, 63, 64, and 73 courtesy of and copyright of the Portable Antiquities Scheme; 24 and 32 Simone Deyts who I have been unable to contact; 44 Dr Fraser Hunter and the National Museums of Scotland; 53 Dr Ann Woodward and Peter Leach; 21 Richard Brewer; 41 RCAHMW; 37 the Pitt Rivers Museum, Oxford; 58 Professor David Breeze; 66 Arbeia Roman Fort (Tyne and Wear Archives and Museums); 46 courtesy of Simon Tutty, Roy Friendship-Taylor, and the Trustees of the British Museum; 70 and 71 Dr Alison Taylor; 65 Shropshire County Council; 34 and 35 Chelmsford Museum; 68 the Museum of London; 54 *Soprintendenza per i Beni Archeologici delle Marche*; and 2 Civic Archaeological Museum of Valle Sabbia, Gavardo.

I have attempted in all cases to track down the copyright holders of images used in the book. In one or two cases attributions of copyright were ambiguous and unresolved. Therefore I would be happy for any copyright holders that I have inadvertently not credited or been unable to contact to get in touch with me via Amberley Publishing.

PREFACE

This book is principally about objects from Roman Britain and about how they were used. It is also about ideas sometimes encapsulated within those objects and in certain artistic images from the province. By objects I mean here largely those items that archaeologists usually call 'small finds', that is objects or artefacts which generally, for reasons of their nature or material of manufacture, have been recorded individually on archaeological sites. On a site of the Roman period this will generally mean objects made of metals such as gold, silver, pewter, copper alloy, lead, and iron, glass objects, excluding vessel glass, ceramic objects, excluding pottery vessels, objects of jet, shale, or cannel coal, objects of bone, ivory, antler, or horn, sometimes wooden objects in the right environmental conditions, and objects made of stone.

The book is not, though, a comprehensive study of all types of Romano-British small finds; such a study could not feasibly be written by a single authority, so specialised are some of the sub-fields of the discipline. Rather it is written in the form of a number of interlinked and often overlapping essays, forming individual chapters, that together raise issues about how certain types of small finds are interpreted once they have been identified to material, type, function, and date. It is also about how sometimes these interpretations can be extended to weave a narrative about certain aspects of life in the Roman past beyond the realm of economics and production, consumers and consumption. Sometimes the viewpoint of the study is panoptic, sometimes microscopic, sometimes both.

A sophisticated culture of the consumption of material goods and a complex, linked system for displaying and interpreting religious signs and symbols were in place in the Roman world and are discussed in this study. I also examine the sometimes extraordinary use of objects and images in a number of religious and ritual contexts in Roman Britain and more widely in the Roman empire. The very presence of certain objects in the archaeological record can often alert us to social and cultural patterns pertaining in the past and, in the case of Roman Britain, this includes objects that might allow us to explore ideas about the self-representation of the individual, about views on the body at that time, about exclusion in society, and about issues relating to race, disability, and age perhaps. In many ways the aim of this book is similar to that of James Deetz's ground-breaking book about American archaeology, *In Small Things Forgotten: an Archaeology of Early American Life*.[1] As Deetz has written:

It is terribly important that the 'small things forgotten' be remembered. For in the seemingly little and insignificant things that accumulate to create a lifetime, the essence of our existence is captured. We must remember these bits and pieces, and we must use them in new and imaginative ways so that a different appreciation for what life is today, and was in the past, can be achieved. The written document has its proper and important place, but there is also a time when we should set aside our perusal of diaries, court records, and inventories, and listen to another voice. Don't read what we have written; look at what we have done.[2]

I would not presume, though, to put forward this study as a Romano-British equivalent of Deetz's book. Perhaps that book is not quite yet ready to be written while there still remains a partial schism in Romano-British archaeology between those who excavate archaeological sites and those who study the finds from those excavations. An examination of any publication on the results of the excavation of a Roman period site in Britain will show that it is still generally divided into two parts, the first dealing with the structural sequence at the site and the second dealing with the finds from the site. This second section is often divided into separate sections on artefacts and on so-called ecofacts, such as human bones, animal bones, charred plant remains, organic material and so on. There will usually be a concluding, third synthetic section or summary discussion of the overall results of the post-excavation analysis of the site records and the finds. The integration of the latter into the discussion in older reports in particular, though sadly not exclusively, is often simply restricted to how the finds inform the site chronology.

Obviously there are exceptions to the rule, but generally it is true to say that the study of small finds from Roman sites has only really come into its own in the past thirty years or so. The first major stand-alone publication of Romano-British small finds from a single site or place, from numerous excavations in Colchester, was published in 1983, to be followed by volumes on Roman small finds from South Shields in 1984, from York in 1995, from Aldborough in 1996, and from Castleford in 1998.[3] The study of Roman small finds has been further promoted in the last two decades by the formation in 1988 of the Roman Finds Group (RFG) whose newsletter, website, regular day-schools, and periodic conferences act as forums for the dissemination and exchange of information among specialists and students.

The Colchester small finds volume of 1983 was also ground-breaking, and consequently hugely influential, in that the system adopted for cataloguing and describing the finds was based not on their material of manufacture – that is, whether they were made of iron, copper alloy, lead, glass, bone, jet and so on – but rather by functional groups, in other words on the basis of what they were used for. Thus the seventeen main categories of finds consisted of: objects of personal adornment or dress; toilet, surgical, or pharmaceutical instruments; objects used in the manufacture or working of textiles; household utensils and furniture; objects used for recreational purposes; objects employed in weighing and measuring; objects used for, or associated with written communications; objects associated with transport;

objects associated with buildings and services; tools; fasteners and fittings; objects associated with agriculture, horticulture, and animal husbandry; military equipment; objects associated with religious beliefs and practices; objects and waste associated with metal working; objects and waste associated with antler, horn, bone, and tooth working; and objects and waste associated with the manufacture of pottery vessels or pipeclay objects.[4]

The beauty of such a schema was apparent from the success of the volume and it was adopted and followed on sites with sufficiently large numbers of small finds to make use of the functional categorisation system, though sometimes with changes to the categories as defined specifically for Colchester. Other additional methods of analysis of small finds assemblages have now appeared alongside the functional categorisation of objects, including correspondence analysis, as first used in studying the Roman small finds from York,[5] and spatial analysis, as used, for instance, in studying small finds from the Romano-British roadside settlement at Shepton Mallet, Somerset, the Roman fort and *vicus* at Castleford, West Yorkshire, and the Roman fort of *Vinovia* at Binchester, County Durham.[6] There has also been much more integration of the results of finds analysis into the overall interpretation of Romano-British archaeological sites, again as at, for example, Shepton Mallet, Binchester, and the Romano-British shrine site of Orton's Pasture, Rocester, Staffordshire, the latter site being discussed at length in Chapter 3 in this present volume,[7] though sadly there are still exceptions to this rule.

In the past thirty years or so, volumes have also appeared on individual categories of finds, such as the Roman iron objects from the collections of the Museum of Antiquities, Newcastle-upon-Tyne and of the British Museum, Romano-British earrings, Roman jet objects from the collections of the Yorkshire Museum, toilet implements, cosmetic grinders, Romano-British brooches, *intaglios* from Roman Britain, and jewellery in general from Roman Britain. Two traditionally structured books on artefacts from Roman Britain as a whole have also appeared.[8]

There is not as well-developed a strain of material culture studies in Romano-British archaeology, and indeed in Roman archaeology more broadly, as there is in prehistoric archaeology in Britain today, and indeed in British medieval archaeology and particularly post-medieval archaeology. Material culture studies first became important in the social sciences before the adoption and adaptation of their methodologies and theories into the field of archaeology and anthropology in the 1980s. Studies of the 'use-life' of objects, the 'paths and life histories' of things, and the 'biographies' of artefacts became common from that time onwards,[9] though surprisingly not in Roman archaeology to any great extent despite its heritage of high-quality excavated data. The trend towards the writing of biographies of objects in a way reached its apotheosis with Neil MacGregor's recent, astonishingly successful radio series and accompanying book, *A History of the World in 100 Objects*, and Edmund de Waal's equally acclaimed family memoir, *The Hare With Amber Eyes*, an account structured around the history and provenance of a collection of Japanese *netsuke*.[10] One wonders, though, if this quite apparent interest in objects from the past and from other civilizations is a generational marker and that the appearance of MacGregor's and de Waal's books marks a tipping point in western European society where technological change has led to a redefinition of which types of 'things' are viewed as being imbued with value by different age groups. These books indeed probably actually appeared in print a good few years after that tipping point had in fact been passed.

For a number of years I used to teach postgraduate archaeology students the introductory session of a course on finds analysis. My session had a tripartite structure. In the first part I would ask the students to write down what they would save from their burning house if they could only save one item, and would then ask them to talk about their chosen item and explain the reasons for their choices. Sometimes the chosen item would be banal and uninteresting, sometimes a student would misunderstand and save a much-loved pet, even though I had already explained that their family and pets had already been saved from the fictional burning building. Most times, though, the answers were interesting and engaging in terms of understanding the sometimes subtle and nuanced meaning of things, and thoughtful and perceptive as to the potential relationships between objects and memory, these factors being brought out by me in the concluding round-up of chosen objects at the end of the session.

The students' saved items included little of actual intrinsic worth, and included much inherited jewellery, glass and ceramics, family photographs, holiday and travel souvenirs, found items off beaches, stuffed birds under glass domes in one case, and a childhood rocking horse in another. Most of these items had stories attached to them; they formed part of a personal narrative for each student. However, in the last few years of teaching this session the answers came back more regularly simply as 'my computer' and in the final year almost exclusively as 'my phone', accompanied by the explanation that 'my whole life is on there'. Answers such as these killed any meaningful discussion of the individual's relationship with objects stone dead; the students' primary relationships were now with a technology facilitated by specific types of functional objects, that is computers and phones, and not with objects themselves. Information and digital data had become 'things' in themselves. The problem, of course, really lay with me, in that I had always expected the answers to link the present with the past and not simply be concerned with contemporary life alone. In many respects the design of many technological media devices today relies upon exhaustive consumer research of the most fundamental, yet old-fashioned, kind into the potential future relationships between people and technology, in the form of 'future forecasting' of material trends, 'cool hunting' for evolving trends, and the netting of trendsetting 'early adopters' who can generate emulative behaviour among their peers and wider and larger social and cultural groups.

The second and third parts of my teaching session continued to have some relevance to the students' lives in terms of making them think about how consumer choices of both objects and, in western societies in particular, food are part of a process of self-definition or group definition of some kind. The students were split up into groups of three or four and each group was then asked to examine the contents of a black bin-bag containing items of pre-selected and sanitised household rubbish, things like plastic sauce bottles, glass jam jars, empty tins of baked beans, empty packets of washing powder, jars of baby food, plastic shampoo bottles, cheese wrappers, and so on. The group then had to try and construct a profile and biography of the individual, individuals, couple, family, and so on who they thought had generated the rubbish in their bag, and justify the deductive foundations of their theories.

Following the construction of the biographies of these fictional rubbish generators, the students then were introduced to the archaeological case study of the recording by the anthropologist Robson Bonnichsen in the late 1960s of the site of Millie's Camp, a contemporary and recently abandoned Cree Indian temporary camp in the central Canadian Rockies[11]. Here Bonnichsen recorded both the physical layout of the camp-site, as if he was surveying and planning an archaeological site, and collected and recorded spatially the artefacts and general discarded rubbish and food waste around the camp. He presented his data as catalogue lists in his published report and then attempted to analyse and interpret his data in terms firstly of identifying who had lived at the camp, when, and for how long, and secondly in terms of reconstructing the economic, social, cultural, and religious or ritual basis of the group or community here. Thirdly he posited the identification of functional zones or sub-areas within the camp where distinct activities were thought to have been carried out. Bonnichsen's experimental 'model' of life at Millie's Camp was then 'tested' by his interrogation of Millie herself, whom he had met while camping in the area and before he hit upon the idea of recording her camp as if it was an archaeological site. Millie was able to confirm some of Bonnichsen's conclusions about life at the camp but also to correct a number of misinterpretations of his data, some quite major and leading to a chain of errors. In this way the students were led through the process of interpretation of an artefact assemblage, albeit a modern one, and shown that the basis of archaeological interpretation is always to do with accurate recording in the first place, systematic cataloguing, and deductive reasoning tempered with imagination.

Reading the report published on Bonnichsen's work at Millie's Camp when it first came out in 1973 had a profound effect on me as a student myself at the time, and opened my eyes to the ways in which material culture could be typologically and spatially analysed, rather than simply catalogued, and the way in which artefacts could be used to construct narratives that touched upon social and cultural issues as well as on economic ones, when viewed in their broader context.

Finds or objects are used in this present book to write an alternative history of Roman Britain in the form of a series of narrative snapshots of the past at certain locations and at certain times. It is not simply a story of daily life illuminated by the study of finds, nor is it a chronological or indeed thematic study of the use of finds. [12] Rather it uses objects to seek to throw light on a number of subjects often on the margins of histories of Roman Britain, about views on the body and the self, on self-representation through the use of images and objects, about culture as a driving force behind urbanisation, about marginalisation and inclusion, and about belief and fear. In writing about Roman Britain it is impossible not to also write about the wider Roman world, and the same is true when writing about Romano-British artefacts. Therefore in the book reference will occasionally be made to finds and artworks from elsewhere in the Roman empire, where their discussion can helpfully shed light on the Romano-British material being discussed or where a continental parallel is more apposite than a British one. Likewise, there will be a number of instances in the book where certain phenomena attested in Roman Britain through the presence of certain artefacts or types of artefacts are best examined through discussion of comparable continental material, particularly if such material is more common or widespread or if its study and interpretation is more advanced than for the British objects.

The book consists of eight chapters, starting with the introductory Chapter 1 on the consumption of goods in the Roman world and on the linked complex systems in place there for interpreting visual information, mainly religious signs and symbols, encoded in some objects. These themes are pursued in Chapter 2 by the setting out of case studies of the artefacts found at two excavated temple sites in Roman Britain, in Chapter 3 by the analysis of medical or anatomical *ex votos* found at Romano-British temple sites, and in Chapter 4 by the examination of the significance of prehistoric stone tools reused in Romano-British ritual and religious contexts and how past and present were here conflated. Chapter 5 is concerned with the role played by Romano-British urban centres in the creation and dissemination of written and visual culture, and of the arts and ideas more generally. In Chapter 6 an examination is made of partial objects and images from Roman Britain and the significance of the fragmented image or artefact in the broader geographical, chronological, and cultural context of the Roman world. In Chapter 7 ideas of the self and of the other are examined, with evidence from Roman Britain being explored with regard to what it can tell us about self-definition at this time, and about the possible marginalisation of certain groups in society, including black Africans, the disabled, and the elderly. The book concludes in Chapter 8 with a return to the consideration of ideas around concepts of consumers and consumption and how objects and ideas have been shown to interact in the world of goods that was Roman Britain. The book also includes academic notes and a full bibliography to allow those interested in any particular topic touched upon in the main body of the text to pursue that topic in more detail by following other sources.

In the process of dealing with these major topics a number of other diverse themes are explored which cut across the individual chapter boundaries. These include: an exploration of the special position of the sick in Romano-British society, placing them perhaps temporarily on society's margins as other; an attempt to examine the way in which self was defined in parts of the province and how this related to views on the body and personal hygiene and grooming; a discussion of how a sense of writing and portraying the self reflected back on those who were perceived perhaps as being other, in this case the idea being pursued through an analysis of the image of the disabled or deformed, the elderly, and the portrayal of ethnic Africans or black people; and an examination of the creation, manipulation, and maintenance of male identity through the demonstration of individual affinity with hyper-masculine figures such as the gladiator and the god Hercules and by the use of phallic symbolism.

The book aims to demonstrate how close readings of the contexts of stratified finds from archaeological excavations, of finds collected during structured field survey, and sometimes of those recovered from less secure contexts such as metal-detector surveys, can enable certain aspects of the past history of Roman Britain to be reconstructed and for some sense to be made of the nature of this world of goods.

I. M. Ferris, March 2011–March 2012
Pembrey, Carmarthenshire, Wales.

A WORLD OF GOODS

Shoppers' Paradise

Why people want to acquire particular things and why they might desire specific objects or perhaps be indifferent to other items are questions that can be asked about members of any society, ancient or modern. How these objects are created or made and then marketed and how people go about acquiring these objects are the very matter underpinning the study of consumers and consumption. Consumption is in many ways a series of rituals, marked by decisions around the acquisition of goods, whether necessities or fripperies and luxuries, or indeed both. Material possessions undoubtedly carry social meaning and help to sometimes convey ideas beyond those connected to their own materiality. Consumption is not only making gestures for marking personal or group status or esteem, it is also a way of marking, forging, or blurring identities, and a way to mark rites of passage, both calendrical, psychological, and religious. In other words, the pattern of a society should be reflected in its recorded and measurable patterns of consumption and in the objects consumed, that is acquired and owned. In this chapter the consumption of goods in Roman Britain will be considered, followed by an examination of the way in which goods in the Roman world could also be carriers of sometimes complex ideas. How these ideas were conveyed and how they might have been received is also discussed.

Frameworks for the interpretation of consumer behaviour and of consumption in general exist among the work of a number of anthropologists, sociologists, and consumer researchers whose approaches to material culture through personal observation and interview provide a dimension alien to the kind of object-led study to which many archaeologists are, by necessity, restricted.[1] In particular, Mary Douglas and Baron Isherwood, in *The World Of Goods: Towards an Anthropology of Consumption*, and Mihaly Csikszentmihalyi and Eugene Rochberg-Halton, in *The Meaning of Things: Domestic Symbols and the Self*, have shown that an understanding of the motives behind the acquisition of goods is crucial to an understanding of the wider social and cultural world and vice versa, for the two cannot properly be separated, and it is perhaps unfortunate that we so often study finds from the past in splendid isolation. Finds are not simply items that can be used to illustrate accounts of the past or to create a generalised narrative of everyday life then. It has been said that 'consumption is the very arena in which culture is fought over and licked into shape'.[2] Goods and objects do make and help maintain social relationships,[3] and they represent certain dynamic processes at work for an individual or within a group and between people and their total cultural environment. These processes can lead to either differentiation or integration of individuals or groups within society.[4] Objects can act as bridges or barriers.

An interdisciplinary approach to the analysis of historic consumption, interpreting patterns discerned by the study of basic historical data in the form of probate inventories – taken at the time of death and recording the household and/or trade goods of the deceased – has been taken by Lorna Weatherill in her ground-breaking study *Consumer Behaviour and Material Culture in Britain 1660-1760*[5] and this study can almost certainly provide a model for undertaking similar work on the material culture of Roman Britain.

While the value of any model lies in the quantity and quality of the available data against which it can be tested, a general reticence among the archaeologists of Roman Britain up to now to undertake theoretical studies of this kind seems untenable given the undoubted value of the database from the province. However, for Roman Britain we cannot to any great extent match the kind of data provided by Weatherill's inventories, with their room-by-room lists of items and possessions providing a snapshot of a particular house's contents at a very precise date, at the time of their owner's death. Of course, full archaeological excavation of a particular house or building can allow an inventory of sorts to be reconstructed for the structure's contents, as has been well demonstrated in classical archaeology in the case of a number of ancient Greek houses. Perhaps the only Roman period archaeological dataset that could possibly equal if not actually surpass such a richness of detail as found in Lorna Weatherill's historic inventory sources is that provided by Pompeii and, to a lesser extent, Herculaneum. Pompeian household assemblages can be reconstructed to a great extent from the *Giornali degli Scavi*, the daybooks of excavation, and the Museum Inventories of artefacts from each house, though these two sources are not without their own individual problems, elisions, and contradictions. It is true to say that artefacts and architecture are only two of the elements that made up the Roman house and the study of one without the other can impoverish our understanding of the functioning of such establishments. Certainly a tension 'may exist between the ideal of the Roman house, as evidenced by architecture and decoration, and the practice, indicated by the range, quantity, quality, and inter-relationships of the household objects. Acknowledgement ... leads to an awareness of the definite role that domestic artefacts had to play in the social and cultural articulation of the Roman house ...'[6]

Weatherill's study principally involved the examination of the acquisition and take-up of new goods in Britain over a crucial one-hundred-year period when an early modern consumer society can be said to have emerged. This she achieved by the identification of key goods which 'had to be reliably and consistently listed in the documents, and they had to be representative of other goods or of people's domestic behaviour'.[7] The goods selected for such further full analysis included 'basic furniture and utensils (tables, pewter, and cooking pots) to newly available things like china. Many of them, like knives and forks or utensils for hot drinks, point towards gradual changes in eating and drinking habits. Some, such as books and clocks, show something of a household's cultural interests and indicate contacts with a wider world.'[8]

Her analysis of her data allowed her to discuss a number of broader issues, both hierarchical and social ones, such as the roles of status, occupation, and wealth in the processes of consumption, as well as geographical ones such as the significance of place of residence, forms of regional variation, and the contrast between town and country. These discussions allowed for some analysis and perspective of changes over time, leading to an appreciation of the processes behind the spread of new goods throughout British society at that time. The potential worth of a model based on Weatherill's work transposed back to Roman Britain is considerable and will be pursued here using a number of archaeological examples. Though quite obviously objects listed in inventories and objects recovered by archaeological excavation have very different values – one is notional, a solid object represented only by lines of writing, the other quite solid and real – the broad framework of interpretation can still be applied.

Weatherill surprisingly found that consumption hierarchies and social hierarchies did not completely correspond, as might have been expected, with traders and merchants being higher in the consumption hierarchy – that is, tending to be the earliest possessors of new types of goods – than the gentry and others of a higher social status, indicating that the often-quoted theory of social emulation and display as a dynamic force behind the acquisition and ownership of certain types of new goods was perhaps too simplistic. Visually, the role of the new object as status symbol cannot be better expressed than in the Bellini painting *The Feast of the Gods*, finished by Titian in 1514, in which the gods dine not off gold and silver plate but off Chinese blue and white porcelain, still a rarity in Europe at that time (Plate 1).

The most obvious way to track new goods in Roman Britain would be to examine which goods were already finding their way from the continent to the elites of the tribes of late pre-Roman Iron Age Britain, and then further plot how such goods might have subsequently become desirable and available to a larger market following the Roman conquest. Such goods principally consisted of Samian pottery (*terra sigillata*), ceramic amphorae and their contents, and metal vessels. Coins are not classed as goods as such. The case of Samian pottery will be briefly discussed here. After its pre-Conquest appearances at elite sites and in elite burials, it might have been expected that this type of pottery retained its cultural cachet for some time afterwards in elite circles following the Conquest. However, this would not appear to have been the case and many non-elite sites in southern Britain are recorded as having Samian present, sometimes in quantity, in the pre-Flavian period before urban development on any scale. Either traders were actively and aggressively opening up new markets very quickly, or previously scarce, therefore perhaps more desirable, goods were arriving at sites through pre-existing networks. Increased supply after the Conquest through military networks was probably mirrored by non-military trading, and thus the status value of Samian soon became devalued in this part of the province. A similar filtering of Samian ownership down through the social hierarchy to sometimes quite remote, non-villa rural sites occurred subsequently a number of

times in areas away from the south through time. A process of status devaluation
that had been completed in the south by the Flavian period cannot be seen to have
ended in, for instance, rural Roman Northamptonshire until the second century.[9]

Samian in circulation may also have played another role in Roman Britain (Fig. 1).
The dissemination of Roman political ideology through the circulation of coinage
and the subconscious consumption of the imperial image and other imagery on these
coins was important. The appreciation of classical art and imagery in general in the
form of depictions on Samian pottery – which circulated in parts of Britain in the
century leading up to the Claudian invasion and in the conquered province up to
the end of the second century in large quantities – must also have been significant in
spreading ideas, even to sites quite low down in the social hierarchy, as has just been
discussed.[10] The role played by the consumption of imagery on Samian pots in the
development of a Romano-British art might well have been crucial.[11]

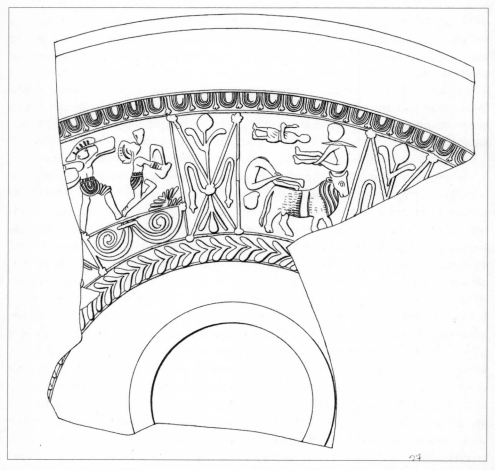

1. A sherd of Samian pottery from Binchester Roman fort, County Durham decorated with
an arena bull-leaping scene. (Drawn by Sandy Morris. From Ferris 2010, Fig. 63 No. 27)

In Roman Britain we can perhaps map also the possible routes for the introduction of certain types of key Roman goods by reconstructing the information processing network of the time. As will be discussed in more detail in Chapter 5 below, a study of literacy in Roman Britain as reflected in the distribution of *graffiti* has found that there were no great regional variations in this distribution, but considerable variations depending on the class of sites represented, with a hierarchy of basic literacy declining from forts and towns to villas and other rural sites or settlements. There is a very real suggestion that villas occupied a lower position in the social and economic hierarchy of the province than the towns.[12] Does the poor showing of the villas in this study suggest, as with Weatherill's findings on the secondary position of the gentry in the consumption hierarchy of her period, that there is some doubt as to the role of villa occupiers as influential social innovators in Roman Britain?

Weatherill's findings on regional patterns of consumption and the possible explanations for regional difference are also of great interest and relevance here. While she could not fully develop the theme, due to the limitations imposed by the nature of her evidence, she noted that 'attitudes to consumption and material goods can usefully be examined at a regional level, for in some areas people may have preferred to spend their resources on special occasions rather than in acquiring household durables',[13] and that in Scotland, for which there exists other documentary sources that can supplement the evidence of the inventories, there are well-documented instances of such conspicuous expenditure. 'Here surplus was consumed in excessive food and drink on a few occasions, rather than on durable goods or even clothing, again characteristic of a "traditional" attitude to consumption.'[14]

The general question of the regionality of cultures in Roman Britain is a topic which has been relatively understudied, with the exception of the study of local or regional pottery industries and traditions. Here discussion will be limited to a brief examination of the situation in the northern military zone where there existed not one homogeneous culture but rather four separate but distinct cultures: Roman culture; a distinct and separate Roman military culture; the indigenous local, native culture; and the culture of the *vicani* – dwellers in the *vici* or civilian settlements outside the forts – who were dependent on the military but who negotiated the space between the two dominant and predominant cultures of Roman and native. It has been suggested that the creation of this situation was brought about by the interplay between two strands of colonial policy at work in the Roman north, one encouraging cultural change but controlling the speed and nature of that change, and the other being the practice of social and cultural isolationism on the part of the immigrants, leading to maintained separate development, though under a unitary political and economic control.[15] There must, though, be a warning of the dangers of assuming the existence of a comprehensive and unswerving policy of Romanisation; there were, perhaps, more elements of *laissez faire* than social engineering at play.[16] In any case, other studies have indicated that the army was not an agent for a policy of Romanisation; rather this was a separate civil and, presumably, emulative process.[17]

The nature of the cultural intercourse between Roman and native in the north has been variously surmised. One authority saw little or no contact between the two dominant cultures and indeed adopted the idea of a more or less seamless indigenous culture with a lifestyle and material culture that changed little from the Iron Age to the post-Roman period. It was thought that some absences of Roman goods on native sites 'might indicate a conscious rejection of these goods by the indigenes'[18] or that 'they could not afford such goods'. A second authority, looking at the area north of the River Tees, thought that the local indigenous peoples 'were denied access to provincial civilisation even if some among them perceived a need to adopt it'[19] and that in the light of this 'the process of acculturation was thereby severely limited'. Once more it was considered whether the possibility of exclusion through poverty could be argued and it was noted that 'the process of pauperisation in many areas, particularly west of the Pennines, is reflected in the failure of the less well-placed communities to attract later prehistoric metalwork'.[20]

In a study of Roman and native interaction in Northumberland it was found that a number of small prestige items of Roman origin, such as *intaglios* (engraved gemstones), appeared on native sites but that few metal objects from the same source were present. However, the later prehistoric culture of the area was also seen to be relatively free of such items and that it was 'probable that north of the Tyne wealth was calculated in terms of cattle or by even more intangible means. Perhaps they concentrated on wine, women and song rather than on decorated metalwork',[21] a point also raised elsewhere with the suggestion of possible penchant for goods that left little or no trace in the archaeological record. Power, status or prestige among native Romano-Britons could have been manifested by, amongst other things, something as intangible and undetectable as the control of followers.[22]

Weatherill's identification of regional or local but otherwise well-integrated cultures, which through tradition retained patterns of consumption based upon more ostentatious and often relatively intangible consumption through display or ceremony rather than on a lower-level acquisition of goods, and evidence for perhaps a similar set of cultural priorities in the Roman north, are interesting to contrast and connect. However, it is almost impossible to define the role played in the mechanics of consumption in Roman Britain by the interplay between the differing value systems of the Roman and non-Roman worlds. The lack of any satisfactory method of gauging the level of poverty, and its effects upon the native population in the Roman north, also make the connection difficult to verify on anything other than a theoretical basis. While poverty does undoubtedly lead to cultural exclusion and dispossession at a certain level of society, the poor can also, consciously or subconsciously, use goods as social fences rather than bridges with the construction of a 'culture of poverty', a term first coined by Oscar Lewis in the 1950s,[23] in which spending on alcohol, on non-essentials, and on conspicuous display, rather than on material goods and often even on essentials, is marked.

In the native cultures of the Roman north we may, in many cases, be looking at sites or settlements so low in the social hierarchy that to use them as indicators of negative contact between Roman and native may be misleading; such sites would be part of what has been dubbed the sub-culture of Romanisation, where little or no cultural change over time should indeed be expected.[24] The true measure of poverty is not in possessions but in the degree of social involvement and the Northumberland data, analysis of which shows a considerable traffic of goods from native to Roman, seem to suggest that, leaving aside the very poor, on a regional basis there is an indication of a level of social involvement in the north perhaps over and above that required simply to satisfy the fulfilment of tax obligations. This brings to mind Heisenberg's principle that an observed system inevitably interacts with its observer.

Perhaps an illustration of how Roman material culture, in its take-up and distribution, did not always follow easily predictable routes in Roman Britain can be provided by briefly introducing two site case studies, both rural. These two sites, Maidenbrook Farm, Cheddon Fitzpaine, Taunton, Somerset and Whitley Grange, Bayston Hill, Shropshire[25] have been chosen not only because of the author's links with the excavations but because the first site demonstrates how regional variations in material culture were significant in Roman Britain and in the second case a type of site usually linked to Romanised culture proves that regional cultural trends could be perhaps stronger than social class.

The site of Maidenbrook Farm was excavated by the author in 1990. Here was found a long sequence of activity dating from the late Bronze Age, through the Iron Age, and into the Romano-British period, with some medieval, post-medieval, and modern activity also represented in the archaeological record. In the Romano-British period a farmstead was sited here, as had also been the case in later prehistory, with floruits of activity in the first to second century and the fourth century. The Romano-British activity was represented by a small assemblage of one thousand, seven hundred and forty-five sherds of Romano-British pottery, weighing around eighteen kilograms; three Roman coins; a jet hairpin and part of a second; part of a Kimmeridge shale bracelet; nineteen iron nails, some of which might well be post-Roman in date; sixteen fragments of Roman vessel glass, including part of a flask and a beaker; just over a kilogram of Roman ceramic tile and brick; two slate tiles, and three stone quern fragments. The Roman pottery assemblage was dominated by local, regional-tradition wares; indeed, only four of the sherds in the assemblage were from Samian vessels. The comparative absence of Romanised items of material culture here could suggest a number of things about the owners of the farming establishment. Firstly they may have been farming at a subsistence level, which did not lead to the generation of a surplus and thus of funds to purchase material goods above and beyond the necessities on the whole. Secondly, if a surplus was available the owners could have chosen not to spend their money on Romanised items that they did not want, with the exception here of the few glass vessels represented and the jet and shale items. While the Maidenbrook Farm site was some distance away from the nearest large Romanised centre, the owners of the farm here would still have had access to a wider range of goods than appeared in the excavated areas of the site.

A study of the broader Romano-British south-west has suggested that there was a discontinuity in the degree of Romanisation detectable on sites of this period to the west and to the east of the River Parrett, with the western sites displaying lesser, and in many cases no, manifestation of cultural change from the later prehistoric period, as reflected in the need to acquire Roman goods, and to adopt Roman styles and habits.[26] Maidenbrook Farm, a site west of the Parrett, presents a more complex example of a Roman site in the region, in that some items of Roman material culture have been acquired by the site's inhabitants, but these are very few in number and quite specific in their nature, being restricted more or less to glass vessels and black shiny jewellery, and there are hints of Romanised buildings having been present nearby.

At Whitley Grange, a site which the author visited several times during its excavation, a Romanised stone building, a villa by definition, with a bath suite range, at least one mosaic pavement, and an imposing presentation façade, was uncovered, with the bath suite built in the third century and the mosaic dating to the fourth century. The bath suite was more imposing than the residential quarters, which consisted of little more than a service corridor and three rooms. However, perhaps surprisingly the amount of actual Romanised artefacts recovered during the area excavation was very small indeed. If items that were structural are discounted, including window glass, iron fixtures and fittings and nails, lead fittings, ceramic and stone tiles, stone column bases and drum, and mosaic *tesserae*, only just over three hundred sherds of Romano-British pottery, weighing around four kilograms, was found on the site, along with one glass bead, four fragments of vessel glass, part of a copper alloy ring, parts of three copper alloy bracelets, a shale spacer bead, part of a shale bracelet, a whetstone, a stone tablet, a quern fragment, and a carved stone figurine.

While rubbish may have been disposed of in pits away from the main house, and the bath suite kept scrupulously clean, it is difficult to account for the paucity of artefacts present on the excavated parts of the site, given the site's undoubted status in the rural settlement hierarchy of Roman Britain. Roman goods would have been readily available for the villa's owner to purchase and well within his or her budget. The Whitley Grange site was very close to and within the hinterland of the major Roman town of Wroxeter, yet that relationship cannot be read from an examination of the finds assemblage from the site. Indeed, the non-pottery artefact assemblage is little different to that found at Maidenbrook Farm and discussed above, and in no respect more Romanised. It has been suggested that this was a relatively underused house, occupied only seasonally or periodically for some reason or reasons, or that a main residential range lies a further distance away from the excavated buildings. Thus a splendidly contradictory statement is being made here by the builder and owner of the Whitley Grange villa. Firstly they are declaring their *Romanitas* through the commissioning of a fine villa building with a show façade, by commissioning the design and laying of a mosaic pavement with a classical image of a Gorgon or Medusa at its centre, and they are bathing here in the Roman style. Yet, much of this is quite literally a façade, behind which this lifestyle choice is being played out.[27]

In many ways the Whitley Grange villa mirrors the situation in the so-called Wroxeter hinterland, a perhaps dubiously conceived modern concept based on economic models alone. Here, away from the undoubtedly Romanised tribal *civitas* capital at Wroxeter, the landscape would appear to be distinctly un-Romanised and lacking in true villas of any sort, even the faux construction at Whitley Grange.

Invisible Architecture

Objects in the Roman world were often bearers of ideas, sometimes encapsulated within images, that transcended the materiality of the objects themselves. Their acquisition and use, their consumption in other words, could have been a more complex process than might appear at first sight, and have taken place on a number of levels. Attention will now be focused on the way in which conceptual frameworks may have operated in the ancient world and the role of memory in the creation of the Roman world view, and it will be argued that the construction of a consensual social memory was an element of great importance in the maintenance of the day-to-day recreation of that world through the use of material culture, a process upon which the system itself depended.

Of course memory and materiality would have also been linked in some way in pre-Roman Britain, but in a different way, in a culturally specific way that reflected the traditions and mores of that society, probably on a tribal or regional level. In Roman Britain there may have been both acceptance and rejection of Roman goods and ideas at different times, in different places, and in different contexts; there may have been understanding of ideas conveyed by goods and artworks on some occasions and there may have been a lack of understanding or indeed incomprehension on some individuals' behalf because of their ignorance of a mental cultural framework in which to interpret and place these ideas. As Frantz Fanon wrote in *The Wretched of the Earth*, when discussing the cultural dilemmas and choices facing a native Algerian intellectual making an original artistic statement in opposition to the French colonial power, 'old legends will be reinterpreted in the light of a borrowed aesthetic and of a conception of the world which was discovered under other skies'.[28] This whole process, of course, would rely on the reuse or rediscovery of native cultural traditions whose value had not been eradicated or compromised through contact with the colonial power. Cultural, folk, or social memory was the key to rediscovery and there may perhaps be times in Roman Britain when we can see such a reclaiming of a pre-Roman cultural heritage taking place, as will be discussed more fully in Chapter 4.

If the culture of the Roman empire is viewed as a text, then an examination or reading of that text can and should be multifarious. Text is always interpreted, and not simply experienced, both by those living it and by observers reading it.[29] We need, therefore, to consider how the self-interpretation of Roman culture depended on a system involving the ordering and control of both mental and physical space, and how each provided the experience and security of returning to the whole. In other words, how could a system of encoding ideas in objects and images, and indeed in architecture and landscapes even, operate and how could those codes be read.

Formal mnemonic systems, devised for the transformation, mental storage, and subsequent recall of information, were used in the Roman world to order knowledge and to train and school the memory. While such systems were also in use in the medieval and early post-medieval periods in Europe, their value was by then being challenged, until they came to be viewed as little more than tricks and deceits. They nevertheless retained their value in some spheres as a tool or technique in teaching and learning. Transformation and recall were based upon an intermediary and the personalised imaging and visualisation of data in mentally constructed 'memory palaces'. The origins and principles of classical mnemonic systems were described and set out by, amongst others, Pliny in his *Naturalis Historia* and Quintilian in his *Institutio Oratoria*, and these authors explained the rationale, workings, and use of such systems in some detail. Quintilian, though slightly sceptical about the value of such methods, noted how chosen images and symbols could be mentally stored in 'buildings':

> these symbols they then dispose in the following manner: they place, as it were, their first thought under its symbol, in the vestibule, and the second in the hall, and then proceed round the courts, locating thoughts in due order, not only in chambers and porticoes, but on statues and other like objects. This being done, when the memory is to be tried, they begin to pass in review all these places from the commencement, demanding from each what they have confided in it, according as they are reminded by the symbol ... What I have specified as being done with regard to a dwelling house may also be done with regard to public buildings, or a long road, or the walls of a city, or pictures, or we even conceive imaginary places for ourselves.[30]

These mnemonic systems were intended for training in rhetoric and oratory, whereby complex arguments and cases, dependent on the correctly ordered marshalling of facts, could be stored and retrieved, not simply by rote learning of a text but by the mental ordering of appropriate images. Other applications were obviously possible.

One of the best examples of such a memory system in use, though in a very different context and at a much later date, is found in the writings of Matteo Ricci, an Italian Jesuit missionary working in China between 1583 and 1610. By this date the value and focus of mnemonic techniques had changed, and there now existed a strong Christian mnemonic tradition focused on memory training as a way to organise spiritual arguments. The life of Ricci has been considered by Jonathan Spence in his book *The Memory Palace of Matteo Ricci* where he states that

> by Ricci's time it had become a way for ordering all one's knowledge of secular and religious subjects, and since he himself was a Catholic missionary Ricci hoped that once the Chinese learned to value his mnemonic powers they would be drawn to ask him about the religion that made such wonders possible.[31]

Here then the system is seen to be almost representative of a wider social network and the way in which it orders knowledge enables it to order the world. As Ricci himself wrote,

> Once your places are all fixed in order, then you can walk through the door and make your start. Turn to the right and proceed from there. As with the practice of calligraphy, in which you move from the beginning to the end, as with fish who swim around in ordered schools, so is everything arranged in your brain, and all the images are ready for whatever you seek to remember. If you are going to use a great many [images], then let the buildings be hundreds or thousands of units in extent; if you only want a few, then take a single reception hall and just divide it up by its corners.[32]

At whatever period, these mentally constructed memory palaces would be filled with images and artefacts appropriate to both the time and the place and to the cultural milieu in which they were constructed; while the images would be individualised they would nevertheless derive their very substance, and ultimately their truth, from the complicity of some social or cultural group which would, if it could be said to have some form of meaningful access to these memory images, recognise its own mores, values, and story in them, for otherwise the images would be so much dead wood and dry straw.

To return to the Roman world, it would be true, if simplistic, to say that Roman power was based on, amongst other things, the ability to order the world through a process of interpretation of often ambiguous and contradictory phenomena, and to translate that interpretation into a new vision of reality. While most obviously this interpretation took place in a military or political sphere it was also achieved through control of the dissemination of ideas and information, through the mediation of art and religion, and through the potentially unifying power of certain elements of material culture.

All these elements coalesced to create a structure for daily life which, if interpreted through experience and memory as a whole and not as a number of random and disparate elements, would allow the individual to grasp, as Bourdieu has suggested, 'the rationale of what are clearly series' and to make it his or her own 'in the form of a principle generating conduct organized in accordance with the same rationale'.[33]

Ecstatic Celebrants

Art could sometimes encapsulate detailed and sophisticated information in an image, whose decoding in a way, perhaps, could be seen as a parallel process to the recall and interpretation of the value-laden images and objects inside the Roman memory palaces. Indeed, the ability to decode certain images, whether in the mind or in reality, was a mark of belonging, the stages of the process of decoding marking the construction of a map by which the decoder could find his or her way. This brings to mind Balzac's aphorism that 'the world belongs to me because I understand it'. Cultural alienation could result from the opposite process, for without a cultural map travelling becomes difficult, if not necessarily impossible.

As an example of the operation of the interpretative process I intend to examine here the research of Valerie Hutchinson on the cult of Bacchus/Dionysus in Roman Britain.[34] Hutchinson, not satisfied with the then-accepted view that the appeal and role of the cult were restricted, even in the Mediterranean world, and therefore that it most certainly must have been purely marginal in a peripheral and less sophisticated province such as Britain, went back to basic principles with the intention of identifying individual objects and works of art relating to the cult in Roman Britain. Although her study is now almost twenty-five years old, and more Bacchic-related items have been subsequently found in Britain, nevertheless it provides a statistical snapshot of carefully analysed data which remains valid, though, of course, in need of updating.

The god, who we will here call Bacchus for convenience's sake – though in the literature he can be found referred to also as Dionysus and Liber – was unknown in what were to become the north-western provinces of the Roman empire before their conquest and assimilation. Before discussing Hutchinson's research, a brief thumbnail sketch of the mythological life of the god will be provided, in order to allow the significance of various iconographical tropes described below to be understood in context.

Bacchus was one of the twelve great Olympian gods, the 'twice-born' son of Zeus and Semele. Twice-born in that he was saved in a premature state from his mother's womb as she died, burned by Zeus's thunderbolt, and sewn into his father's thigh till he reached full term and was born. Even then the life of the infant Bacchus was under threat from the vengeful and jealous goddess Hera, so much so that Hermes was instructed to secretly spirit the child away to Crete to be brought up disguised as a girl by Ino, sister of Semele, and her husband Athamas. The child is said to have consorted with and played with wild felines as he grew up. Almost inevitably Hera discovered his whereabouts and took a dreadful revenge on Ino and Athamas by driving them mad and having them kill their own two sons. Bacchus, though, was protected by his father Zeus, who turned him into a kid to elude bitter Hera, and took him to Mount Nysa to be brought up safely there by the mountain nymphs.

However, Hera's pursuit of Bacchus was unrelenting and continued into his adult life when, despite his adoption of disguises and his occasional shape-shifting, she succeeded in locating him and driving him mad, as she had done with Ino and Athamas. Mentally unhinged he roamed the world, visiting Egypt, Syria, and Phrygia, where he was cured of his madness by Cybele. His wanderings continued, however, taking him as far as India before he eventually returned to Greece (Plate 2). These journeys were not uneventful, and during his exile he enjoyed numerous adventures and encountered both friendly and hostile people, as will be discussed further below. Eventually Bacchus, perhaps surprisingly, became reconciled with

Hera, despite her evident childcare issues, through saving her from imprisonment by her son Hephaestus. Bacchus subsequently travelled to the underworld, from where he snatched his mother Semele who he took back to Olympus to live as one of the immortals. He married Ariadne, after her abandonment by Theseus, and at Olympus she bore him four sons. With the goddess Aphrodite he had a fifth son, the rustic fertility god Priapus. There are numerous other story strands to the myth of Bacchus, too many to go into here, the best known of which are probably his encounter with King Midas of Phrygia, who had helped Bacchus's elderly companion Silenus, and his granting of Midas's wish, more a curse, of turning everything he touched to gold, and with King Lycurgus of the Edonians, who was persecuted in various ways by the god for refusing to recognise and pay feasance to his divinity.

Bacchus was the god of vines and viticulture, of wine, of drinking and intoxication, of ecstatic celebration and ritual madness, of release from the everyday, mundane identity, the latter role also being reflected in his links to acting and the theatre, where masks and impersonation allowed the transformation of identity to seemingly take place. Thus music and dance, drinking, and carousing marked the celebration of the rites of the god, though a darker side to his cult was reflected in the acts of followers who 'sometimes, in their ecstasy, [tore] animals to pieces (*sparagmos*) and [ate] the flesh raw (*omophagia*)'.[35] Like many classical deities he was also imbued with powers linked to fertility and healing.

Thus within this mythological carapace of Bacchus's life can be found life events, exotic locations and travels, numerous gods and mortals, and symbolic tropes including the fragility and allure of youthful innocence, the transforming power of disguise and deceit, the delicate balance between madness and sanity, and between sinning and redemption.

Hutchinson identified over four hundred objects with Bacchic connections from Roman Britain,[36] ranging from mosaics and large-scale statuary to 'small scale statuary, engraved or embossed metal plate, figured glassware, ceramics, furniture appliqués, knife and key handles and other gadgets, ritual items and grave-goods, jewellery, amulets and charms', all displaying iconographic links to the cult (Plates 3–7). These portrayed not only the god himself in his various guises, his main mythical colleagues and attendants – including Maenads, Nymphs, and Satyrs, the latter including his tutor Silenus, usually on his donkey – and the famed Marsyas, his companion Pan/Faunus, his son Priapus, and his enemy Lycurgus, but also animals such as the panther, the lion, the dolphin, the hippocamp, the parrot, and the elephant with a recognised place in the iconography of the cult, as well as ritual paraphernalia such as the *thyrsus* – a wand of fennel rod with a pine cone at the top, ribbons around its shaft and ivy leaves wound around the tip – and *pedum*, and attributes and symbols, such as *canthari* and other wine vessels, and, of course vines and grapes. Lions he was said to have played with as a child and in whose guise he sometimes appeared, as with the panther; the tiger was a symbol of his Indian journey and his affinity with felines in general. Other related figures also appear, including Ariadne, his wife, Semele, his mother, and Methe, female personification of drunkenness, as does the so-called *Risus* or smiling child, masks, infant Bacchi, Bacchic *genii* and cupids. Indeed, in Britain there is represented almost every Bacchic image known in the classical repertoire. The portrayal and context of discovery of a few of the pieces represent instances of an *interpretatio celtica* of the classical cult.

The complexity of the Bacchic story, and consequently the large number of ways in which this could be portrayed or alluded to in religious art – in contexts that must document actual religious activity of some kind, whether public worship, private devotion, or mere superstitious practice on an individual or group level – make it a useful indicator of the processes of dissemination of classical religious ideas in Roman Britain. The ability to decode and understand the significance of some of these objects would be part of the overall experience of being a member or sympathiser of the cult, an experience perhaps indistinguishable from the overall ecstatic and celebratory drama of the cult rituals, while to others outside the cult or outside the milieu in which it operated, their meaning may have been purely visual and lacking any context of interpretation or explanation. It had previously been argued that many such objects would have been produced for purely decorative purposes, but in the majority of instances this cannot any longer be seen as a valid argument and, as Hutchinson has noted, 'an impressively large number of these British *Dionysiaca* are certain to have carried an active cult connotation'.[37]

During decoding, each representation could be seen in the mind as a static image to be transformed by memory into part of a larger pictorial sequence and narrative derived from Bacchic mythology.

Thus, for example, a knowledgeable viewer, not necessarily an adherent of the Bacchic cult, would be able to identify the individual figures and motifs in, for instance, the marble statuary group from the Temple of Mithras, London; the youthful Bacchus, the aged Silenus on his donkey and holding a wine cup, Pan, a Satyr, a Maenad, an accompanying leopard, and a vine branch and grapes. That knowledgeable viewer could then be able to place these individuals and motifs into a memory room in which was held the overall narrative of Bacchic mythology. An uninformed viewer would see simply a genre scene that he or she could not further interpret. A knowledgeable viewer would understand the simple image of a parrot or parrots, for example the pair of Indian parrots depicted on a now-lost Cornelian *intaglio* from Wroxeter, Shropshire and the individual parrots on the bowls of each of three pewter spoons from London. He or she would also recognise the significance of the tiger that appears on a copper alloy pelta-shaped mount from Walker, Northumberland below griffons' heads and of the images on two *intaglios*, one from Corbridge, Northumberland and the other from Caistor by Yarmouth, Norfolk each bearing elephants' trunks holding a palm frond, along with a head of Silenus.[38] That knowledgeable viewer would know that these exotic creatures were of Indian origin and place them in a memory room with other images related to the mythology detailing Bacchus's Indian triumph. An uninformed viewer would simply see respectively an unusual bird they did not recognise, a strange feline of some kind, and a fantastical, exotic creature from some unknown or far-off land or out of mythology.

Indeed, it could be said that Hutchinson's research, while obviously dependent on the systematic location, description, analysis, and interpretation of all relevant material in museums or in the period literature, primarily relied on her ability to decode the hidden texts through her own knowledge of classical mythology and to use her knowledge of Roman religion to place these objects in some overall cultural context. Previous scholars had perhaps not only simply lacked her dedication but also the academic apparatus necessary for understanding. Thus we may see here, mirrored in a modern academic setting, the same process of inclusion through knowledge, mediated by memory, and exclusion through the lack of the mental apparatus to provide a contextualising cultural, social, or religious framework.

Hutchinson mapped her data both geographically and chronologically and was able to make some tentative observations about the operation of the cult, previously thought to be the more or less exclusive preserve of the well-to-do in the major towns and the country villas, and about the mechanisms of its adoption and spread. At the time of writing Hutchinson noted that with the possible exception of the building that had been the Walbrook Mithraeum in London[39] and which might have been turned over to the worship of Bacchus in its final phase, there were no other Bacchic shrine sites then known in Roman Britain. As will be seen in Chapter 2, excavations managed by the present author in Rocester in Staffordshire in the 1990s identified a stone building on the site of Orton's Pasture which may well represent just such a shrine.[40]

Though slightly problematic in terms of the classification of some sites, the percentage breakdown of the distribution of *Dionysiaca* by site type is fascinating. From sites associated with the Roman army, principally fortresses, forts and associated settlements came 37 per cent of the items defined as Bacchic-related in Hutchinson's catalogue; from the major towns, that is the *civitas* capitals, came 28 per cent of the objects, though as she noted, the vast majority of these came from four urban centres only, London, Colchester, Wroxeter and Cirencester; from rural, non-villa settlements came 18 per cent of the items; from villa sites came 9 per cent; and from a grouping of miscellaneous sites came the other 8 per cent, this grouping including Bath, which today would be classed as a specialised small town.[41] Diffusion of cult knowledge would have been via trade and via the army; literature and imperial propaganda in the form of coins[42] would also almost certainly have been important.

Artefacts, Images, and Memory

In this chapter I have alluded to the existence of what may best be called an information system in Roman Britain, as reflected in the distribution of inscriptions, knowledge of the literary classics, the distribution of *graffiti*, and the significance of visual literacy. It has been suggested here that this system may also be further reconstructed through an analysis of the processes of introduction of new goods, that is certain classes and types of artefacts that are representative and redolent of quite specific cultural positions and assumptions. Such goods, most particularly items with religious uses or associations, sometimes could carry, and thus potentially disseminate, complex and sophisticated ideas, concepts, and information.

Of course, the role of oral transmission in the creation and operation of this information system cannot be quantified, nor must it be assumed that the material carriers of this information, such as epigraphic inscriptions, were interpreted solely within the concept of a linear progression of time. Certain inscriptions can indeed be read according to a number of different chronologies; according to 'the expectations of the reader memory orientates the biographical expectations of the reader towards the inscription and allows the reader not only to understand what they read but also to recognise something of their own experiences, and those of others, being addressed through that reading'.[43] Indeed, the power of memory, whether individual or collective, lies in its ability to defy linear time and to allow a version of the past sometimes to exist parallel to the present.

There is a need to distinguish between the structure of memories of dominant and subordinate groups, the dominant placing themselves within a linear trajectory of time, in relation to the past legitimating origins, and in relation to the future creating a sense of the continuity of power, wealth and influence. The subordinate will construct a different history, defined by a different narrative of life with 'a different rhythm [a] rhythm not patterned by the individual's intervention in the working of the dominant institutions'.[44]

The distinction and relationship between past and present in psychology and the way in which this can be reflected in linguistics and in 'primitive' thought is complex.[45] Indeed, the world of overlapping time sequences defining a contemporary reality, as opposed to a world where linearity alone exists, as reflected in certain inscriptions from Roman Britain, is but a step away from the surreal or metaphysical. In their writings and paintings Giorgio de Chirico and Carlo Carra, two artists greatly influenced by psychoanalysis, argued that modern man was driven by the same instincts as his ancestors and that beneath the conscious mind there lay a rich subconscious world of dream and fantasy in which the past and present were one. De Chirico reacted against the concept of reality being defined by physical and visible phenomena alone, a reality from which elements could be selected and reorganised to form a new visible representation. He strove, rather, to widen the definition through the incorporation of psychological facts deposited in the individual or collective unconscious and unearthed in reaction to external symbols (Plate 8).

Memory, then, must be seen as part of a wider cultural system that relies on a collective vision of the world, of reality, or more properly a series of overlapping realities that differ slightly in detail but which correspond in a sufficiently broad way as to present the appearance of a unified whole. In the Roman world there can also be seen to have been two interrelated systems for ordering conquered territories, one through the physical incorporation of landscape, taking place in sequential time, and the other through a mental incorporation of both landscapes and peoples into a shifting and adaptable collective vision of empire, mediated and transmitted by social memory, to which individuals, families, or social and cultural groups could adhere or subscribe, consciously or subconsciously, in whole or in part, or against which people could react, if little or nothing of this constructed memory related to their own situation, vision, or reality.

The developed, or mature, Roman perception of geography involved the taming of landscape by the building of roads and the subsequent creation of an infrastructure, including bridges, fords, causeways, planned and gridded towns, frontier works and so on. 'The geometric layout of the lands is measured, expressed and controlled by the celebration of itineraries across them. The formation of such axes became a familiar aspect of Roman attitudes to the empire, almost to the point of being a doctrine. It is these routes which gave shape and definition to the world,'[46] and along which ideas and information travelled. Added to this was the development of exact topographical recording of landscape. 'Very simply, the Roman perception of the place to be conquered and the process of conquest are so clearly related as to be aspects of the same mentality, and there is no need to disjoin them or to seek more elaborate explanation.'[47]

Creative building upon memory marked a positive step towards the making of new mental maps. Proust noted that 'distances are only the relation of space to time and vary with it', a variation mediated by memory alone until technological innovation became perhaps a more important factor.

It was crucial to the integration of territories into the empire that the native elites subscribed to the maintenance of the physical infrastructure, even if their perception of the rationale behind its creation differed or was relatively unsophisticated. Administrative policy and military and economic expediency were always underpinned by a mentally retained and imperceptibly shifting and mutating vision of the world that depended on adherence to a collective vision or social memory in which the elite of the empire could see their own story, whether expressed through cultural solidarity, social or economic concordance of interests, or religious practice. This was the motor for acculturation and is one factor in creating what has been called 'the unity and diversity of romanisation'.[48] Diverse tongues, objects, actions, and thoughts gave to collective life a collective form. In this situation memory created the only truly human landscape, as solid and structured, as yet inaccessible, inconsistent, and secret as the human personality.

In conclusion, it has been suggested in this chapter that for the Romano-British archaeologist the analysis of objects, goods, and images can tell us as much about ideology and symbolism as can architecture and inscriptions. In this chapter I have attempted to suggest that there is value in the application of anthropologically and sociologically derived models of consumption to the finds data from Roman Britain, and that more imaginative approaches to the writing of archaeological finds texts might result from a greater awareness of the mechanics of the construction of early modern consumer narratives. The understanding of 'the meaning of things' is part of a strategy for belonging or for deliberately opting out of certain parts of the social and cultural packages that constitute the matrix of any particular society. Belonging can also be enhanced by the use of objects in ritual and religion and discussion of this aspect of the individual and group experience of immersion in the world of goods that was Roman Britain will form the basis of the next chapter of the book.

2

A WORLD OF GODS

Dedicating Objects to the Gods

In the previous chapter the study of the consumption of goods in general in Roman Britain was introduced and the concept that certain goods could also carry ideas, not just in the form of decoration, was discussed. In this chapter the use of objects in specifically religious and ritual contexts will be explored, principally through the discussion of the use of certain types of objects as *ex votos* in Romano-British religious practice and through the examination of finds assemblages from two case study sites: West Hill, Uley, Gloucestershire and Orton's Pasture, Rocester, Staffordshire.

There is no documentation from Roman Britain to indicate how the process of dedicating items at religious sites was conducted, though a small number of dedicated artefacts themselves help to provide clues to the operation of this system.[1] The best illustration of the process of commissioning of a work of art for dedication at a temple, in this case a temple to Mars, is provided by a bronze statuette of the god found at Fossdyke, Torksey, Lincolnshire in the eighteenth century and now in the collection of the British Museum (Plate 9).[2] Standing slightly under thirty centimetres in height, the extremely well-modelled figure of Mars, resplendent in a high-crested helmet but otherwise naked, stands on a rectangular base, on the front of which is a long inscription. The god would apparently have originally held something in both of his hands, most probably a sword and a shield, but these items, which would have been made to be detachable in any case, are now missing. This reads, '*Deo Mart(ti) et Nu(mini)b(us) Aug(ustorum) Colasuni Bruccius et Caratius de suo donarunt ad sester (tios) n(ummos) c(entum) Celatus aerarius fecit et aeramenti lib(ram) donavit factam (denarius) III*', translated as 'to the god Mars and the *numen* of the Emperors, the Colasuni, Bruccius and Caratius, presented this at their own expense at a cost of a hundred *sestertii*; Celatus the bronzesmith fashioned it and gave a pound of bronze made at the cost of three *denarii*'.[3]

Thus it appears that the Colasuni brothers, even though they must have been relatively well-off to have spent such a sizeable sum of money as a hundred *sestertii* on the commissioning of the statuette, had struck a deal with Celatus the bronzesmith to save themselves further expense by allowing Celatus to become second dedicatee of the statuette to the god through his own negotiated generosity in waiving the cost of the pound of bronze needed to make the figurine and base. Whether the brothers bought the item off the peg, and then had the inscription added to the base, or whether Celatus was commissioned to make the statuette as a one-off original piece we cannot be sure, though the latter scenario seems more likely.

Another inscription in punched letters on a small ansate bronze tablet, this time from Colchester, records that '*P ORANIUS.FACILIS.IOVI SIGILLUM. EX. TESTA*', in translation 'P[ublius] Oranius Facilis [dedicated] the statuette to Jupiter in his will', the text indicating that the panel had once been attached to a statuette, dedicated in similar circumstances perhaps as the Fossdyke Mars. Other inscribed bronze panels from Roman Britain might also have originally been attached to statuettes in order to advertise the munificence of the dedicatee, for instance one from Caister-on-Sea, Norfolk reading '*A[.]RATTICI A[.]US MERCURIO USLM*' – 'Aurelius Atticianus willingly and deservedly fulfilled his vow to Mercury' or another from Brancaster, Norfolk, '*DEO HER*', 'to the god Hercules'.[4]

While most of these dedicated items were probably intended for gifting to the gods at a temple site or some other kind of formal religious establishment, it is possible that some religious items were intended for use in more private religious practice, that is for dedication and display in a home shrine or *lararium*. A great deal is known about home shrines in Italy, and especially at the sites of Pompeii and Herculaneum. Unfortunately, however, less is known about home or domestic shrines in Roman Britain.[5]

The appearance of certain types of artefacts exclusively at temple sites suggests that they were specifically manufactured for dedication as *ex votos* and in that case they were either specifically commissioned on an individual basis and then brought to the site by that individual or they were manufactured as a series of identical objects and sold for instance in the markets and shops of the towns, again to be then taken to the religious establishment for dedication there. The third alternative is that they were actually on sale at the religious sites – religious establishments and markets having some form of inter-relationship – were bought there, and then dedicated there.[6] At the Temple of Sulis Minerva in Bath there is evidence, in the repetitive formulaic nature of some of the language inscribed on lead curse tablets bought and dedicated there, that professional scribes prepared these tablets upon commission rather than the texts necessarily being written by the dedicatee and brought to the site for dedication. Perhaps this also occurred at other sites, such as West Hill, Uley, where curse tablets were also present.[7] If a business venture like this could be overseen by the temple authorities then the supervised manufacture and sale of *ex votos* is also likely to have taken place.

The criteria for the identification of ritual items is that these are either non-functional or unusual versions of artefacts, that many items of the same type appear in a context or on a site together, or that contextual associations suggest that a ritual interpretation must be bestowed upon a particular object or objects.[8] In Britain the dedication of *ex votos* took place in pre-Roman times at Iron Age temple or shrine sites; it may indeed even be possible to go further back in prehistory to see this as part of a ritual continuum from the Bronze Age dedication of metal items in so-called watery places. The types of *ex votos* known from Iron Age sites most-commonly include coins, both full-size metal weapons and model weapons, jewellery, principally copper alloy brooches, and pottery. Less common are horse harness and cart or chariot fittings and, in one instance, iron currency bars.[9]

In the Roman period the range, number, and diversity of objects dedicated as *ex votos* increased exponentially,[10] along with the number of formal religious sites in both towns and in the countryside. Cult statuary in stone and bronze and stone altars, both inscribed and uninscribed, became part of the celebration of rites at temple sites. Pottery, coins, brooches, and model weapons continued to be significant chosen items as *ex votos* (Plate 10). Other types of models now became more common also. In the north-west Roman provinces as a whole such models are relatively common finds but the sheer diversity in types of object miniaturised is striking.[11] These include, in order of common occurrence, wheels; arms and armour of various sorts including shields, swords, knives, axes, spearheads, arrowheads, gladiatorial equipment, military equipment fittings, even a snaffle bit from horse harness in one case; miniature coins; ceramic and metal vessels; lamps; tripods and stands; tableware; jewellery; other types of tools, and votives relating to travel. A final category is rather more specialised in use and appearance, the so-called *Mithrassymbole*, related to the Mithraic cult. Altogether new, specifically votive items now came into use, such as copper alloy letters, plaques, and sheet metal leaves or feathers in copper alloy, silver or gold, as did the use of inscriptions, formal writing, and *graffiti* on items for those who had acquired the habit or could pay a scribe to render their pleas or thanks to the gods in script. Visual representations of gods and goddesses as statues or figurines, sometimes inscribed, sometimes not, also became important. The range of jewellery items increased significantly, to also encompass bracelets, pins, and finger rings, as did the types of material from which it was made. A wide range of personal items was dedicated at different sites, including spoons, toilet implements, gaming counters, metal vessels, and candlesticks. Miniature pottery and clay vessels, pottery lamps, tazzas or incense burners, triple vases, lamp chimneys, and face or head pots are most often found associated with religious sites. So-called medical or anatomical *ex votos* also now appeared and discussion of these items will form the focus of Chapter 3.

In numerical terms the most common dedicated *ex votos* on Romano-British temple sites are coins and brooches. I do not intend to discuss coins here, as these lie outside my own field of knowledge. Coins as site finds are normally published in excavation reports in chronological sequence, with the individual reverse types also being recorded in the published catalogues. As far as I am aware, no study has taken place in which the emphasis has been on the numerical or statistical analysis of the reverse – that is the non-portrait – sides of the coin assemblages from religious sites in Roman Britain, despite the important role played at such sites by both written and visual literacy. For example, there may be some particular significance in the fact that coins with the *Britannia capta* reverse appear in some numbers in the coin assemblage from the Sacred Spring at the temple of Sulis Minerva at Bath,[12] but there is no easily comparable data available on pictorial reverses from other British temple sites. Attention will therefore be turned briefly to discussion of brooches from temple sites, and particularly plate brooches.

Two particular questions emerge; do brooches have ritual associations and are there certain types of brooches that have these associations exclusively? The answer to both questions is undoubtedly yes, though some authorities would be more cautious about giving such a positive answer without certain qualifications.[13] In this respect, plate brooches in particular are of great significance and interest, it would appear, though only one example of a brooch actually depicting a deity can be cited, a representation of Cernunnos holding two deer on a brooch from Thornborough, North Yorkshire.[14] Plate brooches, most commonly enamelled, take many forms; there are anthropomorphic examples, including one depicting a bearded warrior holding a shield, but most commonly in the form of the so-called horse-and-rider brooches; zoomorphic brooches, including depictions of horses, dogs or hounds, hares, cats, less commonly deer, dolphins and so on; ornithomorphic brooches, including ducks and chickens; insect brooches; and skeuomorphic brooches, most commonly in the shape of shoes or boots. Sometimes plate brooches appear in suggestive combinations, such as a horse-and-rider brooch appearing together with a horse plate brooch and one depicting a raptor with its prey.[15]

A third question regarding brooches can also be briefly addressed. Can certain types of brooches be linked to certain specific deities? One authority certainly believes so and has interestingly argued that certain plate brooch types have links to the cult of Mercury.[16] The suggested Mercury-linked brooches consist most obviously of cockerel brooches, the cock being one of his acknowledged attribute animals, purse and shoe sole brooches in certain contexts, and fly brooches. In addition, she also believes that 'horse-and-rider brooches refer to the Romano-Celtic rider god; horse brooches to the horse goddess Epona; dog brooches to the various gods associated with healing, such as Nodens and Ascelepius; panther, amphora, and flagon-shaped brooches to Bacchus; stag brooches perhaps to the woodland god Silvanus or the horned Cernunnos; and wheel and crescent brooches to the cults of the sun and moon'.[17] I would certainly not be quite so dogmatic in linking these types to specific deities but acknowledge the distinct possibility that this could be true in some situations.

Some years ago I published a paper on horse-and-rider brooches, following discovery of a new example on a site at the New Cemetery, Rocester, Staffordshire, where I was co-directing excavations (Plate 11).[18] It is worth summarising the contents of that paper here and bringing discussion of the distribution of this brooch type up to date and introducing conclusions from recent scientific analysis of some of the more recently discovered horse-and-rider brooches.

Horse-and-rider brooches are small and made of copper alloy, with coloured enamel inset panels in dark blue and red in most cases, generally no longer than about thirty-five millimetres in length. Some of the brooches are silvered. I have suggested that there are two principal types of this brooch, both portraying a male rider seated on a horse riding towards the viewer's right. Other typological sub-divisions can be made based on the application of a scale of simplicity to complexity in the delineation of the image and on the shape and number of enamel cells on the brooch.[19] The first type, in the majority amongst recorded finds so far, is a more simple type in which little attempt has been made to distinguish the body of the rider from that of the horse on which he is mounted. Simple nicks in the metal generally delineate the rider's hair and the horse's mane. The horse is stiff-legged and the rider leans back in the saddle. However, there is a tremendous amount of variation in form and size among brooches in this simple type, from a highly naive example from Lode, Cambridgeshire to a well-cut example from Brettenham, Norfolk. The shape and positioning of the enamel panels can vary, and departures from the most common use of blue and red as enamel colours are recorded, with green and red enamelling being used on an example from Ipswich, for example, blue enamel only on brooches from Brettenham and Lackford, Suffolk and red only on a second brooch from Lackford. A few examples were made just as a flat, un-enamelled plate with tinning or silvering.[20]

The second principal type is less common and is more elaborate in modelling and in finish than the more ubiquitous first type. It is typified by the example from Rocester, Staffordshire. Here the horse is caught posed at a canter and is modelled in a lively and spirited manner, with nicks and incisions indicating its mane. It has a tapering head, with flared nostrils, and caught in profile its right ear and eye are clearly visible. The body of the rider is differentiated from the horse's body much more clearly than in the simple type of this brooch and is larger in scale in relation to the size of the beast. The rider's head in particular is large and out-of-scale to the rest of his body and he sits more upright than on examples of the more common type of this brooch. The rider is quite clearly well-groomed, with a neatly trimmed beard and elaborate capped or limed hair, though it has been suggested, wrongly to my mind, that rather than being hair this is a crested helmet of some kind. He holds a stick or short staff in his right hand, not held as if it was a goad or a prod but rather as if it was a baton or mace, a symbol of authority and power. It has been suggested alternatively that the rider could be holding a sword, but this does not really tally with the evidence of the image.

There are now around 150 of these brooches known from Roman Britain, sixty-four of these horse-and-rider brooches being quite recently discovered at a temple site at Sutton Cheney, Leicestershire, discovered during a metal detector survey of Bosworth battlefield and its environs.[21] These appear there along with possibly two horse brooches, a raptor brooch, and a double axe brooch. An examination of the recently replotted distribution of the sites at which horse-and-rider brooches are found[22] shows that their appearance is biased still towards the Norfolk, Suffolk, and Cambridgeshire part of East Anglia, with the Lincolnshire and Leicestershire area now much more strongly represented from when I first mapped this type due to many brooches from these areas being recorded with the Portable Antiquities Scheme, and the Wiltshire and Somerset area providing a lesser focus (Fig. 2). Were the distribution described on a numerical basis, discussion would be skewed by the size of the cache of brooches in Leicestershire. The majority of the sites at which these brooches occur are recognised as temple sites, or at least as sites where religious activity is likely to have taken place on balance of evidence, even if no formal temple buildings have yet been recognised or excavated there. A number of other brooch find sites are contexts where ritual activity of some kind might have taken place and some, it must be made

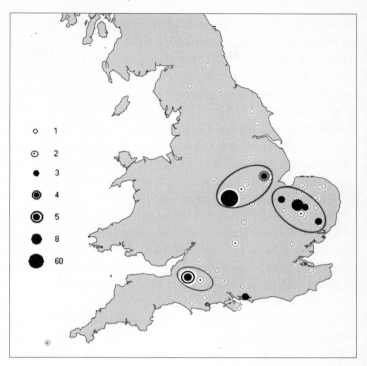

2. Distribution
map of horse-and-
rider brooches in
Britain. (Drawn by
Ruth Fillery-Travis.
From Fillery-Travis,
Forthcoming, Fig. 2)

clear, are sites where there is presently no evidence for religious or ritual activity, as at
the New Cemetery, Rocester. The brooches often appear in multiples, obviously as at
Sutton Cheney, but less spectacularly at Hockwold cum Wilton, Norfolk where eight
examples are recorded, Lamyatt Beacon, Somerset which has yielded five, Hayling
Island, Hampshire and March, Cambridgeshire where three have been found, and
Woodeaton, Oxfordshire, Brettenham, Norfolk, Coddenham and Lackford, Suffolk
and Cold Kitchen Hill, Wiltshire, all of which have produced two examples.

Recent scientific analysis of the large group of brooches from Bosworth[23] has
shown that the majority of the objects were made of leaded bronze, while a small
number only were of bronze or leaded gunmetal, meaning that they 'compare
well with established alloying patterns' for other Romano-British brooches. On
some brooches there was evidence of outlining of parts of the image on the plate
with soldered silver wire. There was no discernible difference in alloys used in the
manufacture of the different main types and sub-types of horse-and-rider brooch
and, perhaps surprisingly, no discernible groupings in the sample by composition,
implying the reuse of scrap metal. This might imply that the Bosworth brooches
represent a collection of some kind, accumulated over time rather than being a cache
of contemporary items from a single manufactory.

Horse-and-rider brooches, though not unknown on the continent, are few
in number there and therefore it must be assumed that they are a more or less
specifically Romano-British object. Dating is broad, with most of the brooches from

secure archaeological horizons being from third- or fourth-century contexts. The general phenomenon of enamelled animal brooches is dated to the second century into the third century.[24] It is interesting to note that enamelling as a technique had its roots in Britain in pre-Roman times and its continued popularity or even its revival in popularity at certain times may have had something to do with cultural recidivism or revitalisation.

With their distribution largely confined to rural locations it is possible that horse-and-rider brooches were linked to some kind of male hunter deity, though the image appears more martial than simply being that of a sporting huntsman. In classical art and mythology the hunt was itself symbolic of the life-course, with death waiting for all of us inevitably at the end of life's chase; this may account for the popularity of the hunt motif in Roman art in general and its ubiquity in many different media in Roman Britain. The so-called Hunting Dogs mosaic from Verulamium represents a good example of this trend, as does the common appearance of hunting dogs on Samian ware, subsequently on Nene Valley colour coat hunt cups, and on Colchester products. The denouement of a hunt, with a hound killing a stag, may be depicted on a relief from Bath.[25]

Hunting became a defining elite male leisure activity in the later Roman empire. A mounted hunting aristocrat appears alongside his two hunting dogs, their elaborately portrayed shaggy coats marking them out as Irish wolfhounds, on the late Roman etched glass bowl from Wint Hill, Somerset, driving their prey, a sprinting hare, into a catch-net set up in a lightly wooded landscape.[26] In the late Roman period such an activity would have been the preserve of not only the aristocratic landowner but also of senior bureaucrats and military officers. Indeed, it is likely that the three altars dedicated to *Vinotonus* and other altar fragments found in the shrine to the god on Scargill Moor, Bowes, County Durham[27] were dedicated by senior military commanders hunting there, probably principally officers from nearby Bowes Fort but also possibly officers from other Roman forts in the region, including Binchester.

If not a hunter deity, then the rider on the brooches could be a Romano-British equivalent of Mars, though he wears no armour, as might be expected of a depiction of that martial deity. He is unlikely to be a male equivalent of the goddess Epona (Plate 12). One local centre of a cult based on devotion to a rider deity has been found at Brigstock, Northamptonshire, where a polygonal and circular shrine of the third and fourth centuries forms the cult focus.[28] A number of bronze statuettes were found here, which portray somewhat belligerent helmeted riders, probably to be equated with Mars. Other bronze figurines and statuettes of male rider deities have been found, for example, at Martlesham, Suffolk, Willingham Fen, Cambridgeshire, from which three statuettes come, Brough and Bourne, Lincolnshire, and Westwood Bridge, Peterborough, Cambridgeshire (Plates 13–14). Two excellent examples have been reported to the Portable Antiquities Scheme, from Stow cum Quy, Cambridgeshire and from somewhere unspecified in Lincolnshire. A relief sculpture of a martial mounted figure spearing a monster has been found at Stragglethorpe, Lincolnshire.[29] The tight geographical clustering of the find-spots of these figurines and the relief ties in East Anglia and Lincolnshire very well with the already discussed apparent grouping of numbers of horse-and-rider brooches in these same two areas.

Of course, images of horses and riders also appear quite commonly in Roman military contexts in Britain both in the form of images on auxiliary cavalry tombstones and other military reliefs and on decorated pieces of parade armour such as the recently conserved Hallaton helmet from near Market Harborough, Leicestershire.[30] I have written elsewhere at length on the significance of this motif in its broader context but as this military image always includes the depiction of a barbarian foe being trampled or killed by the rampant Roman horseman it cannot be claimed to have any particular link to the brooch horseman image under discussion here.[31] However, it has been suggested that the military rider motif may partly have its origins in the use of such images by a Thracian rider cult,[32] though again it is unlikely that a regional cultic phenomenon in Roman Britain, as represented by the horse-and-rider brooches and the artworks from places like Brigstock or Stragglethorpe, would have connections with another regional cult at some remove elsewhere in the empire.

It is much more likely that the image may be part of a suite of visual indicators of the celebration of hyper-masculinity in Roman Britain, as discussed more fully in Chapter 5 below.[33] Images of hyper-masculine deities such as Mars and Hercules, Priapus, and hyper-masculine figures such as gladiators, soldiers and, of course, emperors created, fed into, or tapped into this mentality, as did the use of phallic imagery. As if to illustrate this link, in the Leicestershire/Lincolnshire zone, suggested to be one of three major concentrations of horse-and-rider brooches and of rider images in general, an unusual rider relief has been found. Recovered during field-walking in the 1970s at Long Bennington, Lincolnshire the high-relief carving depicts a male rider mounted on a huge, two-, possibly four-legged phallus, the rider goading on his unusual steed with what appears to be a whip.[34]

A Tale of Two Temples

The theme of objects in service to religious and ritual practice will now be pursued through the presentation of two contrasting, detailed case studies of excavated Romano-British religious sites, at West Hill, Uley, Gloucestershire and Orton's Pasture, Rocester in Staffordshire.[35] These two sites have been chosen because to some extent they represent two ends of the spectrum in terms of type of religious establishment; Uley a bustling religious complex that was run almost like a business, Orton's Pasture a more remote site and more a private shrine rather than a public establishment. Both sites were subject to modern archaeological excavation, although under very different circumstances in terms of the reasons behind the excavations. Both sets of excavations have been fully published and both publications were very much what can be called finds-driven, that is projects where analysis of the finds from the site was central to the interpretation of the site rather than acting simply as dating evidence for the structural sequences there.

Excavation at the ritual complex on West Hill, Uley, sited on the edge of the Cotswold escarpment in south Gloucestershire, took place between 1976 and 1979 and the meticulous examination of around two thousand square metres of the site led to the identification of a sequence of ritual activity here dating from the prehistoric period – the Neolithic period – to the eighth century AD or later. Twenty buildings or structures were identified and 'over 8,000 small finds, 67,000 sherds of pottery ... and a quarter of a million animal bones' were recovered during the excavation. Though it is the activity on the site in the Roman period that is of interest here, the contrast between the later Iron Age rituals carried out here and the accompanying material culture and the Romano-British rituals and material culture will need to be considered. The Uley temple lies in an isolated rural position, some distance off a Roman road and about two to three miles away from the large Roman site at Kingscote.

The Iron Age activity at Uley took the form of a sequence of ditched and palisaded enclosures, set in a probably sacred woodland clearing according to the excavators, inside which were two timber-built shrines associated with large pits containing deposited ritual material. Finds from this phase of activity included iron weapons, bone and antler tools, and votive ceramics in the form of miniature thumb pots. In the Roman period, in the early second century AD, the central timber shrine was replaced by a stone Romano-Celtic temple, which was subsequently enlarged. This temple lasted in use until the end of the fourth century when collapse or demolition took place, with a smaller, modified building then seeing use into the early fifth century. Related ancillary buildings, identified by the excavators as 'living quarters, guest accommodation, and shops associated with the use of the temple', were ranged around the temple. All of these buildings saw long use, modification and, in some cases, rebuilding. The finding of parts of a fine classical stone cult statue of Mercury unequivocally identified that god as the presiding deity at the site in the Roman period. Other specifically religious items recovered by excavation included figurines, altars, and both inscribed and uninscribed lead curse tablets. The make-up of the pottery and animal bone assemblages also betrayed important information about the religious and ritual activities that took place on the site, as will be discussed below.

The publication of the results of this excavation work at West Hill, Uley is important because it was very much 'finds-driven', that is the finds from the site were studied not just from a chronological point of view, that is to provide dates for each individual phase of the site's structural sequence or spot dates for individual contexts and features, as so often takes place in archaeological studies, sadly even today. Rather the finds were additionally studied from a socio-economic point of view, that is to allow a picture to be built up about the economic basis of the site, its trade links, and its place in the wider Romano-British market and economy, and of the social and cultural basis of the site and its inhabitants, which, of course, could quite obviously be seen to be centred around the practice of religious and ritual activity and the role that religious belief played in the structuring of everyday life here over an extended chronological period. Such an analysis was enhanced by the initial methodology adopted during excavation for the recording of finds on the site. At the most basic level, on archaeological sites finds are recorded according to the context and layer from which they are excavated, with all finds from one particular context or layer bearing the same code number assigned to the layer itself. However, often without the requirement of too much more effort, further spatial information about individual finds can also be recorded on site. At Uley the positions of all individual finds, with the exception of pottery and animal bone, which were collected by context, were recorded in at least two dimensions, with scatters of pot, bone and tile being further recorded in later seasons. Finds were spatially plotted on-site (Fig. 3).

By far the most spectacular find at Uley was the head of the cult stone statue of Mercury, found carefully buried in a pit (Fig. 4). Carved in oolitic limestone, the statue is purely classical in form and execution. Other fragments from the cult statue were also found, including parts of the left thigh and lower right leg of the god, stone fragments in the form of hanging drapery or a cloak, and fragments derived from a ram and cockerel, beasts that are usually depicted as accompanying the god as attributes. The reconstruction drawing of the cult statue, which would have been slightly larger than life-size, with the accompanying beasts being smaller than in real life *pro rata*, places a purse in the god's right hand and a *caduceus* in his left, as was standard artistic practice in the classical world, though no stone fragments of these two particular items were recovered at Uley. Part of another stone head was found and, though heavily worn, could be identified as being from a second, smaller statue of the god and part of the knee of a third stone statue was also found. A circular stone fragment may be from a fourth statue, not of Mercury, as may also have been a carved fragment of Italian marble. The god also appears in relatively crude representations carved in relief on two of the three stone altars excavated, one of these altars bearing an inscription, recording both the fact that, in translation, 'Searigillus [son] of Searix made this' and that 'Lovernius set this up and joyfully paid his vow'. Fragments from perhaps a fourth altar were also reported. Copper alloy figurines of Mercury again and of an infant Bacchus or a *putto* were found, along with two small figurines of a goat and a cockerel, and four decorative mounts or fittings; one bearing a bust of Jupiter, a second a bust of Sol, the third a bust of a horned deity, and the fourth a youthful head, which might be of Bacchus. Other overtly religious figurative material included two copper alloy feathered wings and three gunmetal legs, one with feet, and a sheet metal breast, the latter four items being medical or anatomical *ex votos*, a type of object whose significance will be discussed at length in Chapter 3.

Other votive objects recovered included six model *caducei* or parts of *caducei*, again items linked to Mercury, along with two inscribed votive plaques, six sheet metal votive leaves, around twenty sheet metal votive plaques of one kind or another, including one with an embossed biblical scene from the later deposits, fourteen miniature spears, a number of full-size iron weapons including spearheads, bolt heads, and a sword, over fifty copper alloy rings of unknown purpose, a ceramic altar, and ninety-four miniature pots.

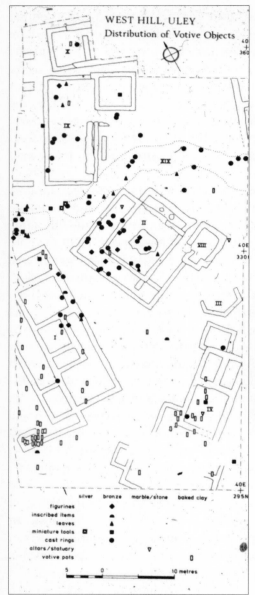

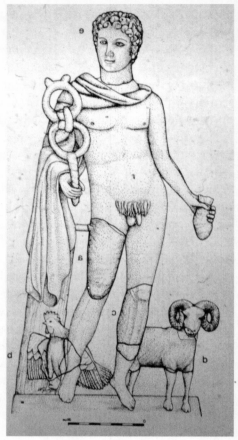

Left: 3. The spatial distribution of votive objects at the temple site of West Hill, Uley, Gloucestershire. (From Woodward and Leach, 1993, Fig. 225)

Above: 4. Reconstruction drawing of the cult statue of Mercury from the temple site of West Hill, Uley, Gloucestershire. (Drawn by Joanna Richards. From Woodward and Leach, 1993, Fig. 76)

Undoubtedly the lead curse tablets found at the Uley temple are of great interest in terms not only of what they can tell us about the nature of healing activity carried out at the site, but also about the nature of such formal cursing in Roman Britain when viewed alongside the similar curse tablets from the excavations of the Sacred Spring at Bath. Both sets of tablets provide social information about the hopes and fears, anger and frustration of those who visited these two sites in the Roman period in order to seek help and divine intervention or give thanks for all having been made good again by the intervention of the gods. One hundred and forty lead tablets were recovered at Uley, of which eighty-six had been inscribed on one or both sides. The majority of the tablets had been rolled and flattened. Some had had a nail driven through them. Many name Mercury. A number of them are concerned with needed interventions following a theft: Cenacus has had his draught animal stolen by Vitalinus and Natalinus, his son; Saturnina has had some linen cloth stolen by an unknown thief – 'whether man or woman, whether slave or free' – and pledges a third of the cloth to the god if recovered; someone has had a gold ring taken from their house it would appear; Biccus curses his thief that they 'may not urinate nor defecate nor speak nor sleep nor stay awake nor [have] well-being or health'; another has had their bridle stolen; another possibly a sheep; another vessels of some kind; Docilinus complains to Mercury of harm done to his beast and asks that the named perpetrators be forced by death or ill health to make recompense; another has had wool stolen; another a cloak and other clothing; poor Honoratus has lost 'two wheels and the cows which I keep and several chattels from my house'; another has lost grain; one asks Mercury for help against 'those who plan evil against me'; one man has been defrauded 'of the *denarii* he owes me' and offers the god one hundred thousand *denarii* for its return while the fraudster is cursed to be made 'half-naked, toothless, tremulous, gouty'; and two pewter plates are recorded on one curse tablet as having been stolen, with half to be given to the god on the plates' return and ill-health to be visited on the thief. It need not be surprising how many of the Uley tablets are concerned with rural life or agricultural practice; for example, with a beast of burden, a bridle, a farm animal which has been bewitched, two wheels and four cows, a sheep apparently, and certainly some wool and two pieces of linen.[36]

There were almost three thousand coins from the site, all redeposited from what would have been their original context inside the temple as offerings. Such a large number of coins, particularly from the period AD 348–64, implies either a massive increase in visitors to the site at this time or the dedication of a large hoard of coins here in one act in this period, or a combination of both.

Other personal items probably dedicated as *ex votos* at the site include thirty-six brooches, perhaps fewer than might have been expected here; six enamelled plates or discs of uncertain function; almost ninety glass beads; five jet beads and one of antler; parts of five necklaces; four earrings; forty-three copper alloy bracelets; twenty-eight jet and shale bracelets; twenty-seven hairpins of silver, copper alloy, jet, and bone; thirty-one metal finger rings; seven jet finger rings; a pendant; some chain; a mirror; fifteen metal spoons; six toilet implements; perhaps fourteen gaming counters; a bone comb, and a razor. Of these three hundred and twenty-three objects, perhaps around two hundred are female-related items, though this figure is somewhat skewed by counting the beads as individual items when many of them together would have made up necklaces.

At West Hill, Uley analysis of the pottery assemblage of over sixty-seven thousand sherds showed that most of the assemblage consisted of coarse-wares of a domestic nature, principally jars, bowls, dishes, and amphorae. Tableware formed a high proportion of the assemblage, while storage vessels were less well-represented. With the obvious exception of a large number of miniature ceramic vessels – almost like thumb-pots – there were no unusual vessels in the pottery assemblage – apart from the occasional example of a pot with a drilled or pierced base, perhaps to allow liquid to escape as part of a libation or to strain something – to suggest that these were anything other than domestic pots produced for the domestic market and only made extraordinary by their final use and destruction here at Uley temple. Almost a thousand pieces of vessel glass were also found, again this assemblage being classed as functional in its make-up.

The Uley animal bone assemblage of over two hundred and thirty thousand fragments provided fascinating information on the activities carried out at the site. The assemblage, unusually large for what is after all a rural site, is dominated by sheep and particularly goat bones, and an unusually high percentage of domestic fowl bones. Among those, the high proportion of male sheep, goats, and fowl, a notable seasonal peak in the killing of these creatures, and a concentration on removing the horn-cores of the sheep and goats all point towards this being largely a votive assemblage derived from selection and sacrifice.

The distribution of finds at the site has been discussed by both the excavators and subsequently by other researchers.[37] In the late Iron Age to Roman transitional period a number of 'offering zones', as they have been termed, were identified by the presence of higher proportions of probably votive finds, one of these foci being a feature identified as a pool or pond of some kind. The artefact assemblages recovered here hinted at a hunting focus rather than a martial one, this feature perhaps continuing into the later Roman period. More Romanised offerings such as coins and amphorae marked the change to a Romano-British religious site.

In the Roman period proper, Structure IV of Phase 4 had an offering concentration of small votive pots, inscribed lead curse tablets and finger rings, pins and many jet/shale items, and could have been a focus for votive dedication. A scatter of items in the courtyard in front of the actual temple suggests its active use. In Phase 5a-c, Structure IX houses the majority of the finds but not votive pots or lead tablets. The destruction levels of Structure I included many pots, inscribed tablets, coins and personal items. As for the temple itself, only in Phase 6 do numbers of votive items occur in any great number, with a concentration of objects towards the rear of the *cella* from Phase 5d-e. Miniature pots and lead tablets are most prevalent up until Phase 6, when superseded by simpler items such as copper alloy rings and metal plaques. A clear front/rear dichotomy existed at the site, on either side of the central, focal temple.

The village of Rocester in east Staffordshire betrays in its place name its origins as a Roman fort. Excavations inside the fort at the New Cemetery site, by the present author and my then-colleague Simon Esmonde Cleary, have shown that there were three successive Roman forts here, their foundations dating to around AD 100, AD 110–130, and AD 140–160 to 200.[38] Outside the fort, to the south, north, and west, lay functionally distinct zones comprising a *vicus* or civilian settlement. The *vicus* area to the south, which includes the Orton's Pasture site, appears to have been a religious zone during one phase of its existence. The author was also involved in the archaeological work at Orton's Pasture and in the publication of the results of that work. Evaluation here ahead of a housing development confirmed that extensive Roman remains were present on the site. An area strip of the topsoil revealed that within the site lay parts of two large enclosures, one lying just ten metres to the south of the other, separated by a trackway. The northernmost enclosure, Enclosure 1, was at least seventy-five metres in length north–south and at least sixty-five metres east–west, with a trackway running outside it to the east; the southern enclosure, Enclosure 2, being at least ninety-five metres north–south and again at least sixty-five metres east–west. Both were defined by boundary ditches, with evidence in places, particularly along the northern boundary of the southern enclosure, for the re-cutting or redefining of the enclosure ditch on at least three further occasions. Large pits lay in clustered groups inside both enclosures. A small, rectangular stone building lay inside the north-east angle of Enclosure 2 (Fig. 5). The creation and use of the enclosures constituted Phase 1 on the site and it is this phase of activity, dating from around AD 95 to around AD 130, which will be discussed in detail here.

In the published report on the excavations I chose to try and interpret the site in two distinct ways – what I called the minimalist interpretation and the maximalist interpretation – and to present each of these interpretations side by side in the report. This was a quite deliberate strategy to demonstrate that overly cautious approaches to archaeological data and the simple presentation of basic data alone – the minimalist interpretation – cannot necessarily allow the archaeologist or reader of a report to fully get to grips with how this data can be used to translate a list of indisputable facts into a narrative account. In the maximalist account I attempted to broaden the interpretation of the basic data to include a number of theoretical perspectives on the evidence and to produce a developed narrative account, and it is this fuller interpretation that I will follow here.

At the Orton's Pasture site, in Phase 1, there were detected repetitive and significant patterns and rhythms within the structural, artefactual, and ecofactual assemblages – some contradictory, some complementary, and some dissonant – whose interpretation can be translated into a story in which a coherent set of actions and activities emerges that encompasses both the sacred and the profane, the banal and the extraordinary, much as life in the ancient world may itself have been structured (Fig. 6).

A basic description of the layout of the two Phase 1 enclosures has already been given above. The key to perhaps understanding, or at least starting to understand the nature of the Phase 1 activity at Orton's Pasture lies in the analysis of the recovered artefacts and environmental material, and the comparison of the material between the two enclosures at Orton's Pasture and with the assemblages from the fort interior excavation at the New Cemetery site. Only then can an interpretation of the structural evidence be offered.

In contrast to the total non-structural finds assemblage from West Hill, Uley discussed above, the total Roman non-structural finds assemblage from Orton's Pasture is very small indeed. It consists of just over seven thousand sherds of pottery; around ninety pieces of vessel glass; a ceramic lamp decorated with an image of Bacchus and a feline; a copper alloy *patera* handle, again decorated with Bacchic motifs; one coin;

two brooches; two glass beads; parts of three bone pins and two copper alloy pins; a copper alloy spoon; a lock bolt; a key; a copper alloy handle; a few studs and mounts; a bone strip; a bone knife handle; perhaps six iron tools, including a chisel and a hoe; part of a stone altar, and a fragment of quern-stone (Plates 15–17). From Phase 1 there were just over two hundred countable animal bone fragments but highly interesting charred plant remains, including those of the Stone Pine (*Pinus Pinea*), dates, grapes, and apple or pear, along with cereal and wild plant remains.

If a very rough comparison is made between the make-up of the overall finds assemblages from the Orton's Pasture site and the New Cemetery fort site at Rocester, some interesting differences emerge in the character of the two assemblages, which may say something about the differing functions of each site. There were too few small finds from Orton's Pasture to allow the kind of grouping by functional category applied so successfully to large Roman assemblages from Colchester and York. So a numerical count was made of all categories of finds from both sites to allow direct

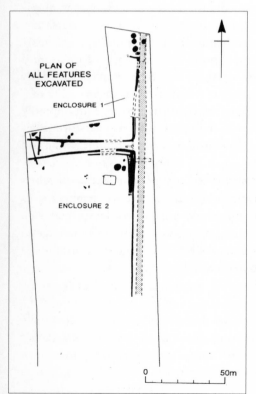
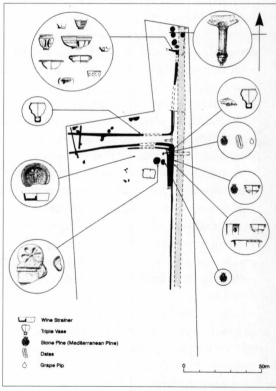

Above left: 5. Layout of the enclosures at Orton's Pasture, Rocester, Staffordshire. (Drawn by Mark Breedon. From Ferris *et al.*, 2000, Fig. 4)

Above right: 6. Spatial distribution of finds at Orton's Pasture, Rocester, Staffordshire. (Drawn by Mark Breedon. From Ferris *et al.*, 2000, Fig. 34)

comparison to be made between them. Samian pottery, amphorae, mortaria, and coarse pottery was quantified and compared by sherd count; coins, iron nails and other iron objects, copper alloy objects, lead, bone, and glass objects were counted; glass vessels were quantified by fragment count. The total number of items making up each assemblage was then calculated and the percentage representation of each category of material or object in each assemblage was calculated. Percentage-wise there was a noticeably greater amount of all types of pottery at Orton's Pasture, with the exception of mortaria. Most of the glass was vessel glass, which at Orton's Pasture was less well represented than inside the fort. Percentages of copper alloy and lead objects were remarkably similar, though at Orton's Pasture there were, percentage-wise, fewer iron objects and nails.

Thus the functional differences between the assemblages can be seen to be quite marked in certain respects. At Orton's Pasture a greater percentage of vessels of one kind or another were in use or were disposed of here, though fewer of these were mortaria and glass vessels. Fewer iron objects were in use and given that objects in this material tended towards utilitarian functions, whether civilian or military in context, this would suggest that certain activities were not carried out at the site. Markedly fewer iron nails perhaps suggests that there may not have been any significant number of timber buildings within the enclosures at Orton's Pasture, and that, though deep ploughing had in certain respects denuded the site over the years, it may not have removed evidence of former timber structures here, as was at one time feared. A generally low number of small finds at Orton's Pasture again probably says something about the nature of activity carried out here, with few personal items being present, only one coin, and only two stone objects, a fragment of an altar and a fragment of a quern-stone, though the appearance of bone objects here, totally absent inside the fort, may be significant. Given that forty-five of the forty-seven stone objects from the fort were pieces of quern-stones, the virtual absence of such utilitarian objects from Orton's Pasture would again seem to be significant. If an additional element of comparison is introduced, by adding the number of animal bones and bone fragments to the totals for each assemblage and then looking at the bone assemblages as percentages of the whole, again an interesting contrast emerges. In the fort, animal bone represents around 11 per cent of the total assemblage by count and at Orton's Pasture less than 5 per cent.

Attention will now be focused on looking at the Orton's Pasture assemblage itself. Certain patterns are immediately discernible among the artefactual and environmental material, and there is a distinct difference apparent between the finds assemblages from the northern and southern enclosures, which may be a reflection of a difference in their functions.

The pottery assemblage includes a higher number of whole or almost complete pots than might have been expected on a domestic or settlement site, and certainly were the site to represent a venue at which rubbish from off-site was disposed of and buried, the reconstruction of these vessels would probably not have been possible. The large average size of sherds from the stratified deposits of Phase 1 and the unabraded breaks on most of the sherds recovered in contexts in pit fills again suggests that the majority of this material was both used on-site, broken on-site, and buried straight after its breaking. In some cases pots were buried whole.

Types of vessels represented both at the fort site and at Orton's Pasture can be broken down into four functional categories: tableware – dishes, platters, bowls, beakers, and flagons; storage vessels – jars and amphorae; food preparation vessels – mortaria; and miscellaneous vessels – tazzas, lamps, inkwells, wine strainers/presses, face pots, triple vases, and miniature pots. Of the overall assemblage at Orton's Pasture, tableware represented around 43 per cent, storage vessels 51.5 per cent, food preparation vessels around 4.8 per cent, and miscellaneous vessels 0.7 per cent. In contrast, at the fort site tableware represented around 47 per cent, storage vessels 40 per cent, food preparation vessels 13 per cent, and miscellaneous vessels around 0.1 per cent. Therefore it can be seen that at Orton's Pasture there were more storage vessels proportionally and fewer tableware, fewer food preparation vessels, and more of the specialised miscellaneous vessels, though it is realised that some types of vessels could be assigned to more than one functional category in this exercise.

The Orton's Pasture pottery assemblage also included more unusual and specialised vessels than might have been expected on an occupation site, whether military or civilian. These included four tazzas; a plain ceramic lamp; an imported ceramic lamp with Bacchic decoration; a fifth tazza, customised to turn it into what would appear to be a candlestick; parts of two triple vases; a face pot; a wine strainer; part of a segmented tray, which it has been suggested could conversely have been inverted to form a ceramic stand or table or even have been a portable offerings stand, and a copper alloy Bacchic-associated *patera* handle (Plate 18). The presence of these more exotic vessels, though in some cases they were recovered from residual or unstratified deposits, nevertheless marks out the assemblage as being in many ways unusual. Inside the fort unusual vessels were not entirely absent though, with a plain ceramic lamp, a tazza, a ceramic wine strainer, and a copper alloy Bacchic-motif-decorated jug handle being present.[39]

Tazzas and lamps are relatively common finds on temple sites and in contexts where religious and ritual activity is presumed to have taken place. They are also found, however, in domestic contexts, though this is altogether less common, though as noted above occurring inside the Rocester fort. One of the best examples of these vessels being unequivocally tied in to religious practice is at the so-called triangular temple at Verulamium from where, amongst a significant assemblage of religious material, a number of tazzas and what were considered to be tazza lids were recovered, as well as ceramic lamps.[40] Much of the other pottery from the site, though, was strictly utilitarian and would not have been out of place in a domestic context, something that can generally be observed of most temple site pottery assemblages. The characterisation of a ceramic assemblage as being connected to a religious site must then be based on the overall make-up of the assemblage and of its association with other materials, though even then definite assignation is not always possible, as was discussed above in relation to West Hill, Uley, and as also applies in the case of Henley Wood, Somerset. The Verulamium triangular temple site also provides a parallel for the appearance of Stone Pine in a ritual context.[41]

Some interesting observations have been made on the occurrence and distribution of various types of unusual pottery vessels found in York.[42] Tazzas, although interpreted as being 'clear indicators of ritual activity', their commonly burned interiors suggesting their use as incense burners, have a distribution across the city determined more by the date of activity rather than by functional zoning apparent in the archaeological record. However, the distribution of ceramic lamps and head pots is markedly biased at York towards the extramural zones and the Blake Street site, 'both of which had high levels of ritual activity'. Ceramic candlesticks would again at York appear to be related to zones of ritual activity. The relative rarity of both face pots and triple vases in the massive York pottery assemblage, while it may reflect a cultural choice not to use such vessels, may more likely serve to highlight the unusual nature of their appearance as part of the Orton's Pasture pottery assemblage.

There are also noteworthy spatial concentrations at Orton's Pasture of either whole vessels that were probably buried in this state or of particularly distinctive ware types. In the latter instance, the very fact that the majority of the stratified green-glazed pots came from a re-cut ditch seems to suggest that this was a particularly significant feature, or that burial of selected and chosen material here marked the completion of a significant sequence of acts and actions. This feature also contained the largest single assemblage of Samian on the site, including three out of the five examples of Samian sherds bearing *graffiti* on the site. Interestingly at the site of Nettleton Shrub, Wiltshire – the site of a shrine dedicated to Apollo – there was recorded a pattern in the pottery assemblage recovered from the backfill of the pre-shrine first-century enclosure ditches and associated features, which suggests that colour, as well as form/function may have been one of the deciding factors in the selection of vessels for use and disposal there at the time. The excavator noted that the 'comparatively rare', imported green-glazed St Rémy ware, of which eighteen sherds were recovered, representing sixteen vessels, came almost exclusively from this enclosure complex.[43]

Other patterns are discernible in the differential distribution of Samian across the Orton's Pasture site. From the backfill of the ditches of Enclosure 1 came one hundred and thirty-two sherds, from internal pits of that enclosure came seventy sherds, a total of just over two hundred sherds. From the backfill of the ditches of Enclosure 2 came forty-one sherds, and from internal pits of the enclosure came forty sherds, a total of just over eighty sherds.

Of the more unusual coarse-ware vessel types, most of which were stratified, there was a notable concentration of these vessels inside, and in the backfilled ditches of the southern Enclosure 2. The plain ceramic lamp came from a pit here; two tazzas and a white ware beaker with a painted symbol that may be the top of a *caduceus* came from an enclosure ditch; a third tazza came from a ditch re-cut; a face pot came from an enclosure ditch; while unstratified fragments of a wine strainer and the decorated Bacchic-motif ceramic lamp came from the cleaning of areas within Enclosure 2.

A similar concentration of environmental 'exotics' was also centred on Enclosure 2. When looking at the charred plant remains from the site it was apparent that there was a significant difference between the types of material associated with the boundary ditches and internal pits of the northern Enclosure 1 and those from the southern Enclosure 2. The more exotic material, including the fragments of cone and nuts from the Mediterranean or Stone Pine and the dates, is exclusively from the southern enclosure, in two pits and an enclosure ditch in the case of the former and from two pits for the latter. Grape pips came from a pit here as well, though these need not necessarily be derived from the fresh fruit, and indeed in the circumstances they are much more likely to be from dried raisins. Also present in the southern enclosure were other wild foods including apple/pear, hazelnuts, and sloe.

If one examines, though, the full lists of charred material recovered from two of the Enclosure 2 pits some further interesting observations can be made. In all three pits tree or shrub buds were recovered, and in addition immature cones/catkins. Buds were also present in another pit to the north of the northern enclosure. If all, or even some of this material was from its contemporary horizons, and therefore was not residual, then it can be fairly surmised that these deposits were laid down in the spring. It defies the laws of probability that charred buds could have reached all of these features simply by accidental incorporation and it may therefore be useful to look for any parallels to such an occurrence and then seek to make an interpretation or explanation. The issue of seasonality and its relationship to the Roman religious character is an interesting topic.[44] Whether dedications and offerings at Romano-British religious sites can be tied in to a seasonal pattern and thus reflect the existing literary evidence for a calendar of religious festivals and observances in the wider Roman world is unproven. Both epigraphic and archaeological evidence is relevant here and from the former it would provisionally appear that there was a suggestion that certain times of year may have been avoided as inappropriate times for the dedication of religious monuments.

At Jordan Hill, Dorset a repetitive pattern of deposition of artefacts was apparent in a third- to fourth-century well or shaft dug in the courtyard of the temple there, thus probably reflecting cyclical time. At the first-century enclosure at Ashill, Norfolk a number of wells or shafts were encountered, the complex possibly being a focus of ritual activity. In one of the shafts a repeated pattern of deposition was again apparent, and again reflected cyclical time. The deposits included a large number of pottery vessels, animal bones, iron objects, copper alloy brooches, a whetstone, leather shoes, and organic material, including leaves, twigs, and nuts from the hazel tree. Either the deposits containing twigs and nuts were deposited in the autumn over a number of years, with the feature being capped and protected during the interim periods, or all the deposits were laid down in a single season of weekly or monthly events. In one of the Orton's Pasture pits there was evidence for a number of interleaved deposits of charcoal and clean sand, which suggests a deliberate and conscious closing off of each of the burned horizons towards the base of the pit by the deposition of thin layers of clean sand. Such a sequence could also have been created by the periodic capping or closing-off of the pit.

Among organic material in features such as those at Jordan Hill, Ashill, and Orton's Pasture there might be indicators of seasonal deposition: the presence of nuts and berries might suggest autumnal activity; buds on twigs and branches would hint at spring deposition; animal bones might also hint at seasonal slaughtering patterns, as already discussed at West Hill, Uley and at the Harlow temple site, Essex, though in a less pronounced pattern there.[45]

As to the animal bone assemblage from Orton's Pasture it is characterised as having a profile consistent with its being military, as opposed to reflecting civilian dietary patterns of the time. While assemblages of bone from temple sites can be so inherently biased in terms of the assemblage being dominated by one particular species almost to the exclusion of all others that its religious context can be established beyond all reasonable doubt, as at West Hill, Uley, less clear-cut examples may be difficult or even impossible to detect. At the Uley temple complex, a site dedicated to Mercury, an indisputably votive bone assemblage was found, as discussed earlier in this chapter, comprising exceptionally large numbers, and thus a heavily skewed percentage, of sheep/goat bones and domestic fowl. No such clear pattern existed for Orton's Pasture. However, it must be borne in mind though that Uley was a formal temple complex while Orton's Pasture was the site of a simple shrine, possibly dedicated by one individual officer or a group of officers from the nearby fort, and perhaps relatively short-lived in its duration of use.

The annual religious calendar, by which the army functioned, called for numerous events of sacrifice and/or dedication, and it is likely that many different kinds of animal sacrifice occurred regularly throughout the year. While the so-called *suovetaurilia*, that is the triple sacrifice of a cow, a sheep, and a pig, was more associated with imperial piety, similar sacrifices of these beasts in particular, or singly, or together in twos and threes, would also have taken place (Plate 19). Following sacrifice of the animals, the carcasses would have been butchered, one assumes in the standard Roman manner, and then the meat would have been cooked and eaten as part of a feast that usually formed an integral part of the overall religious rite.

Cattle certainly were being slaughtered and dismembered at Orton's Pasture in Phase 1 or nearby, as the evidence from the analysis of the excavated bones themselves shows, with a selection of most skeletal elements being present, with a 20 per cent higher level of butchery being discernible on this site than on the bones from inside the fort. There were also some individual contexts on site where butchery levels were particularly high, all of these being backfills of stretches of the southern, northern re-cut, and eastern enclosure ditches of the northern Enclosure 1. That there was also a distinctive pottery assemblage from the re-cut northern ditch has already been mentioned. The fact that there was also a concentration of cattle scapulae displaying hook damage recovered from the backfill of the eastern ditch further emphasises the spatial patterning here. It is quite possible therefore that the northern enclosure could represent a zone for the corralling, slaughtering and butchering of cattle and perhaps other animals, either under military or civilian supervision, perhaps to also supply meat to the fort to the north. It is also possible that animals could have been corralled here prior to their ritual slaughter as part of the military calendar of religious observance, which required animal sacrifice as a necessary part of the ritual process.

Parallels for certain elements represented in the Orton's Pasture animal bone assemblage and collection of charred plant remains were found at the site of Great Holts Farm, Boreham, Essex.[46] At this site finds were made of both Stone Pine and another exotic plant, olives, not found at Orton's Pasture, and cattle bones from large, perhaps imported, beasts. The religious activity at Orton's Pasture dates to the second century AD while the Great Holts Farm site dates principally to the fourth century. The former is a shrine site, the latter a villa. At the villa, the majority of the unusual finds came from the backfill of a well and could therefore represent structured deposition. This phenomenon in the Roman period is perhaps best represented at the Roman fort site of Newstead, Melrose, in Scotland and at the Roman fort and *vicus* site of Castleford, West Yorkshire.[47]

At both sites there were recorded episodes of pit digging and rubbish disposal, which to the excavators appeared to be in some respects unusual and yet at the same time much as one would expect to find on sites where the hygienic disposal of tons of domestic and everyday refuse in a safe and efficient manner would have occupied some considerable and continual effort and expense of time. At Newstead large open areas were exposed within an enclosure, interpreted as an annexe, which lay to the south of the main fort complex. Both within as well as outside the annexe boundary ditches a number of huge pits were excavated which were originally interpreted in some cases as wells that had naturally gone out of use, perhaps with the contamination of the water therein, and which had then been used as ready-made rubbish pits in which material from the forts could be dumped and backfilled. Within the annexe there were no diagnostically military buildings: indeed, at certain periods the interior of the annexe must have been largely empty, the only archaeologically detectable activity being the digging of pits and the sinking of wells, and the subsequent disposal of rubbish into these features.

However, the diversity and range of material dumped in some of these pits/wells was such that questions had to be asked about the definition of rubbish when applied to the contents of the pit backfills. Not only was there a range of domestic pottery vessels represented but also metal vessels, wooden artefacts, in some cases well preserved in the waterlogged conditions which existed at the basal levels of some features, and some more extraordinary objects, including the renowned cavalry parade helmet, which would appear to have gone into the ground in a virtually mint condition. There was also animal bone and other types of environmental material such as wood and leather. In the case of Newstead, the direct physical relationship between the fort and enclosure ditches and the particularly large quantity of military artefacts and equipment recovered during the excavations, meant that there was no hesitation in the site being characterised as a military annexe. It was later that the ritual aspects of the site were brought out in academic discussion, with the structured deposition taking place there alongside the more profane aspects of the use of the site.

More examples of such 'Newstead pits', as they have become known to archaeologists, were subsequently excavated there. While no objects quite as unusual as those uncovered by James Curle in 1905–10 were recovered in the later campaigns of excavation, nevertheless a significant new dataset was added to the pit groups and allowed for a reinterpretation of some of the patterns of waste disposal at the site to be undertaken. In Newstead's south annexe the pits excavated would seem to have been in use for the disposal of rubbish and deposition of other material around the middle of the second century AD. A pattern of the use of these pits was established, which suggested that they were not all in use at the same time, with perhaps fifteen to twenty pits being open at any one time. At some period other activity connected with metalworking took place within the annexe at the same time as some of the pits were in use for rubbish disposal. While undoubtedly the majority of the material dumped into the pits could be defined as rubbish, nevertheless some items certainly could not, including the aforementioned parade helmet, perfectly serviceable tools, and so on. Certain types of material seemed to appear only in pit contexts, as opposed to the activity areas examined by the later excavators. They concluded that 'some material clearly had a possible ritual significance' and observed that 'while some items deposited in the Newstead pits were complete, even damaged or fragmentary artefacts may have represented deliberate deposition of significant items'.[48] Their re-examination of the Newstead pits phenomenon identified trends in the selection of material for disposal, patterns of structured deposition and, in addition, recognised the existence of 'special deposits' in some pits. The context for these deliberate acts remains uncertain, however, for specifically religious items were seldom included amongst the dumped material.

At Castleford fort and *vicus* analysis of the finds from pits suggested that there was a discernible pattern of rubbish disposal within the pits, as at Newstead, and that there was undoubtedly both selection of specific types of material for disposal in this way and some cases of what must have been complete, or almost complete pottery and glass vessels. Once more it was suggested that 'something more than utilitarian rubbish disposal may have been going on in these pits, and that they may reflect some form of ritual or religious activity in this area',[49] and viewed this as being part of a wider phenomenon that includes the common, though obviously not exclusive use of pits, wells and shafts on Romano-British sites as foci for formalised and structured deposition of material as part of a religious or ritual action.

The recognition of instances of structured deposition in a Romano-British context is not new and indeed similar deposits had earlier been identified in the Middle Walbrook Valley site in London.[50] A very useful summary of votive and ritual deposits in Roman Britain exists[51] and includes many examples of structured disposal or placing of pottery and other finds in ditches, pits, shafts, and wells.

The Newstead, Castleford, and Walbrook examples tend to suggest that the pattern of well and/or pit digging and the disposal of rubbish and other more significantly construed material at Orton's Pasture is part of a more widespread Romano-British phenomenon. In the case of the southern enclosure at Orton's Pasture it can perhaps be demonstrated to be a phenomenon sometimes also connected with specifically religious acts and observances. At least one, and possibly all three of the pits in the north-eastern corner of this enclosure should then perhaps more properly be called *favissae*, a *favissa* being a pit dug for the disposal of *ex votos* and other items, sometimes quite ordinary and mundane, used within a temple or its precinct. The controlled disposal of such material inside the precinct would allow for its religious significance to be otherwise retained. Alongside the repetitive acts of rubbish deposition it could also be said that the re-cutting and redefinition of parts of the enclosure boundary ditches of both enclosures here represented a significant, repetitive action. Marking boundaries is accepted as a significant rite, sometimes associated with marking out by ploughing (Plate 20).[52] In plan, this remarking appears most markedly around the north-east corner of southern Enclosure 2. The very fact that this re-cutting is around the angle of the enclosure which contains and protects the small stone-footed building that constitutes the only building on the whole site in this phase seems to be rather more than a coincidence when viewed alongside all the other evidence for a distinctive character to the activity here. It does not require a great leap of faith to identify this small stone building as a shrine, and the enclosure as its *temenos* or precinct.

If this building was a shrine, in the absence of firm evidence for its use as such, it is possible to find a small number of parallels for similar structures found elsewhere in Roman Britain.[53] Such structures are categorised as 'rectangular religious buildings' and are relatively rare, though more common on the continent.[54] All the known examples are simple structures, in some cases with an internal sub-division, as at Orton's Pasture, and in one case with a porch or extension. Other such buildings are known from Springhead and Richborough, both in Kent, Wycomb, Gloucestershire, and Bowes, County Durham. The size of such buildings varies but the Orton's Pasture building, with dimensions of around eight metres by four metres, would fit into the general size range of these simple shrine buildings.

The shrine at Bowes was of drystone construction, the majority of the others being constructed with bonded masonry walls. Nevertheless it is likely that all of them had simple, gabled roofs and few internal fixtures or fittings. A number contained no finds to confirm their religious function beyond doubt, and this has been assigned based upon indirect association and context, as is the case at Orton's Pasture. It must be assumed that the worked sandstone backfilled into or dished into the top of a nearby pit inside the southern enclosure at Orton's Pasture had originally formed part of the superstructure of the building. Other building stone from here had probably subsequently been dispersed by ploughing over the years.

Among this worked but otherwise undiagnosable stone was a single recognisable fragment of an altar. The exotic ceramic vessels and the exotic and other foodstuffs from the three pits here and patterns of deposition within the re-cut enclosure ditches, not to mention the re-cutting evidence itself, point towards the carrying out of religious and ritual rites here. Such ceremonies could have taken a number of forms and have been carried out in a number of different ways appropriate to different situations.

A formal procession to the site of the shrine can be envisaged. Entrance into the defined enclosure precinct would have made the crossing of boundary lines a significant act itself, with the individual moving from a world of human experience and endeavour into the world of the gods, where dealings between men, women, and their gods could be mediated by prayer, sacrifice, and ceremony. Upon arrival at the shrine, offerings of food would have been made on an altar and burned. Prayers may have been offered and gifts dedicated to the gods. Libations of wine may have been poured, herbs and incense may have been burned, candles or lamps may have been lit, particularly as daylight ebbed away towards the end of the day, animals may have been slaughtered, and a feast or meal may have been consumed.[55] Afterwards the remains of the meal and the offerings, perhaps also the vessels used in its preparation and consumption, would have been, like the libations, returned to the earth by their burial, perhaps following on from their breaking or ritual killing, as is attested at a number of temple sites, although such material is more or less absent from Orton's Pasture.

Containers to bring food to the site need not necessarily have been anything other than ordinary domestic vessels – jars, bowls, dishes, amphorae – and this point has been made quite clearly also at West Hill, Uley and Henley Wood where analysis of the pottery assemblages showed that most of the coarse-wares were domestic in nature.[56] At Uley, with the exception of a large number of miniature ceramic vessels, there were no unusual vessels in the pottery assemblage, apart from the occasional example of a pot with a drilled or pierced base, to suggest that these were anything other than domestic pots. At Henley Wood the same applied, though analysis of this material by form did allow some intra-site variations to be reported and for comparison to be made between Henley Wood and Uley, where tableware formed a higher proportion of the assemblage, while storage vessels were less well represented.

It is perhaps, then, in a way remarkable in terms of contrast that at Orton's Pasture, with the exception of the Bacchic-inspired *patera* handle and lamp, and the altar fragment, there were no specifically votive objects present at the site, yet at Uley they were extremely common. It was the case that items either dedicated as *ex votos* at temple sites or shrines, and items otherwise connected to the religious rites there, were not removed from out of the religious precinct, whether that precinct was bounded by a formal *temenos* wall or, as here, defined by a boundary ditch, possibly originally with an associated bank.

Some imagination is required to recreate the setting of the shrine at Orton's Pasture. It is in a physically liminal position, as well as performing a liminal role between the world of men and that of their gods. The field in which the shrine building lies was found by excavation to have been subject to apparently regular seasonal flooding. While the regimes of the River Dove will have altered, perhaps quite drastically, since Roman times, nevertheless there is some evidence that some Roman features were cut into a tail of alluvium, helping to define the zone of the river's encroachment at some stage around the first or second century AD. Towards the very bottom of the field, to the south, there was recorded a build-up of about a metre of alluvium deposited by the floodwaters of the River Dove. This suggests, then, that at certain times of the year much of the ground to the immediate south of the shrine building would have been underwater, giving a spectacular and dramatic context to any activities carried out at the shrine in the period of the late autumn to early spring each year.

It may have been this remarkably evocative scene, with the upper parts of trees sticking out above the water's surface and so on, that first alerted the dedicatee of the shrine to the site. The suitability of the habitat to attract water birds may also have provided an extra filip in the form of the opportunity to pursue wildfowling here, hunting and religious observance often having a slightly symbiotic relationship in the Roman world. Rural shrines in general were not large or particularly grand, and indeed it has been observed that there was often a form of inverted cachet associated with the hut-like simplicity of the shrine at its most unpretentious, a classical influence on Roman Britain which has been described as 'sacro-idyllic'.[57]

Few such shrines have been recognised in Britain and even one of the more remote and inaccessible of these, the shrines of Vinotonus on Scargill Moor, near Bowes, in North Yorkshire, despite their impressively isolated and wild location nevertheless were provided with a suite of impressive altars by its patrons, military officers from the nearby fort at Bowes who must have come to the moor to indulge their pleasure for hunting and for wild unfettered landscape. Here Vinotonus is equated with Silvanus, a deity of woodland, groves, and hunting, just as a similar dedication of an altar to Silvanus was made by another Roman army officer on Bollihope Common, Weardale, again in northern England, though it is uncertain whether this equally remote spot was the location of a formal shrine.[58]

Given the physical setting of the Orton's Pasture shrine, with the potentially dramatic, almost theatrical, effect created by its proximity to a flood-prone area, it is also worth considering the question of the deliberate integration of this feature into the very landscape itself. There was a commonly shared Roman and British veneration of natural features in the landscape such as rivers, springs, woodland and so on, and away from the towns and major road routes this would have been a deciding factor in the location of the smaller religious sites. This would seem to be partially the case at Orton's Pasture, the site being both in the landscape and of the landscape, quite literally, while at the same time also being linked potentially to the site of the adjacent fort. A study of religious and ritual practices in Roman Gaul has also considered the location of temples and other types of religious sites in relation to 'the mythical geography of the landscape'.[59] Amongst other favoured natural locations, the significance of the sites of springs, rivers, and brooks, and of 'particularly the sources, confluences and intersections with land roads' could also be demonstrated in the case of Gaul, as with Roman Britain. While scarcely major rivers it should nevertheless be remembered that the rivers Dove and Churnet meet less than a kilometre to the south of the Orton's Pasture site, while a main crossing over the Dove must also have been immediately close by, in order to take the road route eastwards towards Little Chester, near Derby. These locational factors are likely to have been determinants in the choice of such a propitious site for a shrine.

The question now needs to be briefly addressed as to whether the shrine at Orton's Pasture was dedicated to the worship of any one particular deity, something that is often discernible through the nature of epigraphic evidence, artworks, or the finds record. Unfortunately the single altar fragment is not from the part of the altar that would have been expected to carry an inscription, if indeed the altar was inscribed at all. There are likewise few *graffiti* on pottery vessels or on other objects from the site, perhaps surprisingly in a possibly military context where a high degree of general literacy amongst the officers and soldiers would be expected. Seven *graffiti* in all were recorded. There would appear to have been no or few exchanges between mortals and their gods here mediated through written materials, as is found on other types of religious sites in Roman Britain, such as at West Hill, Uley, discussed earlier in the chapter.

There are, however, the two decorated objects from the site: the copper alloy *patera* handle and the imported ceramic lamp fragment, which might have been re-utilised as an *oscillum* after its breaking when in use as a lamp. Both these objects bear Bacchic and Bacchic-associated imagery which must be assessed within the framework of analysis established some years ago by Valerie Hutchinson in her in-depth study of the evidence for the Bacchic cult in Roman Britain, which was discussed at length above in Chapter 1. Hutchinson found that knowledge of the cult or use of its imagery, rather than necessarily adherence to the cult, was much more widespread in Roman Britain than previously had been thought. Bacchic-associated artefacts have been found on sites ranging in date from the first to the fourth century, and in both town and countryside, in both civilian and military contexts. They have also, of course, been found in both domestic and religious contexts. Hutchinson has noted that *paterae* decorated with Bacchic imagery 'on the basis of form alone merit consideration as religious artefacts'.[60] She also considered lamps as a general category of object that, decorated or undecorated, were more likely to be used in non-domestic contexts than as objects for everyday lighting.[61] In her catalogue Hutchinson listed 159 Bacchic-related objects from military sites in Roman Britain, and twenty-eight objects from sites that possibly represent rural shrines. Given that three Bacchic-related objects have now been found at Rocester – the two from Orton's Pasture under discussion here and a copper alloy jug handle from the New Cemetery site, which lies inside the Roman fort complex to the north of Orton's Pasture – there would certainly seem to be the suggestion that in the later first century or early second century there was a small group of cult adherents stationed in the military establishment here or at least associated in some way with the military, if the Orton's Pasture items belonged to one of the *vicani* (Plate 22).

Whether the exotic foodstuffs and plant remains from the southern enclosure can themselves help provide clues to the deity worshipped or invoked here also needs considering. It is unfortunate that routine environmental sampling as an integral part of archaeological excavation pre-dates many of the more important Roman temple excavations in Britain. There is, for instance, no environmental data available for consideration in Hutchinson's study of the Bacchic cult in Britain. At West Hill, Uley there was little information provided by the analysis of the plant macrofossils, and certainly nothing to enhance the interpretation of the religious function of the site. The presence of mulberry in one deposit there may imply the importation of this fruit as a foodstuff or as an appropriate offering for religious purposes. Stone Pine has previously been found at two temple sites in Britain, the Temple of Mithras in London and the Triangular Temple in Verulamium, as well as on a handful of non-religious, domestic sites. At two of the latter, Chew Park and Great Holts Farm, this material came from well deposits, which may be of significance in itself, as has already been suggested above. Two other finds of Stone Pine can also be seen to be in potentially ritual rather than domestic contexts. The presence of seeds of *Pinus Pinea* was recorded in a mass of charcoal in a cremation from Mucking, Essex while two complete Stone Pine cones came from excavations at Number 1 Poultry, London.[62]

The extremely low level of finds made of metal and bone at Orton's Pasture, and the complete absence of objects of jet or shale and so on, that is both ordinary domestic items and those which might have been transformed from the ordinary into the extraordinary by their dedication as *ex votos*, and of specifically manufactured *ex votos*, argues for this being a private shrine rather than a public place of worship and sacrifice. Such a distinction needs to be made in the case of religious establishments and their users. It is, though, perhaps significant that two of the three copper alloy brooches from the site come from a pit inside the southern enclosure, and that these brooches can certainly be considered therefore as *ex votos* rather than simply casual losses. Indeed, as discussed at the start of this chapter certain types of brooches are now recognised as having regular association with ritual sites and deposits rather than simply being utilitarian objects re-contextualised or transformed by their use in ritual or religious activity. Given that no characterisation can therefore be made of the pattern of *ex voto* deposition at Orton's Pasture, as was attempted in the publication of West Hill, Uley, this too would seem to be a dead end in terms of identifying the cult or cults linked to the shrine here.

Public and Private Vows

In this chapter it has been considered how objects such as brooches and other kinds of *ex votos* were dedicated at Romano-British religious sites where alongside the vow they acted as intermediary manifestations of individual dealings between men and women and their gods and goddesses. An attempt has been made by the presentation of two contrasting site case studies to show how the excavation of different types of religious site can generate different types of assemblages of finds of one kind or another, depending on the nature of the activity that took place there in the Roman period. The large but isolated temple complex at West Hill, Uley, dedicated to Mercury, would appear to have been a focal point for a large constituency of travellers or pilgrims seeking the intercession of the god in business ventures, in disputes, and in providing healing services. The temple establishment was well appointed and probably run along the lines of a business. In contrast, the small, rather rustic shrine at Orton's Pasture, probably dedicated to Bacchus, was probably a more private religious establishment, built and maintained by an officer or officers from the nearby auxiliary fort and a site where the ecstatic celebration of the rites of the Bacchic cult married sacred duty and profane enjoyment in equal measure. At both sites the study of objects found allows a reconstruction of activity there to be attempted.

Of course, there were many highly varied types of religious establishment in Roman Britain different to Uley and Orton's Pasture, but space precludes discussion of more examples of other types here, though more formal healing shrines will be discussed in some detail in Chapter 3. Such sites again often betray their function through the make-up of the finds assemblages found there by archaeologists. For example, finds from what must have been a local healing shrine came to light at Llys Awel, Abergele, Conwy, Wales.[63] The fourth-century hoard of material consisted of over five hundred coins, a copper alloy statuette of Mercury, two copper alloy figurines of seated dogs, a third copper alloy running dog, three votive plaques, two decorated with images of dogs, and a twisted wire bracelet (Plate 21). It can be assumed that the coins and bracelet were *ex votos* from the shrine which was dedicated to Mercury. Mercury was one of many gods in the Roman world who had healing powers. Indeed healing as a subsidiary role to other responsibilities seems to have been the god's situation at the Uley temple complex. Dog images are extremely common on healing sites in the Roman world, most famously in Roman Britain at the healing complex at Lydney Park, Gloucestershire, and it is likely that live dogs played some role in the healing process, thus explaining the potential power probably imbued in images of such ritual beasts, both at formal healing shrines and at other types of sites where occasional healing rituals might have been required to be carried out. A carved jet handle in the form of a dog from Binchester Roman fort may indeed have been the handle from a medical instrument or from a ritual knife of some kind (Fig. 7).[64]

Healing shrines were also sites where images of broken or sick bodies or body parts were often found and these anatomical or medical *ex votos* will form the topic of the next chapter.

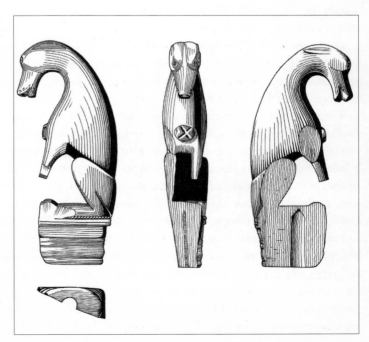

7. A carved jet dog, possibly a knife handle, from Binchester, County Durham. (Drawn by Sandy Morris)

THE COMFORT OF STRANGERS

Body Parts

As seen in Chapter 2, in the Roman period the range, number, and diversity of objects dedicated as *ex votos* at temple sites in Britain increased exponentially, along with the number of formal religious sites in both towns and in the countryside. Some of the least common but most interesting of these new types of dedicated *ex votos* are the so-called medical or anatomical *ex votos* and discussion of these items will form the focus of this chapter.

While the sick in Roman Britain generally suffer in silence in the archaeological record, on occasion individual voices can be overheard or detected in dialogue with the gods. In the Roman world the development of a system of rational medicine, mostly derived from the Greeks, did not, as might have been expected, banish irrational recourse to the healing gods but rather 'healing deities flourished alongside scientific medicine in an almost parallel development'.[1] This is perfectly illustrated by the dedication of a Greek doctor serving in the Roman army at the northern fort of Binchester of a sculptural panel bearing an inscription to the healing god Aesculapius and his daughter Salus. Here both rational and irrational medicine meet (Plate 23).[2]

However, it is not the purpose of this chapter to consider the evidence for medical practice in Roman Britain, but rather to present and contextualise the evidence for specific dealings between men, women, and the gods, dealings beyond the realm of the formalised and scientific healing art.

The purchase and offering of votive objects or *ex votos* at religious sites in Roman Britain carried on, or at least did not interrupt, a similar Iron Age tradition, as noted in Chapter 2,[3] a tradition with an even longer pedigree at so-called watery places,[4] but in many instances new forms of *ex voto* were introduced. As has been noted, 'it is exceedingly difficult to assess the implications of these new artefacts for Celtic religion, as they may all be no more than new forms of votives introduced by the Romans, which do not conflict with any Celtic beliefs'.[5] One such type of new votive was the medical or anatomical model, which could nevertheless have been acceptable in the context of the generally recognised Celtic use of miniaturisation in religious situations.[6] These objects in Roman Britain were both custom-made and customised.

Though I am concerned here with discussing the use of anatomical or medical *ex votos* in Roman religious practice at healing shrines and other religious sites principally in Roman Britain, almost inevitably reference will also have to be made to their more widespread and common use in Roman Gaul and elsewhere in the Graeco-Roman world. The emphasis of discussion here will be both on the objects themselves and on the ideas and concepts that they represented and perhaps encapsulated, particularly ideas related to the position of the sick in society and to views on the human body. In order to consider the potential complexities of these ideas, reference will also be made to the later, well-documented and well-studied healing roles of Breton saints in the medieval and early modern period, and to some anthropological or ethnographic studies of healing cults that throw significant light on the mechanisms of religious observance at Roman period sites.

Anatomical or medical *ex votos*, models or representations of human body parts made in various materials, were dedicated at healing shrines or sanctuaries throughout the Graeco-Roman world, though with perhaps significant chronological, geographical, and representational variations. Creation and use of such *ex votos* possibly had independent origins in Greece and the Italian regions of Etruria and Latium in the fifth and fourth centuries BC.[7] In Italy the dedication of anatomical *ex votos* had become a less common custom by the first century BC, though it did occur as a manifestation of Graeco-Roman practice at numerous sites elsewhere within the empire well beyond this date, of which the Gallo-Roman healing shrines of *Fontes Sequanae* at the Source of the Seine, near Dijon, and the *Source des Roches* at Chamalières, Auvergne represent the best-known examples, and I will be discussing the finds from the Source of the Seine later in this chapter (Plate 24).

Generally, the perceived lack of artistic merit or aesthetic value of anatomical *ex votos* has meant that their significance has often been overlooked or underestimated in site reports. As has been noted by one commentator, writing on anatomical *ex votos* from the Greek world, 'that beauty was not the primary concern of the dedicators and the manufacturers of these objects, seems to have been little understood'.[8] Again, the emotional subtext behind their dedication has been little explored, perhaps in the mistaken belief that considering emotions is somehow alien to historical culture studies rather than being an intrinsic and necessary part of the study of every society. Unfortunately the emotion encapsulated in these medical or anatomical *ex votos* is fear: fear of sickness, fear of infertility, fear of social exclusion or ostracism, and, of course, fear of death. These items were tools in strategies of fear management, containment, and alleviation.

I first wrote on this subject almost twenty years ago and have previously published a list of the relatively few anatomical *ex votos* then recorded from Britain.[9] I concluded then that the number of these recovered by excavation at various religious sites was then perhaps significantly small compared to numbers recovered from other areas such as Italy[10] and Gaul, though, of course, no strictly comparable sites to, for example, the Sources of the Seine have been identified or excavated in Britain. While conditions of deposition may have led to the absence from the archaeological record of *ex votos* fashioned from certain organic materials it should not be assumed that such objects, for instance in wood, actually ever existed in Roman Britain; at the sacred spring at Bath and at Coventina's Well, sites where the context would have been sympathetic to the survival of organic matter, no such items have yet been found. Indeed, I previously suggested a trend towards the customisation of other artefacts to create anatomical *ex votos* in Roman Britain, rather than there being a significant industry making these items to order, as occurred elsewhere, and I see no reason now to question this thesis.

The preparation of this present chapter has allowed me to return to that previously compiled list and to try to bring it up to date. For simplicity's sake I am omitting a number of perhaps highly equivocal items that I discussed in my earlier paper, such as the tin mask from Bath which could have been a piece of religious paraphernalia worn by a priest or could equally have represented, according to Martin Henig, 'a visitor to the shrine who came to be healed in body or mind',[11] but which I now think are not true anatomical or medical *ex votos*. The most convincing anatomical *ex votos* listed previously come from religious sites at Bath and Lamyatt Beacon in Somerset, West Hill, Uley and Lydney Park in Gloucestershire, Wroxeter in Shropshire, Springhead in Kent, and Verulamium in Hertfordshire, from which sites come more than one item, and Muntham Court in Sussex, Woodeaton in Oxfordshire, Winchester in Hampshire, Harlow in Essex, and Segontium in Wales, from which come one item each.

These items comprise, listing the multiple find-spots first: a pair of carved ivory breasts and a sheet bronze breast from Bath; a bronze leg and a bronze hand, 'originally holding a sceptre' according to the excavator, perhaps customised from cut-up figurines, from Lamyatt Beacon, and one wonders whether stone statuary fragments, of a foot, a foot and leg, and a portion of a leg from the site could also be significant; a copper alloy plaque with a repoussé breast in the centre and three lead model legs, one with a foot, and a silvered bronze plaque bearing a foot in relief from West Hill, Uley (Fig. 8); a bronze arm and a bronze leg and foot, again possibly customised from figurines, from Lydney Park, from where also comes a bone plaque on which is incised the figure of a naked, possibly pregnant woman, an item that the site's excavators believed could have been dedicated by 'some female worshipper who had received relief in childbirth'; a pair of eyes made from a sheet of beaten gold, a fragment of an eye in bronze sheet, between thirty and eighty plaster eyes, and, least convincingly, an eye fashioned from a sherd of Samian pottery, all from Wroxeter; a bronze thumb, bent at the joint, a bronze arm and hand, originally thought to be custom made but now considered by others to be a customised fragment of a statuette, and a bronze hand with clasped fingers which may originally have held a now-lost object, once more possibly customised parts from figurines, from Springhead; and three unpublished miniature bronze feet, two ending around the ankle and the third including some part of the lower leg, from Kathleen Kenyon's excavation at the theatre at Verulamium, these items appearing to be custom-made anatomical *ex votos*.[12]

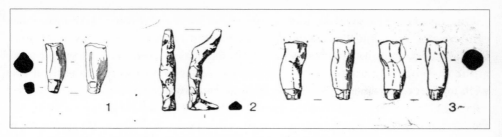

8. Some cast lead model legs from West Hill, Uley temple site, Gloucestershire. (From Woodward and Leach, 1993, Fig. 88)

The single items comprise: a miniature clay leg with foot from the temple site at Muntham Court; a small statuette of a naked woman with her arms crossed over her breasts from the temple at Woodeaton, Oxfordshire, a find that the excavator noted could be connected to childbirth; a bronze leg 'attached to a ring and either worn as an amulet or used as a votive' from Winchester; a miniature ivory and bronze breast from the temple at Harlow; and, finally, a stylised clay foot from Segontium. A 'tiny bronze child's foot' from Woodeaton might also be a customised anatomical *ex voto*.[13]

Perhaps unsurprisingly, few further anatomical *ex votos* have been found or recognised from excavations in the last twenty years or so, with the exception of two, possibly three, plaster eyes from Arbeia Roman Fort, South Shields. The two most convincing eyes have been roughed out as a circle in one case and an oval in the other, with a central area of the plaster at the front being gouged or hollowed out to form the eye's pupil. These come from unstratified layers in the *vicus*. The third plaster eye came from a courtyard house inside the fort and is perfectly circular and pierced right through the middle by a cleanly cut circular hole.

As to other votive objects found since 1993, I have chosen to prevaricate over the find of a small bronze male head from West Wight, whose uncertain provenance does not necessarily suggest a votive context for this find, though it might well be votive. This means that only six further recent finds, all from the Portable Antiquities Scheme database of metal-detected finds, can be added to the list with certainty: a copper alloy eye from Caistor St Edmund, Norfolk; part of a copper alloy eye from Market Lavington, Wiltshire; a copper alloy arm and hand from Hambleden in Buckinghamshire, either a fragment from a figurine or an actual votive; a life-sized copper alloy finger from a possible votive hand from North Kesteven, Lincolnshire; a cast lead foot cut off at the ankle from South Cambridgeshire; and a 275-millimetre-long lead foot sole, almost like a 3D impression of a human foot, from Berkshire. Around a dozen other PAS listed items, including six copper alloy feet or legs, some copper alloy arms and hands, and a copper alloy ear would appear to be figurine, statuette, or statue fragments, as suggested by the finds liaison officers who examined and catalogued the objects and these may or may not be customised medical *ex votos* (Plates 25–26).[14]

One significant site whose finds have not been considered for inclusion in the catalogue of anatomical or medical *ex votos* from Roman Britain is Coventina's Well at Carrawburgh, Northumberland. No medical *ex votos* as such were found at the site but two particular classes of object recovered from the backfill of the well, miniature masks and leather shoes, may have fulfilled a similar intermediary role between the sick and their goddess here. The three small bronze masks from the well again could be of significance, if one accepts the previously quoted but rejected interpretation of the Bath tin mask as a medical *ex voto*, though of the three it is believed that one was probably a bucket or cauldron mount, that a second had a similar function or was a mount for a bowl or item of furniture, and that the third was also a mount,[15] though the portrait-like quality of this third mask has previously been commented on by one authority.[16] A number of leather shoes, or rather leather shoe soles, also came from the well, including two shoes which must have belonged to children. The cataloguer of these items noted that 'the discovery of shoes in votive deposits is not unknown' though 'these shoes might have found their way into the well as rubbish'. However, it was also accepted that they could in fact be medical *ex votos* 'thrown in as a request to Coventina to cure some malady of the foot'.[17]

Other finds of interest also come from probable healing shrines at Chedworth Roman villa, Gloucestershire and Box villa in Wiltshire. Again, as with the masks and shoes from Coventina's Well, the objects from Chedworth and Box cannot be firmly classified as medical or anatomical *ex votos*, though they might have been used as such given the function of the sites at which they were found. At Chedworth villa, suggested to have been a healing shrine in its later life, were found three stone statue bases, all consisting only of feet, in one case shod in sandals and in another wearing some kind of boot. A bronze plaque fragment, so broken as to only display a panther and a pair of feet, and a life-sized bronze thumb cut from a statue also come from the site.[18] Could these all in fact have been customised for use as anatomical *ex votos*? And what of the full-size silver eye, possibly from a bronze head of a cult statue found at the Box villa, another site suggested to have become a possible healing cult centre in later life?[19]

Manufacture of medical *ex votos* is difficult, if not impossible, to detect from the archaeological record, especially as in Roman Britain it is suggested that the customisation of pieces of statues and statuettes or figurines seems to have been a generally acceptable practice at some sites, a process with perhaps a further significance of its own, as has been suggested with regard to the fate of statuary from Roman London.[20] At Verulamium two bronze limbs, one a lower leg and foot and the other a model arm and hand with a prong for possible attachment, were recovered from behind the cellar wall of a building in Insula XIV and may have been derived from an earlier bronze-smith's workshop on the site (Fig. 9). Though these may have been pieces collected for the melting pot they may as easily have been intended as votive objects.[21] At the Mill Street site, Caerleon a number of fragments of pipeclay Venus figurines was found, represented by three or four sets of feet, torsos,

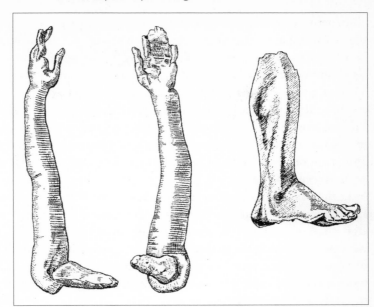

9. A copper alloy leg and arm from Verulamium, Hertfordshire. (From Frere, 1972, Fig. 49)

and separate heads; these are reported to have been cleanly broken or cut, though publication of this material does not highlight this aspect of the items.[22] Given the well-attested evidence for the customisation of artefacts for religious purposes in Roman Britain it might be worth reviewing the contexts and significance of other classes of material regularly found at religious sites, including face pots and pins with human head terminals.

Seeking a Cure

The total number of certain, probable, and possible anatomical *ex votos* from Roman Britain, omitting the Bath tin mask and finds from Coventina's Well, Chedworth villa, and Box, is therefore sixty-seven to one hundred and seventeen items, comprising between forty-two and ninety-two eyes (vagueness here is caused by the fact that many of the Wroxeter plaster eyes are described as ranging 'from the possible to the dubious'), fourteen legs and/or feet, seven arms and/or hands, four breasts or pairs of breasts, and two 'whole people' represented by the Lydney Park plaque and the Woodeaton statuette. These items come from nineteen separate sites or locales, mainly in southern, south-western, and central England, with an outlier in Wales and one in the north-east at South Shields/Arbeia Roman fort.

To put this in a broader perspective, Simone Deyts, in one of her studies of the remarkable collection of dedicated *ex votos* and statuary from the Source of the Seine site,[23] has tabulated and quantified the occurrence here of different kinds of representation in different types of material, that is stone, bronze, pipeclay, and wood, and compared this assemblage with those from other Gallic healing sanctuaries. At the Source of the Seine there is a large number of representations of what might best be termed here, awkward though it is, 'whole people', a total of ninety-seven to one hundred and two men, women, unsexed representations, and swaddled infants. There are two hundred and twelve busts and heads, one hundred and seventy-two torsos and pelvises, a figure which includes twenty-five female breasts or pairs of breasts, as well as a number of both male and female lower torsos with sexual organs, fifty-seven internal organs, one hundred and forty-nine legs and feet, fifty-four hands and arms, one hundred and nineteen eyes, a ratio of body parts to whole people of around seven to one.

At the other three Gallic sites quantified by Deyts, that is Alesia, Essarois, and Halatte, ratios of body parts to whole people are respectively two hundred to one, eleven to one, and two to one. Comparison of the Source of the Seine assemblage with the assemblage of anatomical *ex votos* from the Republican healing sanctuary of Ponte di Nona near Rome is also interesting, in that more internal organs and more individual representations of sexual organs, both male and female, appear at the Italian site.[24] Models of sexual organs are absent from Romano-British sites, though as will be discussed in Chapter 6 the phallus was in itself a very common image in Romano-British life.

Anatomical *ex votos*, along with other categories of *ex votos* dedicated at religious sites, signify the making of a contract between a man or woman and their gods, in this case related to petitions for the restoring of health to a sick individual through divine intervention or in thanks for health having been restored in answer to a prayer or previous visit to the site. Every type of *ex voto*, anatomical or otherwise, through purchase or commissioning and by dedication, relates to an individual person. Anatomical *ex votos* obviously and very specifically relate to that individual's body and in many cases to highly specific parts of that body.

The sick in the Graeco-Roman world have been described by one medical historian[25] as being viewed as temporarily or permanently stigmatised, depending on the nature or duration of their illness. Seeking a cure for the sick body was not only linked to issues of personal health, it was also a way of seeking reintegration back into society. 'The position of the sick among primitive people is a magicoreligious one … the position of the sick in Greek society during classical times was of quite another type', with health in the Greek world being seen as the highest possible blessing and sickness as a stigma or curse, either temporary or permanent, depending on the nature of the illness. Such a value system was largely adopted by the Romans. Ill health and disease are culturally defined phenomena and it is possible to define reactions to them and to understand their cultural definition through archaeological evidence. The special tension inherent in many assemblages of *ex votos* between emotion and feeling on the one hand, representing self, and documentation on the other, mirroring their time of creation, is somewhat allayed by the overall sense of structural order in the way they were used. Religious practice here helped to maintain the fundamental social structure of society and ultimately maintain the individual's sense of reality. Here the healer's role was a mediating one, that of a cultural broker, and certainly it can be seen that in most cultures religious rites often concern what has been called 'the management of fear' in this way. Dialogue with a deity would at least have allowed private emotions, and perhaps an otherwise marginalised passion, to be given a more public voice.

I recognise that with the Romano-British material discussed here that I have pulled this material out of its context. That is, I have isolated items according to my own categorisation of anatomical or medical *ex votos* as being significant to my study and have omitted discussion of the other items with which they appeared in the archaeological record. It is though, in fact, the very rarity of anatomical *ex votos* from Roman Britain that makes their appearance of especial significance, and in some cases their presence can help us to understand certain aspects of health provision in Roman Britain, particularly with regard to specifically female medical problems and dilemmas being addressed at some sites and curing specialisation for both sexes being attested at other sites.

From Bath came a pair of breasts carved in ivory which might indicate that the petitioner suffered 'from a breast complaint such as mastitis',[26] a sheet bronze breast, and the well-known tin mask from the culvert of the baths. As already mentioned above, it has been suggested that while the mask could portray a deity, it could equally be a medical *ex voto* representing 'a visitor to the shrine who came to be healed in body or mind',[27] a suggestion which could have implications for the interpretation of other masks, both full-size and miniature, found in religious contexts elsewhere. I am here seeing the mask as an item of religious paraphernalia rather than as a medical *ex voto*. Given the nature of the sacred spring deposits at Bath it seems relevant to wonder here whether some of the gemstones from the site, if they do not represent simple losses or the deposition of a bag of gems by a *gemmarius*,[28] could betray in their subject matter a text relevant to this present study. In the published catalogue of finds from the site, six of the gems are listed as portraying deities especially concerned with fecundity, while two others include motifs, in the form of corn-ears and poppy-heads, which refer to the same theme. Could not the subject matter of these gems have been particularly chosen for dedication at the spring by women wishing to conceive, already pregnant and desirous of a safe delivery, or in thanks for a problem-free birth?

The women who dedicated the models of breasts at the temple at Bath, and others at West Hill, Uley and Harlow, chose to represent themselves in this way, as a disassociated body part, rather than through using a female-related item of personal adornment such as hairpins or bracelets, as would certainly appear to have happened at the Lydney Park temple site. At Lydney, an unusually large number of female-related items such as these were recovered and the site might therefore have been one specialising in female medical problems. The full range of items at Lydney will now be considered. These included a bronze arm, with the hand's thumb and forefinger in such a position as to suggest to the excavators that the hand originally held the apple frequently found in this position on ornamental pinheads,[29] a bronze leg and foot from the early excavations conducted by the Reverend Bathurst there,[30] and a bone plaque on which is incised the figure of a naked, possibly pregnant woman, though one authority later took issue with this interpretation of the figure's state[31] and thus with the excavators' statement that the plaque could have been dedicated by 'some female worshipper who had received relief in childbirth'. A fourth possible *ex voto* is represented by a bronze-shod foot, obviously broken off a statuette, but deemed by the excavators to have no further significance. The excavators also believed, following the interpretation of similar material from Epidauros, that the presence of large numbers of specifically female objects, like pins and bracelets, related to dedications connected to women's medical problems. The images of dogs from the site were linked to the healing properties attributed to dogs' saliva at healing shrines, though (Plate 27).

Such specialisation in female cures has also been suggested as occurring at Great Witcombe villa, Gloucestershire where a healing shrine might have existed in a later phase and where unusually large numbers of female-related small finds such as hairpins and bracelets were recovered during excavation. It is possible that at Lydney, Great Witcombe, and other British healing sites the hairpins were actually secondary dedications by individual women, following the cutting off and dedication of their hair there.[32]

It is relevant here while discussing female health problems in Roman Britain to introduce mention of the unique finding of a tablet of some kind, a charm tablet rather than a curse tablet, though in this case the charm, written entirely in Greek, is on a rectangular strip of gold leaf. Dated by the style of cursive writing to between AD 250 and 350, the find was made south of Oxford in an area where no Roman site is presently recorded. The text of the charm, introduced by two and a half lines of magical signs reads in translation, 'Make with your holy names that Fabia whom Terentia her mother bore, being in full fitness and health, shall master the unborn child and bring it to birth; the name of the Lord and Great God being everlasting.'[33] This object is so far without parallel in Roman Britain, though it has been noted that it can be compared to 'an unspecific uterine amulet made of haematite and an inscribed lead phylactery against a "wandering womb"'.[34]

The Gods could also be asked to curse as well as cure. One of the lead curse tablets from Bath asks that someone 'be accursed in [his] blood and eyes and every limb, or even have all [his] intestines eaten away', while another tablet, from Lydney, specifically entreats the deity not to grant any of the family of Senicianus health. A third tablet, this time from London, curses the 'life and mind and memory and liver and lungs mixed up together' of Tretia Maria.[35] While it is tempting to suggest the possible extension of the practice of cursing to also include the magical use of models of the cursed person's body parts, there is no evidence to support the existence of such a process in Roman Britain and indeed a warning has been given that the curses from Bath were 'petitions for justice, not magical spells'.[36]

In terms of identifying other Romano-British sites that might have specialised in providing cures for particular specific illnesses or for a specific medical market, it is possible that the anatomical *ex votos* of eyes from Wroxeter and South Shields and legs from West Hill, Uley point towards specialisation there, even though find numbers are relatively few. At Uley, three lead model legs, one with a foot, and a silvered bronze plaque bearing a foot in relief suggest an allusion 'to Mercury as the god of wayfarers' and 'as an appropriate deity to cure diseases impeding movement'.[37] At Wroxeter, during the excavation of the uppermost levels in the baths basilica area, a number of eyes fashioned from plaster were found; at least thirty positive identifications and some fifty other examples which 'range from the possible to the dubious' are represented. The eyes are in some cases carefully modelled, with pupil, iris, and tear duct easily distinguishable, but others are crudely and roughly fashioned. They range in size from large and heavy examples to tiny, almost delicate pieces.[38] There was also found an eye made from a sherd of Samian pottery. From the same area, and found at a different time, came a pair of eyes made from a sheet of beaten gold[39] and a fragment of an eye in copper alloy sheet. From what structure all these objects derived is uncertain but they obviously relate in some way to a religious healing site. The South Shields plaster eyes are all unfortunately equally difficult to interpret, one being from a robber trench inside Arbeia fort and two being unstratified in the *vicus* there. It is worth noting that from the apse of the basilica at Cirencester came a larger-than-life-size bronze eye and lid,[40] most probably derived from a statue; caution forbids any speculation about the significance of this find as another example of the presence of an eye specialising healing centre here, as at Wroxeter and South Shields (Plate 28).

A note of caution does need to be struck over making perhaps simplistic connections between eye troubles and Wroxeter and South Shields and leg or foot problems and Uley as evidenced by finds there. Such finds cannot always be taken at face value. Representations of eyes at other Graeco-Roman healing sites could have stood not for visual problems or impairment but rather for the importance of visual experience in the mysteries of seeking a cure or even have acted as an allusion to visions seen in dreams. They could have represented the all-seeing eyes of the gods or even symbolised requests for the deity's gaze to be directed upon the supplicant's prayer. Likewise representations of feet could simply have acted as proof or memento that the owner of the feet was there, that they were going on a journey for which they sought safe passage under the protection of the gods, or indeed they could have alluded to the divine feet and presence of the god or goddess themselves.

Fear and the Gods

Not all of the Romano-British sites from which anatomical *ex votos* come are classifiable by function, though most were temple or religious sites – some, though not all of them the sites of healing shrines; nor can all of the identified religious sites be assigned to the worship of a particular deity, though Bath, West Hill, Uley, Lydney Park, and possibly Lamyatt Beacon are exceptions. It must be remembered in this respect that 'many or most of the gods could heal'[41] and therefore that healing could take place at any kind of religious site. An analysis of the roles and attributed powers of the numerous saints of Brittany[42] raises some very interesting points about the potential complexity of analysing healing deities in the context of a competing 'world of gods' such as also existed in Roman times, many of these deities being highly local in their operation. In Brittany there are two hundred and sixteen individual saints with healing powers: of these, one hundred and eighty-five are relatively specialised in their attributed powers. For instance, of those saints dealing with skin complaints, Sainte Flamine of Gestel in the Morbihan area is one of only ten saints who deals exclusively with eczemas while of those seventeen saints specialising in eye problems Saint Clair of Derval, Loire-Atlantique is one of eleven saints concentrating exclusively on these. Only forty-five saints are seen as dealing with all medical problems, while others have quite diverse portfolios of attributed roles: for instance, Saint Cado deals with ears, rheumatic pains, faintness, breakdowns, eczema, and sores or ulcers. A dedication of an *ex voto* to Saint Cado, for example, if not specific in its form to the complaint for which a cure was being sought, would be difficult to interpret correctly without full knowledge of his range of attributed medical responsibilities.

Some authorities see anatomical or medical *ex votos* as simple to interpret, with the objects being dedicated either in seeking help to obtain a cure or in thanks for having secured one, and occasionally for both. However, there would appear to be a number of concomitant factors in addition to choosing the right deity at the right site that made the process of dedication more complex, not the least of which must have been the individuality of each and every act of dedication, though at the same time dedication would also have been an intensely social act. The *ex votos* themselves can be seen both as instruments and as texts, in the latter instances carrying coded messages, of belief, hope, fear, or alienation, or any combination of these. Human motives are seldom subsumed or revealed in the drama of ritual itself and therefore some attempt to contextualise these objects has to be made using other classes of source material and using an extended geographical and chronological framework. 'Ill health and disease are culturally defined phenomena'[43] and it is impossible to define reactions to them or to understand the cultural definition by reference to the archaeological record alone.

The Roman religions had developed a system whereby individuals could 'come to terms with the gods by a process of oath-taking, and fulfilment of contracts',[44] a system evocatively demonstrated in the case of Roman Britain by many of the contract-like texts on the lead curse tablets from the sacred spring at Bath.[45] On a simple level anatomical *ex votos* could be viewed as indicators of the initiation of a contract, dedicated as part of the process of seeking a cure, or at its completion, with the dedication being an offering in thanks for the cure. However, even if in a diluted or mutated form, the stigma attached to the sick in classical society – defining them as somehow being less worthy and almost outside of polite society – applied in Roman Britain, and the pressure and need to obtain a cure by any means, including by means of contract with the gods, would have been particularly intense. It is indeed true that 'who a person is and where he is located in the social and institutional structures strongly influence who presents an illness, or at least the signs that are interpreted as illness, for treatment'.[46] This may be significant where the sick person, in addition to being outside the world of the healthy and/or in pain, may be culturally construed as being somehow alienated and dispossessed. In such a situation the dedication of a medical *ex voto*, either before or after any cure, would also carry an additional meaning relating to the suppliant's desire for re-entry or reintegration into society. The situation is similar to Emile Durkheim's positive theory of ritual, in which religious practices help to maintain the individual's sense of reality.[47] Here the healer's role is a mediating one, that of a cultural broker, and certainly it can be seen that 'in most cultures religious rites often concern the management of fear' in this way.[48]

How sickness and what was construed as sickness particularly affected women's roles in classical or Roman society is difficult to ascertain, though social pressures on women to conform with the expected norms of child-bearing and child-rearing must have been considerable. For the elite, and this may also have applied to the native Romano-British elite, the need to assure the survival of the male line of a family may have been a significant motor in social and sexual relations,[49] and it is known that barrenness was a justification for dissolving a Roman marriage. An actual or perceived stigma attached to the childless woman may have led many such women to seek help from the gods and goddesses, whose involvement in these instances could therefore again be viewed sometimes as being on more than a purely medical level. Dialogue with a deity would at least allow private emotions, and perhaps an otherwise marginalised passion, to be given a more public voice, and there is no evidence to show that the gods in such a situation were any less accessible to women, or less of a perceived comfort to them, in times of real or construed illness or overbearing social and family pressures.

While the essential individuality of each dedication has already been stressed, it would nevertheless seem churlish not to turn now and examine the large body of epigraphic material relating to the dedication of medical *ex votos* in the Greek world. For here, among the surviving inscriptions are expressed instances of timeless and universal hopes and fears, and possible insights into the motives and mechanics of dedication. It must be noted that the dedication of *ex votos* was often inextricably linked to prayer and sometimes to sacrifice, with the votive representing on occasions, evidence not for a single religious act but rather for one of a number of acts in an often extended process of dialogue. An *ex voto* could be said to be a prayer made visible.

At the Asklepion in Athens, inscriptions tell of the occasional dedication of complete representations of individuals along with the more normal dedications of *ex votos* in the form of single body parts. An invaluable catalogue of the Greek material has been compiled, and its compiler has suggested that in such an instance the dedicator 'may be overcome by an acute awareness of the vulnerability of his mortal body, perhaps even heightened at the sight of numerous similar dedications in the sanctuary. It would not seem such a bad idea, then, to commend one's entire body to the benevolent attention of the god'.[50] In many cases pain will have become fear and, in extreme cases, fear of death, for 'disease forces us to recognise the place of destiny in our lives. It activates our spiritual sensitivity. It directs our gaze towards the eternal.'[51] From the same site come other inscriptions that show that on occasions more than one example of the same body part was dedicated or even that dedications were sometimes made on someone else's behalf,[52] instances of a subtlety that would be otherwise lost in the archaeological record. From the sanctuary of Aphrodite, again in Athens, comes an inscription which implies that the dedication of a pair of breasts is connected with childbirth rather than with any specific breast problem.[53]

At the sanctuary of Demeter and Kore at Eleusis, the dedication of a marble plaque showing a woman's face and neck under a pair of eyes possibly relates not to a plea for the recovery of lost sight or impaired vision or the cure for an eye infection, but rather to the Eleusinian Mysteries, a 'primarily visual experience' for which 'eyes would be appropriate'.[54] Eyes also appear in an unusual context at the Amphiareion at Oropos in Boetia, on a curious relief dedicated by Archinos. Again here the eyes are not linked to a medical problem but rather they 'render thanks for the vision he saw in his dream', which is the main subject of the relief.[55] At the healing shrines were to be found both dreams and health, and contact could be made with the gods there both by the dedication of images 'because that was where the gods lived' themselves and 'beyond their images ... through sleep ... [and] dreams'.[56] It should be further noted that in both the Greek and Roman worlds, dedicated eyes were in some instances intended not as models of afflicted parts but as the all-seeing eyes of the gods, requests for their gaze to be directed upon the suppliant's prayer, in the same way that the listening ears of the gods could also be petitioned through the dedication of votive ears.[57] Greek sites also produce evidence for footprints, either represented as carvings or simply outlined, dedicated not only with reference to a cure but also either 'as proof and memento that the owner of the feet was there' or in representation of 'the divine feet' as is attested by inscriptions (Plate 29).[58]

In the classical world the definition of the medical *ex voto* occasionally went beyond the use of models or representations of body parts, and encompassed clothes, sometimes worn by women during pregnancy or childbirth,[59] clipped or shorn hair,[60] cakes in the shape of the affected body parts,[61] and shells 'in the shape of the womb, suitably filled with dough or clay'.[62] Ethnographic and wider archaeological studies could probably show an even broader definition in other cultures and societies, and a greater variety in the use of materials, with *ex votos* often being made of cheap and perishable materials which in most situations would not survive in the archaeological record. From Roman Britain medical *ex votos* made from gold, bronze or copper alloy, pottery, clay, plaster, and ivory are known. We know that terracotta was particularly favoured in Italy for such items, as seen at sites such as Ponte di Nona and Nemi,[63] both near Rome (Plates 30–31). Wood was likewise seemingly particularly esteemed in Gaul, as revealed in the remarkable groups of carved wooden *ex votos* from, for instance, the Source of the Seine.[64] The use of wax is attested from the medieval period onwards.[65]

The eventual disposal of *ex votos* would itself have been a practice with as many variants as their dedication. Retention of *ex votos* after dedication would seem to have been a necessity, in that they were, even long after their dedication and after their specific original context of meaning had been exhausted, both ornaments and advertisements for the place of dedication.[66] Votive and sacred items could be deposited in a *favissa*, a pit for the reception of such objects that were no longer needed but still dedicated to a deity, and we must envisage such a clearing-out of *ex votos* happening at regular intervals. Whether in Roman Britain objects of precious metal were ever recycled or melted down to enrich the religious establishment where dedicated, something attested in the Greek world and also much later in the medieval period,[67] we cannot say. Such possibilities of extended retention, delayed ritual disposal, or even destruction and recycling of *ex votos* make chronological or typological discussion of the relatively small group of Romano-British *ex votos* impossible. That the latest of them probably came from Lydney Park and date to the fourth century either shows the longevity and constancy of the idea behind their use, almost a linearity of a particular strain of ancient Greek and Roman belief and ritual, or a conscious revival at that time of an earlier practice, adopted and subsequently discontinued by those sections of society in Roman Britain most open to religious acculturation. This scenario might suggest that the act of dedication was at the earlier period more ubiquitous than the limited archaeological survival of material would seem to indicate. It would be interesting to see if the well-attested later ritual reuse of earlier statuary in Roman Britain, part of what one commentator has called 'the final pirouette of Romano-British civilisation down the road to barbarism',[68] was rather part of, in certain but not all instances, a conscious revival of another classical idea. Could this process not also have links to the theory of an elite-driven 'revitalisation movement' in later Roman Britain?[69]

Model Bodies, Real Bodies

Despite the academic fashion of the 1990s for looking at the history of the body in the classical world there has not really been a concerted attempt to carry out such a study using data from Roman Britain, including finds data, as well as art historical data and, perhaps most obviously, burial data. Indeed, at a number of conferences I have heard doubts expressed on more than one occasion that a history of the Romano-British body could be written using archaeological data. Contrary to this cynicism, some recent finds studies in fact suggest that the appearance and distribution of toilet implements in the late pre-Roman Iron Age and Romano-British period reflects a chronologically recognisable change in perceptions towards bodily hygiene and maintenance and thus of the individual's view of his or her own body, though I will return to this very subject in Chapter 7.

There must be a reason or reasons why anatomical or medical *ex votos* are not common finds on religious sites in Roman Britain. And likewise, when they are found we need to be careful about interpreting their significance. Their relative rarity when compared to finds of large numbers on a few sites in Gaul and of smaller numbers at many sites there suggests that there is a major cultural difference between the sick or cured pilgrims or worshippers at Gallo-Roman and Romano-British sites, due to a difference in the way that the body is conceived in those societies. Being unable or unwilling for whatever reason to accept the concept of the body as being a series of conjoined parts might be a Romano-British cultural trait. Perhaps those who dedicated anatomical *ex votos* in Roman Britain were from elsewhere in the empire (Plate 32).

It is hoped that some new light has been shed on the crepuscular world of the healing deities in Roman Britain in this chapter. It has been suggested above that the subtlety and potential complexity of the process of dedicating anatomical or medical *ex votos* needs to be recognised. The definition of the special position of the sick within society, and of sub-groups among the sick based on culture, class, or gender, creates a new perspective that may allow more anodyne interpretations of the significance of the healing cults to be reassessed. The reading of signs and symbols, for such are anatomical *ex votos*, can be as superficial or as profound as the reading of any text. But if we define symbols in Baudelaire's sense as the means by which man can aspire to penetrate the temple of nature, then perhaps we are as close to the truth of the past in this instance as our distance from it will allow.

If looking at anatomical *ex votos* provides some insights into views on the body in Roman Britain then perhaps further insights can be gained by looking at evidence for personal grooming and hygiene. This could be done by looking at architectural evidence, that is the distribution and spread of bath houses, and by looking at artefactual evidence in the form of objects used in personal grooming, that is items known collectively as toilet implements in the archaeological literature, and items associated with bathing.

Perhaps anatomical *ex votos* were not particularly regarded by Romano-Britons as acceptable parts of the religious rites at healing shrines, and, indeed, it might be suggested that a reason for this could be a failure on their part to engage in mental strategies of disassembling bodies into body parts, as was required as part of the process, as will be discussed further in Chapter 6. Following on from this, an examination of the published volumes of the definitive sculptural corpus for Roman Britain – *Corpus Signorum Imperii Romanum* – suggests that busts and portrait heads, in other words representations of whole individuals by partial portrayals, are again not well represented among the art from Roman Britain. Does all of this imply that the image of the fragmented body and the concepts behind it were anathema to most of the people of Roman Britain? If so, this would appear to represent a perhaps significant difference in perceptions of both the individual and the body, and the role of art in articulating such perceptions between Roman Britain and other parts of the empire.

A recent study of the patterns of fragmentation of cult statues in Roman Britain[70] has again raised interesting issues with regard to possible Romano-British attitudes towards the body and in particular the body in pieces or fragments. While the main thrust of this study was not in this direction – it was very much aimed at debunking iconoclasm as a catch-all explanation for the breaking of many cult and imperial statues – it nevertheless showed that some element of positive or negative selection of certain body parts of these statues took place when the complete or whole statue was no longer deemed, for whatever reason, to be any longer valid as an object. It would be most interesting to see such a study extended to take in non-cult or religious images, though once one eliminates cult and imperial images from the catalogue of free-standing statuary from Roman Britain there are relatively few examples of representations of individuals to work with. Individual representation seems to have been more acceptable through the use of inscriptions or often stock funerary reliefs.

It can be asked whether the images of the fragmented human body discussed in this chapter represent part of a broader coherent pattern or trend in belief or value within the Roman or Romanised societies which created and consumed such images. I would argue that this would certainly seem to be the case and I will return to this theme in more detail in Chapter 6. Are there in fact any conceptual links between individual body parts dedicated as *ex votos* at healing shrines and wax *imagines*, images of ancestors in the form of masks worn at Roman funerals, and portrait busts? Both *imagines* and busts, like anatomical *ex votos*, are after all partial images representing whole bodies. While in Greek society and art the body remained an almost inviolable whole, in Roman art the fragmentation of the body in images when it occurred perhaps reflected the permeability of boundaries in Roman society and culture between life and death, sickness and health, Roman and barbarian, past and present, and class status and lineage.

It can perhaps be argued that the active manipulation of the fragment in the Roman world created a new whole, and in so doing not only stressed the indivisibility of the present from the past but acted as a metaphor for their conscious dissociation. Wax ancestor masks or *imagines* were used to keep the memory of notable ancestors alive in the present. They were also didactic devices for demonstrating to the young the moral qualities of earlier generations of Romans. Together these elements provided society with the experience and security of returning to the whole, a process of interpreting often ambiguous and contradictory phenomena and translating that interpretation into a new vision of reality. Partial representations in portraiture allowed the same process to be extended to other classes of Roman society and to other parts of the empire, and for this to occur in other social and cultural situations, often linked to funerary commemoration. Anatomical *ex votos* were used in a process of both trying to seek a cure and reintegration back into society and in a way were props for seeking a return to the whole through reincorporation within the social body, as indeed they have been and are in many other societies (Plate 33).

No matter how much metamorphosis is reinforced by the dividing, deforming, and fragmenting of the body as an image in Roman material culture and art, the inherent tension between inner and outer reference always remains, as does the extension and even preservation of tradition in the face of what might be considered almost avant-garde technique. The metaphor of containment or inclusion frequently used was basically an image of possession, of things taken from the world, dematerialised, and made to belong to society itself. In some instances the corporeal body was reduced to the status of an artefact.[71]

The sick do not suffer any longer in silence in the archaeological record from Roman Britain. The growing number of anatomical or medical *ex votos* now recognised from Romano-British sites adds a human dimension to the picture. Finds of medical equipment and medical-related items like occulists' stamps further add to the emerging picture of the state of health of the inhabitants of the province of *Britannia*, as indeed does the vital study of human skeletal remains from both cremation and inhumation burials, a topic well beyond the core subject of this book. Lead curse tablets, principally from Bath and West Hill, Uley, provide a remarkably personal insight into how ill health could be viewed by some individuals as a weapon to be used by the gods in seeking vengeance against an enemy or the perpetrator of a crime of some sort.

As already noted, most studies of the classical body have dealt with the whole body, with issues of gender and representation, health and medical practice, or exclusion through disability or other perceived differences, but once we start to consider the concepts behind an empire in pieces perhaps other types of analysis may be required to be brought into play. In some of the situations presented above the human body was not simply modified, it was transformed into a series of unrelated parts. The social body had in certain contexts approved the dismemberment of the corporeal body as images in order for the whole body to be cured and restored to society. There was an undoubted 'tension between the belief in the body as an ideal form, and the body as dehumanised parts'.[72] In many ways some of the sick presenting themselves at healing shrines in Roman Britain were hoping to induce their gods to manipulate time on their behalf, to help them deny the reality of the present, and return them to a former time in the past when their health was good. The creation of other narratives of Romano-British life that conflated the past and the present to attempt to body forth new realities forms the subject of the next chapter.

DISCOVERED UNDER OTHER SKIES

The Present Past

Following on from the discussion of medical or anatomical *ex votos* in the last chapter, in this chapter an attempt will be made to analyse another seemingly relatively minor aspect of ritual behaviour during the Roman period, as occasionally evidenced by archaeological finds in both Britain and Gaul, namely the reuse of prehistoric stone and flint tools, so-called lithics, in certain well-defined and well-regulated archaeological contexts. Arguments about the credibility of the evidence from Britain on a site-by-site basis will be eschewed here in favour of a more broad-brush approach to the subject, without in any way minimising the importance of establishing contextual security for such finds. It will be argued that there is now a sufficiently credible body of data about such instances of reuse to enable problematic and possibly residual material to be eliminated and discounted from such a study and for new frameworks of explanation and interpretation to be advanced that take cognisance of evidence for other types of engagement between the Romano-British present as it then was and the British prehistoric past. Indeed, recent finds from the site of Ivy Chimneys in Essex are of such great significance as to move forward an academic argument of over twenty-five years' standing that had become bogged down in the quite necessary questioning of the minutiae of the stratigraphical credibility of each find in turn.

This is not then an entirely new area of academic study and debate. The presence of Neolithic polished stone axes on Romano-British sites was first the subject of an academic paper in 1985, wherein was discussed what the authors saw as the significance of this presence backed up by a gazetteer of forty sites on which finds of axes had been made, the types of sites including not only temples but also towns, forts, and kiln sites. The paper drew both praise and criticism. While being lauded as definitive by one authority, another almost at the same time was calling into question the validity of the criteria used for compiling the gazetteer. It was asserted that eighteen of the forty listed instances of site finds were dubious, and that a further ten were to be, as the critic put it, 'treated with some reserve'. Indeed, it was therefore asked whether there was, in fact, any pattern of deposition to be studied.[1]

In this chapter I will refrain from reopening the debate about individual entries in the 1985 site gazetteer, but will rather discuss a small number of additional case studies instancing the reuse of prehistoric material, and not just Neolithic axes, in non-domestic Roman period contexts, publication of the more interesting examples in any case post-dating the compilation of the gazetteer and its subsequent critique.

By far the most important and intriguing find has been made at the site of Ivy Chimneys, near Witham, in Essex. Between 1978 and 1983 forty-one certain and three possible Palaeolithic flint hand-axes were recovered during controlled excavation at the Romano-British ritual and religious site there. The majority of the axes came from within, or around, two large depressions, the digging or creation of which the excavators dated to the Roman period,[2] although the gravel infills of these depressions were quite distinct from each other and had obviously been deposited during two discrete episodes of backfilling. The earlier of the two infills was dated to the second to mid-third century AD, a period when it was believed there was no temple on the site[3] and the later infilling to the early fourth century onwards. Away from the depressions, eight other definite axes and one possible axe were recovered, one notably from a context of the early to mid-first century and another from a horizon broadly contemporary with the earliest depression. The hand-axes from the depressions were mostly of so-called Wymer Type E,[4] that is not particularly finely made (Plates 34–35).

The detailed analysis of the axes demonstrated beyond all doubt that this was a mixed assemblage of geographically and typologically diverse artefacts whose presence at the site could only be explained by their having been brought together deliberately and systematically. The excavators concluded that 'the sum of evidence makes the alternative explanation that they were accidental imports untenable'.[5] Indeed, they later wrote that 'they may have been recognised as hand-made by Roman stone masons experienced in the properties of flint. The best axes may have been kept for special ceremonies, while more ordinary Type E axes were deposited in the depressions.'[6] There is also the possibility that 'such items may have held significance also for their pure antiquity value, which may itself have been endowed with magical imagery. Neolithic flint axes are known in Merovingian graves ... and may have possessed the same kind of reverence value.'[7]

If twenty fully trained professional archaeologists were instructed today to go forth and find just five Palaeolithic axes, despite their knowledge of prehistoric sites and landscapes and their ability to identify such objects as artefacts, it is unlikely that this group of experts would return to base any time soon with even one axe, never mind the forty-plus buried at Ivy Chimneys. The amassing of such a collection at Ivy Chimneys must have been an extended process and one involving a vast network of contacts who knew that such items were being collected there.

A brief discussion of the wider significance of the find is offered in the published report on the axes. It can be asked whether the traditional schema of interpretation offered – that axes equal thunderbolts and that thunderbolts equal Jupiter – is perhaps flawed, and whether the reiteration of this interpretative framework consciously or subconsciously denies the application of other parallel or different analyses. In particular, little is made of what would appear to be the longevity of the practice of collecting and disposing of axes on the site. At Ivy Chimneys 'a single large, isolated post-pit may represent evidence for a ... timber Jupiter column here',[8] but that does not necessarily link the presence of the axes to an entirely hypothetical Jupiter monument at Ivy Chimneys.

A medium-sized assemblage of two hundred and thirty-four post-Palaeolithic worked prehistoric flints also came from the site,[9] though in the published final report these are simply discussed in terms of their being residual finds from a ploughed out or otherwise disturbed and obliterated prehistoric settlement here. The two most highly worked items, part of a polished flint axe and a barbed and tanged arrowhead, came respectively from a ditch infill to the west of the main enclosed area and from the fill of a depression to the north-east of the main site, but not one of the two large depressions that contained the Palaeolithic axes. The outlying positions of the features from which these items came might just possibly suggest that they were placed here as boundary markers.

The sequence of structural activity at Ivy Chimneys begins with a settlement of some kind here in the Iron Age, with very large late Iron Age ditches and other evidence pointing towards at least part of the site having had a religious function. The nature of the earliest Roman activity here is not altogether clear, though two large depressions dug at this time mark the beginning of Roman religious activity on the site, while in the third century a Romano-Celtic temple was built here, with a sophisticated water regulation system and isolated timber columns. In the fourth century a new temple was constructed, contemporary with which was another man-made depression and a pottery kiln. The site possibly saw Christian worship in the mid-fourth century, returning to pagan worship in the late fourth to early fifth century. Leaving aside the coins and personal items from the site which might represent *ex votos* of one kind or another, specifically religious items recovered included: a copper alloy votive letter V;[10] a copper alloy moulded head, possibly of a priest figure;[11] an iron, copper alloy, and gold model of bull's horns;[12] a stone cult figure[13] in the form of a double-sided stone with a possibly male figure in a tunic in a niche representing a temple building on both sides; and a fired-clay phallus.[14] Analysis of the animal bones recovered by excavation at the site suggested that leaving aside bones linked to domestic species and bones providing evidence for bone/animal processing here at some time, the presence of bones of larger-sized cattle and of slaughtered horses probably related to ritual activity.[15]

A similar find, cited as a parallel in the Ivy Chimneys report, comes from the nearby site of Kelvedon, also in Essex, where a Palaeolithic hand-axe was again found in association with Romano-British material. Exact details of the find are unclear, in that it is reported as having been found amongst a group of material from 'one or more pits, said to be 2m deep and full of charcoal'.[16] The Roman material found included *tesserae*, several copper alloy letters, a silver necklace, an *intaglio*, lengths of copper alloy rod, and part of a human skull. This assemblage was associated with the possible site of a temple and is clearly votive in character and in the nature of its deposition. The general consensus would seem to be that the axe in the pit was part of a deliberate deposition in the Romano-British period.[17] The pit containing the object was obviously a *favissa*, that is a pit dug to take *ex votos* removed from inside a temple building.

At the Iron Age and Romano-British temple site on Hayling Island, flint tools, principally scrapers of Neolithic/Bronze Age date, occur in some quantity. A Neolithic polished stone axe and a Mesolithic axe came from topsoil deposits, and, as will be discussed further below, a Bronze Age bronze spearhead has also been found here in a more secure archaeological context. The excavators of the site are in little doubt that 'these objects from earlier prehistory, perhaps found casually during the Iron Age as a result of activity that disturbed earlier material, were brought to the site as votive offerings'.[18] It is interesting to note in passing that prehistoric lithics specialists usually interpret scrapers as being tools redolent of settlement sites where hearth-based activities such as skin scraping would have taken place, ethnographically such tasks being female roles in the community economy.[19]

To return briefly to the 1985 gazetteer,[20] it should be noted that a flint axe was deemed to be a votive offering at the temple of Springhead, Kent, where a miniature bronze socketed axe was also found, while material at the temple of Farley Heath, Surrey – 'a flint chisel, two stone axes and a reworked axe' – was said to have been 'found in a heap inside the enclosure of the temple', a surely significant context, though this is one of the examples subsequently deemed dubious on the grounds of there being other Neolithic artefacts found on the site.[21] At Lancing Down temple site in Sussex a prehistoric axe was possibly a ritual object.

The next example comes from an excavation of a Romano-British pottery production site at Newland Hopfields, near Malvern, Worcestershire. The excavation located and examined a single kiln producing Severn Valley ware and a number of associated features and structures.[22] Close to the kiln was a laid stone working surface, partially damaged by recent agricultural activity on the site, consisting mainly of imported river cobbles, but including amongst its components a Neolithic polished stone axe.[23] Little other prehistoric material was recovered from what was an extensive open-area excavation here, and some explanation for the presence of the axe in the floor surface must therefore be sought in the activities of the Roman period. Again, it is worth noting two entries in the 1985 gazetteer for the finding of a stone axe at the kiln site at Durobrivae and of a 'polished stone adze ... found in the 1st-century lining of a pit' at the Brockley Hill kiln site in Hertfordshire,[24] though I have not been able to check the context of these finds in the site archives (Plate 36).

Prehistoric material has also been found in a small number of Romano-British burial contexts. While the temple site represents the dividing line between the lives of men and women and their gods, the burial site represents the dividing line between the living and the dead. Both types of site, nevertheless, are controlled through – and relationships there mediated by – ritual activity. Robert Philpott's work on burial practices in Roman Britain[25] has provided a useful summary of the phenomenon of the reuse of prehistoric material.

Philpott writes that[26] 'worked flint flakes or tools were deliberately included in a number of graves in chalk regions while prehistoric tools are occasionally found.

These should be distinguished from the cremations where flint was used to pack the grave or urn, or were placed inside the urn ... the presence of ... flint flakes and tools ... in graves is frequent enough not to be accidental.' His amalgamation of flints found in graves with instances of the finding of fossils and pebbles, and their discussion together as 'amuletic objects', would seem to close off discussion of other possible interpretations of the presence of such objects. It also very much follows the work of Audrey Meaney[27] on similar material found in Anglo-Saxon contexts.

In his gazetteer Philpott lists, and here his descriptions of the artefacts have been followed: three flint chips in a cremation urn at Haslemere in Surrey; a flint flake in a cremation at Canterbury, Kent, and a Bronze Age arrowhead in a second cremation at the same site; a Neolithic scraper in a burial at Ford, Reculver, Kent; and a Neolithic arrowhead and four small stones in the cremation burial of a child at Gatcombe, Somerset. He is more vague about the nature of flints used to pack burials, although it is assumed that these are generally natural, unworked nodules, with the exception of two examples, one at Seaford, East Sussex where 'cinerary urns were surrounded by flint flakes and a scraper' and the other at Skeleton Green, Hertfordshire where 'a similar packing of the urn with flints' was reported. Not included in Philpott's list are further examples recorded from, for example, Bradley Hill, Somerset,[28] where a flint scraper was recovered from the fill of a grave, and from Bradford Peverell, Dorset[29] where flint nodules were used to pack a grave.

As for fossils, Philpott records a belemnite included in a cremation at Fordington, Dorchester and fossil sea urchins in a number of inhumation burials at Frilford, Oxfordshire.[30] I am aware of only one instance of a fossil being used as raw material for the creation of an artefact, in the Roman period, though the dating and perhaps genuineness of this piece is certainly also open to question, given that it was a stray find, said to have come from a field at Great Bedwyn, Wiltshire. The object is a roughly carved female head made from an ammonite fossil,[31] with the outer, ridged ring of the ammonite forming the woman's hair. If a genuine Roman article, the fossil might have been selected for aesthetic purposes rather than for its amuletic or other significance.

It is difficult to know at present what to make of the burial data. The presence of flints in cremations must represent deliberate deposition, but there must always be a question mark over the context of flints recovered from the backfills of graves, as opposed to their having been recorded as being deliberately positioned within a grave. There is no evidence whatsoever to suggest that we are talking about a coherent burial rite, on a geographical, chronological, cultural, social, ethnic, religious, or gender basis.

To turn briefly to Gaul, there is considerable evidence for the finding of prehistoric stone tools in Gallo-Roman religious contexts, and this seems to be generally accepted on the continent as being a genuine phenomenon. A gazetteer of Romano-Celtic temples in continental Europe lists thirty-five instances of stone tools having been found at such sites, alongside other objects of an undeniably votive or religious character,[32] while in the Ivy Chimneys report it is stated that 'at least twenty-six continental temple sites have produced such finds'.[33] Unlike the British examples, with the exception now of Ivy Chimneys, the quantity of prehistoric material from some of these Gallic sites immediately discounts its identification as being residual or inadvertently imported. For example, from Essarts comes a hoard of seventy Palaeolithic and Neolithic stone axes, found with fossils and other material; from La Mare-du-Puits come twenty polished stone axes and twenty-two fossil sea urchins; from Phase B of Saint-Aubin-Sur-Gaillon come twenty flint axes and, again, some fossils; from Louviers come eleven flint axes and tools; from Vertault come five or six polished stone axes, and so on.[34] Other types of prehistoric flint tool, generally blades and arrowheads, are also listed in the gazetteer as having been found in Gaul, but these appear in smaller numbers and might therefore be residual, along with the instances of the discovery of single axes.

It would require special pleading to accept the continental evidence for the deliberate curation at temple sites of prehistoric stone tools but to reject the self-same practice as having occurred at the British site of Ivy Chimneys.[35]

There is also some evidence for Bronze Age socketed axes and other Bronze Age items to have been curated in the Iron Age[36] and to a lesser extent in the Romano-British period.[37] In the southern British Iron Age bronze objects, already hundreds of years old, appear deposited at sites:

> with a pre-existing monumentality [which] may suggest that objects and places were felt to share 'otherwordliness'. These items and places may have been used to construct esoteric knowledge through reference to spirits but it is also likely that particular acts of curation and deposition created genealogical associations, incorporating ideas of the mythical past into the context of the present.[38]

A study of this phenomenon identified twelve possible sites in England and Wales at which curation of Bronze Age items is attested, involving hundreds of individual items, a figure skewed by the occurrence of over five hundred objects of this date in the Salisbury hoard.[39] Although a second hoard site in this list, the so-called Batheaston hoard, again contained over three hundred individual objects only a few were of early or middle Bronze Age date. In the Lexden tumulus, Colchester, a suite of grave-goods accompanied what is generally considered to be the burial of a later Iron Age tribal leader. Among these was one 'out of time' item, a Bronze Age bronze palstave axe, seemingly carefully wrapped in a cloth for protection, and one startlingly contemporary item, a medallion of the Roman emperor Augustus.[40]

Of most interest in the context of this chapter is the finding of a broken mid-Bronze Age bronze spearhead in one of the entrance post-holes of a circular timber temple structure at Hayling Island, Hampshire, a site where religious buildings follow one after another from the Iron Age into the Romano-British period. The presence at the site of what have been interpreted as curated prehistoric flint tools has already been mentioned above. The late Iron Age and Romano-British temple site at Ashwell, Hertfordshire has also produced 'numerous' Bronze Age metal items from early

Roman contexts. Bronze Age items at Hengistbury Head might equally have been deposited there in the Roman period. Also worthy of note here is the possibility that the large bronze cauldron excavated from a pit at the Sheepen, Colchester site in the 1930s, and dating from 1400–1100 BC, could have been deposited here in the Roman period and thus have been over one thousand years old when finally buried. Again, some of the Bronze Age metalwork found at the Harlow temple site could allegedly date to the Romano-British temple phase at the site.[41]

In Roman Gaul parallels can again be found for this phenomenon: at Fesques a Bronze Age socketed axe was found along with a flint arrowhead, and a Bronze Age flanged axe came from a burial of a woman near Boutae, Annecy. At Mont-Beuvray a bronze axe was found along with one and a half polished jadeite axes.[42]

Miniature socketed bronze axes, that is models of Bronze Age artefacts, are now thought to have been made in the late Iron Age or earlier Roman period in Britain, perhaps as part of a regional phenomenon centred on present-day Wiltshire and southern England more generally.[43] It has been pointed out though that some of these models may be copies of contemporary Iron Age axe types.[44] These items may have been dedicatory *ex votos*, in common with other model objects, or, perhaps less likely, they may have been worn as amulets.[45] In the Roman period other types of miniature or model axes have also been found at sites like Springhead, Kent where prehistoric stone tools have also been recorded, or in ritual-associated contexts, and it is vaguely possible that this could be in some way related to the practice of collecting and displaying Palaeolithic, Neolithic, and Bronze Age axes at Romano-Celtic temples or sanctuary sites.[46]

A Mythical Past

A certain degree of scepticism has already been expressed about the often employed postulate that in the Roman mind a stone axe equalled a thunderbolt, and that this, in turn, somehow alluded to Jupiter. Martin Henig,[47] in his definitive book on religion in Roman Britain, treats such objects as being more to do with superstition than formalised religious practice and, once more, introduces the concept of parallels with folkloric identifications of arrowheads as 'elfshot'. This interpretation arises, of course, from the fact that there is some confirmation of the axe-equals-thunderbolt view in certain classical sources, including the writings of Pliny, who calls such stones *cerauniae*, from the Greek for thunder.[48] The view that the psychology of life in Roman Britain can be better understood today by reference to classical texts is debatable, and there remains in any case a problem in defining how widespread was a knowledge of such written sources in Roman Britain itself or whether the classical sources reflected wider public views on these objects.

Ethnographic studies have shown that prehistoric stone tools are found reused in numerous cultures, at different times and for different purposes, though it cannot be denied that probably the most commonly found explanation for their origins concerns their identification as thunderbolts or so-called thunderstones. A considerable body of folklore also surrounds such material and its supposed origins and physical properties. In the Pitt Rivers Museum in Oxford a collection of such stones is on display. A perusal of the display captions shows that individual stones were also variously used as: a charm to ward off lightning; a protective charm when in battle; a love charm; a charm to protect women during childbirth; a charm to protect cattle, the stone in this case being boiled in water which was later drunk by the cattle; a protection against thieves when placed in front of a house; and as a medical charm which was rubbed over the bodies of the sick. However, lore surrounding such prehistoric stones is not always quite so simple to unravel, as an example from Haiti demonstrates.[49] Here stone axes are believed to be the residences of the *loa*, or gods, having been hurled from the sky as lightning. According to research here the *loa* stones 'are passed from one generation to another … in this way the *loa* who inhabit them are inherited … sometimes, but rarely, stones are sold'.[50] Thus the stones also inextricably become associated as much with the ancestors as with the gods. There are also accounts of prehistoric tools 'being buried in fields to ensure success of the crops, or kept in granaries to increase the store of rice. In Thailand they were used as a charm against lightning, and to sharpen the artificial spur of fighting cocks, as well as just to sharpen knives.'[51] Again, it is worth noting here the frankly astonishing phenomenon in seventeenth-century Spain, where silk copies of prehistoric stone axe heads and arrowheads were made and then worn as amulets (Plate 37).[52] While similar ephemeral amulets are unlikely to survive archaeologically they attest to a different, less tangible medium for a singular form of expression.

The appearance of prehistoric stone tools in bona fide Roman contexts marks the end result of a series of processes in which the material has been located, collected, and curated before being disposed of. The significance of these objects in religious contexts goes beyond their form and function and date of manufacture. The latter would seem to have been an irrelevant factor. These objects, in fact, now had no practical value other than in terms of an emotional currency. They were thus redefined in terms of their new usage and their contemporary context, and thus became as much a part of a Roman religious assemblage of artefacts as, for instance, a lead curse tablet or a copper alloy pin dedicated as an *ex voto*. The role of such objects in the drama of ritual must always be viewed as having been active rather than passive, the objects actively being used as props for mediating between men and women and their gods. Stone or flint objects, because of what must have been viewed as their otherness, would have represented 'the distant, the hidden, the absent'. In other words they acted as go-betweens between those who gazed upon them and the invisible from whence they came.[53]

The group of stone tools at Ivy Chimneys, and those at the Gallic sites, constitute collections, and as such may benefit from the discussion of their significance within the theoretical frameworks applied in interpreting the culture of collecting and, in particular, through those developed by Krzysztof Pomian.[54] Pomian[55] defines the drive towards the creation of collections as being 'an attempt to create a link between the visible and the invisible', something that would be particularly emphasised within a religious, ritual, or somehow official context. His definition of a collection as 'a set of natural or artificial objects, kept temporarily or permanently out of the economic circuit, afforded special protection in enclosed places adapted specifically for that purpose and put on display' would fit the cycle of Roman religious drama, in which an object is forever redefined by its dedication as an *ex voto*, by its display inside or on the walls of a temple or shrine building, and by its eventual disposal by regulated burial, again a form of curation, in a *favissa*.

Within a collection, objects become what Pomian terms 'semiophores', and this applies as much to 'relics of the past and objects found in the natural and exotic world' as it does to works of art. Semiophores are objects 'bearing meaning, on their production, their circulation and their consumption'. The collection also brings into sharp focus the question of temporal relationships. Jean Baudrillard[56] has written that:

> It is by their discontinuous integration into series that we put objects at our disposal, that we possess them ... Objects not only help us to master the world, by their insertion into instrumental series; they also help us, by their insertion into mental series, to master time, making it discontinuous and organising it in the same way as habits, submitting it to the very constraints of associations which govern the arrangement of space.

The collection methods employed in bringing together single or a few prehistoric stone artefacts could have relied upon the chance finding of this material during agricultural activity, building work, gravel extraction, or quarrying. The identification of the material as being exotic, unusual, or somehow other would have led to its retention and possibly to its introduction into the religious milieu through the gift or dedication of an individual or group. But there must also have been occasions when material was disturbed from visible archaeological sites.

To see the bringing together of a large group of such material as that found at Ivy Chimneys – albeit material probably disposed of, if not actually collected, in a number of temporally distinct episodes – as the sum of a large number of chance finds and subsequent dedications would seem improbable. As was noted by the excavators[57] the assemblage here appeared to represent the end result of a sophisticated process of selection. The objects must either have been sought deliberately, or it was known that objects such as these would be accorded special status at this site and were thus brought here for that very reason, though by whom and for whom is unknowable.

More hypothetical still is the notion that in the pattern of selecting certain stone objects, some knowledge of their true nature may be discerned. It has been[58] suggested that Roman stonemasons would have been quite familiar with the techniques of working both stone and flint in those areas of the country where the latter occurred naturally, and, of course, this familiarity is well displayed by the regular use of flint in building work at southern villa sites in the flint/chalk belt, in towns such as Verulamium and Colchester, and even in the later Roman period at the Saxon shore fort of Burgh

Castle where carefully knapped flint blocks formed wall facings. Flint tools would appear to have formed part of the toolkit of workers in the Roman Kimmeridge shale industry of Dorset, particularly a diagnostic squat flint flake,[59] and quite recently at the site of Norwich Road, Kilverstone, Norfolk the probability has been raised that in the later Roman period flint flakes were being produced for use in a threshing sled or machine of some kind,[60] perhaps a *tribulum*.[61] The Kilverstone Roman flintwork came from a single feature and consisted of a single deposit of over eleven thousand pieces of worked flint, mostly so-called micro-debitage, that is minute waste material from the knapping process, most of which was under ten millimetres in length. The knapping episode or episodes represented here seemed focused on the production of small flakes only. According to the lithics specialist who examined and reported on this material 'the technology employed in the generation of the Roman assemblage is highly idiosyncratic and makes it easily distinguishable from the prehistoric material which litters the site. Experimental attempts to replicate [this] suggest that the flakes were detached with a metal hammer'.[62]

It is also worth noting that it is now accepted in some quarters that flintworking to produce tools was also a facet of late Bronze Age and Iron Age society in some areas, most usually in the domestic sphere on a local level,[63] and it has even been suggested that evidence of the knapping of broken glass fragments in the Romano-British period to produce small hand tools not dissimilar to prehistoric artefacts indicates that old techniques continued in use, opening the way perhaps for the identification of occasional Roman flint tool making[64] at sites like Kimmeridge and Kilverstone most obviously and at other sites such as York, Honeyditches Roman Villa, Seaton, Devon, and Wooton, Bedfordshire, all sites where there is little doubt that recovered flintwork is Roman in date.[65]

Some allusion has already been made to the idea that prehistoric artefacts could have been collected and curated because of a recognition of their otherness. This does not necessarily imply that they were actually recognised for what they were, although this is not surely beyond the bounds of possibility. Rather, it may mean that they were seen to be representative of activity that was outside the direct experiences of the finder and of the society to which he or she belonged. A link may have been made with natural phenomena or with the gods, but it may also have been made with the past and the ancestors, with otherwise ill-defined times before the Roman conquest. Given the prestige value assigned to certain types of stone axes in the Neolithic period[66] and attested for similar artefacts in ethnographic literature, it must be asked whether in post-Neolithic contexts these objects retained any emotional currency that allowed for their retention and curation or for their continued circulation, or for a reinvention of these practices.

Richard Bradley, in his seminal academic paper *Time Regained: the Creation of Continuity*,[67] considered what he termed 'the striking juxtaposition of prehistoric and early medieval monuments observed at Yeavering and other sites', something which he interpreted as 'attempts by a social elite to legitimise their position through reference to the past' rather than 'showing a continuity of ritual'. This idea, that there was a concept of the past in the past, raises interesting points about the way in which sites and possibly, by extension, artefacts can be used as temporal points of reference. These reference points, if cited in times of social, religious, or political crisis need refer only to the otherness of the past and, by implication, to its seamlessness. Memory by its very nature unites and contextualises. Veracity is not necessarily required and is seldom possible.

Of some considerable relevance here is the work of Adrienne Mayor who, in her strikingly original book *The First Fossil Hunters: Paleontology in Greek and Roman Times*,[68] convincingly makes the case for a return to the idea that the roots of palaeontology lay in the classical world rather than in the Renaissance period. Although some might see this as somewhat of an academic straw man, nevertheless her evidence would appear compelling in terms of demonstrating that the Greeks and Romans were familiar with fossils as the remains of once living beings and that there is indisputable archaeological evidence for fossil collecting in the ancient world. She shows that in the Roman world collections of natural curiosities such as large vertebrate fossils were frequently recorded as being on display in temples and in other public places, citing, for instance, the early example of Augustus's museum of giant bones at his villa on Capri, as will be discussed further below, and a much later display of similar 'giant bones' in Constantinople. According to Mayor, 'people brought curious objects to sanctuaries, not just as private offerings to gods, but in the spirit of creating communal museums where men, women, and children could contemplate natural wonders and try to puzzle out their meaning'.[69] It is important to note, however, that though such displays generated intense interest and speculation they were nonetheless sensationalised events, presenting exhibited natural curiosities as relics of some mythical past, the remains of giants or mythical creatures no longer walking the earth. These fossils were interpreted and presented as being 'of the past' but not of the real past; they allowed viewers to reconcile the ancient myths with contemporary life and to grapple with the concept of a physical, pre-political chronology. If Roman foundation myths helped to underpin the legitimacy of the authority of the Roman emperors from Augustus onwards, then the contemplation of the chronological scale of times past linked people to pre-foundation mythology and to the roots of a popular, oral, folk tradition. It allowed what might at first sight be an irrational world view to co-exist with the Roman imperial world view.

It is known that in 31 BC Augustus was responsible for the plundering of what were allegedly the giant tusks of the legendary Calydonian Boar from a temple at Tegea in Greece and their display as trophies in Rome. Even less convincing as genuine natural relics would have been the bodies of a giant and giantess he had displayed in Sallust's Garden in Rome. However, it is instructive to consider here the palaeontological museum set up by Augustus on Capri. As Adrienne Mayor so convincingly puts it, 'according to his biographer Suetonius, it housed "a collection of the huge limb bones of immense monsters of land and sea popularly known as giants' bones, along with the weapons of ancient heroes". This offhand statement is an important milestone in palaeontology, because it shows that Suetonius, writing in the early second century AD, was aware of the *animal* origin of the prodigious remains conventionally ascribed to humanoid giants.'[70]

But what has any of this to do with Roman Britain? A number of authorities have noted how in fourth-century Britain there would appear to have been a resurgence, some have called it a reinvention,[71] of certain Celtic religious traditions. This is reflected not only in the number of new Romano-Celtic temples constructed at this time but also in the increase or reappearance or commencement of various types of ritual activity, not always in a strictly defined religious context. Some have, for instance, highlighted the phenomenon of the deposition of what they rather awkwardly call 'head objects' in the fourth century, and the third- and fourth-century increase in the use of pewter in ritual contexts.[72] Others[73] have seen a link between the prehistoric deposition of metalwork in so-called watery places and the later Roman phenomenon of burial of silver plate or lead tanks. Finally, a marked increase in the level of Roman material found on prehistoric sites in the fourth century has been detected, and this has been seen as a revival of the use of such sites, possibly as a way of connecting with the idea of a non-Roman past.[74] Such links can also be found in other countries such as Spain.[75] Artefact studies in particular have a crucial role to play in isolating, identifying, and elucidating such social and religious trends as these.

Footsteps into the Past

Interest in collecting and analysing evidence for some kind of Roman activity taking place on prehistoric sites has grown considerably in the last few years. The placing of shrines and temples might have been in some cases predicated upon a desire to either acknowledge continuity or a link with the past or by physical association to create a schism with the past, to usurp memory by the supplanting of an alien structure to mark a new beginning. This phenomenon was first written about at length by Ann Woodward[76] who identified at least three distinct categories of prehistoric site at which this can be seen to have occurred. Firstly, a high frequency of Roman temples can be seen to have been located within the defences of former Iron Age hill-forts, as at Maiden Castle, Dorset, or adjacent to hill-forts, as at West Hill, Uley, Gloucestershire. Others were sited over or in close proximity to prehistoric barrows, as occurred at Mutlow Hill, Cambridgeshire for instance, where a circular shrine was located adjacent to a Bronze Age barrow and other burials. Woodward saw this juxtaposition as being somehow anomalous in style to the now widely accepted phenomenon of the deliberate use of prehistoric barrows for the insertion of secondary burials in the Roman period, in the south-west of England alone represented by at least twenty-five instances in Wiltshire, Gloucestershire, Somerset, and Dorset, and for the finding of Roman coins, pottery, and other artefacts in long barrows. Thirdly, some Roman temples were located within or close to prehistoric henges, Woodward listing at least five such sites at which Roman structures or features have been found, along with pottery, and two more at which pottery only has been found. Of course, Roman-style temples in stone often succeeded Roman timber temples which in turn, as at Hayling Island, Sussex, had themselves been built over the site of a timber Iron Age temple or shrine.

The Roman temple/Iron Age hill-fort relationship displays a south-western geographical bias and 'may have been part of a regional manifestation of religious beliefs. There are more ubiquitous associations between temples and a variety of other older monuments and features ... and the link with hill-forts could be seen as just one facet of this phenomenon.'[77] In terms of the Roman engagement with prehistoric mounds in Britain it has been suggested that we might even consider whether Roman period burial mounds themselves constitute an active, monumentalised engagement with the past through the restating of an old burial monument type.[78]

Ronald Hutton has further extended the debate by analysing three further groups of prehistoric sites where a presence of some kind can be attested in the Roman period: caves in the Bristol Channel area, the chambered tombs of the Cotswold-Severn region and the Peak District, and the Wessex monuments of Stonehenge, Avebury, and the Uffington White Horse.[79]

Such Roman period activity would seem then to fall into three broad categories: activity at temple sites, artefact deposition, and burial.[80] This may be a geographically restricted phenomenon, concentrated in the Cotswolds, Wessex, and the Peak District, and more thinly scattered over lowland southern and eastern Britain. It would appear to me though that if this dual use of sites is looked for in more areas it will in fact be found. Chronologically such activity spans the whole Roman period, though hoard and artefact deposition at prehistoric sites tends to be a later Roman phenomenon. Recently a great deal of interest has been taken in 'ephemeral monuments' and their link to the performance of rites concerned with social memory, group identity, and ancestral worship. The principal case study usually cited in print concerns the highly elaborate cremation involving the building of a number of temporary structures carried out at the Folly Lane, Verulamium site in the first century AD, a site viewed in terms of the ancestral celebration embodied there in subsequent, more permanent structures built on the site. 'A striking feature of the Folly Lane ceremonies was the almost obsessive care with which everything connected with the funeral was systematically destroyed'[81] so that something new could be created quite literally over the ashes.

Less convincing to me, but nevertheless interesting as a concept, is the idea that there was some kind of hero cult in early Roman Britain, centred on Romano-Celtic temples of the early Roman period in Britain, principally the first century AD. These temples were often associated with 'indications of elite mortuary use in and around them'[82] or were associated with ritual pits and wells, or with both mortuary use and pits/wells, suggesting to one authority that the active links being made at these sites between the realm of the living and the world of the dead ancestors related to the celebration and commemoration of a native, pre-Roman past through the agency of memory, memorialisation, and indeed monumentalisation. That is not to say that the idea is altogether *outré*, rather that it is certainly a seductive interpretation when applied to the archaeological evidence of two particular sites at Folly Lane, Verulamium and Gosbecks, Colchester/Camulodunum but less so when more widely interpolated.

It would appear to have perhaps been a local or at best regional phenomenon, and perhaps also a specifically first-century phenomenon, when the reality of conquest and occupation and political and cultural change was affecting the previously held certainties of existence for many tribal people in south-eastern Britain, and was a lived reality as well as a memory. As already mentioned above, at Folly Lane, on a hill overlooking Verulamium, a mortuary enclosure was excavated where evidence was found of the laying out, cremation, and interment of a member of the local native elite of the Catuvellauni tribe, in the years immediately following the Claudian invasion of Britain. After a few decades had passed a Romano-Celtic temple was constructed there, directly over the cremation site. Ritual shafts outside the enclosure contained both human remains and items suggesting some form of head cult being significant here. There can be no doubt that the temple commemorates this important individual. Less easy to understand is why such a commemoration was allowed under Roman eyes; some kind of official approval for this taking place so close to the emerging new urban centre of Verulamium must have been sought and yet perhaps the site may have acted as a focus for anti-Roman sentiment and activity. At Gosbecks, Colchester there is again found a Romano-Celtic temple placed within what was thought by some to be a mortuary enclosure perhaps dated to just before the conquest of AD 43. This area subsequently saw a theatre built nearby and a road set out linking it to the *colonia*, suggesting its importance as a locus. Some authorities see this mortuary site as the final resting place of King Cunobelinus, who died before the conquest and whose commemoration here in this way would not in itself necessarily be a form of anti-Roman exhibition.[83]

An example from my own experience is also worthy of consideration here. Aerial photography and archaeological area excavation at Bromfield Quarry, just outside Ludlow in Shropshire, showed that a mid-first-century Roman military marching camp had been sited in such a position in relation to a Bronze Age round barrow as to suggest that the fort's incorporation of what would have been at the time a still-upstanding monument into its south-west corner was a deliberate act. In plan, during excavation, it could be seen that perhaps astonishingly the V-shaped ditch of the marching camp had just clipped the outer ring ditch of the barrow (Plate 38).[84] Was this incorporation a physical metaphor for the conquest of the past by the present? Did Roman military intelligence and reconnaissance gather information to show that this monument had some kind of significance to the local tribal peoples here, and acted as some sort of link with their ancestors? Was the barrow enclosed within the fort – captured, incorporated, emasculated – in an attempt to sever those links, to tear some kind of hole in the local chronological continuum of folk or tribal memory? It is difficult not to see this as having been the case.

Fragments and Memory

The idea that 'the fragment' could be part of 'an enchainment' of memory is now widely accepted as a theory for interpreting certain social practices attested in archaeological contexts on some prehistoric sites.[85] Such enchainment involving artefacts can be seen quite widely in Anglo-Saxon contexts in England, of which the inclusion of Roman items in Anglo-Saxon graves as grave-goods is the most obvious example;[86] indeed, a drawing is reproduced here of some Roman glass beads incorporated into a necklace of amber and glass beads from a mid-sixth-century Anglo-Saxon inhumation burial of a young woman within the bounds of the former Roman fort at Binchester, near Bishop Auckland, County Durham (Fig. 10).[87] The Roman beads here represent either heirloom objects of some kind or found items retained for talismanic or amuletic purposes, perhaps because of their link to the relatively recent past. At Binchester this burial, most likely in a marked grave, was located next to the crumbling, abandoned shell of the large bath suite forming part of the mid-late-fourth-century commandant's house or *praetorium*. One of the stone

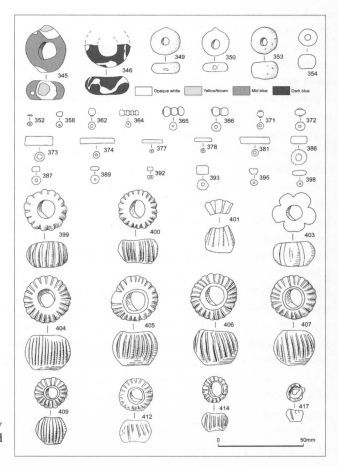

10. Roman glass beads from Binchester Roman fort, County Durham. Nos 372, 378 and 398 were reused in an Anglo-Saxon necklace and placed in a burial of the mid-sixth century here. (Drawn by Mark Breedon, John Halstead *et al.* In Ferris, 2010, Fig. 86)

arches inside the bath house was subsequently robbed out and perhaps was used, along with other stone from buildings inside the fort, to build the nearby Anglo-Saxon church at Escomb, a few miles across the Wear Valley. Back at Binchester fort it would appear that the presence of the burial site of the woman acted as a focus for the establishment here of a more formal Anglo-Saxon cemetery, consisting of possibly hundreds of burials spanning the eighth century to the eleventh century.

Another example of the reuse of Roman items in the Anglo-Saxon period can be given here, again illustrated by a photograph, and comprises the discovery of two very large, heavy, roughly pierced stones inside a later Anglo-Saxon timber building of some kind at the so-called Owen Owen Department Store site in central Shrewsbury, Shropshire.[88] These items are interpreted as being stone anchors for use in boats on the River Severn, which flows through Shrewsbury, and are undoubtedly made from neatly sawn sections of Roman stone columns either from a Roman villa nearby, though villas are very rare in this area, or more likely from the Roman town of Wroxeter – Viroconium – about three miles away (Plate 39).

Since I first wrote about the link between the British prehistoric past and Roman Britain, the amount of evidence for such links has continued to grow. Nevertheless it is still true to say that the reuse of past monuments by a later cultural group is more noticeable as a phenomenon in the Anglo-Saxon period in Britain than it is in the Roman period. It has been suggested that 'this early medieval period monument re-use seems to be strongly influenced by practices introduced from Scandinavia and northern Germany but they could have an indigenous component'. If so, then perhaps we should see attitudes to ancient monuments representing a form of ritual continuity across the Roman/medieval transition.[89]

In conclusion, it is suggested that certain types of prehistoric artefacts could have been used in the Roman period as semiophores, announcing cultural otherness and establishing links with the past and with the ancestors. There is certainly no coherent or conclusive evidence for this interpretation, but is the thunderbolt theory any longer a convincing and acceptable explanation in all those situations where it is deemed that explanation for the presence of prehistoric stone tools on Roman sites is necessary? Or is it possible to see in the evidence from Ivy Chimneys a phenomenon with roots pre-dating any form of Roman religious activity here, and thus a phenomenon in need of a new framework of explanation? It is surely for finds researchers to try to decode the use and meaning of objects in the past rather than to collaborate in the perpetuation of systems of analysis which aim to explain away apparent contradictions in the way the past is presently constructed.

It is possible that the use of prehistoric stone artefacts was only a localised phenomenon and that the caches of Palaeolithic stone axes at the Ivy Chimneys site reflect a strong Gallic influence in the same way that Roman Gaul probably was the primary external influence on Romano-Britons expressing themselves in Roman form, but a form already diffused with local characteristics in Gaul.

Certainly site and settlement evidence is pointing towards an active link between past and present, perhaps not a real past but instead an imagined or mythical past, in the Roman period in Britain. It is also possible that memory was the overriding factor here, linking present people with distant ancestors or with heroic past figures. Religion certainly played a major part in all of this but it is not altogether certain whether it acted to establish links or to distort or even sever them. Organised religion in the Roman period was very much a tool and an artefact of Romanisation, if that word can still be used to define the concept of cultural conquest. Certainly, if in the Neolithic period certain classes of artefacts were viewed as symbols of power, then it is possible that prehistoric objects could have been viewed as holding some symbolic power linked to a mythical past or to the ancestors. It is not altogether impossible to think that such a power to link the past and the present together in religious devotion could also have had a political dimension, that such items could have been used as symbols of resistance in some cases. Dispute over the very ownership of both the sites of the past, thinking about the legal wrangling over the Kentish woodland which will be discussed in Chapter 5,[90] and control of its narrative must have occurred at every level of Romano-British society and in every region of the province. We should perhaps not just look for examples of the memorial linking of past and present remembering in Roman Britain but we should also look for evidence of schism, of exclusion, or even of destruction – forgetting in other words.[91]

CITIES OF IDEAS

Collage and Spectacle

In the first part of this book discussion was centred on objects in Roman Britain and on their acquisition and use in certain often quite specific contexts. In this second part the emphasis will be on the circulation of ideas in the province, these ideas often though being conveyed by or through objects, by material culture in its broadest sense. As an archaeologist I have always viewed material culture as including art, and in this chapter I will examine the role played by urban centres in Roman Britain in the spread of written and visual literacy and as foci for the production and consumption of art.

While there exist highly detailed and important book-length studies of both the large towns and the small towns of Roman Britain[1] which include reviews of the evidence for the adornment of both public and private buildings and spaces in the towns, no explicit attempt has been made in these works to explore the role of art in Romano-British towns and indeed the role of towns as centres for the display of art and the articulation of its associated underlying ideologies. The same general absence of discussions of art in an urban context in Roman Britain is also apparent in the numerous shorter papers on Romano-British urbanism which also exist.[2]

The town was both a venue where art was created and displayed, and a space in which various spectacles were enacted in which art played an important part. Whether there was in fact a specifically urban art in Roman Britain, as distinct from art in the towns being part of a wider Romano-British art, and whether similar situations existed in both the large towns and what archaeologists call the small towns, are questions that need to addressed here.[3] The opportunity will also be taken to flag up some potentially new and exciting avenues of research on the subject of the inter-relationship between art and urbanism in Roman Britain and the wider Roman world.

It is perhaps not altogether surprising that, leaving aside the British fascicules of the *Corpus Signorum Imperii Romani* (*Corpus of Sculpture of the Roman World*) project so far published,[4] the only Romano-British town for which individual studies of its art and architecture have been produced is London, for which there also exist two general surveys of the city's Graeco-Roman artworks[5] and a detailed study of the art objects from the London Mithraeum.[6] In addition, some brief consideration has been given in print to aspects of architectural embellishment in Bath[7] and to the possibility that Carlisle was home to a school of sculptors in the Romano-British period.[8] Urban art from Roman Britain has, again, not been considered as an explicit phenomenon in synthetic studies of the art of the province.[9]

Of course, much consideration has been given over the years to the role played by the towns of Roman Britain in the production of art. D. J. Smith's argument that schools of mosaicists worked out of various towns in the fourth century is still persuasive,[10] if still as yet unproven by archaeological work. Workshops of sculptors probably were based in Bath and Cirencester,[11] perhaps with a linking figure at one stage being the *scultor* Sulinus, mentioned in inscriptions from both towns. Other urban schools have been suggested at Lincoln, the small town of Ancaster,[12] and Carlisle.[13] However, all of these urban artists and artisans were probably mostly engaged in fulfilling private commissions in both town and country, rather than constructing civic monuments alone.

Urban Art as Ideology

If urbanisation was part of the package of becoming Roman,[14] if the 'idea' of the city or town was an integral part of the overall rhetoric of Roman imperialism, as numerous studies attest was the case across the empire,[15] then it would seem appropriate to try and understand what role, if any, was played by the use of art in this programme.

In order to do so, 'we must consider the city as both the major cultural construct and conveyancer of Roman imperialism abroad'.[16] If the urban centres of Roman Britain were then the motors, or rather were intended to be the motors, of a process of change, then it might be expected that the archaeological evidence to support the role of culture and art in this process could be found. This might take the form of architectural innovation and the development of an urban style and form of building, with an accompanying level of architectural ornamentation and artistic embellishment, a demonstrably higher degree of literacy and cultural awareness in the towns, or an ideological programme of art that was exclusively urban in either its form or its message and in its intended audience.

It is generally accepted then that the city or town was part and parcel of the cultural package that was classical civilization. Rome the cosmopolis was to be the mother of an extended family of cities which would act as centres for a civilizing force around its empire. Certainly the city was first and foremost a bureaucratic concept, a place where business could be conducted, goods made, sold, or exchanged, and taxes could be most easily extracted from a large client population, especially in the furthermost provinces. The city also became a focus for the redirection of the support and opposition of the provincial elites of the empire, or so it was hoped by the imperial court. Concomitant on all this was the theory that the city would ultimately become a centre for the circulation and exchange of ideas and concepts which underpinned its workings and those of the Roman empire as a whole. Such a system was intended to apply in Roman Britain as elsewhere in the empire, though local and regional conditions and processes would have created a considerable variation in the way urbanisation actually happened on the ground in different provinces.

A number of other, perhaps at first sight esoteric, ideas were also apparently linked to urbanism and these can be examined through studies of artefactual evidence from Roman Britain. The first idea is the creation and expression of the concept of the social self, as reflected in the celebratory representation of private individuals operating in the public sphere through both visual, principally sculptural, representation and through epigraphic dedication. In certain urban situations the advertisement of the social self could conversely imply selflessness, an immersion into the whole, the social body of the tribe or group, into the town, into the province, into the empire. The second idea is the benefit of literacy, both written literacy and visual literacy. In the Roman world both provided a code for understanding, and understanding was intended to engender a sense of belonging.

Viewing the City

At the centre of each Romano-British town there would have been a standard suite of civic buildings,[17] principally the forum and basilica complex, perhaps with associated temples. In some towns other structures were also erected, including public baths, market halls, theatres and amphitheatres, sanctuaries or temple compounds away from the civic centre, monumental arches, Jupiter columns, and other types of votive columns. There also would have been large-scale imperial statues at some urban centres, as represented, for example, by the head of Hadrian from London, cuirass statues like an example from Cirencester, or equestrian statues, as at, for instance, Lincoln and Gloucester. Gates could also bear sculptural schemes, as in the case of the Bath Gate at Cirencester, from which a life-sized representation of Mercury is probably derived.[18]

Astonishingly, little is known of the decoration of the fora, basilicas, and public bath complexes of the major towns of Roman Britain. That we know that the *curia* in the basilica at Caerwent had a mosaic panel and painted walls with architectural perspectives is exceptional. Indeed an academic's lament of a few years ago that we do not in fact know as much about the plans and layout of the British fora as we might[19] still largely holds true. The survival of evidence for the painted ceilings of some of the rooms in the market hall at Leicester is again almost unique. Of the known theatres – at Canterbury, Colchester, Gosbecks, and Verulamium, and the possible theatre site at Brough-on-Humber, few have well-provenanced associated art. Once more the same applies to the amphitheatres at Dorchester (Maumbury Rings), Caerwent, Silchester, Cirencester, Chichester, Caister St Edmunds, and London, as well as at the small town of Charterhouse and at the religious centre at Frilford, and to the amphitheatres in York and Leicester, known only from inscriptions. Are we to infer from all this that these sites were not well appointed with artworks?

1. Giovanni Bellini
and Titian, *The Feast
of the Gods*, 1514.
(National Gallery of Art,
Washington)

2. The Indian triumph
of Bacchus portrayed
on a two-handled
ceramic vessel from
the Roman necropolis
of Lugone, Salò,
Lombardy, Italy. (Photo:
Civic Archaeological
Museum of Valle Sabbia,
Gavardo)

3. Bacchic and marine scenes on the great silver dish from the Mildenhall Treasure from Suffolk. (Photo: Copyright Trustees of the British Museum)

Above left: 4. Marble statuette of Bacchus and feline companion from a grave near Spoonley Wood villa, Gloucestershire. (Photo: Copyright Trustees of the British Museum)

Above right: 5. A Bacchic motif on a copper alloy jug handle from the New Cemetery site, Rocester, Staffordshire. (Photo: Graham Norrie)

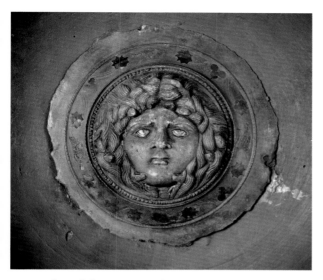 

Above left: 6. Head of a Bacchic Medusa on the central medallion of a copper alloy *patera* from Faversham, Kent. (Photo: Copyright Trustees of the British Museum)

Above right: 7. Bacchus on the handle of a copper alloy *patera* from Brompton, Shropshire. (Photo: Graham Norrie)

8. Giorgio de Chirico, *L'archeologo* (*The Archaeologist*), 1927. (Private collection, USA)

Left and above: 9a & b. A copper alloy figurine of Mars from the Foss Dyke, Lincolnshire, with a close-up of the inscription on the base. (Photo: Copyright Trustees of the British Museum)

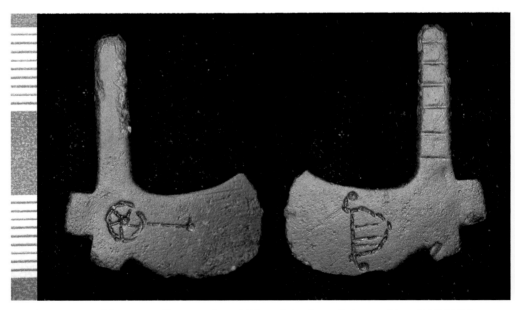

10. A votive model copper alloy axe from Melton Mowbray, Leicestershire. (PAS LEIC-88ADC3. Photo: Copyright Portable Antiquities Scheme)

11. A horse-and-rider brooch from the New Cemetery site, Rocester, Staffordshire. (Photo: Graham Norrie)

12. A copper alloy statuette of Epona seated between two horses from Wiltshire. (Photo: Copyright Trustees of the British Museum)

13. A copper alloy statuette of a rider figure from Lincolnshire. (PAS YORYM-C2A231. Photo: Copyright Portable Antiquities Scheme)

14. A copper alloy rider figure from Westwood Bridge, Peterborough, Cambridgeshire. (Photo: former School of Continuing Studies archive, Birmingham University)

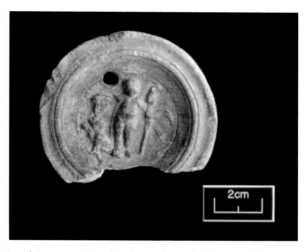

Above left: 15. A copper alloy Bacchic *patera* handle from Orton's Pasture, Rocester, Staffordshire. (Photo: Graham Norrie)

Above right: 16. A Bacchic design on a ceramic lamp from Orton's Pasture, Rocester, Staffordshire. (Photo: Graham Norrie)

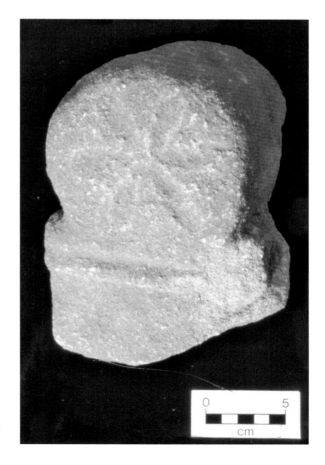

17. An altar fragment from Orton's Pasture, Rocester, Staffordshire. (Photo: Graham Norrie)

18. A selection of votive pots from Orton's Pasture, Rocester, Staffordshire. (Photo: Graham Norrie)

19. A scene of *suovetaurilia*, ritual sacrifice, on one of the decorated bases from the *Decennalia* monument. Now in the Roman Forum, Rome. (Photo: Author)

20. A copper alloy model plough team of an ox and cow from Piercebridge, County Durham. (Photo: Copyright Trustees of the British Museum)

21. Finds from a healing shrine at, or near, Llys Awel, Abergele, Conwy, Wales. (Photo: Richard Brewer. National Museums and Galleries of Wales)

Above left: 22. Close-up of the Bacchic face on the copper alloy *patera* handle from Orton's Pasture, Rocester, Staffordshire. (Photo: Graham Norrie)

Above right: 23. Altar dedicated to Aesculapius and Salus, from Binchester, County Durham. (Drawing from Hooppell 1891)

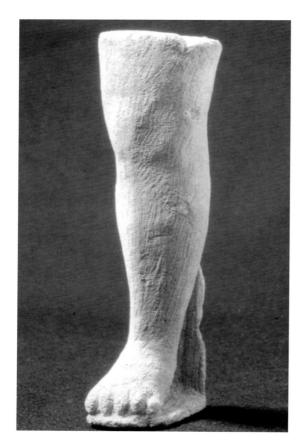 

Above left: 24. A stone medical or anatomical *ex voto* of a leg from the Source of the Seine. (Photo: from Deyts, 1994, 109)

Above right: 25. A cast lead votive model foot from South Cambridgeshire. (PAS BERK-98EFC8. Photo: Copyright Portable Antiquities Scheme)

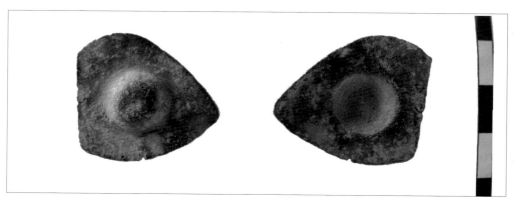

26. A copper alloy votive model eye from Market Lavington, Wiltshire. (PAS WILT-1F1EB2. Photo: Copyright Portable Antiquities Scheme)

Left: 27. Copper alloy dogs, a copper alloy arm, and other votive items from the Lydney temple site, Gloucestershire. (Photo from Wheeler and Wheeler, 1932, Plate XXVI)

Above: 28. A pair of votive sheet gold eyes from Wroxeter, Shropshire. (Photo: Copyright Trustees of the British Museum)

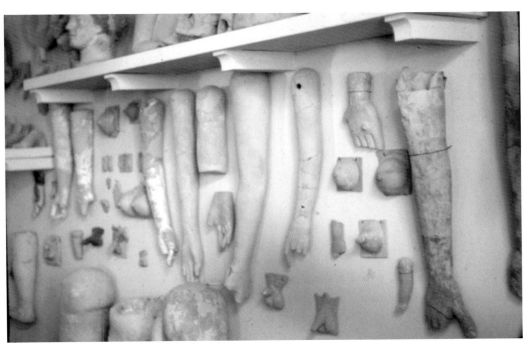

29. Medical or anatomical *ex votos* in Corinth Museum, Corinth, Greece. (Photo: Author)

Above left: 30. A terracotta medical or anatomical *ex voto* of internal organs from a healing shrine in Italy. Third–first century BC. (Photo: Copyright Trustees of the British Museum)

Above right: 31. A terracotta medical or anatomical *ex voto* of an ear from a healing shrine in Italy. Third–first century BC. (Photo: Copyright Trustees of the British Museum)

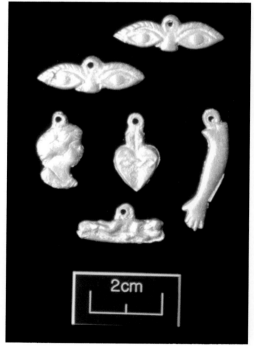

Above left: 32. A stone medical or anatomical *ex voto* of a breast from the Source of the Seine. (Photo: from Deyts, 1994, 79)

Above right: 33. Contemporary Mexican metal medical or anatomical *ex votos* in author's own collection. (Photo: Graham Norrie)

34. A selection of the Palaeolithic flint hand-axes from the Roman temple site at Ivy Chimneys, Essex. (Photo: Chelmsford Museum)

35. A selection of the Palaeolithic flint hand-axes from the Roman temple site at Ivy Chimneys, Essex. (Photo: Chelmsford Museum)

36. A Neolithic polished stone axe head from the Romano-British pottery production site of Newland Hopfields, Worcestershire. (Photo: Graham Norrie)

37. A group of seventeenth-century Spanish silk amulets in the form of prehistoric axe heads and arrowheads to protect against thunder. (Photo: Pitt Rivers Museum, Oxford)

38. A linear Roman marching camp ditch cutting the outer, curving ring ditch of a Bronze Age round barrow at Bromfield, Shropshire. (Photo: Author)

39. Two Anglo-Saxon stone anchors made from reused sections of Roman stone column lying *in situ* during excavations at the former Owen Owen store, Shrewsbury, Shropshire. (Photo: Author)

40. Bacchic figures on a capital from a votive column from Cirencester, Gloucestershire. (Photo: former School of Continuing Studies archive, Birmingham University)

41. Statue base inscription to Tiberius Claudius Paulinus from Caerwent, Monmouthshire, Wales. (Photo: Royal Commission on the Ancient and Historical Monuments of Wales)

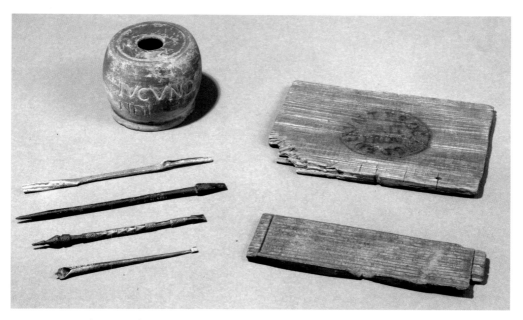

42. A selection of Romano-British writing equipment, including an inkwell, styli, and writing tablets. (Photo: Copyright Trustees of the British Museum)

43. A complete copper alloy enamelled seal box from Mareham on the Hill, Lincolnshire. (PAS LIN-E12F25. Photo: Copyright Portable Antiquities Scheme)

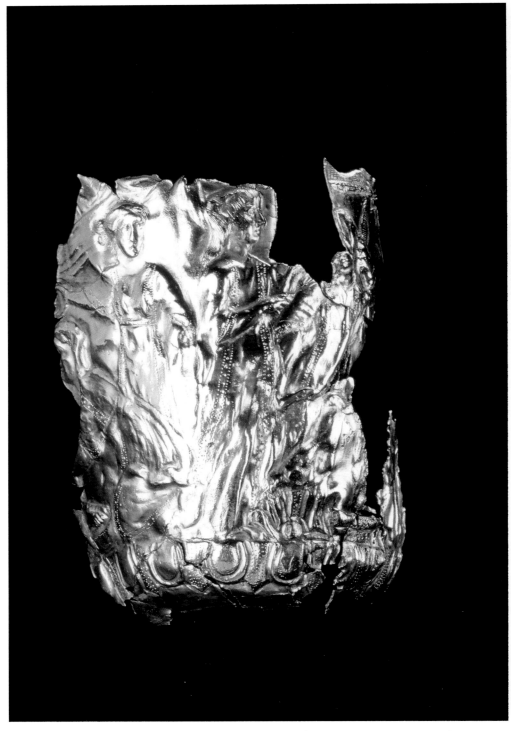

44. The recognition of Ulysses, a scene on a silver vessel from Traprain Law, East Lothian, Scotland. (Photo: National Museums of Scotland, Edinburgh)

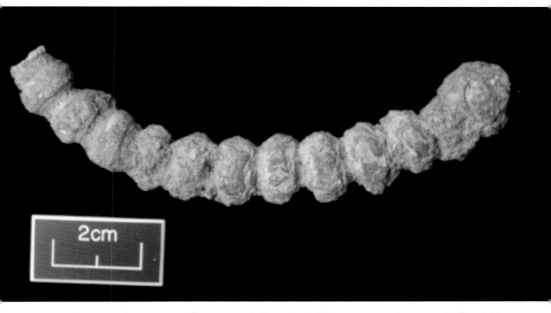

45. A copper alloy torc, a military award, from the Mill Street *vicus*, Rocester, Staffordshire. (Photo: Graham Norrie)

46. A copper alloy clasp knife handle in the form of a gladiator from Piddington Roman villa, Northamptonshire. (Photo: Courtesy of Simon Tutty, Roy Friendship-Taylor and the Trustees of the British Museum)

Top left: 47. Silver-gilt statuette of Hercules from near Birdoswald, Cumbria. (Photo: Copyright Trustees of the British Museum)

Top right: 48. Gold Hercules club earring from Walbrook, London. (Photo: Copyright Trustees of the British Museum)

Bottom left: 49. Kurt Schwitters, *Bild mit heller Mitte* (*Picture with Light Centre*), Painted collage, 1919. (Museum of Modern Art, New York)

50. The so-called Barberini togatus statue. *Museo del Palazzo dei Conservatori*, Rome. (Photo: Author)

51. A head pot from Piercebridge, County Durham. (Photo: Author)

52. The beheading of a gladiator on a relief from Due Madonne, Bologna, Emilia Romagna, Italy. *Museo Civico Archeologico di Bologna*. (Photo: Author)

53. The head of the cult stone statue of Mercury during excavation at West Hill, Uley, Gloucestershire. (Photo: Ann Woodward and Peter Leach)

54. The conserved Cartoceto bronzes on display in the *Museo Archeologico Nazionale delle Marche*, Ancona. (Photo: *Soprintendenza per i Beni Archeologici delle Marche*)

55. Albert van der Eeckhout, *A Tarairiu or Tapuya Woman*, 1641–1643. (National Museum of Denmark, Copenhagen)

Above and below: 56a & b. A copper alloy votive model in the form of splayed human legs, displaying male genitalia on the one side and female on the other, from Cliffe, Kent. (PAS KENT-30CF10. Photo: Copyright Portable Antiquities Scheme)

57. A phallic symbol carved on a stone in the bridge abutment at Chesters, Northumberland. (Photo: Author)

58. A relief of Silenus from Bar Hill, Dunbartonshire, Scotland. (Photo: David Breeze)

Top left: 59. The Horsey Toll pot, Cambridgeshire. (Photo: former School of Continuing Studies archive, Birmingham University)

Bottom left: 60. The Horsey Toll pot, Cambridgeshire. (Photo: former School of Continuing Studies archive, Birmingham University)

Bottom right: 61. The tombstone of Callimorphus and Serapion from Chester. Grosvenor Museum, Chester. (Photo: Author)

62. A copper alloy cosmetic grinder with stylized animal head terminals from Hockwold cum Wilton, Norfolk. (Photo: Copyright Trustees of the British Museum)

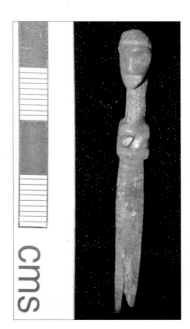

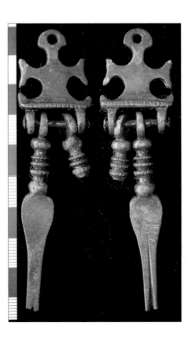

Right: 63. A decorated copper alloy nail cleaner from Norton, Northamptonshire. (PAS NARC-733D28. Photo: Copyright Portable Antiquities Scheme)

Far right: 64. A copper alloy chatelaine with intact attached nail cleaner from Narborough, Leicestershire. (PAS LEIC-8572C4. Photo: Copyright Portable Antiquities Scheme)

Above: 65. A silver mirror from Wroxeter, Shropshire. (Photo: Shropshire County Council)

Right: 66. Tombstone of Victor from South Shields. (Photo: Arbeia Roman Fort (Tyne and Wear Archives and Museums))

67. A cast copper alloy oil flask with African head motif from Bayford, Kent. (Photo: Copyright Trustees of the British Museum)

68. A Samian lamp in the form of the head of a black African male from London. (Photo: Museum of London)

69. Detail of the Rudston Venus mosaic, Rudston villa, East Yorkshire. (Photo: Author)

70. Grave-goods from a child's burial at Arrington, Cambridgeshire. (Photo: Alison Taylor)

71. Grave-goods from a child's burial at Arrington, Cambridgeshire. (Photo: Alison Taylor)

72. An ivory statuette of a hunchback. Hellenistic, probably later second century BC. (Photo: Copyright Trustees of the British Museum)

73. A copper alloy figurine of Priapus from Thorrington, Essex. (PAS ESS-E6F9E3. Photo: Copyright Portable Antiquities Scheme)

 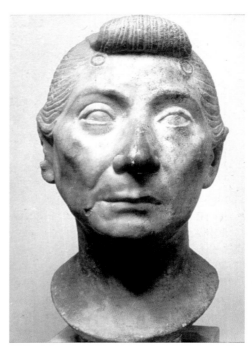

Above left: 74. Portrait of an elderly man from Otricoli, *c.* 50 BC. *Museo Torlonia*, Rome. (Photo: former School of Continuing Studies archive, Birmingham University)

Above right: 75. Portrait of an elderly woman from Palombara Sabina, *c.* 30 BC. *Museo Nazionale delle Terme*, Rome. (Photo: former School of Continuing Studies archive, Birmingham University)

76. The Chi Rho silver amulet from Shepton Mallet, Somerset. (Photo: Graham Norrie)

Civic arches, so often the medium for extensive artistic programmes of a political or didactic nature elsewhere in the empire, were rare monuments in Roman Britain for some reason. At Richborough there was erected a Claudian victory arch, though thought to have been constructed in the reign of Domitian, and in London was another that may have been an entrance to a religious enclosure of some kind. At Colchester the Balkerne Gate was originally a free-standing arch, while at Verulamium three arches are known. An inscription refers to an arch at Ancaster which may, like the London arch, have been linked to a religious site, as may also have been one at York. The very form of the monumental arch and its attested appointment with Italian marble cladding at Colchester, Verulamium, and Richborough created both a conceptual and actual link with Rome and Italy.[20] There may intriguingly have been a link between the arch at Verulamium and the nearby triangular temple where decorative marble debris recovered hints at their both being part of a unitary scheme of design and construction.[21] Fragments of bronze sculpture found in proximity to the Richborough arch may be all that remains of an imperial figure in an equestrian group originally positioned on top of the monument.

As for Jupiter columns,[22] there were probably two, and possibly three, at Corinium (Cirencester), possibly one at Wroxeter, and, perhaps surprisingly, one at the small town of Great Chesterford. The best representative of this type of monument in Roman Britain is the second- or third-century inhabited Corinthian capital with Bacchic figures from the *civitas* capital of Corinium (Plate 40).[23] Despite this being one of the canonical pieces of art from Roman Britain, and therefore one of the most discussed in print, its sheer size and its air of stylistic accomplishment and iconographic sophistication still make it a sculpture worthy of further consideration here. The fact that academic identification of the four individual figures on the capital – Bacchus, Lycurgus, Silenus and Ambrosia – was, until relatively recently, contradictory, suggests that in Roman Corinium to have read and understood the significance of the iconographic scheme on the capital would also have been a matter of being sufficiently well versed in the classical canon.

Pioneering research work some years ago by Valerie Hutchinson,[24] discussed at length above in Chapter 1, uncovered evidence for the cult of Bacchus to have been much better known in Roman Britain than had been previously supposed, and that a sophisticated accompanying artistic repertoire of representations, signs, and symbols allowed cult adherents to allude to the sometimes complex elements of the Bacchic myths in a way that suggests that understanding of these allusions contributed to a sense of inclusion. Memory and mnemonic systems were often interlinked elements in the cultural sphere.

That this monument, or another column in the town centre, still had some form of emotional currency in the fourth century is attested by its repair and consolidation by L. Septimius, governor of *Britannia Prima*. Perhaps by then, even if its original significance may have been lost on its later viewers, the monument nevertheless was an item of civic pride whose restoration was seen as an essential prerequisite for urban regeneration and renaissance. Analysis of the almost purely classical iconography of the sculptural programme of the so-called *Porta Martis* in Rheims in Roman Gaul[25] has suggested that 'the sculptural decoration was an expression of the public ideology of the Remi' – the local tribe[26] – and that whether the arch was erected through local initiative and munificence or through imperial patronage is not an issue affecting interpretation of the sculptures as 'they can only be meaningfully understood if the ideas depicted were sustained by the local community'.[27] Conversely, the fate of the temple of Claudius at Colchester[28] demonstrates how architecture and art could also symbolise dissension and act as the engines of their own destruction. The importance of monumental inscriptions – having 'the epigraphic habit'[29] – similarly relied on both the understanding[30] and complicity of the viewer[31] and on the power of group or social memory,[32] as will be discussed further below.

Building complexes associated with religious cults would have been found in most Romano-British towns, and perhaps many of these establishments relied for their very existence on the cosmopolitan nature of many of the towns and the money to be found there. The link between art and religious practice in the Graeco-Roman world is well known,[33] the most significant examples of this in Roman Britain being the Temple of *Divus Claudius* at Colchester and, of course, the extensive religious complex associated with the hot spring and the temple of *Sulis Minerva* at Bath.[34] Indeed, it seems likely that in Roman Britain the attested guild-sponsored repair and repainting of the façade of the Four Seasons at Bath represented an example of a more common and popular form of architectural munificence than the building and repair of public and administrative buildings.[35] An inscription from London records the restoration of a temple or shrine to the *matres* by one of the city's *vici* or districts.[36]

The extramural areas of towns do not appear to have been areas where the display of civic art was deemed appropriate,[37] with the obvious exception of the urban cemeteries, a very specific forum for the display of identity, status, position, ambition, and standing through the commissioning of monumental inscriptions, tombs, and gravestones. These cemeteries were quite possibly one of the few areas within an urban environment, though of course outside the walls, in which women could use art to make statements about their position in society, their status, and their aspirations. The urban environment itself may have been a focus, along with the military forts of Roman Britain, for the overt celebration of a form of hyper-masculinity, a theory developed further below.

The phenomenon of the provision of mosaic pavements in town houses in the second century in Roman Britain,[38] a truly urban phenomenon here, should not mislead us to believe that this represents public munificence of any kind when rather it represents private initiatives and conspicuous consumption on behalf of the elite. The same can be said of the appointment of town houses with wall or ceiling paintings.[39] If there was an ideological motive here it was more linked to elite values than to state ones, though obviously at times, probably as much by necessity as anything else, there was some degree of overlap between the two sets of values,[40] as perhaps shown by the inscribed statue base of Tiberius Claudius Paulinus at Caerwent, a work of art dedicated by the *Civitas Silurum*, and the only example of the civic honouring of a named individual in Roman Britain who was not a member of the imperial family.[41]

The expression and advertisement of the social self takes two principal forms elsewhere in the Roman empire: the commissioning of portrait sculpture for public display, and the naming of individuals in formal public inscriptions. There is surprisingly little evidence recovered to date from Roman Britain to suggest that the commissioning of portrait sculpture and the setting up of dedicatory public inscriptions by named individuals or in celebration of named individuals was common, or rather as common in many other provinces.

There is a great deal of evidence to suggest that what has has been called architectural munificence, that is the funding of public buildings in the major towns, was noticeably less marked among the elite of Roman Britain than it was in the Mediterranean region and in parts of Gaul.[42] When buildings were sponsored, dedicatory inscriptions suggest that collective munificence rather than individual generosity was more usual in Britain. Fewer public buildings were erected than in many other provinces and in general the buildings erected were longer-lived, smaller, and more modestly appointed. If fewer public buildings were erected, then it naturally follows that in Romano-British towns there would concomitantly be less art commissioned as part of the overall schemes. Of course, a number of significant sponsored architectural commissions are known from epigraphic dedications, and indeed a number of such buildings are known only from the inscriptions marking their existence, including possible amphitheatres at York and Leicester, a theatre at Brough, and an arch of some sort at Ancaster, the latter being an unusual instance of architectural munificence at a small town in Roman Britain. An arch into a religious complex in York was sponsored by Lucius Viducius Placidus, a merchant from Rouen, thus a native Gaul rather than a Romano-Briton.

Turning from the major urban centres of Roman Britain to the smaller ones, some years ago an attempt was made to quantify art from the small towns of Roman Britain, in order to examine whether there was any discernible difference between the use of a 'classical' or 'Celtic' grammar of imagery at these sites that could allow the culture of the small towns to be examined through the medium of art.[43] While I am sure the author of the study would probably agree that this early attempt to quantify archaeological data from Roman Britain is now very out of date, not least because of the increased level of excavation in small towns seen since the paper was published in 1977, but nevertheless certain of the conclusions of the study are worth considering here.

Over two thirds of the art objects quantified in this study were pieces of portable art, that is art that would have appeared in the private sphere. The others comprised principally sculpture, mosaics, and architectural ornament, in that order. That decorated architectural fragments totalled only eight pieces, coming from the walled towns of Ancaster (one piece), Irchester (two pieces), Wall (one piece), Water Newton (two pieces), and the small town/temple complex at Springhead (two pieces),[44] mirrored the hierarchy of urban sites from *civitas* capitals down to unwalled small towns. Sites lower down the scale had fewer or no pieces of non-portable art. Attempts were also subsequently made by this particular author to look at changing tastes for classical art over time in Roman Britain.[45]

Collage

In many respects the classical town represents a collage, created over a number of years, and perhaps viewing Romano-British towns from this standpoint might offer new insights into the use of art in an urban context at this time. The phenomenon of the use of *spolia* – reused sculpture or other stone fragments – is well attested in the later Roman period, though whether the appearance of sculptural stonework derived from a monumental decorated arch and a decorated screen depicting deities reused in the later defensive Roman riverside wall of London[46] really can be classed as being part of this phenomenon is open to debate. Such a pagan monument might have been 'redundant in the 4th century, under Christian emperors'[47] but, equally, the idea that a monument could be imbued with the power of place and that both could incorporate the ideological aspirations of the urban elite, an idea considered above in relation to the Arch of Mars at Rheims, might colour its reuse with some ideological significance.

Other occurrences of the reuse of architectural and sculptural fragments are attested at Chester, as discussed more fully in Chapter 6, and at Lincoln where inscribed tombstones were built into the *colonia* wall, and 'plain mouldings, engaged fluted pilasters, and a decorated cornice' into the fourth-century west gate.[48] In London, material built into two external towers consisted of almost exclusively funerary material, including the well-known Julius Classicianus tombstone, though some of this material might have been derived from a religious precinct, including 'a column shaft decorated with lattice work and overlapping leaves which could have formed part of a small, votive column'.[49]

It has been suggested that funerary monuments were demolished to make way for the building of the walls and in fact lay in their path, but the incorporation of fragments of these monuments into the very fabric of the new build could have been an altogether more complex choice than simply one of necessity.[50] Indeed, 'in Spain and Britain it was exceptional for town defences to incorporate material from structures other than tombs',[51] while elsewhere in the empire 'the types of monuments from which masonry was taken and reused include: tombs and gravestones; temples and religious precincts, and altars; public buildings such as forums, baths, and arches; and milestones'.[52]

Writing and Reading the City

The evidence for written literacy in Roman Britain is provided by two main sources of information: epigraphic evidence, that is formal inscriptions on stone; and the evidence provided by *graffiti*, informal writing or sometimes defacement on numerous media, including stone, wall plaster, pottery, tiles, glass, metal items, and so on. In addition, the presence or absence of writing equipment such as ceramic inkwells, metal styli or pens, and metal seal boxes on archaeological sites can act as an indicator of literacy, sometimes in the service of bureaucratic endeavour. At the northern fort site of Vindolanda, the excavated caches of wooden writing tablets provide a more or less unique insight into army life, both of individual soldiers and of the organisation of certain official aspects of army life, and records such as these must also have existed in the towns as part of their role as administrative, legal, and tax collection centres. A small number of writing tablets from urban contexts is however known.

The so-called epigraphic habit, that is the use of formal, cut inscriptions in Latin in stone to commemorate an individual, a group, an event, an army unit, an emperor, or a deity, was an indicator of the acceptance of the visual literacy of inscriptions to forge social and group cohesion, as well as providing a platform and medium for the individual to be celebrated in a societal context.

A detailed study of the inscriptions of Roman Britain was carried out a number of years ago by the Hungarian scholar M. Biró.[53] Though over thirty-five years have passed since then and new inscriptions have been found, nevertheless Biró's study provides a valuable analysis, the methodology and broad statistical conclusions of which will still hold firm. The inscribed stones studied included all categories of inscribed objects, including tombstones, a total that was even then noted as being very modest compared to totals of material from other provinces. Of the inscriptions forming the database of the study, only around 5 per cent of these were found in urban contexts, in the large towns or *civitas* capitals. Large numbers of inscribed stones came from London, the provincial capital, and from Bath, a religious urban centre. The legionary fortresses accounted for around 12 per cent of the total epigraphic material from Roman Britain. The evidence in this study would therefore appear to suggest that the section of Romano-British society most linked to the commissioning and consuming of inscribed stones, in other words those who had acquired the so-called epigraphic habit, were principally members of the mobile military aristocracy of the empire when stationed or residing in the province of *Britannia*. Local tribal elite figures, based in the *civitas* capitals and in some of the rich villas in the surrounding countryside, would not seem to have acquired the epigraphic habit to anywhere near the same degree.

Perhaps astonishingly the only such formal dedication to a private individual comes from the town of Caerwent in Wales[54] where it is now housed in Caerwent Church (Plate 41). Discovered in 1903 in a reused context, the inscription, in Bath stone, reads: '[*Ti(berio) Claudio] Paulino legato II Aug(ustae) proconsul(i) prouinc(iae) Nar(r)bonensis leg(ato) Aug(usti) pr(o) pr(aetore) prouin(ciae) Lugudunen(sis) ex decreto ordinis res publ(ica) ciuit(atis) Silurum*', translated as 'to [Tiberius Claudius] Paulinus, legate of the Second Legion Augusta, proconsul of the province of Narbonensis, emperor's propraetorian legate of the province of Lugudunensis, by decree of the council, the Canton of the Silures [set this up]'. The inscription dates the stone to shortly before AD 220. Whether the inscription was accompanied by a portrait sculpture of Paulinus is uncertain, though likely.

Comparing the British evidence for dedicatory inscriptions, or rather the relative paucity of such evidence, to the numbers of dedicatory inscriptions on public buildings in the provinces of Gaul and Germany it was found that the situation in Britain was anomalous.[55] This would seem to indicate that despite an expected official encouragement to do so the Romano-British elite chose not to embrace the idea of celebrating and memorialising the social self through the setting up of dedicatory inscriptions in an urban context and rejected the idea of integrating their deeds within the communal experiences commemorated in the fora of the towns. Whether the elite chose instead to express their individuality, their wealth, and their dedication to the urban project and ideal through the building of luxury town houses, a phenomenon in Roman Britain from the mid-second century onwards, is possible, though in many other provinces municipal munificence and the building of luxury town houses were not mutually exclusive phenomena.

When it comes to the evidence of *graffiti* we are again fortunate in being able to draw upon the conclusions of two pre-existing studies of the distribution of *graffiti* in Roman Britain, carried out by R. G. Collingwood in 1937[56] and Jeremy Evans in 1987.[57] Once more, certain aspects of these studies are now slightly out of date but as with the study of inscriptions discussed above it is accepted here that the broad statistical patterns discernible in the *graffiti* data in particular may still hold true.

Collingwood examined four hundred items bearing literate *graffiti* of some kind. Of these, around 84 per cent came from urban contexts, with around a quarter of these coming from Roman London. Just over 6 per cent came from military sites and just under 8 per cent from villas. Only 2.5 per cent came from other rural sites of different kinds. Evans was concerned not so much with the *graffiti* themselves but rather with their geographical distribution, their relative levels of occurrence on Romano-British sites of different types – that is at large towns, small towns, villas, non-villa rural sites, and military sites – and their quantification by date. Therefore his aim can be seen to have been to not only map patterns of *graffiti* and thus of implied literacy but also, by chronological filtering, to potentially map the spread of literacy within the province. The overall conclusions of this study are of considerable interest here and help to support some of the conclusions reached by Biró some years before with regard to the distribution patterns of inscribed stones in the province.

Evans confined his dataset to *graffiti* scratched on pottery vessels and found that there were significant concentrations of numbers of potsherds bearing *graffiti* at large towns, military sites, principally though not exclusively fortresses, forts, and villas. The data comprised around four hundred examples of *graffiti* found between 1969 and 1982. A pronounced proportion of numbers of *graffiti* could be seen to come from *vici*, *civitas* capitals and, to a lesser extent, forts. Low numbers came from rural sites in general, though more were recorded at villas than at other types of rural site. Nevertheless it would appear from this evidence that villas were lower down the social and economic hierarchy than the towns, though as has been noted elsewhere in this chapter there were other ways for villa owners to demonstrate their cultural literacy, knowledge, or awareness than by writing *graffiti*. The results were less clear-cut chronologically, though in general it could be concluded that basic literacy was a constant through time at the sites recorded, with perhaps a fall-off of literacy rates in the later Roman period at fort sites. Over 75 per cent of the *graffiti* used in Evans's study were personal names, most often in the genitive case, implying that they were marks of ownership.

While a great deal of the *graffiti* from Roman Britain, as from the other provinces of the empire, is in the form of illiterate marks, much of it is in the form of written names. Certainly the deliberate marking of one's name on an item is not only a signifier of some degree of literacy on the part of the writer but is also a way of again of writing the self, of asserting ownership of an item, of claiming an act of vandalism for oneself, for asserting one's membership of a group of some kind. A ground-breaking study of *graffiti* from Pompeii, sadly not yet replicated for Roman Britain, has shown how *graffiti* provided the individual with a way to literally leave his or her mark on the urban fabric as well as on individual objects within the town. The Pompeian study[58] suggested that the *graffiti* caricatures common on the walls of the town acted as a socio-semiotic system that operated in opposition to so-called erudite wall painting. Caricature, the study concluded, served to sometimes criticise those in positions of power, to reinforce social and class distinctions, and in general to act as an expression of self-esteem and of an individual's consuming interests and passions.

There is very little similar *graffiti* from Roman Britain, though I illustrate three interesting examples of caricature *graffiti* from Britain here, only one of them being an urban *graffito* as such (Fig. 11). A grey-ware potsherd from London has been found incised with a *graffito* scene of a man being attacked by a large bird, probably a goose. The man is possibly a dwarf or even was intended as a pygmy. His nose takes the form of a phallus. The letters *CAVII* appear alongside the scene, perhaps being short for 'cave [*malum*]', 'look out for trouble'. Interestingly, a similar phallus-nosed man

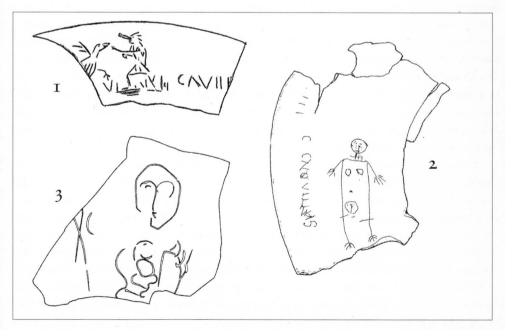

11. *Graffiti* caricatures from 1. London, 2. Blackwardine, Herefordshire, and 3. Binchester, County Durham. (Compiled from RIB II 2503.100, RIB II 2417.4, and Ferris, 2010, Fig. 71 No. 14)

holding a basket appears scratched on a potsherd from the amphitheatre at Caerleon, Wales, again depicted in confrontation with a large bird, perhaps a crane or stork. The second caricature, this time in the form of a naked woman with crudely delineated breasts and vagina, is scratched on the rim of a pewter plate from Blackwardine, Herefordshire, the figure again being accompanied by incised letters spelling out 'C CNOVILL', perhaps a personal name. With the third example I would certainly like to think that a rough *graffiti* drawing on the surface of a ceramic tile recovered during excavations at Binchester Roman Fort, County Durham, is a bored soldier's caricature cartoon of an officer supervising a work detachment at a military tilery.[59]

It is both unfortunate and frustrating, though perhaps reassuring for the prudish among my readers, that the author of the infamous *graffito* from a second-century town house in Leicester – '*ac quis te cinae[de] ...; equa elle; culo*', 'and who, catamite ... you; ... that mare; ... arse' – did not accompany his coarse invective with some drawings. A number of other crude or obscene partial *graffiti* on wall plaster from Britain include, in translation: 'you are shitting' from Alresford villa, Essex; and 'may you be thrashed' from Silchester. On a slate tablet from London a *graffito* refers to 'the eleven or more virile members of Nonius', while on tiles from Farmingham, Kent and Colchester, Essex *graffiti* refer to 'Attius's bugger' or 'Attius you bugger' and 'buggers' respectively.[60]

As for writing equipment, again an indicator of literacy, sometimes of individual literacy, sometimes of group literacy represented by the keeping of written records, Romano-British sites have produced numerous examples, in the form mainly of inkwells, styli, and seal boxes (Plate 42). The majority of inkwells found are in Samian ware, the rich, red-coloured fine-ware pottery imported from Gaul. As a form the inkwell is relatively rare, as has been shown by a recent study of their geographical distribution in the province, though they are found in sufficient numbers to make their analysis as a group worthwhile.[61] However, the distribution pattern to some extent mirrors the distribution of inscriptions and *graffiti* in that most inkwells from Roman Britain occur on military sites, with a still sizeable proportion coming from the large urban centres of the province, particularly from contexts associated with the administrative forum-basilica complexes of those towns.[62]

Styli, generally made of iron or copper alloy, though bone examples are also known, were implements designed for writing, with a pointed tip at one end and a spatulate eraser head at the other. Four principal iron types are known from Roman Britain. These are relatively common site finds on sites of all types in Roman Britain and there has not yet been any overall study of styli as a separate type of artefact, so no overall figure for numbers found in Roman Britain can be advanced here or any detailed comment be made on their geographical or chronological distribution outside the southern, civil zone of the province. Here styli appear on rural sites right across the south-east, particularly at villa sites, though perhaps not in such great numbers as might have been expected there, and at many non-villa rural establishments including small farmsteads, indicating at least record-keeping right down the social scale and therefore perhaps literacy too.[63] Certainly styli often crop up on individual sites in quite large numbers, seventy at Hambleden, Buckinghamshire and twenty-nine at Barnsley Park, Gloucestershire for example, often in association with iron ox-goad points, suggesting at such sites that record-keeping associated with the buying and selling of large numbers of cattle was taking place there. The possession of styli, perhaps as prestige items, can even be attested on a small number of late pre-Roman Iron Age sites in the south-east. Their presence here, though, need not necessarily imply a pre-Roman use of Latin in Britain among some elite individuals.

Seal boxes were generally made of copper alloy, and while plain examples are common, more ubiquitous still are examples with patterned enamel inlay on the lids (Plate 43) . Early bone examples are known on the continent but as far as I can ascertain none has been found in Britain. These seal boxes consisted of a hollow body and a hinged lid. Five principal types of box are known from Roman Britain – ovate, lozenge-shaped, square, leaf-shaped, and circular – with two further types, pyriform and triangular or polygonal, known from the Continent.[64] The continental types have been further subdivided to recognise twenty-five sub-types of box. Their purpose is generally accepted as having been to enclose a wax seal attached by string to a letter of some kind, the seal box preventing tampering with the letter itself. The seal box would thus be broken open at its final destination by the recipient of the missive, this being the reason why most seal boxes found in archaeological contexts consist of only one piece of the original box. The wax seal protected by the seal box would most likely have borne some kind of official or personal visual seal impressed on the hot wax by an *intaglio* ring. At the site of Wroxeter in Shropshire a seal box was found with some beeswax residue still inside the box and the impression of the threads of a string on the underside of the wax.[65] Received wisdom is that letters or dispatches sealed in this way would principally have been official post sent as part of the working of the provincial administration and of the army, utilising the so-called *Cursus Publicus* system of official mail transportation. Thus the majority of seal boxes might be expected to be found in the province's administrative centres, that is the large towns, and at military sites and sites of the *mansiones*, which formed staging posts on the *Cursus Publicus* routes. Any private letters so sealed must have had recourse to a private delivery system, by slave or paid messenger, a system about which we know nothing. Private post might account for the find-spots of seal boxes away from the towns, forts, and *mansiones*. In addition, it has been suggested that on the continent there is a notable link between finds of seal boxes and shrine sites[66], suggesting that the seal boxes may have been used at these sites to seal personal vows written on wooden or lead tablets by individual literate worshippers or by paid scribes in employment at the sites to act as intermediaries between the illiterate worshippers and their gods.

No countrywide study of the distribution of seal boxes in Roman Britain is presently available, although it is understood that this situation will soon be remedied.[67] In the interim it is therefore of interest to look at a study of seal boxes from Roman London[68] to see if any patterns emerged from this work. At the time of the study in 1995, forty-four examples were known from excavations in the city, the Roman provincial capital, with seventeen further examples known of then but not classified in the study. How many have subsequently been found here is not known to the writer. Eighteen of the seal boxes could be seen to be associated with administrative or military areas of the capital, six from the area of the Basilica, two from the Forum, seven from the Bucklersbury area, one from a possible *mansio*, and two from military establishments.

The assemblage of forty-four seal boxes from Roman London pales somewhat into insignificance when compared to the assemblage of one hundred and thirty-eight seal boxes found at the site of Augst or Augusta Raurica, in Switzerland, the largest number of seal boxes known from a single site anywhere in the empire. The larger sample size and the secure site provenance of most of the boxes mean that their analysis can potentially throw further light on the use of these items in the Roman world and thus ultimately in Roman Britain as well perhaps. While extensive area excavation of the public buildings and spaces of Augst has not taken place, nevertheless the absence of finds of seal boxes in these areas when trenching had taken place might be of significance. Three seal boxes were found within the perimeter of an urban religious sanctuary. The vast majority, however, came from private residences and residential areas within the town, suggesting that the accepted link elsewhere between the presence of seal boxes and the operation of the imperial *Cursus Publicus* system might not necessarily be correct.[69] Whatever the use of the seal boxes – in public or private post or more likely both together – both in Britain and on the Continent their presence and distribution can still be analysed to help map the spread of Latin literacy, a piece of evidence among a suite of indicators in the process of becoming Roman. On the Continent, seal box distribution analysis has been used, for instance, to convincingly map the spread of literacy via returning auxiliary veterans to rural settlements on the Rhine frontier.[70]

The keeping of written records is likely to have been an integral part of the administrative bureaucracy of the province, as well as of the Roman army, as evidenced by the kinds of information recorded on the Vindolanda wooden writing tablets. It would appear, though, that record keeping, even if it only consisted of the keeping of written tallies rather than a more sophisticated record, also occurred in rural contexts, as the multiple occurrences of styli on rural sites attests, as discussed above.[71]

The record, on a wooden writing tablet from the Garden House site in the former Walbrook valley in the City of London, of a legal dispute over the ownership of a tranche of land in Kent provides evidence of the urban legal system at work in *Britannia*.[72] The thirteen-line text, though the first part only of a longer document, is still the longest stylus tablet text so far recovered from Roman Britain, at least up until 1996. The tablet is both an intriguing find and one that creates a feeling of academic exasperation. Intriguing because it is the only document of any kind from Roman Britain which alludes to the nature of landownership in the province and to a land deal of some kind. Its creation is a testament to the necessarily pedantic nature of Roman imperial bureaucracy, which underpinned the working of the province even down to the smallest parcel of land. Exasperating because the text gives a tantalising insight into the minutiae of conquest and change on a more human level than that of the grand historical narratives of historians such as Dio Cassius and Suetonius.

Because of the length of the document text, a translation only is given here:

> In the consulship of the Emperor Trajan Hadrian Caesar Augustus for the second time, and Gnaeus Fuscus Salinator, on the day before the Ides of March [ie 14 March AD 118]. Whereas, on arriving at the property in question, the wood *Verlucionium*, fifteen *arepennia* more or less, which is in the canton of the Cantiaci in Dibussu [...] parish, [...], neighbourhood by the heirs [of ...] and the heirs of Caesennius Vitalis and the vicinal road, Lucius Julius Bellicus said that he had bought it from Titus Valerius Silvinus for forty *denarii*, as is contained in the deed of purchase. Lucius Julius Bellicus attested that he [...].

The Celtic-sounding name of this forty-denarii patch of woodland – *silvum Verlucionium* – suggests that the land was named some time before the Roman conquest and that it may have been a sacred grove of some kind, given how unusual it seems for a small patch of land such as this to have a name at all. It has been suggested that following the conquest this land, which should have become imperial property, was sold to a private individual, was subsequently acquired by Valerius Silvanus, and was then bought later in good faith by Julius Bellicus. The legal challenge against Bellicus's ownership might have been brought by another interested individual party – this part of the document is missing – or more likely by the provincial procurator on behalf of the Roman state or by the local tribal *civitas* authority reasserting their original ownership of the land in pre-conquest times. As neither of the named owners of the land in the document has a name suggesting a British origin, a dispute with the tribal magistracy of the *Cantiaci* seems likely.

This document therefore can be seen to represent perhaps the tip of the tip of the iceberg with regard to the records kept by a judicial authority in the provincial capital, backed up by a record-keeping secretariat. Perhaps a farm-by-farm record of post-conquest land transactions was maintained for the whole province, either in London or at each of the *civitas* capitals for their own tribal region, though perhaps such documentation was only maintained when legal ownership became a matter for dispute.

Other types of evidence for the expression of literacy in Roman Britain would have to include the occurrence of mosaic pavements whose use of stories, images, and tropes from classical mythology would imply both literate creators of these images and literate, rich consumers, or perhaps in some cases those who aspired to be seen as being literate consumers. A knowledge of the literary classics of the Graeco-Roman world in Roman Britain is implied here but not proven.[73] Such evidence is found in both urban and villa contexts. Only the works of the writer Vergil can be attested as being known in a small number of contexts in Roman Britain, and then only his *Aeneid*. For example, an inscribed ceramic flue tile from the town of Silchester bears the scratched Vergilian phrase '*conticuere omnes*'

– 'all fell silent'. Knowledge of Homer's *Odyssey* can be read by the appearance of a scene depicting the recognition of Ulysses on a silver flagon from Traprain Law, East Lothian, Scotland (Plate 44). Again, knowledge of classical mythology can be mapped. As might be imagined such knowledge, in the absence of a particularly large number of surviving wall paintings as are found in Rome, Italy, and certain other provinces, is best demonstrated in mosaic art. This did not mean, though, that such knowledge was confined to a rural elite in their luxury country villas, as many of the mosaics reflecting knowledge of the classics come from town houses. Perhaps the greatest concentration of such pavements was in the town houses of Corinium, Roman Cirencester, where mosaics depicted scenes from Bacchic lore and the fate of Actaeon, the hunter turned into a stag as punishment for his spying on Diana as she bathed naked. Another urban centre where knowledge of the classics was displayed to their guests by a number of town house owners was Verulamium, Roman St Albans.

New Directions

But what new research directions could there be for studying art in the towns of Roman Britain? The extraordinary omission of discussion of both religion and art from the otherwise excellent recent research agendas document for Roman Britain might lead the casual reader to imagine that there are no viable future directions. The study of art is omitted from the document on the not altogether convincing grounds that 'spectacular discoveries like the Cramond lion are not easy to foresee'.[74] In the same volume it is noted with regard to public buildings that 'there are also questions of both how such structures were used and how they structured everyday experiences',[75] with little elaboration on this observation. It is also pointed out how little analysis there has been of the use of ritual space in towns. Yet, in the past few years ancient historians and art historians have been examining the town as a space for performance and spectacle, indeed for such activities to be as much a part of the fabric of a Roman town as the marble, stones, and mortar that constituted its very essence.[76] There is certainly the scope to look at the towns of Roman Britain from this perspective.

   In trying to understand what Romano-British towns looked like we can create virtual reality models and draw upon a long tradition of reconstruction drawings, going back to the time of Alan Sorrell. Yet so often, as noted above, our evidence for the appointment of the interiors of these buildings is lacking. Marble usage and the meaning of colour has been explored briefly in an important and perhaps overlooked paper by Raphael Isserlin,[77] based on his doctoral thesis. Marble would have provided additional sensual dimensions to the visitors' aesthetic experiences of a building, leaving aside any accompanying sculptural programme or dedicatory inscription. Colour would have seduced the eye, while the tactile experience of touching the surface of the polished stone might have provided an additional stimulus to the overall experience.

Civic art in Rome could also sometimes serve a didactic purpose with regard to the definition of the roles and moral responsibilities of women.[78] Whether there was what might be called moralising art aimed at the women of Roman Britain or even if we can identify gendered space in the urban plan is open to question. However, once more such avenues of research might throw new light on the programme of urban foundation and growth in Roman Britain. Expanding briefly on this particular topic there perhaps must be raised the issue as to whether the public bath houses of the towns were exclusively male spaces and if this was reflected in their adornment; it is, of course, possible that male gendered space need not have been necessarily dominated by heterosexual men; indeed, the bath houses may well have provided queer space for homosexual liaisons and a model for a small enclosed world without women.[79] The preponderance of images of men, and most often images reflecting masculinity, in the Roman world must have been striking; emperors, senators, magistrates, soldiers, gladiators, and gods were everywhere. That the concepts of what constituted manliness probably changed between the time of the earlier Roman empire and the late empire, the period often called Late Antiquity, is beyond dispute. That there were probably also geographical and cultural changes should also be borne in mind. As has been noted by Natalie Boymel Kampen:

> throughout late antiquity contention about the nature of power and where it was to be found required public self-representation by the various contending parties, whether they were emperors or bureaucrats, bishops or holy men. Whoever they were, they had a stake in connecting their images with the visual ideals of masculinity circulating in their part of society and in asserting those images as normative.[80]

On coinage one is instantly struck by the images of many of the emperors of the third century onwards who present themselves to an understandably jittery populace by the use of portraits of bull-necked, close-shaved, crop-headed, hard-faced military men who might, just might, be good men to rely on and turn to in a crisis. This was to change to a certain degree with the advent of the House of Constantine, where familial reliability, even if only conveyed through the similarity of the emperors' names – Constantine, Constantius, Constans and so on – became more of a trait situated in the needs of the peoples of the empire. This was a harking back to the days when the emperors looked like gods and age in portraits was a flexible concept.

A great deal of the hyper-masculine display being discussed here inevitably was linked to the army and, as such, at first would have been largely confined to the forts and fortresses of the province, perhaps until the time when veterans regularly took up residence in non-military communities, mainly in the *coloniae* and other large towns. Images of emperors, of fellow soldiers, of martial figures such as Jupiter the Thunderer, Mars, and Hercules; of the eagle, of predatory beasts such as the lion and mythical griffon; of phallic symbols, and of dead or dying barbarian foes enforced the masculine aesthetic here. Yet Victory would have been there too, perhaps making her the most masculine of female deities. The male aesthetics engendered in the army uniforms and weaponry, the parade equipment, the military awards, and so on have been little considered. Was the Roman army veteran whose high military award, a copper alloy torc of little intrinsic value,[81] was found in the *vicus* at Mill Street, Rocester, Staffordshire living here and trading on his past (Plate 45)? Did he see his younger self in the retained object? Was it both a source of great pride to him and a symbol of hyper-machismo?

The popularity of the image of the gladiator and of gladiatorial combat throughout the Roman world is striking, given that the gladiator 'possessed a kind of excess of masculinity that ultimately put him at the margins'. The Latin word *gladius*, for sword, was indeed used coarsely in demotic terms to mean penis.[82] As this cipher, this meta-man, the gladiator's image was paraded before both men and women in the private sphere as much as in the public arena. Given the otherness of the real-life gladiator, his link to the depravities of slavery or criminality, his public role as a base entertainer and showman, his barbarity, and his sexual attraction for both Roman men and women, it is surprising to see his image given such prominence in domestic contexts both in town and country in Roman Britain.

In Roman Britain, where gladiatorial games would have been a largely urban or military phenomenon and were unlikely to have been particularly common events, images of individual gladiators and of combat appear in wall paintings, on mosaic pavements, on a stone relief from Chester and a ceramic plaque from Colchester, metal, pottery and glass vessels, and in the form of figurines or statuettes in not only metal but also in ivory in one instance. A panel depicting gladiators fighting forms part of a wall painting scheme in a town house at Colchester. It has been suggested that 'it is unlikely that a house-owner would have commissioned a wall-decoration involving gladiatorial scenes unless he had some personal familiarity with, or enthusiasm for, the entertainment of the amphitheatre'.[83] However, this need not necessarily be the case as noted already, given that the choice of such a scene could equally have been a way for the house owner to display his own liking for and identification with the kind of hyper-masculinity represented by the gladiator. Perhaps the most famous appearance of images of gladiators in Roman Britain is on a mosaic from Bignor villa, Sussex where are found *putti* or cupids dressed up as gladiators and gladiator trainers. Here sweaty hyper-masculinity is at least diluted with humour. A gladiator *emblema* forms the centre of a mosaic floor at the later first-century Eccles villa in Kent and two gladiators appear on a mosaic at Brading villa, Sussex.

Two copper alloy figurines of gladiators have been found in London, while a splendid bone or ivory figurine of a *murmillo*, a heavily armed gladiator, naked apart from a loin cloth and armour, holding a shield on which scenes of gladiatorial combat also occur in an inter-textual manner, comes from Lexden, Colchester and probably dates to the first or second century, and is now in the collections of the British Museum. A first-century volute ceramic lamp from London, again now in the British Museum, bears gladiatorial combat scenes. Copper alloy clasp knife handles in the form of gladiators come from Corbridge, Northumberland, and from a third-century context at Piddington villa, Northamptonshire, and in ivory from South Shields (Plate 46). Gladiatorial combat in the arena was also a popular theme on imported Samian pottery vessels, and on vessels produced in Britain in Colchester and in the Nene Valley, the circulation of this pottery spreading the image much more widely than the other image-bearing items discussed here. Glass cups depicting gladiatorial contests are known from many urban centres, including London, Colchester, Wroxeter, Dorchester and Leicester and in smaller numbers away from the towns. A painted glass bowl from Vindolanda bears a design of a combat between two gladiators overseen by a *summa rudis* or referee.[84]

Another hyper-masculine figure with whom some men in the ancient world might have wanted to identify with is the hero god Hercules.[85] As might have been expected perhaps, many of the images of Hercules from Roman Britain are found in military contexts where the linking of martial activity with the brave labours of the god perhaps went deeper than might at first sight appear. Indeed it must not be forgotten that in the second century the emperor Commodus became somewhat obsessed with the hero god and was often portrayed in his guise, most famously in the bust of the naked torso of the bearded emperor with a lion skin draped over his head, the paws tied across his chest and holding a club over one shoulder, now in the *Museo del Palazzo dei Conservatori*, Rome, and a cult of Commodus-Hercules developed in the army in the provinces. In the latter centuries of the Roman empire the image of Hercules sometimes became linked to ideas of salvation, of earthly struggle and effort, of the triumph of good over evil, though more often other figures such as Orpheus or Mithras were used to convey such concepts. Individual images of the god are found in numerous media and contexts. Representations of the Labours of Hercules, of individual labours, or of mortals, other gods, animals or objects associated with one or more of the labours appear relatively commonly in Roman Britain as well. The god appears on the reverse of many coin issues but no attempt has been made to discuss or quantify these here, save to report that coins in this case would have acted as a medium for the circulation of such images.

From the northern military zone come a number of major artworks depicting Hercules. At High Rochester, Mars and Hercules flank an inscription panel of *Legio XX Valeria Victrix*. A naïve carving of Hercules and his protector the goddess Minerva appear on a sandstone relief from Corbridge, Northumberland, a scene in which he may be killing the Lernean Hydra, and which may have been one panel in a larger frieze depicting all of his labours. From Rudchester comes a now-damaged statue, though easily identifiable as the god-hero by the apple and club he holds, as well as his lion skin and quiver. From Housesteads comes an altar with three of its faces bearing in relief a carving respectively of Hercules and the Nemean lion, of the Lernean Hydra, and of the apples of the Hesperides. From Housesteads comes a small stone figure, though without the god's standard attributes. From Netherby comes a small statue of a man hooded with a lion skin. He is depicted on a gravestone from Chester rescuing Hesione. A silver-gilt statuette found near Birdoswald may depict the emperor Commodus in the guise of Hercules (Plate 47). The god-hero appears represented as five small bronze figurines, two from South Shields, one from Piercebridge, one unprovenanced, and one from York.

On a fragment of a silver bowl from the Traprain Law treasure was a head of Hercules as a central *emblema*, with various beasts around towards the outer edge. On one of the skillet handles from the treasure found at Capheaton, Northumberland a plethora of images depicting Hercules is found: his head and face appears at the end of the skillet while his wine cup and club flank him, then there are also depicted the corpses of the slaughtered Nemean lion, the Keryneian stag, and the Erymanthian boar. On the base in the centre is a flaming altar, the apple tree of the Hesperides with the hero's quiver and bow case leaning against its trunk, two of the Stymphalian birds, and the Lernean Hydra. Hercules also forms the *emblema*, while figures of him wrestling Antaeus also appear here, along with the lion skin and club and a draped female figure, now damaged, who presumably is his goddess guardian Minerva.

From the civilian parts of the province, finds depicting Hercules are again numerous. A headless statue of Hercules with a club and lion skin tied on the chest was found at Sibson, Huntingdonshire. Hercules appears with Jupiter on one side of a stone block from Bath, a similar stone with Hercules and Apollo being now in Compton Dando church, Somerset. From a villa site at Colerne, Wiltshire comes a rectangular carved stone block, on the front of which is a concave niche topped by a shell canopy; on it is a crude large male figure of Hercules battling the Hydra. From London comes a fine classical bronze of Hercules firing his now-lost bow, presumably at the Stymphalian birds. Another classical representation is recorded as having come from Ford Green, Northamptonshire. The god is depicted heavily bearded and carrying a wine cup and his trademark club from the temple site at Bruton. From East Anglia come a very large number of small figurines of the hero god in various guises, comprising two from Ely, one each from Sutton near Ely and Icklingham, Suffolk, five from Colchester, one from Cowlinge, and a metal detector find from Suffolk. Two small bronze figurines come from Verulamium, and another from Bedfordshire.

On a mosaic pavement at Bramdean, Hampshire, Hercules is depicted lifting the giant Antaeus, again overseen by Minerva. A drunken Hercules, supported by Satyrs, carouses with Bacchus and Silenus and others on the great silver dish from the Mildenhall treasure from Suffolk, and on the handle of a complete imported jug from the Welshpool hoard artistic licence is taken with the chronology of the hero's labours, in that we see depicted here the boy Hercules holding one dead serpent while a second lies on the escutcheon at the base of the handle. Of course, rather than being a boy, as here, this feat in the chronology of his mythology was carried out when he was just a baby. Again, the boy on the Welshpool jug is depicted wearing the trademark lion-skin hood which in mythology he did not adopt until after he had, as an adult, slain the Nemean lion whose skin he then wore.

A fine copper alloy strigil handle from Caerleon is decorated with the Labours of Hercules; he also appears on an ivory knife handle from Eccles, Kent, a copper alloy handle of a folding knife from Lincolnshire on which he wrestles with Antaeus, and on a possible handle from Hertfordshire. A strigil handle from Reculver, Kent takes the form of Hercules's club. A copper alloy head of the lion-skin-hooded hero-god, filled with lead, comes from Hertfordshire and was probably a steelyard weight. Small-scale representations of the club also appeared at Thetford, probably a charm worn around the neck, and at London, and in gold at Birdoswald and Ashstead, Kent (Plate 48).

Hercules on his own, slaying the Nemean lion, attacking a monster, and so on are common themes on decorated Samian vessels, though it is not possible to quantity the numbers of occurrences of the hero-god on vessels found in Roman Britain, though it is undeniable that these must have acted as inspiration for the decorative schemes appearing on many subsequently produced Romano-British decorated pottery vessels. On pottery beakers or cups from the Nene Valley potteries, Hercules appears hunting the Cerneian hind, as on a pot from Lincoln, battling with a monster to rescue the naked Hesione who is depicted tied to a rock on another pot, and fighting the many-headed Hydra on a pot from Welney, Norfolk. On a beaker from Verulamium appear Mithras the hunter, Hercules and Mercury. On a yellow-green beaker from Cirencester an appliqué figure of Hercules with a club appears, along with representations of a Maenad and possibly Mercury. An archer figure appears on a mould from Stibbington-cum-Sibson, Huntingdonshire and this may be Hercules. In burial contexts, a bronze statuette from an inhumation burial at York depicts Hercules holding a dead serpent and an apple. A white pipeclay figurine of Hercules was one of a number of different types of figurine in the so-called child's grave at Colchester.[86]

While the appearance of Minerva alongside Hercules in a few of the artworks listed above might have made his image acceptable to female viewers, the sheer testosterone-fuelled vitality of the majority of the images of the hero-god from Roman Britain and the Roman world more widely must have been aimed to appeal squarely to a male audience.

Art and Urban Discourse

Until all of the volumes in the *Corpus Signorum Imperii Romanum* for Britain have been published it will not be possible to produce a definitive quantification and distributional analysis of art in Roman Britain, and to fully address differences between art in the towns and art in the countryside and issues relating to the ideological role played by art in towns. In contrast, urban art and architecture in Roman Gaul has received perhaps fuller and more sophisticated academic attention in terms of assessment of their cultural significance.[87] A very brief quantification of what can be called urban art from Gaul, produced from perusing the volumes produced by Espérandieu,[88] suggests that urban art played a more significant role in Gallo-Roman life than it did in Romano-British society. This view has been further reinforced in the author's mind by recent study visits to the museums and *lapidaria* of French urban centres such as Lyons and Dijon, where the sheer quantity of artworks cannot simply reflect differing patterns of survival and recovery in the two countries.

If one accepts the notion that the town was experienced, and therefore conceived, in different ways by different people at different times then the history of towns could be written from a number of discrepant parallel perspectives, each different but each equally as valid as the other.[89] Perceptions of a town or city would have as much to do with the individuality of the buildings there and their artistic adornment as to whether it had a thriving market or was home to a particular industry. The concept of the urban hinterland relies for its existence almost entirely on the town being an economic centre at the hub of a rationally organised landscape, rather than also as an oasis where carefully managed and staged aesthetic and religious experiences, mediated by art, could be enjoyed by the inhabitants, as well as by visitors.

It was lamented some years ago how poor much 'urbanistic discourse' was. 'The way in which space is occupied is much studied, but exclusively in physical terms of occupation and amenity. The psychological space, the cultural, the juridical, the religious, are not treated as aspects of the ecological space with whose economy the urbanist is concerned [even though they] impinge on the symbolic world of the citizens.'[90] If the idea of urbanism in the Roman world was linked to the psychological impact of the urban space and everything within it, then art was not simply part of the fabric of the town, rather it was part of a wider ideological package behind the idea of the town.[91] Urban space was not simply to be passively enjoyed, it was to be actively engaged with.

The evidence presented in this chapter would appear to corroborate the thesis that the large towns of Roman Britain acted as the motors for the spread of ideas in the province, that they were cultural as well as political and economic centres. The same type of evidence also is present at the Roman army forts in Britain, as might have been expected. The evidence of finds also shows that there was a very distinct urban culture in Roman Britain, as elsewhere in the empire, a culture reflected in the visual and written literacy that can be demonstrated to have been a particular feature of towns in the province. If the idea and actuality of the town or city ultimately did not appeal to Romano-Britons or at least maintain its initial appeal, then it might be that this was as much a cultural rejection as a social or political one. The momentum behind the creation of the Romano-British urban culture was apparently not enough to sustain it within a political vacuum. As the contemporary urban theorist Richard Florida has pointed out, cultural production can exist within and sustain a failed urban environment and can even be the motor for eventual regeneration of both political will, civic pride, the urban economy, and the urban fabric.[92] Though Florida's theories are mostly germane to post-industrial societies today and to the broader concepts of post-modernism, nevertheless they provide some kind of theoretical continuum from the writings of Antonio Gramsci for whom the indivisibility of culture and political power was self-evident.[93] Discussions of Roman art and culture only occasionally feature prominently in broader discussions of Roman imperialism and of Romanisation and acculturation when perhaps they should take a more central role.

In conclusion, it can be suggested that there was a distinct strain of art and a distinct use of that art in an urban context in Roman Britain. Urban art was not apparently embedded in the Romano-British psyche as a vehicle for ideas and ideologies, in the way that it was at Rome and in Italy more generally[94] and perhaps also in parts of Gaul. The Romano-British elite would appear on the whole to have invoked a choice not to commission and consume civic art, in a way that they also chose to embrace, or not to embrace, other elements of Roman material culture.[95] While some art became specifically associated with urban situations in Roman Britain, for instance the mosaics and wall paintings of second- and third-century town houses, truly urban art, that is art which played some role in the very rhetoric of urbanisation, did not appear to have become either part of the fabric of the city in the province, perhaps surprisingly even at the *coloniae*, or part of the very idea of the city, as appeared to have happened elsewhere within the empire. The cities of Roman Britain, though, were as much made up of poetry, pleasure, philosophy, and dreams as they were of politics, business, and architecture. Though small compared to urban centres today, the city loomed large in the Roman imagination; indeed the idea of the city might be said to have been more important then than its physical structure.

6

AN EMPIRE IN PIECES

The Psychology of the Whole

In Sigmund Freud's London house in Maresfield Gardens, Hampstead, is a collection of archaeological objects that includes a number of pieces of Greek and Roman sculpture. One of the criteria set by Freud for acquiring such items for his collection was apparently that they should be complete,[1] a condition imposed by him for purely aesthetic purposes, rather than through any concern about the perhaps ambiguous state of the fragmentary image.

There is something almost seductively unreal about complete objects to many archaeologists, and a great deal of time and effort in our profession goes into reconstructing the wholeness of the past, in sticking broken pots back together, in estimating vessel equivalents from a pottery assemblage of individual sherds, and in honing sampling strategies that will allow us to believe we can understand a whole site or a whole landscape from our supposedly scientifically selected samples. Perhaps, as some academics have suggested, under the influence of the psychoanalytical theories of Jacques Lacan and Melanie Klein, we need to return to the whole in this way in order to understand our own lives, to fulfil some inner need, some innate desire buried deep within us.[2]

But while so much of the evidence for the past is all too often fragmentary, broken, damaged, or incomplete, a certain amount of this material was in this state before it entered the archaeological record, so that any biographies of such fragments must include consideration of both their once-complete state as artefacts and their existence as fragmented objects. Fragmentation may have taken place immediately prior to these fragments being disposed of or buried, or the fragments may themselves have been employed or used in some way other than in their previous form, before fragmentation took place. The process of fragmentation and the significance of the fragment have been the subject of academic enquiry in prehistoric archaeology for some time[3] and Roman archaeologists are now tentatively engaging with the subject and bringing new lines of enquiry into play on their own data.

This chapter will deal specifically with images of fragmented bodies, although many of the methods of enquiry employed could equally be applied to artefact studies, and indeed are used so in a number of case studies in the chapter. While in Greek society and art the body remained an almost inviolable whole, in Roman art the body became something that could sometimes be portrayed simply by representing the head or bust of an individual. The cropping of images of people often occurred in wall paintings and on gemstones. Body parts of statues were sometimes intentionally interchangeable by design. Portrait heads could be re-carved, sometimes out of economic necessity, other times for more political reasons. The sick could represent themselves at healing shrines with *ex votos* portraying their diseased or affected body parts, as has been demonstrated in Chapter 3. The human body in these instances was not simply modified, it was transformed into a series of unrelated parts. There was evidently a tension between beliefs in Roman society, mirrored in Roman culture, of the body as an ideal form and the body as a flexible image.

This fragmentation of the body, when it occurred, perhaps reflected a permeability of boundaries in Roman society and culture, particularly between life and death, and sickness and health. The social body in certain contexts condoned and acquiesced in this dismemberment of the corporeal body into images. In some instances the corporeal body was reduced to the status of an artefact, and it is this process which will be examined here using evidence from around the Roman world but anchoring discussion on evidence from Roman Britain when such evidence is available.

Theorising the Body

There has been a considerable amount of attention paid to the body in antiquity and perceptions of the human body in the ancient world, not only by archaeologists but also by ancient historians, classicists, and art historians.[4] Perhaps rather tellingly, the majority of work on the body in the ancient world was undertaken in the body-conscious, not to say body-obsessed 1990s, and much of it was concerned with issues of gender identity. A more recent strand of research has concentrated on male identity and the male body in particular.[5]

Many of the previous studies of the classical body have dealt with the whole body, with issues of gender and representation, health and medical practice, or exclusion through disability or other perceived differences. How studies of the classical body fit into a wider body history has been neatly summarised by one authority, though the balance of this historical overview of the field of study is not without its own inbuilt biases. Interestingly she argues against what she sees as a false historical watershed, around 1800, when many body historians, including Michel Foucault, see fundamental changes in attitudes to sexuality and homosexuality as having taken place, or even indeed for these concepts only to have emerged around about that time. She also quite rightly questions the idea that pornography only came to be associated with obscenity in relatively recent times, that is after 1500.[6]

In thinking about analysing the fragmented body, consideration needs to be given to psychoanalytical approaches to the viewing and reception of fragmented and fragmentary images of the body, approaches principally championed by Melanie Klein and Jacques Lacan, and in the field of classics by Page Dubois.[7] The psychoanalyst and social theorist Julia Kristeva has been involved in an art historical research project, centred on the exhibition *Visions Capitales* held at the Louvre in 1998 and its accompanying catalogue of the same name.[8] Through an exploration of the image of the severed or disassociated head from prehistoric contexts up to its inclusion in the art of Andy Warhol in the 1960s, the project provides a broad context for perhaps understanding the varying cultural situations in which the image has been employed. A great deal of relevant material can also be found in writings on the subject of the fragment by the art historian Linda Nochlin, and on collage by the artist Kurt Schwitters.[9] Together, these sources have perhaps helped to provide me with a theoretical framework for looking at such images in the context of the classical and Roman world. While Nochlin's work on fragmentary images, principally in painting, is of great relevance to this study, it is again a study that, by tying the use of fragmented images to the birth of modernism, indeed by her seeing the fragment as' a metaphor of modernity', creates another possibly false watershed in body history.

Kurt Schwitters is perhaps best known for his collages of the first quarter of the twentieth century, utilising train tickets and postage stamps, coins, newspaper clippings and advertisements, printed numbers and fragmented words and phrases, found objects, and pieces and fragments of wood, metal, glass, paper, card, and cloth (Plate 49). Schwitters created his collages through a process of what he called *Entformung*, a process involving, through assembly, both the metamorphosis and the dissociation of fragmentary or fragmented objects and materials which he viewed as possessing what he called *Eigengift*, 'their own special essence or poison'. This *Eigengift* would be lost during and as a result of their *Entformung*. The intention was not that these materials should now function as if they were transformed into some other kind of material, rather that they now formed part of a new whole, a collage that was more than simply the sum of its parts. The crucial thing to Schwitters was that through the creation of art he could order and rationalise the world and thus understand how art and the processes of creation could work against the decay of meaning in things, and how timeless order could be created out of temporal chaos. Time and again, in the chapters above, we have seen instances of both contemporary and older objects in Roman Britain and the Roman world more generally being used in some way to create just such a new reality, often in a religious or ritual context. Below, in this chapter, further examples of this almost collagist process will be discussed in terms of the use of fragments and fragmented images to create a new whole.

Images of Ancestors

The creation, display and use of wax masks – *imagines* – of noteworthy male ancestors who had held magisterial office was a well-attested aspect of social display among the aristocratic classes of Rome from the early Republic onwards, and may have had its origins in Etruscan or pre-Roman Italic social practices,[10] though the tradition of using masks in a purely theatrical context obviously goes back to the Greeks. Discussion of the display of such masks in the home and their more active use in funeral processions, where they were worn by mourners playing the role of the deceased ancestors, has centred on their origins and significance as status symbols and their possible influence on the development of Roman portraiture, with its concentration on the head and face, at the expense of the whole person. The use of such masks at Roman funerals was both a piece of social bonding with the idea of the ancestors and, of course, a piece of political theatre.[11]

In Roman art, from the time of the Republic onwards, portrait heads and busts proliferated as a medium for the representation and commemoration of the individual, both men and women, at first in sculptural form only[12] but subsequently in two dimensions on funerary reliefs, sarcophagi, mosaics, and gemstones. This truncated representation of the human body probably owed its origins wholly, or in part, as has just been mentioned, to the Roman aristocratic tradition of commissioning wax ancestor masks as a form of social display, although the Etruscan and Italic traditions of manufacturing terracotta heads was also an undoubted influence on developments in Roman portraiture.[13] It can be assumed that sculptural portrait busts of ancestors were common in the houses of the aristocracy in the same way that the wax *imagines* had been, although portraiture became an artistic medium not confined to aristocratic patrons alone (Plate 50). A good depiction of a pair of ancestral busts on display in a wooden cabinet appears on a cylindrical funerary altar from Brescia, northern Italy.[14]

The origins, development, and use of Roman portraits in the form of busts and heads are again linked to funerary situations, not only at Rome and more broadly in Italy, but also further afield within the Empire, as in Egypt where the painted Fayum mummy portraits represent a significant and vibrant variation on this practice.[15] As has been pointed out,[16] many portrait busts were intended for display on the outside of tombs and one must try to remember that in this context their viewing was only a small part of the overall sensory experience of walking down a street of tombs, looking at the structures themselves, viewing portraits and reading the biographical detail given in the accompanying inscriptions. The same would have applied to the display of busts in niches inside *columbaria* such as those at Vigna Codini in Rome.[17] Perhaps accessing all this information together allowed the viewer to reconstruct the life and appearance of the deceased ancestor from these fragmented commemorations of their lives.

Portrait busts also appear in later Christian contexts, such as on the fourth-century mosaic in the Basilica at Aquilea, by the so-called Master of Portraits, where ten portrait depictions in roundels of men and women, cut off mid-torso, appear. These portraits probably represent affluent members of the Christian community in the city and benefactors of the Church.

In Roman Britain it may be that face pots and particularly head pots in some way were intended to represent a deity or an individual person. Indeed, head pots are found less in domestic contexts than face pots and may therefore have had some especial ritual or religious function linked to celebration or commemoration (Plate 51).[18]

Alchemy of Suffering

Anatomical *ex votos*, models of human body parts made of various materials, were widely dedicated as offerings at healing shrines and religious sanctuaries throughout the Roman world, as seen in Chapter 3. Above I compared *ex votos* from the Republican healing sanctuary at Ponte di Nona, near Rome with those from the Gallo-Roman religious site at the Source of the Seine, near Dijon, and consideration was given to the differences between these sites as reflected in the relative numbers and types of body parts represented at each. The role played by anatomical *ex votos* in the process of seeking a cure at such sites and the significance of the representative body parts themselves – heads, torsos, eyes, ears, hands, arms, legs, feet, sexual and internal organs – must be viewed in the context of the special position of the sick in the classical world.[19]

At Ponte di Nona, the huge collection of mainly terracotta *ex votos* of body parts – over eight thousand were recovered by excavation in the mid-1970s – represented all the most common body parts found at such sites: over thirteen hundred heads; over two thousand three hundred feet; just under a thousand limbs; just over six hundred hands; just under four hundred eyes; forty-four ears; one hundred and sixty male genitals, and eight breasts. But also included were twenty-seven uteri, seven models of intestines, a tongue, a mouth, hearts, kidneys and vaginas, which suggests a much deeper knowledge of human anatomy than seen at many other healing shrines.

Portrayals of individual body parts cannot, though, always be taken at face value, as can be demonstrated in the case of a stone *ex voto* from Rosinos de Vidriales, Spain, and in the *Museo Provincial de Zamora*.[20] On it are depicted the soles of two pairs of feet, the right-hand pair with toes facing downwards and the left-hand pair with them facing upwards. Rather than being an anatomical *ex voto* of the kind dedicated at healing shrines, this may in fact represent a dedication by a gladiator, a gladiator trainer, or an organiser of gladiatorial games at a *Nemeseion*, a shrine to Nemesis, signifying entering and leaving on good feet, that is, surviving in the arena in a gladiatorial contest.

Brief consideration should also be given here to some instances where individual body parts of deities appear in Roman art, in contexts where the healing power of the deity is being invoked. The most common, though still relatively rare, example of such an image is connected to the cult of Sabazios, a deity most often represented *in absentia* by his hand only, a good example of such a *mano panthea* coming from Brescia, Lombardia, Italy and on display in the *Museo della Citta*, Santa Giulia.[21] Again, the right hand, palm outwards and with fingers splayed out, depicted on a stone votive from Quintanilla de Somoza, León, Spain, and now in the *Museo de León*, may similarly be linked to Zeus-Serapis, as indicated by a Greek inscription on the stone, rather than being a depiction of the hand of a dedicatee seeking a cure. Finally, in a Christian context, the hand of God appears twice emerging from out of the clouds on one of the apse mosaics in the church of *Sant Apollinare in Classe*, Ravenna.

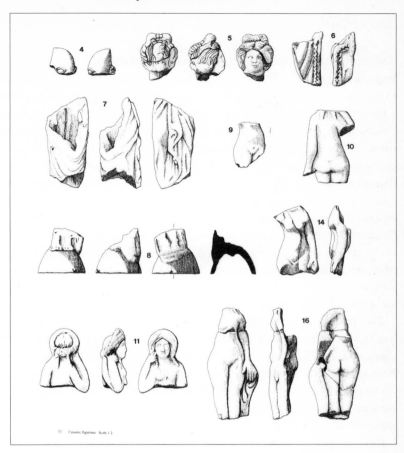

12. Broken Pseudo-Venus pipeclay figurines from Mill Street site in Caerleon, Gwent, Wales. (From Evans, 2000, Fig. 72)

However, if one looks at the case of the Bronze Age figurines from Keros, an island in the Cyclades of Greece, a study from outside the Roman world and from an earlier period, then further complexities of interpretation could perhaps sometimes be inherent in studying broken objects.[22] On Keros a number of special deposits were found of quite carefully broken figurine fragments buried in small pits; none of the hundreds of fragments conjoined, nor were there chippings or smaller fragments present that would suggest that the breaking of the figurines had taken place here. The excavators have suggested that the figurine fragments were already broken when brought to the site for ritual burial and that the act of burial here was the final stage of an extended process of creation and use of whole figurines, breaking of those figurines after some time and for some unknown reason, and pilgrimage to Keros bearing the retained and curated figurine fragments. A possible guest-house for the accommodation of pilgrims was found on an islet nearby. Could similar complex motives have been behind what appears to have been the ritual breaking of pipeclay Venus figurines at the Mill Street, Caerleon site discussed in Chapter 3 (Fig. 12)?[23]

Body Politics

The barbarian enemies of Rome were common subjects in Roman art from the Republic to the late Empire and I have written on their portrayal at great length.[24] From the reigns of the emperors Marcus Aurelius and Commodus onwards there was a growing trend towards the dehumanisation of the barbarian in Roman art, as most dramatically exemplified by the images of slaughtered and beheaded barbarians on the Column of Marcus Aurelius in Rome and a similar scene of the beheading of a prisoner, his hands tied behind his back, which occurs on the Bridgeness legionary distance slab from the Antonine Wall in Scotland.[25] These gruesome images must be examined, along with earlier head-hunting scenes on Trajan's Column, again in Rome, and the historically attested appalling post-mortem treatment of the severed head and hand of the Dacian king Decebalus,[26] in order to try to understand the significance of these acts of ritualised bodily dismemberment in the context of the wider study of fragmentation of the body in Roman art. That there was not a trend among the Romans for depicting themselves in a similar way suggests that they may have made some distinction between the bodies of Romans and those of non-Romans.

The issue must be raised as to whether any of these images of mutilation of barbarian bodies represents a strain of pornographic or sexual violence, and whether there was some element of sadism inherent in these depictions. The common Graeco-Roman sculptural subject of the punishment of the satyr Marsyas, who had the temerity, or foolishness, to challenge Apollo to a musical contest, could also be seen as perhaps being part of such a strain, although in this case the subject matter was purely mythological. Having lost the musical contest, Marsyas had to submit himself to Apollo's chosen forfeit, for the satyr to be flayed alive by his Scythian servant. While pre-Hellenistic representations of this story generally concentrated on the musical contest, leaving the appalling aftermath to the imagination of the viewers, Hellenistic and Roman sculptures, perhaps all derived from the Hellenistic original known today as the *Hanging Marsyas*, depicted the distressed and anguished Marsyas strung up in a tree, hanging by his hands, positioned above and behind his head, and awaiting the cut of the Scythian's knife.[27]

These head-hunting scenes and scenes of beheadings should perhaps be seen in the wider context of Roman attitudes towards the games and towards judicial punishment.[28] A particularly gruesome example of a beheading scene during a gladiatorial combat can be seen on a relief from Due Madonne, Bologna, dated to the second half of the first century BC (Plate 52).[29] On the left of the surviving part of the relief is a gladiator with raised right arm looking to strike at an opponent who must have appeared on the now-missing part of the relief. But it is the scene on the right-hand side of the stone that is of relevance here. A third gladiator, clad in a short skirt-like garment held in place with a thick belt, boots, a wrist-guard, and a helmet, holds up an oval shield in his left hand and moves his right, the sword hand, down towards his waist, having just struck a swingeing blow to behead a fourth gladiator who kneels on the ground to his right. The kneeling figure, hands held passively behind his back, is headless. His head, still encased in his helmet, falls to the ground to his right, his shield discarded behind him.

The subject of Roman judicial savagery has been academically scrutinised. The number of crimes for which capital punishment was to be meted out rose considerably in the period after AD 200, and some crimes that had previously merited decapitation now were subjected to supposedly harsher punishments such as 'crucifixion, burning, or wild beasts'. Eusebius' accounts of the judicial mutilation of Christians by the breaking of legs, the cutting out of an Achilles tendon, the putting out of an eye, or the cutting off of an ear or the nose are of note. Under Constantine some corrupt officials could have their hands amputated, punishment also recorded as commonplace under Valentinian and in the army under Theodosius. Mutilation was not a formal judicial penalty before A. D. 300. 'Amputation, whether loss of a foot for a deserter, of a hand for the destroyer of public buildings, or of sexual organs for the pederast (under Justinian)', proclaimed 'symbolically the particular evil being punished'.[30]

Metaphor and Metamorphosis

A very specific type of fragmentation is the destruction associated with the concept of *damnatio memoriae*.[31] Pliny, in his panegyric to Trajan, related the feelings of those who had attacked images of the emperor Domitian: 'it was our delight to dash those proud faces to the ground, to smite them with the sword, and savage them with the axe, as if blood and agony could follow from every blow'.[32] Such vandalisation of images in the Roman world, principally of statuary, is relevant both in terms of this official and overt political process of *damnatio memoriae* (the condemnation of an emperor by the Roman senate, leading to the destruction, mutilation or alteration of his images) and the more covert activities of iconoclasts whose motives are less susceptible to generalised analysis.[33] Both strains of destruction must be considered in terms of investigating how and why such acts of vandalism were organised, how they were carried out, and particularly which parts of the images were targeted, and in what ways.

In a recent study of the fragmentation of Roman statues in Britain it is not specifically addressed whether there are possible differences of motive and motivation that may have led to the destruction of religious statues as opposed to political statues.[34] It can, though, be demonstrated quite conclusively that there are statistically significant biases in the archaeological record towards the survival of certain parts of the bodies of statues, implying in some cases a careful and deliberate targeting of specific parts of some statues and a marked process of selection, even curation, of broken statue fragments. The problem lies in how to interpret individual finds of parts of statues and place them in a convincing explanatory structure of interpretation, as the next four short, diverse examples may help to demonstrate. A fifth example, that of the so-called Cartoceto Bronzes, follows at more length.

The fate of the cult statue of Mercury from the temple complex site of West Hill, Uley, Gloucestershire, portions of which were found during excavations in the 1970s, is interesting. The head of the cult statue was found carefully deposited in a pit sealed beneath a rubble platform outside the very late Roman or post-Roman Structure VIII of excavation Phase 7,[35] while other parts of the statue were also found in the same phase, in a clay spread (Plate 53). There can be no doubt that these fragments, especially the statue's head, were treated with some degree of post-fragmentation respect; indeed, that they were curated, ending in their careful burial.

The second example concerns a cache of sculptural material excavated from Sector 16-P in Antioch, consisting of twenty-five fragments of arms and hands in white marble and twelve legs and feet in the same material, 'along with several other [unspecified] statue fragments'. The catalogue publication of this material notes that the material came apparently from a sculptor's workshop 'in the immediate area of … an oven that may have functioned as a limekiln … and [they] may have been destined for destruction in the limekiln or for reuse by the sculptor'.[36] Such an explanation hardly seems credible, given the biased composition of the assemblage of statuary body parts. Some conscious selection of statue body parts had clearly taken place here and been caught *in stasis* in the archaeological record.

The third example is a bronze head of Augustus, obviously cut off a full-size statue of the emperor, found at Meroë in the Sudan, and now in the collections of the British Museum. This was obviously booty of some sort, it has been suggested, perhaps from the capture of Roman Syene by Ethiopian forces in 24 BC,[37] and was found under the entrance staircase into a temple of victory probably dedicated a few years after the victory at Syene. In this case the destruction of the original, complete statue of the emperor was motivated by anti-Romanism, though the carrying off the head of the statue shows a recognition of the power of images, a power then presumably further insulted by a ceremonial burying of the broken image.

A fourth example is provided by a head and single foot from a more or less life-size bronze statue excavated from the same level in Zone C, Ercavica, Castro de Santaver, Canaveruelas, Cuenca, Spain.[38] Bronze statue fragments are, of course, much more likely to be recycled, by melting down, than are stone statue fragments. The survival of just these two body parts therefore once more implies selection and curation post-fragmentation of the original statue.

While political and religious motives probably account for most of the destruction or mutilation of statues, images, and inscriptions in the Roman world, other motives may equally have applied. It has been has pointed out that 'the harming of people through private magic by the mutilation (or binding, or burying) of images of them was one manifestation of the widespread and well-known habit of … enchantment … in the ancient world'.[39] Indeed, the texts of curse tablets are often composed in such a way as to target enemies' bodies, and quite often specific parts of those bodies, commonly the eyes, as has been discussed in Chapter 3.

The Cartoceto gilded bronzes represent one of the most impressive survivals of a bronze statuary group from classical antiquity. These gilded bronze figures were discovered largely in fragments 'piled on top of one another'[40] in 1946 during groundworks on a farm at Santa Lucia di Calamello, near Cartoceto, in the commune of Pergola, Pesaro, in the region of Marche in eastern Italy, close to the *Via Flaminia*.[41] Their conservation and display today constitutes a remarkable achievement in itself. In terms of survival, the Cartoceto gilded bronzes rank alongside the few other life-sized gilded bronzes from the Roman world, such as the equestrian statue of Marcus Aurelius from Rome, the Horses of San Marco, Venice, and the imperial portrait heads from the *Capitolium* at Brescia.[42]

The circumstances leading to the burial of the statues at Cartoceto and the potential motives behind their careful disposal inevitably are the subject of much academic speculation. Questions of the meaning of certain gestures, and of gender and power are also raised by the unique composition of the group.

The date of the statues has generally been accepted as being between the second half of the first century BC and the latter half of the first century AD, though 'life-size gilded bronze sculpture is uncommon until well into the Roman imperial era'. But, as the results of scientific analysis of the head of one of the Cartoceto horses have indicated that the gilding of the bronzes in this group was achieved by 'glueing leaf to the surface of the metal', rather than their having been gilded in the strictest sense of the word,[43] technically a date early in this range cannot be discounted.

The statues in the Cartoceto group consist of two men, two women, and two horses, the men being represented as equestrian figures with outstretched right arms and the women portrayed with veiled heads and standing upright in the so-called *pudicitia* pose (Plate 54). The statues are larger than life-size, something which is obviously of some significance in terms of defining the perceived power of the individuals and of the family portrayed. The number of individual statues in the group, their costly gilding, the use of the equestrian motif for the males, the manner of their attire and poses, and their transportation from somewhere in Latium, if not actually from a workshop in Rome – though more recently it has been suggested that they could have been made in Rimini[44] – all allude to the wealth, prestige and status of the statues' commissioning patron.

There was differential survival of the statues, which were recovered in many fragments in some cases, with only the two most complete figures of one of the women and one of the men being found with their portrait heads intact or reconstructible. It has been argued for the identification of the statuary group as being that of the family of Domitius Ahenobarbus.[45]

The arrangement of the figures in a formal posed group, proposed by both Stucchi and Pollini, can be seen in the *Museo Archeologico Nazionale delle Marche* in Ancona, where the newly conserved statues are now on display, and in the form of a full-size set of copies displayed on the terrace of the museum. In both instances the two mounted male figures are arranged in the centre of a tableau, with the women standing one on either side of the men, though Pollini places each individual woman on opposite sides of the group to their positions in the displays. It has been suggested that there may have been a potential fifth bronze statue in the group, but, as Pollini has pointed out, this is pure speculation.[46]

Most previous academic discussion of the Cartoceto group has focused on the possible identifications of the family represented by the four gilded bronzes, despite the fact that there was no inscription or dedicatory plaque found with the statues. The identifications have either been of members of the imperial family in the early Empire, a Roman aristocratic family of the late Republic or early Empire, or of members of a local, provincial Italian aristocratic family, again of the late Republic or early Empire. Of the imperial identifications, the extant male portrait has been suggested variously to have been Julius Caesar, or one of either Nero Julius Caesar or Gaius Caligula, despite it being of a middle-aged man, while the extant female portrait has been likened to Livia, the wife of Augustus, or to his mother Atia.[47]

The imperial identifications would now appear to be generally discounted. Again, while alluding to a then-unpublished prosopographical study of local aristocratic families undertaken by Filippo Coarelli, Pollini declined to accept the identification of the Cartoceto figures with any of these families, and instead suggested the family group as being the powerful and influential Roman *Domitii Ahenobarbi* family, that is Gnaeus Domitius Ahenobarbus himself, his mother, his father Lucius and his wife. A more controversial and altogether less credible identification, already refuted, has recently been put forward that the best-surviving male rider figure is the politician, lawyer, and inveterate letter writer Cicero.[48]

The destruction of the statues as part of a process of *damnatio memoriae* has been discounted by John Pollini who suggested that the statues, for whatever reason, were interrupted in transit and then destroyed, and that they were never actually set up in position anywhere, something that he surmised from an 'absence of lead tenons in the feet for erecting the figures'.[49] An analysis of the significance of the breaking-up and fragmentation of the statues in a broader theoretical context would almost certainly provide fresh insights to their study.[50] In many ways the motives behind their destruction may be hidden from us by our inability to identify who the statues were of.

The equestrian male statue type in the course of the first century BC 'became the primary tool for propaganda for the Roman senatorial class', eventually to become the sole preserve of the imperial family, beginning with a series of equestrian statues of Augustus, as depicted on coins. Over two hundred equestrian statues are recorded by historical and literary sources in the classical world, while the fourth-century *Cataloghi Regionari* records the presence of twenty-two imperial equestrian statues in Rome itself, some of which are referred to as being '*equi magni*', presumably a reference to their larger-than-life size. Such statues can be expected to have been present in many, or even most, of the cities and towns of Roman Italy at this time.[51] The gilding of the Cartoceto bronze statues would presumably have placed them in a category of higher opulence than other non-gilded bronze or indeed stone equestrian statues.

The Cartoceto statue group makes a very specific statement about the power and status of the family and the individuals portrayed. It also makes a statement about gender relations within the group, and within the aristocratic families of provincial

Italy, away from Rome. The very existence of the female statues in the group showed that 'women of such a family could be honoured with public images' in the late Republican period in provincial Italy.[52]

A statue of a veiled woman, posed similarly to the most complete of the Cartoceto female figures and represented in re-cut half-figure, is in the collection of the *Museo Gregoriano Profano* in the Vatican.[53] The Cartoceto and Vatican figures are represented in the so-called *pudicitia* pose, a common female pose alluding to chastity, piety, and humility, and most often associated in the modestly veiled form with older women.

Elite women playing some public role in civic life in the Roman empire, principally through benefaction or religious observance, may have then done so following 'the example of the women of the imperial court, who were particularly prominent and autonomous in the Julio-Claudian, Antonine, and Severan periods'. Most interestingly, such women 'seemingly paradoxically ... had a much more conventional public image ... [often being depicted] as *Pudicitia* and other traditional female virtues associated with harmonious families ... [an ambivalence] justifying both political power and a retiring persona'.[54]

Substantial inheritances were sometimes left to women in the Roman world, an arrangement which would have allowed them to use their wealth in the same way as men to enhance their power and prestige through civic benefaction. That women often did act as civic patrons in the Roman world is attested by epigraphic evidence, as in the case of Aurelia Leite of Paros, honoured for repairing a gymnasium in the city at the start of the fourth century AD, although, of course, women could not serve as magistrates. Much of the evidence for the patronage of women comes from Roman Greece, where 'the "physical" presence of female benefactors in the form of statues must have been quite impressive. Greek cities were filled with statues of wealthy men and women. Those of women stood not just in or near temples, the only area of public life traditionally belonging to women as well as men, but in conspicuous places all over the city.' But 'women could only act within the framework created by their male relatives'. One notable instance of the honouring of an elite woman was when the city of Naples buried, at public expense, a woman called Tettia Casta and 'the senate voted a statue to her to be erected'.[55]

Perhaps the most widely discussed of these female civic benefactresses in the Roman world is Plancia Magna of Perge in Asia Minor, known from a number of inscriptions in which she is referred to as 'daughter of the city'. Two statue bases for now-lost statues, dedicated to her by the city's council, assembly, and council of elders, attest to the visual celebration of her life, position, achievements, and largesse. Her major public work of benefaction would appear to have been the renovation of the highly decorated southern gate into the city between AD 119 and 124, inscriptions on two of the statue bases referring to 'M. Plancius Varus ... father of Plancia Magna' and 'C. Plancius Varus ... brother of Plancia Magna'.[56]

It would appear that there is unlikely ever to be a conclusive identification of the four individuals portrayed in the Cartoceto bronzes group. Equally, they could date from any time between the latter half of the first century BC and the second half of the first century AD and a more precise dating may remain elusive. There would though now appear to be a consensus that these statues do not represent members of the imperial family, but rather that they represent either a powerful Roman aristocratic family or, perhaps more likely, a rich and politically engaged local elite family associated with one of the Roman cities in the region in which the statues were discovered.

The financial outlay invested in such an unusually large and opulently finished statuary group, even if they are not deemed by some authorities to represent works of the highest artistic quality, nevertheless makes them an impressive visual statement about the power, status, competitiveness, and aspirations of that provincial aristocratic Italian family. That the statue types represented, that is equestrian males and females in *pudicitia* poses, represent archetypes respectively for male aristocratic and later male imperial power, and female aristocratic and later female imperial virtues, makes their appearance together a juxtaposition that says much about gender relations between the men and women portrayed in the Cartoceto group.

It has been suggested that rather than assuming that the group represents the family of a powerful local male aristocrat, it could perhaps be viewed in a more nuanced manner, with the totality of the group, the unity of the family, and the strength resulting from that unity, being the intended messages. There is a considerable body of mainly epigraphic evidence for elite women in some instances playing significant public roles in the Roman world, and not just in the Greek east, and such powerful women we know were on occasions honoured for their civic contributions by the commissioning, erection, and dedication of statues to them. They may indeed have honoured themselves, their families, and their ancestors by setting up statues themselves.

In Roman Britain, one of the most intriguing examples of what may well be large-scale iconoclasm centres on the Roman military fortress at Chester and a collection of over one hundred tombstones and recognisable tombstone fragments built into the north wall of the fortress. Any number of explanations could account for this event. At the time of the rebuilding of the wall in the later Roman period, good building stone was at a premium for some reason and retained tombstones saved after the levelling of a military cemetery were simply reused, implying nothing other than practical considerations in the use of this material. Alternatively the tombstones from a cleared military cemetery were built into the wall for ideological reasons, imbuing this *spolia* with the power to unite past and present and stress the continuity of Roman military authority here. Some acknowledgement of the professional ancestry associated with these stone memorials may also have been made here.[57] Certainly the use of *spolia* in the late Roman period, most famously in the construction of the Arch of Constantine in Rome, has been little considered as an ideological concept also at play in certain contexts in late Roman Britain, as was noted in Chapter 5.

Much more intriguing, however, is the theory that the Chester-based legion *Legio XX Valeria Victrix*, for whose existence there is no epigraphic evidence after the end of the third century, supported the British usurper Carausius and as a consequence was disbanded in disgrace following his murder and the restoration of legitimate imperial control in Britain.[58] This disbandment of the legion would have included military and judicial sanctions and punishments against individuals and, according to the theory being summarised here, ideological sanctions against the legion as a unit along the lines of a *damnatio memoriae*. Thus the clearance of the *Leg. XX* tombstones and grave memorials at Chester, their clear defacement and desecration in some cases, and the incorporation into a new defence would have been officially sanctioned rituals and rites. The additional incorporation of some earlier *Legio II Adiutrix* stones at the same time might argue against such an explanation. However, their reuse might have been accidental, these few stones being pulled down during the clearance of the majority *Leg. XX* tombstones. The presence of some memorials to women here, most famously the tombstone of Curatia Dionysia, could be explained by their having been spouses of *Leg. XX* soldiers or members of their families.

Real Bodies

Burial in the Roman world represented an arena in which the inert body was transformed by cultural practice and custom into a signifying artefact, whether by cremation or by inhumation. It can be argued that mortuary ritual and the post-mortem treatment of the body may sometimes have mirrored the processes of fragmentation of the body into disassembled images, as seen in Roman funerary art, and which perhaps had its origins in Etruscan society.[59]

It must be asked, though, whether there was not, in parts of the Roman world, a distinct process of post-mortem manipulation of human body parts before inhumation burial. Certainly in prehistoric Britain there may well even have been a cult of human relics, as identified by Ann Woodward,[60] that could have continued in some form into the Roman period or have been revived then. As well as examining such links, consideration also needs to be given to the significance of the Christian cult of relics[61] that developed in the later Empire and which spawned its own accompanying decorated artefacts, in the form of reliquaries, to house bones and other relics of the saints.

When General Franco died he was clutching the relic arm of Saint Teresa of Avila. This is one of the more high-profile and later examples of the cult of relics which had its origins in late antiquity and perhaps reached its height in the figure of Philip II of Spain, who amassed a collection of over seven thousand holy relics, including one hundred and forty-four heads, three hundred and six arms and legs, and ten whole bodies. Philip, as he lay on his deathbed in his palace at El Escorial, selected the arm of St Vincent and the knee of St Sebastian from his collection to bring him solace.[62]

Collecting and curation of body parts is attested in many other cultures, and for many different reasons. In the mid-seventeenth century the Dutch artist Albert van der Eeckhout, in his painting *A Tarairiu or Tapuya Woman*, in the National Museum, Copenhagen, recorded a cannibal woman in Brazil, naked save for a strategically placed piece of vegetation probably added by Eeckhout, calmly looking towards the viewer (Plate 55). She holds in her right hand a severed human hand, while sticking out of the basket held by a strap over her head is a human foot.[63]

Robert Philpott, in his survey of grave treatment and furnishing in Roman Britain, has discussed the phenomenon of decapitation as a burial rite,[64] and has recognised three variations in the rite across a sample of seventy individual sites on which decapitation has been recorded. These variations are: burials with the head missing or buried separately nearby; burials with the head placed in the correct position at the neck of the torso; and examples where the head has been placed in the grave but usually by the feet or lower legs. Though there are one or two isolated earlier examples, Philpott dates this rite to the later third century, with most examples being of a fourth-century date. Slightly more women than men are represented in Philpott's catalogue of ninety-eight decapitated burials, with older women being well represented. He concluded that the linking factor must be 'social status, caste or kinship affiliations'. Geographically, most are found in rural cemeteries. When such burials occur in urban contexts they are at the peripheries of the cemeteries, as is indeed also the case in rural locations. In a very few cases mutilation of the body seems to have taken place along with the decapitation. Philpott cites examples where skull and body parts had been moved and replaced in the grave, and one instance at a cemetery in Dunstable where a right foot had been removed but still buried with the body.

Skulls are often found in non-burial contexts, as are other stray body parts. As part of a paper on special deposits at Roman Heybridge, Essex, given at a conference I attended in Durham, a speaker briefly alluded to the discovery of the articulated remains of a human arm in the fill of a ditch. The arm had obviously been carefully buried, but no other possible explanation for this unusual burial was given, other than the supposition that the arm might have been torn off in an agricultural or industrial accident.[65] Full details of this discovery have not yet been published.

Human sacrifice may have taken place in Roman Britain, and in such circumstances it would have been part of a process of placation of the gods that may have replaced a more symbolic act of controlled violence, including 'the smashing of pots, the bending of weapons, and the killing of animals'. There are a number of examples of possible human sacrifice where the excavated remains have been of partial bodies only, though the implications of this possible additional evidence for dismemberment are uncertain.[66]

It is worth briefly considering here the question of how familiar the Romans were with the human skeleton and whether the appearance of skeletons and skulls in Roman art represents part of the same phenomenon of fragmentation of the body being discussed in this paper, with the unfleshed body being seen as distinct and divorced from the live body. Almost certainly there was a developed medical knowledge of human anatomy, much of it derived from dissection carried out in Alexandria[67] or from chance opportunities for doctors to study uncovered skeletons. In later antiquity it would appear that anatomy lessons centred on a study of human cadavers were ubiquitous, one such scene being portrayed in a fresco on one of the catacombs in *Via Latina* in Rome.

The skeleton was a relatively common motif in classical art, particularly in the context of the appearance of skeletons at a feast or banquet, in scenes which were principally intended to remind diners of their own mortality.[68] This trend led to a relatively short-lived liking for comic images of animated skeletons, best exemplified by their appearance on the Boscoreale silver cups, and to the limited use of skeletons in funerary art starting in the first century BC. Of the few examples of Roman art where the skeleton can be taken as representing the dead body, there is a second- or early third-century relief from Rome itself, now in the British Museum, in which a skeleton is laid out full-length under a panel containing an inscription.

The Epicurean theme identified by research certainly would appear to account for the vast majority of appearances of skeletons in Roman art, though one or two other appearances are worthy of further discussion here. A realistic rendering of a decaying corpse is inconceivable within pre-Hellenistic Greek art. But even in more realistic Hellenistic and Roman art such a representation is not at all common as a way of rendering the dead in art. The question of the origin of the image of the dead as a skeleton is therefore tied up with the contexts in which such images appeared. There can be identified, though, a distinct use of the image of the skeleton in funerary art. Almost all instances of the skeleton in Graeco-Roman art are late Hellenistic, Republican, Augustan, or early imperial. As with the skeleton, so with the skull motif, most famously appearing along with a mason's level and other items as the *emblema* of a mosaic pavement from Pompeii and on tombstones being contemplated by a philosopher.

However, of considerable relevance here is the evidence for an extraordinary instance from Roman Britain of the possible use of the '*os resectum*', literally 'cut bone', burial rite at a cemetery in Lincoln, a rite known from Roman literary sources but not otherwise known archaeologically in the western empire.[69]

Three separate Latin sources – Cicero, Varro, and Festus – allude to the rite, and one of them to the removal of a finger from the dead body before cremation can properly proceed; the finding of the ritualised burial of finger bones in different contexts on a small number of Italian sites has suggested that the rite was indeed carried out in Rome and some other areas of Italy. What actually constituted the whole rite is uncertain, but scholars believe that the retention of the cut bone, presumably still fleshed, for a period after the cremation of the rest of the body, allowed the deceased – represented by the body part – to be part of the extended post-cremation purifying and cleansing rituals in the household, which would have helped to bring mourning to an end. The cleansing could have involved purification by fire, at which stage the retained bone might be ceremonially burned, but not cremated. Later it would be buried.

The Lincoln burial, a cremation at 43 Broadway excavated in the 1950s and in store since then, dates to the late second to mid-third century AD. Modern analysis of this and other Lincoln burials showed that the Broadway cremation was unusual and perhaps unique in Roman Britain. The burial consisted of 'the cremated remains of a single adult ... but sex was not assigned due to a lack of identifiable sexually dimorphic features'. The colour of most of the cremated bones was white but three hand phalanges, 'with sizes consistent with their belonging to the same single finger', stood out as being completely dark grey in colour. They also stood out as not having encountered any or much shrinkage due to exposure to the pyre fire, as could be noted on the other bones, 'indicating that they had not been heated to the same high temperatures as the other remains'. A third reason to see these finger bones as standing somehow apart from the other bones in the cremation was the fact that no other upper limb bone fragments were present here; in other words, the finger represented here indicated 'differential treatment of body parts' as part of this specific cremation rite.[70]

Sexual Fragments

The phallus was one of the most common motifs in Graeco-Roman art, appearing in numerous artistic media across the Roman world.[71] While it was most often probably used as a protective or apotropaic symbol, it was also, nevertheless, a ubiquitous reminder of the dominant social position of the sexualised male in Roman society.[72] The phallic motif needs to be discussed in terms of its numerous meanings and its contexts of use, but it must also be considered from the point of view of its more provocative role in representing a generalised male dominance.[73] It is one of a suite of images linked to the display and celebration of hyper-masculinity, as has been noted in a number of the chapters in this book. 'Walking down a city street in Pompeii, you would have been surrounded on all sides by images of the erect penis – stamped on walls and paving stones, decorating shop signs, worn as amulets by children.'[74] The same impression comes from a perusal of the study of Pompeian street signs.[75]

Sexual body parts could also be evoked by vocabulary, either spoken or written, and one example from Roman Britain provides a good case study of this. On one of the lead curse tablets from the Romano-British temple site of West Hill, Uley, Gloucestershire, discussed at length in Chapter 2, is a plea to the god Mercury to secure some punishment against some textile thieves, made by a man called Mintla Rufus. As was noted by the transcribers of the Uley text, 'the name may or may not have had an intentional sexual connotation. The second part [i.e. Rufus] is unexceptional, but the first part is a colloquial Latin word for phallus. If it was not a neutral second name it may have been a composite name, "Redprick"'.[76] A rough carving of a phallus and pine branch on a stone slab from Vindolanda is accompanied by the incised inscription *HP III*, perhaps standing for '*h[abet] p[edes] III*', 'it is three feet long'.[77] This too could be an example of sexual boasting or mocking linked to the phallus.

Studies of sexual symbolism in the Graeco-Roman world have perhaps too often placed discussion of the use of the phallus completely beyond the issue of sexuality by categorising all such imagery as part of a broader category of erotic art.[78] This has, of course, helped to move the definition of such material away from nineteenth- and earlier twentieth-century views of its being obscene but in so doing has perhaps created a false dichotomy itself. It can surely no longer be sustainable to argue that the motif of the phallus was not largely concerned with the construction of maleness and the place of men in Roman society. Ideas relating to fertility and protection, linked to the phallus, are nevertheless also linked to male sexuality and being.

While certain strategies were employed at different times to emphasise the power and potency of emperors – Augustus appearing with numerous children on the *Ara Pacis* in Rome; the ever-youthful portrait types of Augustus and Trajan; Trajan as 'the father' of his country on the Benevento arch; the bull-necked coin portraits of some of the third-century military emperors – the employment of the image of the phallus in an imperial context did not take place. Nevertheless, many examples of such sexualising of rulers' bodies in other ancient societies can be found.[79]

While the phallus was undoubtedly a ubiquitous symbol and motif in the Graeco-Roman world, female genitalia were also employed as images in certain contexts, though such uses were nowhere near as numerous as those of the phallus.[80] Very occasionally the two were juxtaposed together (Plate 56). Mention has already been made of models of female genitalia being found at healing sanctuaries as anatomical *ex votos*, but it is true to say that female sexuality and fertility is more usually represented in the Roman world by the portrayal of the female breast, often the suckling breast.

Sometimes body parts could be conflated, as in an example of a small bronze amulet from Palencia and in the *Museo de León*, Spain, in the form of a winged phallus, at one end of which is a hand making the obscene gesture known as the *fica*.[81] Another amuletic bronze from Lancia, again in the León museum collection, has one end formed as a pair of testicles and the other by a hole in the object which may represent a stylised portrayal of a female sexual organ. Again, the phallus and the so-called evil eye were also often conflated, as in the case of a small terracotta in the British Museum depicting two animated phalluses sawing an eye in half.[82]

In Roman Britain the symbol of the phallus was probably as common as it was in other parts of the empire and compiling a catalogue of its many appearances is quite beyond the scope of this study. However, a few observations will be offered here on a few of the types of phallic representation found in the province, on the types of objects on which such representations appear, and on the contexts in which these images and objects are found. The use of phallic symbolism, it has been noted, generally is related to one or more of the following: fertility or ancestral celebration or commemoration; erotic display; apotropaic or protective power; the confirmation of sexual identity in rites of passage; and the advertisement or celebration of male social power.[83]

There was certainly not any kind of phallic cult in Romano-British religion, though the assumed potency of male deities and their presumed ability to intervene on a supplicant's behalf in matters of infertility is apparent at some healing centres. Certainly the god Priapus was known in Roman Britain, as will be discussed in Chapter 7, but he must always have been a fringe figure in Romano-British religion.[84] Phallic symbols do crop up at a few religious sites, as at the temple of Ivy Chimneys, Essex where a fired-clay phallus and a model of bull's horns were recorded.[85]

Very often, though, images of phalluses were used as protective symbols at boundaries, either geographical boundaries or more local boundaries such as household thresholds. This was probably the case with the phallus carved on one of the stones in the abutment of the Roman bridge at Chesters, Northumberland and was certainly the case with two copper alloy herms of Priapus to be discussed in Chapter 7 (Plate 57).[86] Phalluses on pottery vessels are also known and may have been protective symbols here also.[87]

It is particularly interesting to see the wide range of personal items from Roman Britain on which the phallus appeared and the way that the symbol is deployed there. Such items are found perhaps most commonly on Roman military sites and in urban contexts, though certainly not exclusively. At least one plate brooch in the form of a phallus is known to me and one woman's hairpin. A phallus appears on a gold finger ring from Faversham, Kent and on a bronze ring from London. Phallic pendants, amulets, and mounts made of various materials, including bone and antler, are very common indeed, and perhaps in East Anglia had a particular resonance of some kind. Such pendants and amulets may have been hung around the necks of male children for their protection (Fig. 13).[88]

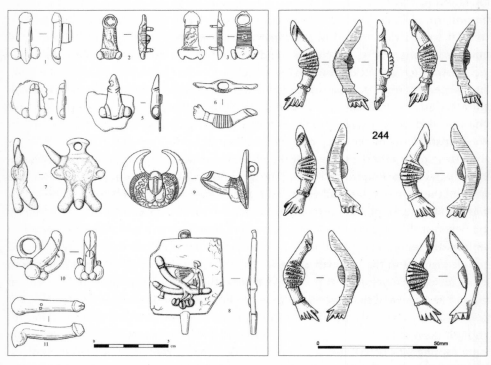

Above left: 13. A selection of phallic objects from Suffolk. (Drawn by Donna Wreathall. Copyright Suffolk County Council. From Plouviez, 2005, Fig. 1)

Above right: 14. Copper alloy hand-and-phallus amulets from Catterick, North Yorkshire. (Drawn by Eddie Lyons. Copyright English Heritage. From Wilson, 2002, Fig. 260)

Hand-and-phallus pendants mark a variation on this theme and would seem to have been particularly favoured in the Roman military north, though a group of four such pendants or amulets in bone is known, for instance, from Verulamium. At Catterick six copper alloy amulets bear depictions of both male and female symbols, one end having a clenched fist with pointed index finger and a bracelet on the wrist, the other a phallus, with a perforated shell motif at the centre (Fig. 14). Five further such amulets were apparently also found together in a child's burial there.[89]

It must not be forgotten, though, that phallic images could also be employed in a humorous way and that ribald, not to say scatological, humour, was very much part of Roman culture, and not just at a plebeian level. Three particular phallic-decorated items from Roman Britain suggest that sexual humour also had its appeal to some at this time. The first object to be discussed here is one of three similar and probably contemporary carved stone figures from the Roman fort of Bar Hill, Dunbartonshire, Scotland (Plate 58).[90] All three figures appear to be bearded and all have been suggested to be either Silenus, the usually drunk older companion of Bacchus, or a male native deity. The man holds a drinking cup on one on the stones. On the other two, in one instance he holds one of his arms across his chest with the middle finger out in a phallic gesture to ward off the evil eye, or interlopers, or perhaps here barbarians, and in the other folding both arms across his chest with the *fica* gesture being made by his hands. Where these three sculptures would have been displayed is unknown but for their viewers they must have provided some amusement.

The second Romano-British phallic item whose intent was probably to engender laughter from its viewers is a copper alloy plaque from Icklingham, Suffolk, decorated with an elaborate scene comprising a small figure riding on the back of a winged triple phallus, holding it in check with reins as if it were a racing chariot.[91] Whether this was intended to be a satirical comment on the reining-in of rampant male sexuality, something that would be particularly apposite if the rather androgynous rider was in fact a woman, or it represented a metaphor for hyper-masculine power cannot be said. In a similar vein, a stone from Long Bennington, Lincolnshire bears a carving of a man riding a large, two-legged phallus and has already been discussed in Chapter 2,[92] while a relief has been found at Wroxeter showing a winged phallus dragging a cart loaded with phalli.[93]

The third and final phallic item from Roman Britain to be discussed here is generally known as the Horsey Toll Pot and comes from Cambridgeshire (Plates 59–60).[94] It is now in the collections of Peterborough Museum. Made at the Nene Valley pottery, probably in the third century, it represents an extraordinary sexual or erotic variation on the signature 'hunt cups' for which this pottery was particularly known. It must have been produced as a one-off, a special commission from an individual customer. Readers of a nervous or excitable disposition, or those who might perhaps be easily offended, are advised to look away now. The hunt or chase here involves two naked human figures; a tumescent, ejaculating male running towards a bending female figure, or so it is generally identified, who is gesticulating to the man to hurry and enter her from behind. In her other hand she holds a giant phallus. Any number of interpretations could be put upon this scene. It could have been intended to be erotic or arousing, an ancient sex aid. It could have been intended to be simply amusing. It could have been somehow satirical, either in terms of satirising male and female sexual relations in general or the sexual tastes and performance of a particular man, woman, or couple. The male figure, rather than being human, could have been the image of a fertility god, though it is difficult to marry this interpretation with the figure's wasteful spilling of his seed on the ground rather than during the sexual congress being anticipated and encouraged by the woman. It could have been a bitter, biting comment on the bluster and failed promise of male hyper-masculinity.

This pot very much reminds me of a fifth-century BC Greek red-figure wine jug, decorated with a scene in which a victorious Greek male, holding his erect penis, strides towards a defeated Persian male who bends over to be buggered.[95] Otherness, defeat, sexual subservience, and femininity are here being conflated in the figure of the Persian. Greekness, victory, sexual potency, and hyper-male superiority reside together in the image of the Greek male. Given the androgynous appearance of the bending figure on the Horsey Toll pot, I wonder how interpretation of the vessel's significance would change were that figure to be identified as a male youth?

Returning to the Whole

It can be argued that while the various case studies presented above do not represent a coherent, all-encompassing theory for understanding the widespread use of the fragmentary or partial image of the human body in Roman art, nonetheless there are many linking threads between these contexts and situations which could be further investigated and illuminated by the introduction of analogous material from other chronological periods and different cultural contexts.

There has only been space here to touch upon a number of issues relating to fragmented remains and only in a few instances has it been possible to include discussion of material from Roman Britain. I have chosen to look principally at the fragmented body as an image in Roman art, and so have perhaps already restricted discussion of wider issues relating to the conception of the body in Roman society and in Romanised societies. The broad-brush approach adopted here also makes it difficult to identify temporal and chronological difference and, importantly, temporal and chronological change. The focus on art means that language and literature have been necessarily omitted, although it is quite obvious that conceptions of the body in any society will be reflected in many aspects of that culture, and not just in its art.

In his study of sexual ambivalence in the Graeco-Roman world, Luc Brisson noted that in classical mythology there are a number of examples of severed heads coming back to life in their own right and delivering prophecies.[96] He recounts the story of Polyclitus who, after his death, returned to Aetolia as a ghost and killed his recently born hermaphrodite child. Having torn the child apart and eaten most of its body,

Polyclitus departed, leaving only the child's head intact. The head then begins to speak and deliver an oracle to the assembled people of Aetolia. Of course, the best-known story of such a talking head is that of Orpheus,[97] but the Polyclitus story is particularly noteworthy in terms of its intertextual references to cannibalism – the eating of human body parts – and hermaphroditism – the physical state of having what were viewed as the wrong set of sexual body parts. As Natalie Boymel Kampen has noted, in discussion of two faience vessels in the form of sleeping or reclining possibly hermaphroditic figures, 'the ongoing fascination with the hermaphrodite speaks … to a sometimes unconscious concern with boundaries, for the objects make the distinction between male and female as unclear as those between childhood and maturity'.[98]

A strain of interest in a 'rhetoric of dismemberment' has been identified in Neronian poetry,[99] particularly in the works of Seneca and Lucan. As has been noted 'there is not a single tragedy in the Senecan corpus in which the mutilation and amputation of human bodies does not play a significant role, even at moments where neither the literary tradition would seem to require it nor common sense to tolerate it'. While there are individual passages in Greek tragedies and early Roman epics that describe mutilations, these tend to be isolated incidents and ones that are few and far between. The only real precursor to the Neronian trend is found in the *Metamorphoses* of Ovid. In trying, though, to find an explanation as to why the Neronian period should mark a trend of literary interest, even obsession, with dismemberment, we must perhaps look to the Stoic beliefs of many of the writers and their interest in the boundaries between human behaviour and that of animals, perhaps centred on the games in the arena. Stoic writers on philosophical science like Galen and Philo saw the body, both human and animal, as being an accumulation of parts 'held together by a sustaining force'. Seneca's 'choppy' style of composition may even have mirrored, or been mirrored by, the dismemberments of human bodies in his text.

Literary and linguistic evidence, however, for the broken body being used as a metaphorical device is not restricted to the canonical writings of the Neronian period. For example, the language used in Coptic texts suggests, through the use of metaphor, 'the disjoining and fragmenting of the body along gender lines'.[100] Consideration will also need to be given to the Latin sexual vocabulary in any fuller study of the fragmented body.[101]

At a more demotic level there can perhaps be seen in the *graffiti* caricatures from the walls of Pompeii another explicit trend towards the reduction of the human body to a set of signifying, disconnected parts, though here we may be seeing humour and spite as the driving forces behind these creations, rather than any complex philosophical reasoning. Most of the caricatures relied upon the exaggeration of certain features, almost always, though not completely exclusively, on facial features, particularly 'hair, beard, eyebrow, lips, jaw, nose, ear and neck',[102] each of which, according to recent analysis, had connotations relating to aspects of laughter, power and authority. Interestingly, many of the caricatures could be seen as being reactions to the Neronian era's 'culture of *nouveau riche* freedmen' and 'introspection by local elites'. 'These people not only did criticise people in power but also used their own stylistic and symbolic creativity to carry on this critique'. The broad contemporaneity of the creation of the Pompeian *graffiti* images and the poetic images of dismemberment mentioned above provides an interesting potential insight into views on the body in the Neronian period.

The ideas expounded in this chapter about the processes behind the fragmentation of the human body into images of partial bodies in Roman art hopefully will not be seen as being esoteric art-historical musings, of no relevance to the study of Roman artefacts, the theme of this book. Rather, it should be stressed that essentialising statements about the experience of the body being culturally unmediated, often found in studies of the classical world, ignore the simple concept that a study of the fragmented body – this archipelago of corrupt fragments – as with a study of fragmented objects, is fundamentally a study of ideas and concepts underpinning Roman culture and society, possibly contributing towards an understanding of the way in which the Romans differed from the Greeks in their conceptions of the body and of the world. An attempt has been made above to examine how bodily and artefactual fragmentation as a reality and as a cultural concept might be identified in Roman Britain, with the creation and use of anatomical or medical *ex votos* and the identification of certain unusual burial rites and practices being the best examples of this process in operation there. A general rarity of fragmented images of the body, perhaps a reflection of a general Romano-British reluctance to imagine the disassembling of the whole body, even as an image, might indicate a cultural schism from the centre based on differing views on the construction of the self in Romano-British society, as will be discussed further in the next chapter.

THE SELF AND OTHERS

The Self

In this chapter an examination will be made of the concept of self in Roman Britain, as reflected in the representation of private individuals in the province, through visual, principally sculptural, representation. The primacy of group dedication of inscriptions celebrating architectural projects in the province over individual dedication has already been discussed in Chapter 5. Visual self-representation through commissioning of images and epigraphic dedication by an individual were undoubtedly linked phenomena. In certain urban situations the advertisement of self could conversely imply selflessness, an immersion into the whole, the social body of the tribe or group, into the province, into the empire. Reflections of self could also be made through the presentation of a physical self-image, and brief consideration will be given to how this might be reconstructible through archaeological evidence. In the much longer second part of the chapter, discussion will focus on three specific groups in Romano-British society whose absence from analysis and sometimes even mention in many books on Roman Britain might suggest to readers that these groups were somehow marginal in Romano-British society in some way, or even were considered at the time as being somehow other. This possible marginalisation or otherness of black Africans, the disabled, and the elderly in Roman Britain will be questioned.

Evidence to be considered, then, for the expression and advertisement of the self takes two principal forms: portrait sculpture, and the naming of individuals in formal public inscriptions. Having set up this discussion it might now appear slightly perverse to acknowledge that there is surprisingly little evidence recovered to date from Roman Britain to suggest that the commissioning of portrait sculpture and the setting up of dedicatory public inscriptions by named individuals was common, or rather as common as in many other provinces.

In the volumes so far published in the *Corpus Signorum Imperii Romani* for Great Britain[1] only a handful of sculptures are classified as formal portraits of private individuals. While there are probably a few dozen sculpted stone heads both of male figures and, lesser in number, of female figures from Roman Britain which might be portrait heads, the majority of these can probably be discounted as being more likely to have been representations of male and female deities rather than mortal private individuals. Certainly a number of imperial portraits both in stone and bronze are present in the archaeological record from Roman Britain, but this is hardly surprising given the numerous official military and civil venues in which the exhibition of such portraits would be expected to take place.

Certainly there is a growing body of recovered tombstones from Roman Britain on which images of the named deceased appear – not portraits as such – but these are not strictly relevant here, though important in helping to demonstrate the role that post-funerary display could play in the formation of the post-mortem social self. I have chosen to illustrate this point with the tombstone of Callimorphus and Serapion from Chester,[2] which utilises the funerary banqueting couch motif to locate the two deceased as part of a thriving community where stones displaying this motif are unusually common, with at least seven examples being recorded from Chester (Plate 61). By choosing this locally significant motif, Callimorphus or his heirs were making a very specific point about being members of a social group, about their individual identities being part of, but subsumed within, this group identity. The inscription on the tombstone tells us that Flavius Callimorphus lived to forty-two and the child Serapion, who is depicted on his knee, to three years and six months. The stone was dedicated by Thesaeus. The names suggest that the men are Greeks and they may either have been merchants or freed slaves.

Why then is there so little portrait sculpture from Roman Britain? A number of individual explanations have been advanced for this phenomenon over the years by various scholars. Some of these explanatory theories may be right, some may be wrong, or some or all of the theories could have applied in tandem, perhaps with other as yet indiscernible reasons.

Though the origins of Roman portraiture can be traced back to the creation and use of wax *imagines* by the upper echelons of the Roman republican elite to commemorate and venerate their ancestors, as was discussed above in Chapter 6, the conceptual link between the present and the past represented by the very medium of portrait art was probably lost by the time the consumption of portraits filtered down the social scale and interacted with other cultural traditions in the individual provinces of the empire. In those provinces there may have been other media, other items of material culture, through which connections with the ancestors could be made. These may have included natural features in the landscape, specific prehistoric sites, and actual prehistoric artefacts, as has been discussed in Chapter 4 as being the case in Roman Britain and Gaul.

Until relatively recently, the two sculpted marble heads and busts of bearded males from Lullingstone Villa in Kent, found together in a basement room there, were taken to be the best examples from the province of the family veneration of portraits of the ancestors. Though the busts were carved in Greek Pentelic marble, and therefore must have come to Roman Britain as finished pieces, nevertheless they appeared to indicate that an elite non-Briton or a particularly rich elite Briton identifying with Roman ancestral ideology lived here. However, it has now been shown to be more likely that these portrait heads are not of private elite individuals but rather that they are portraits of the emperor Pertinax, who served as *Legatus Augusti* in Britain after Ulpius Marcellus, and his father P. Helvius Successus, based on a striking similarity between what can now be called, with some confidence, the Lullingstone Pertinax head, and a portrait head of the emperor from Aquileia in northern Italy.[3]

Perhaps private individuals were represented by two portrait heads from Bath, Somerset and Blackheath, near Colchester, Essex. A larger-than-life-size stone head of an elderly woman with an elaborate and fashionable Flavian period hairstyle was found at Bath in the eighteenth century, in an area outside the formal town boundary, where some kind of funerary monument may have been set up to this individual. Though the woman could represent one of the women of the imperial court at the time, the find-spot of the head and the fact that it is carved in local Bath stone argues against this and for her identification as a local elite individual.[4] The second portrait, from Blackheath, is this time of an elderly man, a small head carved in marble.[5] Though doubts have been expressed about its provenance, and it has been suggested that rather than it being a contemporary Romano-British object it is in fact a lost souvenir from the Grand Tour of more recent times, it may still have come from a proper archaeological context. If so, it is one of only a few portraits of an elderly elite individual from the province. These particular portraits will be discussed further later in this chapter.

My own feeling is that the paucity or lack of portrait sculpture in Roman Britain has something to do with the fact that the concept of the portrait providing a link with ancestors, and thus acting as an indicator of family status, simply meant nothing to the elite of the province, the very people who would have had the financial resources to commission portraits had they so desired. Equally, as has been discussed at length in Chapter 6, the conceptual idea behind the portrait bust, that an image of part of the whole person can be taken to represent to the viewer an image of the whole person, appears to have been anathema to the Romano-British imagination. Fragmentation such as this might have been acceptable in other spheres of Romano-British life, particularly the religious or ritual, but not in the realm of the self. Such a vision of the fragmented body did not chime with Romano-British society's concept of the inviolability, the indivisibility, of the body at that time.[6]

There is no denying that sculpture in stone would have appeared to have mattered, that is had some social or cultural value, to only a relatively small audience in Roman Britain, in the fortresses and forts of the province principally and in the large urban centres. As the majority of sculpture from Roman Britain is in some way religious or votive, there must be some particular explanation for this phenomenon. It has been argued that once the main military and urban audience for stone sculpture in Roman Britain has been discounted from the picture, then there is an undeniable correspondence and therefore a link between the distribution of stone sculptures remaining and geological deposits of good or at least reasonable stone suitable for carving. If sculpture linked to religious sites and sculpture of a religious nature made for private individuals is then discounted, few dots would be left on the distribution map.[7]

Not wishing to celebrate the self through the commissioning of portrait sculpture or through being linked to architectural munificence by the setting up of an inscription must be linked phenomena. As Peter Stewart has recently observed with regard to sculpture from Roman Britain, there is 'a conceptual distance between naturalistic or refined works in the classical tradition and their provincialised imitations. That mental gap ... could result from differences of expectation as well as limitation in technical knowledge ...'[8] Indeed, there would appear to have been significant conceptual differences, in a number of areas of cultural and social life in Roman Britain, between Roman and indigenous, that were more to do with non-acceptance or rejection of certain concepts – rather than necessarily opposition to them – than with purely technical issues.

While the control of images could be a way in which individuals could project a version of themselves to others, a similar effect could be achieved by the styling of their own bodies and the presentation of those bodies in public. Some of those bodies might even have borne tattoos, though this is unlikely in later Roman Britain, given the general association in the Roman world of tattoos with slaves, prisoners of war, and criminals. However, some soldiers and veterans might have worn tattoos acquired during service.[9] And, of course, dress, clothing, the adoption of particular hairstyles, and adornment with jewellery such as hairpins, earrings, necklaces, bracelets, and finger rings would have been significant, though this will not be discussed here. Evidence for styling the body in Roman Britain comes variously from the presence of bath buildings, and from the use of numerous objects such as toilet implements, cosmetic grinders, combs, and mirrors.

Baths are, of course, purely Roman cultural architecture, but some of the types of small grooming items appeared in smaller numbers and in different styles in the pre-Roman Iron Age in Britain. The great prestige value of decorated mirrors in the British and continental Iron Age is well known. Certain types of cosmetic grinders and toilet implements continued to be produced and used from the Iron Age into the Roman period, attesting to some continuity of traditional culture and a tradition linked to personal and group appearance and identity (Plate 62).[10] Toilet implements represent perhaps the best-studied of these grooming-related artefacts (Plates 63–64).[11] These are rare in Britain before the first century AD and usually occur in a restricted geographical area where they probably represent prestige objects. After the Roman conquest they became more common, though their distribution pattern, which shows concentrations in the small towns and other minor settlements rather than in the large towns, suggests their identification as native British grooming implements rather than their being linked to a Romanised regime of body styling and cleaning.[12] Again, the bifid nail-cleaner would appear to be a specifically British type of toilet implement, continuing in use as a common type from the Iron Age in Britain into the early fifth century AD.[13] There is also evidence for regional styles of implement and implement decoration, probably reflecting cultural or tribal groupings and their aesthetic preferences.[14] It is interesting to see that personal identity and cultural, group, or tribal identity might have been conflated here, as was the case with the individual shunning of celebrating the self by architectural munificence in the towns of Roman Britain and thus of the use of the epigraphic habit to celebrate individual generosity in favour of group architectural sponsorship on occasions.

No clear pattern of gender attribution has emerged from the major study of these toilet implements in late Iron Age and Roman Britain, and indeed without more burial data allowing us to link sexed cremations and skeletons from inhumation burials to grave-goods, which might include items such as toilet implements, combs, and mirrors, discussion of such matters will have to remain in abeyance (Plate 65).[15] However, worthy of note here is a recently published study of boxwood combs from the Roman fort at Vechten in the Netherlands.[16] Here a small assemblage of twelve wooden combs survived in environmentally kind conditions that guaranteed their survival. Their presence here suggests that the combs were in this particular context male items, used by soldiers to comb and clean their hair and perhaps in some cases beards, and to keep them free of hair and scalp parasites. Such a grooming routine may have been a requirement of military discipline that dictated the precise appearance as well the behaviour of all serving soldiers, thus engendering their group identity as a military community and fighting force. The presence of other assemblages of wooden combs at Vindonissa in Switzerland and most notably at Vindolanda in Roman Britain, from where sixty-one of the one hundred and fifty-three such combs and comb fragments from the province have so far been recorded, including one still in its original leather carrying case, perhaps suggests that these were standard military-issue items,[17] though such combs have also been found in non-military, urban contexts. Again, personal grooming with such combs in a military context implies individual obeisance and subservience to a group identity.

Others

In the first part of this chapter and in the preceding chapters there has been a certain amount of discussion about the perception of self in the archaeological record from Roman Britain, pursued through a consideration of the cleaning of the physical body by bathing and grooming and of the healing of the sick body and the fear of its cultural exclusion through illness. The fragmentation of the physically inviolate body through artistic representation and images has also been discussed. All of these issues relate to the self. I have written elsewhere at considerable, and some might say excessive, length about the use of art and images to portray the other, those outside or on the fringes and margins of Roman society both during the Republic and the Empire, and how the creation and dissemination of such images was really another form of self-definition for Roman society. My focus for exploring attitudes to others was almost exclusively though through analysis of depictions of barbarians of one sort or another, and it is not intended here to return to this particular aspect of the study.[18]

Some years ago the feminist ancient historian Phyllis Culham quite rightly asked 'did Roman women have an empire?', so frustrated was she at the absence of women from so many contemporary mainstream academic studies of the Roman period.[19] While that situation may have been remedied to some extent in the interim period there is still a tendency for some academics to pay only lip service to equality, for instance by introducing discussion of imperial women's hairstyles rather than of their power, or other such minor, diverting topics. Equally, today one could ask 'did black Africans have a Roman Britain?' or 'did the disabled have a Roman Britain?' And what about the elderly? These are three groups of people hardly ever mentioned, let alone discussed in books on Roman Britain. Are they not discussed because they actually were marginal groups in that society, somehow deemed to be other? Or do we simply not have enough evidence to discuss their presence in Roman Britain and this is why they are seldom mentioned by scholars? I will therefore take the opportunity here to examine evidence for the presence of black Africans in Roman Britain and evidence for attitudes towards the disabled and the elderly in the province.

Black Africans

Studies of the ethnic make-up of the population of Roman Britain are very much in their infancy, perhaps because there is so little information available to study this particular topic, though analysis of ancient DNA is helping to revolutionise our understanding of diasporas in the Roman world.[20] At the simplest level there were two groups in Roman Britain; those who were native to the province, with roots going back to the pre-Roman Iron Age tribes and in most cases further back in prehistory, and the non-Britons who came as conquerors and soldiers, as administrators and bureaucrats, and as merchants and traders and carpetbaggers in the wake of the invasion and so on. Some of these incomers would have been in the province only temporarily, some for a longer period before moving on, and some would have died here or settled here permanently. As the decades passed after AD 43, the situation would have become more complex, with inter-marriage and both emigration of Britons and further immigrants arriving for various reasons. By the fourth century the ethnic mix, particularly in the large towns, would be difficult to unravel comprehensively due to the mobility and migration which had characterised the empire and sustained its workings.

The presence of non-Britons in *Britannia* is most obviously indicated by the existence of inscriptions recording their presence or by funerary monuments using particular, non-British visual styles. Sometimes the form of a name written in *graffiti* might also suggest a non-British origin for its inscriber. There is evidence for the occasional or extended presence of members of many individual ethnic groups in Roman Britain, including Nubians, Moors, and other black Africans, North Africans, Scythians, Syrians, Mesopotamians, Greeks, and Egyptians, leaving aside Italians and Romans, Gauls and Germans, Spaniards, Thracians, and ethnic groups from the Low Countries. Pioneering studies by Vivien Swan of the pottery from certain northern sites, where overseas units from North Africa were attested by epigraphic evidence as having been stationed at certain times, have identified specifically ethnic foodways there.[21] Two main episodes of North African military units coming to Britain are recorded. In around AD 149–150 they were likely to have joined troops returning to Britain from the emperor Antoninus Pius's Mauritanian war and probably were subsequently billeted or stationed at sites on the Antonine Wall in Scotland and at Chester, Holt, and Bowness-on-Solway in northern England, going on to form a unit, *Numerus Maurorum Aurelianorum*, which was then put together at Burgh-by-Sands.[22] Later, in AD 208, Septimius Severus launched his campaigns in northern Britain, among the troops being African detachments from *Legio II Augusta*. Men of this legion are attested as being present at York in particular but also at Caerleon in Wales, on Hadrian's Wall, and in Scotland. Survivors of the campaign are in a number of cases attested by inscriptions as having returned to North Africa. Further evidence for North Africans in Carlisle has also been found.[23] North African units were unlikely though to have been composed of black Africans, though some may have been present, as will be seen below. The voting of Emperor Septimius Severus 'best black Briton' some years ago was hopeful at best and disingenuous at worst.[24] The presence of various ethnic groups, including black Africans, in the Roman north is now receiving a great deal of academic attention.[25]

According to a history of the life of Septimius Severus,[26] the emperor, on returning to his quarters after a victory in Britain, was thrown by encountering an Ethiopian soldier carrying a bough of cypress, both the soldier and the vegetation being taken by him as an unpropitious sign, a pre-shadowing of his death. The soldier was ordered out of his presence. This text is worth quoting here in full, given that it is the only textual reference we have to black Africans in Britain in the Roman period, though the incident is as likely as not to be a fictional construct:

when he [Severus] was returning to his nearest quarters from an inspection of the wall at Luguvallum [Carlisle] in Britain, at a time when he had not only proved victorious but had concluded a perpetual peace, just as he was wondering what omen would present itself, an Ethiopian soldier, who was famous among buffoons and always a notable jester, met him with a garland of cypress-boughs. And when Severus in a rage ordered that the man be removed from his sight, troubled as he was by the man's ominous colour and the ominous nature of the garland, the Ethiopian by way of jest cried, it is said, 'You have been all things, you have conquered all things, now, O conqueror, be a god.' And when on reaching the town he wished to perform a sacrifice, in the first place, through a misunderstanding on the part of the rustic soothsayer, he was taken to the Temple of Bellona, and, in the second place, the victims provided him were black. And then, when he abandoned the sacrifice in disgust and betook himself to the Palace, through some carelessness on the part of the attendants the black victims followed him up to its very doors.

However, the best evidence for the presence of black Africans, or certainly one black African, in Roman Britain comes in the form of a highly decorated tombstone from South Shields,[27] found in two parts but otherwise complete apart from some damage to the face and head of the image of the deceased on the stone (Plate 66). Victor is portrayed in a common format for certain civilian tombstones, lying on a couch with a goblet or glass, presumably of wine, in his hand. Below, the tiny figure of a serving boy proffers Victor another goblet of wine. Above, in a triangular-shaped pediment are the image of a lion's head with a ring through its mouth and to either side portrait busts. The inscription reads '*D[is] M[anibus] Victoris natione Maurum [a]nnorum XX libertus Numeriani [e]q[u]itis ala[e] I Asturum qui piantissime pr[ose]qu[u]tus est*', translated as 'to the spirits of the departed [and] of Victor, a Moorish tribesman, aged twenty, freedman of Numerianus, trooper of the First Cavalry Regiment of Asturians, who most devotedly conducted him to the tomb'. It must be considered whether the seemingly isolated damage to the face of Victor on the tombstone was targeted vandalism of some sort or whether this damage took place at the same time that the tombstone was broken into two pieces and disposed of.

A small bronze figurine of a bearded male rider from London had for many years been interpreted as being a depiction of a western barbarian, with long, heavy locks of hair. It is now thought that this figure, in his cloak, tunic, and boots and holding a circular shield is in fact a representation of a Moorish cavalryman serving in an auxiliary unit of the Roman army.[28]

Other artworks from Roman Britain depicting black Africans include: a copper alloy steelyard weight from Redcross Street, Leicester in the form of a young black boy, his chest emerging from a calyx of stylised leaves; a small lead statuette or weight in the form of a crouching black boy holding his arm up, perhaps an acrobat caught in the act of performing a move, found at Wall, Staffordshire; a lead statuette, broken around the waist, of a black youth from near Bath; a carved amber head of what has been described as 'an Ethiopian or pygmy' from Grave 278 in the Butt Road cemetery, Colchester, Essex, a figure with an exaggerated, perhaps phallic nose which might be of further significance in itself; a bronze oil flask with a black male's head motif on it, found with two bronze strigils and therefore which can be assumed to be part of a bath set from a rich burial, including other grave-goods, excavated at Bayford, Kent in 1877 and now in the British Museum (Plate 67); a reported, but not yet fully published, boxwood scoop with a black male's head on it from excavations at the Thames Exchange Building, Upper Thames Street, Southwark Bridge, London; and a red-glazed ceramic lamp from Moorgate Street, London, shaped on the top like an African man's head, with its elongated chin forming the lamp's nozzle and its open mouth being intended to receive the wick (Plate 68). The lower part of the lamp is in the form of a camel's head.[29]

The database of the national Portable Antiquities Scheme lists four further items: a well-modelled copper alloy figurine of a sleeping or seated, waiting African youth from Uttlesford, Essex, perhaps from a steelyard or a lamp holder (Fig. 15); a steelyard weight in the form of an African or Egyptian head from south Oxfordshire; a copper alloy mount in the form of an African face from Kings Sutton, Northamptonshire; and a cast copper alloy head with African features, perhaps from a statuette, from Bury, Greater Manchester.[30]

Also of note are a few examples of mould-blown glass vessels in the form of whole heads of black African males, found relatively commonly around the empire, an example in signed yellow green glass coming from Caerleon, Wales, with a head of Sol on the base. A second example in deep blue glass, the bottom part of a flask or beaker, possibly, though not certainly, comes from South Shields. A third example comes from London. Deep blue glass fragments of what are suspected to be two further beakers come from Caersws and Camelon.[31]

Also relatively common in the classical world was the portrayal of African pygmies, most usually depicted in combat with cranes or in Nilotic scenes on wall paintings and mosaics and on pottery.[32] In Roman Britain, images of pygmies occur only on imported Samian pottery. A relatively brief search of published corpora of Samian produced examples from London, Cirencester, Piercebridge, Newstead and Inveresk, suggesting that such images were reasonably well circulated and may have engendered discussion among the viewers of these vessels. The pygmies either appear alone, or as armed fighters, with wild, exotic animals such as a panther or as hunters of animals such as bears.[33]

It is now generally recognised that stylistic influences from Roman North Africa can be detected in some of the images and compositions used in the late-third- or fourth-century mosaics at Rudston villa, East Yorkshire. The owner of the Rudston villa may have lived in the region at some time and thus may have come into contact with many more different ethnic groups there than would have been encountered in Roman Britain, as citizens, soldiers, traders, and slaves, from both inside and outside the empire. It is interesting therefore to note here in passing that the lower body shape of the figure of the so-called Rudston Venus on one of the villa mosaics resembles that of a Khoisan woman with *steatopygia*, a genetic characteristic manifested in a very high degree of fat accumulation around the buttocks and the elongation of the labia (Plate 69). In the nineteenth century a grotesque fascination with black African women with this natural physical attribute was reflected in the exhibition around Europe of a number of individuals in what were billed as freak shows, of whom Sara or Saartjie

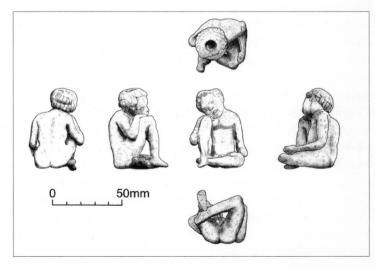

15. A copper alloy figurine of a sleeping black African youth from near Saffron Walden, Essex. (PAS-ESS-6F60D3. Drawing by I. Bell: Copyright Essex County Council and Portable Antiquities Scheme).

0   50mm

Baartman, her given slave-name, was perhaps the most famous, appearing as *The Hottentot Venus.*[34]

Perhaps not a great deal can be read into the presence of these eighteen items in Roman Britain, and of the pygmy image pots. Certainly the images they bear are part of a trend for the depiction of black Africans in Graeco-Roman and Hellenistic art which has long roots.[35] The presence of the items does not imply the presence of black Africans in Roman Britain, though other evidence for their potential presence does exist and has already been mentioned above. Unlike the few images of figures of western barbarians known from Roman Britain, none of the representations of the black Africans discussed here shows them in overtly subservient positions, that is bound, evidently acting as slaves, giving obeisance to Roman emperors or, like the most extreme of the western barbarian depictions, being killed by Roman military forces. In other words there is no narrative of black African subjugation being presented here for the delectation of the citizens of the province of *Britannia*. However, as has been pointed out by a number of authorities, genre representations of black Africans in the Roman world often portrayed them as slaves working in the bath house or attendant on a master.[36] There has also been identified a trend for the depiction of hyper-sexual black males in bath house mosaics of a number of Augustan houses in Pompeii, though here these figures may be apotropaic rather than erotic.[37] Images of black males also appear in wall paintings there. It has even been suggested that in the so-called House of the *Triclinium* in Pompeii one particular set of wall paintings depicting banqueting scenes has a sexual subtext. In these paintings appear the owner of the house, his friends, and the household slaves attendant upon them. The sexual subtext lies beyond that immediately apparent, from a power imbalance in the master-servant relationship. John Clarke sees in the first painting in the series an exclusively male event, with male diners and male servants; physical contact is being made between a balding man and a black boy – the man lays his left hand on him – and between a vomiting man and a small servant who supports him. 'To an ancient viewer, [the] black slave-boy [here] represented an expensive and exotic trophy, meant, like any boy slave, to serve his master in every way – especially sexually.'[38]

The Romano-British objects depicting black Africans are all depictions of black males, most of them youths. The figurine of the auxiliary cavalryman remains an exceptional portrayal among this assemblage. The tombstone of Victor tells us that he was a freed slave while it is likely that the Wall and Uttlesford youths fall into a category of genre depictions of slaves providing entertainment and slaves waiting for their masters respectively. Tasks of house slaves often involved lighting lamps, attending at the baths, and serving food and drink, and in these contexts it is probable that the London ceramic lamp, the Bayford oil flask, and the glass African's head beakers, are also generic images of slaves. We can therefore perhaps read some negative connotations into many of the portrayals of black Africans from Roman Britain, though the transformative element to Roman ideology that allowed Victor to become a freedman commemorated, in image and epigraphic dedication, and the Moorish rider to become a member of the Roman army, with all its cultural, social, and financial benefits, should be noted.

The existence or non-existence of racial prejudice in the Roman world is presently quite a contested topic of academic debate.[39] In Roman Britain, if anything, we only see overt prejudice flare up in the dismissive talk among Roman soldiers of the '*Brittunculi*', the 'wretched little Brits' on one of the Vindolanda writing tablets.[40] Some military inscriptions also appear dismissive of their enemies. On an inscription from Carlisle, Hercules is thanked by the prefect Publius Sextanius for safeguarding troops of the cavalry regiment Augusta 'after the slaughter of a band of barbarians'. On an altar from Corbridge Quintus Calpurnius Concessinius, prefect of cavalry, thanked the deity (not known here) 'after slaughtering a band of Corionototae'.[41]

The Eye of the Beholder

Moving on to a consideration of the disabled in Roman Britain, there is little evidence for their presence other than that provided by the analysis of skeletal remains from Romano-British burials. One of the most pathetic, using that word in its truest sense, is the burial of a child found in a lead coffin and accompanied by grave-goods at Arrington, Cambridgeshire in 1990 (Plates 70–71).[42] The examination of the surviving skeletal remains, principally the skull, as most of the other bones were badly eroded, led to the following conclusions about the child, an infant of about nine months old according to the evidence of the teeth and ten to eleven months old from other indicators. The skull was particularly enlarged, indicating that the child suffered from a serious disability. However, 'despite the child being no older than one year, the reconstructed skull vault [was] enormous, being comparable in size to that of other archaeological specimens of four years old. The vault [was] low, the greatest size increase having been in width, particularly in the frontal region; the bregmatic fontanelle [was] very large, and the bones [were] thin.' This was identified as a case of hydrocephalus ('water on the brain') and it was deemed 'almost certain that this condition caused the death of the child'.[43] The hydrocephalus here was probably congenital rather than acquired. Symptoms of the condition in an infant could have included poor feeding, vomiting, fretfulness and irritability, seizures, and sleepiness. As the condition progressed, with the enlarging of the skull under pressure, the child's eyes would have appeared to gaze downwards, and a lack of reaction to stimulation from its surroundings and a general torpor would have set in. General weakness in movement and shaking arms would have developed.

Hydrocephalus need not necessarily be a disabling condition today, with the fitting of shunts and so on, but in the past most certainly would have been. There is no suggestion in the published report on the skeletal remains that the Arrington child displayed signs of any intrusive medical intervention to try and relieve the condition, and its suffering, and that of its parents, must have been prolonged and painful.

The dead child received a normative burial in some respects but an unusual one in others. The burial appears to have taken place at an isolated site off Ermine Street where there is presently no evidence for a settlement or other burials. The nearest Roman site is over a mile away. The body was wrapped in a dyed, striped woollen blanket or cloth and placed inside a lead coffin which itself was inside a wooden outer coffin. There were traces of what has been suggested to be incense inside the coffin. What was probably a wooden box containing grave-goods was placed on top of the coffin in the grave. A great deal of care and attention had been lavished on this burial and a great deal of money spent.

The grave-goods, dated to AD 130–160 and having continental affinities, consisted of eight pipeclay figurines: a mother goddess seated in a wickerwork chair; a bust of a smiling bald infant; a bust of a long-haired child; a seated, naked male figure, perhaps in the form of a *'spinario'*, that is pulling a thorn out of his foot; a cloaked male figure wearing an eastern, Phrygian cap; two rams; and an ox or bullock.[44] Interpretation of the figures as a coherent group would seem to be impossible; indeed, they could have been a collection of figurines from the family's home household shrine, accumulated over time for specific individual reasons. If they were a group chosen specifically for dedication with this burial it must be asked how they were obtained and where. Did they represent specific manifestations of ideas consigned with the child to the world of the dead? Some of the figures could be deemed to be overtly religious – the mother goddess, the male eastern deity, and perhaps the rams and the ox as representations of sacrificial animals. Less easy to interpret are the busts of children and the *spinario* figure. Interestingly it has been suggested that these three figures together constitute three stages of the life-course the Arrington child did not achieve, from infant, to older child, to adult. Conversely, the two busts could represent the child on its life-course and its mother and father could have been represented by the Mother Goddess figurine and that of the *spinario*.

In his ground-breaking book *The Eye of the Beholder: Deformity and Disability in the Graeco-Roman World*, published in 1995,[45] Robert Garland in a way threw down the gauntlet to academics to extend the study of disability in the ancient world into other fields and regions not covered in his work (Plate 72). Unfortunately, it is only relatively recently that an attempt has been made to synthesise evidence from Roman Britain relating to the disabled in that society. Ongoing research into disability in Roman Britain, by William Southwell-Wright,[46] is apparently attempting to question whether the present-day concept of disability is anachronistic when applied to this alien past society. The so-called Social Model for examining disability in society allows for an awareness of historic context. Disease and ill health, as has been argued elsewhere in this book, may sometimes have affected the social status of affected individuals, but it is unclear at present whether impairment or disability, two quite distinct states, also did this. Even if it did, this might have been on the level of individual cases rather than being applied to the disabled across the board. Perceptions of what constituted difference through disability might have varied in different parts of Romano-British society and, of course, may also have changed over time.

In the virtual absence of depictions of the disabled from Roman Britain, the principal source for this new study is skeletal evidence from the examination of human remains excavated in principally third- and fourth-century inhumation cemeteries at Bath Gate, Cirencester, Gloucestershire, Dunstable, Bedfordshire, London Road, Gloucester, and Poundbury and Alington Avenue, both in Dorchester, Dorset. At these five case study sites, there was found to be evidence for both indications of esteem invested in some burials of those who could be defined as disabled and evidence for in some other cases the disabled being treated differently at their time of burial and by their burial in marginal locations in the cemeteries or by the use of different, indicative burial rites. Southwell-Wright has found evidence for individuals suffering from congenital dwarfism, deafness, ankylosis, traumatic injuries, tuberculosis, gout, syphilis, and poliomyelitis. The Poundbury cemetery was notable for containing some burials of impaired infants. At the Alington Avenue cemetery, also at Dorchester, was found the burial of a young adult with mesomelic dwarfism, who would have stood just four feet and three inches tall, but whose burial was normative, that is not distinguished in any way from the mainstream form of burials in the cemetery. Apparently a second individual with dwarfism was represented among burials at Derby Racecourse cemetery, but this example is as yet unpublished and no specific details of the case can be given here. These individuals lived in some cases into adulthood, so it can certainly be seen that infanticide was not perhaps as widely applied to the disabled in the classical world as once thought. As he noted: 'the impaired were neither entirely marginalised nor institutionalised'.[47]

Two Romano-British objects that might be of relevance here are a steelyard weight in the form of a human head found in Lincolnshire and a decorated pottery vessel from Colchester. The steelyard weight head, on the database of the Portable Antiquities Scheme, has been described as a grotesque head that might be in the form of a caricature.[48] However, it might just be in a category of object relatively common elsewhere in the Roman world, where exaggerated images of disabled or somehow deformed individuals were deployed in a supposedly humorous fashion for the delectation and amusement of others. The decorative scheme on the Colchester pottery vessel, indeed, has been described in print as being the depiction of 'a comic situation'.[49] On the pot appears a stylised *venatio* or animal hunt being conducted by a party of *venatores* composed of at least three persons, one a naked individual with a hunchback – suffering from what is technically known as non-congenital gibbosity – carrying a long knife, and their hunting dogs. The quarry comprises a bear, a hare, and four human hunch-backed dwarves dressed in the long hooded cloaks most commonly worn by the so-called *genii cucullati*. Two of the dwarves lie on the ground, either dead, injured, or exhausted by the chase, a third is depicted in the process of falling to the ground, and the fourth is shown being menaced by one of the snapping and snarling hounds. As has been pointed out by Robert Garland, 'certain categories of deformed persons, such as hunchbacks and dwarfs, were valued collectively for their talismanic qualities as averters of evil ... still today in the Mediterranean and Middle East it is considered lucky to touch a hump'.[50]

Depictions of the Roman fire god Vulcan, and his Greek equivalent Hephaistos, are probably the rarest in numbers of the depictions of the major deities of the

Graeco-Roman world for some unknown reason. Vulcan/Hephaistos was a disabled deity, with either a club foot or a mangled or damaged foot, something quite overtly shown in some Greek works, though not during Roman times. Those aware of the god's back-story, through knowledge of classical mythology, would have been aware of his otherness created by the supposed occasional mockery of Hephaistos by some of his fellow gods. Images of Vulcan from Roman Britain are few. A votive relief from Keisby, Lincolnshire shows the god standing by his anvil. A now-lost relief from Duns Tew, Oxfordshire may have depicted the god. A copper alloy statuette of Vulcan came from excavations at Bainesse Farm, Catterick, North Yorkshire and others from Richborough, Kent and North Bradley, Wiltshire. He appears on two gold ring settings from Newark, Nottinghamshire and Brant Braughton, Lincolnshire. He is a relatively common figure type on Central Gaulish Samian pottery, though I have not tried to find and list all the pots and sherds from the province on which he occurs; an example from Wroxeter is well known. Most often on Samian he appears with one leg standing on a block, something that is likely simply to be a standard pose rather than an attempt to stress his disability. There are a number of images of a smith-god on pots from Roman Britain, most famously on the mould from Corbridge, but as this deity was probably separate from but equated with Vulcan I will not discuss these further here. Vulcan appears on two of the votive plaques in the so-called treasure from Barkway, Hertfordshire and is mentioned in the inscription on one in the Stony Stratford, Buckinghamshire cache of religious material. Two inscriptions on altars from Old Carlisle and Chesterholm/Vindolanda refer to Vulcan.[51]

Classical mythology also tells us of the rustic god Priapus, son of Dionysus/Bacchus and Aphrodite/Venus, abandoned by his mother shortly after his birth because of her shame at his grotesquely huge phallus. This permanent deformity became a focus for his worship as a god of fertility and plenty, of orchards and gardens, and as a protector of boundaries. Priapism today is classed as a medical emergency, though if recurring or frequent it becomes a functional disability. Representations of Priapus or priapic males are not particularly common in the Roman world and relatively uncommon in Roman Britain. Small copper alloy statuettes of herms of Priapus, that is small-scale representations of boundary markers, come from Pakenham, Suffolk and Haxey, Lincolnshire. A statuette of the tumescent god, holding grapes, from Thorrington, Essex and a bronze of an older but still priapic Priapus from Ingham, near Bury St Edmunds, Suffolk have been recorded by the Portable Antiquities Scheme (Plate 73). A lead figure of Priapus from near Telford, Shropshire and a copper alloy Priapus figurine from Helmsley, North Yorkshire have been recorded on the UKDFD website database. A number of *intaglios*, carved gemstones, from Britain carry images of Priapus. A stone slab from the Scottish fort of Birrens, Dumfries and Galloway, Scotland bears an image of a horned Priapus, along with the partial inscription '[P]*riapi M[entula]*', translated as 'Phallus of Priapus'. A now-lost relief sculpture of Priapus is recorded by antiquarians as having been found at Binchester Roman fort, County Durham.[52]

Thus some tentative connections can be made between Priapus and northern military contexts and rural contexts in Suffolk and perhaps East Anglia more broadly. It is interesting to note here the relative ubiquity in Roman Suffolk of phallic ornaments, suggesting some regional phenomenon that is difficult to interpret at the present time.[53] Rather than view these images of Priapus as relating somehow to narratives about disability we should perhaps view them as part of the broader Roman and Romano-British narrative relating to the display and celebration of hyper-masculinity, as discussed more fully in Chapter 5.[54]

Acting Their Age

In their recent book, *Growing Up and Growing Old in Ancient Rome: A Life Course Approach*, Mary Harlow and Ray Laurence have written that 'our understanding of the Roman concept of old age, unlike much of the life course, is informed by the personal voices of the elderly', or rather perhaps that should have read by the personal voices of *some* of the elderly, those relatively few men in fact who wrote philosophical treatises, 'the focus of many of these [being] their experience of old age'.[55]

As noted by Harlow and Laurence, the age at which one was considered to be old in ancient Rome varied considerably from 'anywhere between forty-six and sixty', with an individual's physical and mental health being significant factors in determining in individual cases when being viewed as old commenced.[56] Being viewed as old meant that social expectations of you changed. In the words of Harlow and Laurence, for the old or elderly 'their role and obligations as citizens reverted to those of a child'. There was considerable potential therefore for the marginalisation of the old, particularly of elderly women, though Roman society undoubtedly recognised and celebrated the contributions made in the past by the elite elderly, principally through the veneration of civic duty in the case of men and motherhood in the case of women.[57]

Harlow and Laurence's study is principally based on the analysis of written sources, and though illustrated with a very small number of black and white photographs of works of art depicting individuals at different stages in what they term the life-course, analysis of visual representations of ageing is otherwise largely absent from the book.

It is perhaps curious that as far as I am aware there has been nothing written on ageing or on the concept of old age and the position of the elderly in Roman Britain. There is a great deal of information which can be gleaned from artworks about such matters in Rome and Italy but portrait art is largely absent from the province, as discussed above. Perhaps the only arena in which archaeological study can make age a socially visible aspect of life here is therefore that of burial and funerary commemoration. Examination of skeletons from Roman cemeteries usually allows an approximate age at death to be estimated, usually within a date range, and sometimes age at death is recorded on a tombstone.[58]

In Roman Britain, as in the rest of the Roman world, when the life of the individual buried was further commemorated by the erection of a tombstone, details of age at death were normally given in the accompanying inscription. Mortuary inscriptions also appear on a small number of other types of object, such as coffins and so on. Examination of the tombstone and mortuary inscriptions published in the two volumes of *The Roman Inscriptions of Britain: Inscriptions on Stone*[59] records two hundred and fifty-three instances of age at death being recorded, or rather being readable on the surviving stones, some of these inscriptions recording the life details of more than one individual, giving a total of two hundred and seventy-three individuals for whom we have a recorded age at death. Of these, eighty-two are soldiers, and these individuals will not be considered further here, and one hundred and ninety-one are civilians in Roman Britain. Of these civilians, forty-four are children of or under the age of fifteen, seventy-seven are men and sixty are women, and ten are of uncertain gender due to instances of partial survival of the inscriptions only.

The majority of the men recorded, fifty individuals, died before the age of fifty, with peaks in the age ranges 31–40 and 41–50. Twenty-seven of the men lived beyond fifty, twenty-one of these beyond sixty, seventeen of these beyond seventy, eight beyond eighty, and one man is recorded as living to 100 years of age. Those who reached or passed eighty were a veteran former *decurion* of the *colonia* at Gloucester who died at Bath (RIB 161), Annius Felix and Cassius Secundus, two veterans who died at Chester (RIB 517 and RIB 526), a man from Caerleon (RIB 3101), and […]*alis* from Brougham (RIB 3236), all five aged eighty at death, and […]*nus* from Chichester who died aged eighty-five (RIB 93). Aurelius Timotheus of Chester died aged ninety (RIB 3161). The centenarian, Julius Valens, was commemorated on a tombstone from Caerleon, Wales set up by Julia Secundina, his wife and his son Julius Martinus (RIB 363), and is described in the valedictory inscription as being a veteran of the Second Legion Augusta. Incidentally, we are also fortunate in having the tombstone of Julia Secundina, on which she is recorded as having died at the age of seventy-five (RIB 373).

The majority of the women recorded, fifty-one individuals, died before the age of fifty, with peaks in the age ranges 21–30 and 31–40. Nine of the women only lived beyond fifty, five of these beyond sixty, three of these beyond seventy, and two beyond eighty, the oldest women being recorded as living to eighty and ninety years of age. These were respectively Iuccittia of Caerleon (RIB 382) and Claudia Crysis who is recorded on a tombstone from Lincoln (RIB 263).

Thus, taken together in our sample of one hundred and thirty-seven adult civilians from Roman Britain whose ages at death were recorded in inscriptions, the majority, around three quarters of the sample, died before they reached fifty years of age and only around a quarter of the adults in the sample lived beyond this. The fact that on the memorial inscriptions all the ages were recorded exactly in multiples of five years suggests that the ages given were in all cases approximations. Some of the ages recorded, though, were astonishingly precise. At the Lankhills cemetery, Winchester, Hampshire osteological study showed that just over a fifth of the skeletons were of people thirty years or older.[60] At the Poundbury cemetery, Dorchester, Dorset only half of the men and a third of the women whose skeletons were analysed lived to forty or older.[61]

There is no evidence from the inscriptions and from the cemeteries that the more elderly members of society were treated or commemorated any differently at death than younger citizens. However, an inscribed lead plaque found in a burial in a Romano-British cemetery at Clothall, Hertfordshire[62] bears the text, in translation: 'Tacita, hereby accursed, is labelled old like putrid core', something that is unlikely to have come from a well-wisher or grieving family member with respect for their elders.

The study of ageing in Roman society in general can be greatly enhanced by the analysis of works of art that portray individuals of a mature age and the elderly, such as the canonical Republican portrait of an old man found near Otricoli. This portrait head, with its veristic rendering of the physical evidence of ageing in the form of deep lines and heavy wrinkles, is perhaps a metaphor for 'the experience and wisdom of the sitter' and a reflection of the esteemed place in Roman society of elderly aristocratic men such as this.[63]

In contrast, under the Empire it is possible to identify a conscious strategy of avoiding the depiction of the emperors Augustus and Trajan as ageing or aged men. The famous Prima Porta statue of Augustus, showing the emperor seemingly in his twenties, when at the time of its production he was in his early forties, illustrates well his regular depiction as an eternal youth.[64] Trajan's portraits, following his accession to the purple at the age of forty-five, show him forever at this age. He was, as Diana Kleiner has dubbed him, 'the ageless adult'.[65] The opportunity will be taken here to briefly examine these and other artworks which suggest a complex mesh of representations perhaps reflecting tensions in Roman society between celebrating old age and denying its physical onset, while recognising the value to the state of experience and lineage. A small number of selected works of Roman art from the late Republic and early Empire up to the time of Trajan which individually portray certain aspects of Roman attitudes to the physical signs of ageing will be examined in the following pages. Collectively, study of these might provide insights into how choosing to depict these signs or not to depict them in portraits was part of a formal strategy for manipulating depictions of age for personal and political ends.

The so-called Barberini *togatus* statue of the late first century BC, now in the *Museo del Palazzo dei Conservatori* in Rome, represents one of the most significant and important pieces of evidence for the way in which ancestral portrait busts may have been used in ceremonial practices in Roman society.[66] Though restored, with another ancient portrait head grafted onto the original statue's shoulders, the work is otherwise complete and portrays a middle-aged or elderly togate male, his clothes marking him out as a member of the Roman elite, standing in an upright pose with a portrait bust of a mature or elderly man held in each hand. The busts face forward and the viewer's gaze is invited to move between the faces of the two busts and that of their owner in an almost triangular movement. There is a sense of anticipation in the piece, as if the man is about to join a procession or walk into a room.

The male figure is holding portrait busts probably modelled in terracotta, and is not holding *imagines*, images in the form of wax masks of dead ancestors who had held magisterial office, as they have been incorrectly identified by a number of authorities in the past.[67] Such busts would have been kept in the home, like the *imagines*, and possibly would have been carried in funeral parades, just as the wax *imagines* were worn at funerals 'by those who seem most like the deceased in size and build', according to Polybius. Ancestral portrait busts and wax *imagines* were thus originally used as props by the Roman elite to define schemes of male ancestral lineage and reflected in their veristic nature a linking of the idea of male ageing with civic virtue.

Another broadly contemporary piece of sculpture is the marble portrait head of an old man from near Otricoli and now in the *Museo Torlonia* in Rome (Plate 74). It probably dates from the late Republic, around 50 BC. The man, probably a patrician, is portrayed staring directly at the viewer, his face, neck and forehead being heavily and deeply lined and furrowed, his cheeks sunken, his hair balding or thinning. The effect has been described as being 'almost a topographic map of the face', although the face in this case is strong and characterful, the depiction quite powerful. Indeed, as has been said, 'the furrows and wrinkles, which stand for the experience and wisdom of the sitter, become the subject of the work of art'.[68]

Also dating to the time of the late Republic is a marble portrait of an elderly woman from Palombara Sabina, now in the *Museo Nazionale delle Terme* in Rome (Plate 75). Like the Otricoli patrician she is frontally posed, directly facing the viewer. The viewer's eye is at first drawn immediately away from the woman's face towards her hair, and in particular to a highly fashionable pronounced roll or *nodus* of hair over her forehead. When attention returns to the woman's face it can be seen that though she was likely to have been roughly the same age as the Otricoli patrician when she sat for the artist, the physical signs of ageing on her face are significantly less pronounced. Nevertheless, her thin face, slightly sunken cheeks, bags under her eyes, and creases at the corners of her mouth can be taken to represent her experience and status as an elite matron.[69]

In terms of setting these so-called veristic portraits in a broader Graeco-Roman context of traditions of portraying the elderly, perhaps the single most significant work of art against which to judge them is the black marble sculpture found in Rome and known either as *The Dying Seneca*, *The Old Fisherman* or, based upon its present home, *The Louvre Fisherman*.[70] Interpretation of the work is almost entirely dependant on whether one believes it was intended to portray an actual person, the Roman philosopher Seneca caught in stasis in the act of committing suicide, having opened his veins and stepped into a warm bath to help facilitate his exit from the world, or an unnamed elderly fisherman either caught wading ashore from his boat or wading out to a boat. The latter interpretation generally now holds sway, and indeed the statue found in Rome is simply one of a number of examples of similar statues, but most certainly is technically the most accomplished and the most dramatically composed. It is likely to be a Roman copy of a Greek original of the Hellenistic era, probably between 200 and 150 BC.

As this is a full-length sculpture and the figure of the old man was probably originally portrayed naked, the artist has addressed head-on the effects of ageing on the whole body rather than simply on the face, as has already been seen in the case of the Otricoli man and the Palombara Sabina woman. The stooping, somewhat emaciated body, with its haggard face, is perhaps difficult to view as an essay in wisdom and experience, as has been suggested as the motive behind the sculpting of the face of the Otricoli man. It has been suggested that at first sight this genre of Hellenistic sculptures, amongst which can also be included 'haggard or drunken old women in the market [and] emaciated old shepherdesses', represents either Hellenistic sculptors taking 'a frank hard look at what they saw around them' or that 'these figures express an aristocratic contempt for the ugliness of the low-born'.[71]

But just as we can cite the previous few examples of portrayal of the old or elderly in an academic, almost anthropological manner, so we can equally come up with a number of instances where art is used to subvert or even invert time in pursuit of acceptable images. The first two examples of such a process involve strategies for the later portrayal in portrait form of the emperors Augustus and Trajan in a way that defies chronologies of ageing. Indeed they have respectively been dubbed 'the eternal youth' and 'the ageless adult'.[72]

Perhaps the best known portrait statue of Augustus is the so-called Prima Porta Augustus found at the Villa of Livia at Prima Porta, just outside Rome. Dating to probably 20 BC, the portrait head of the statue itself defines a portrait type for Augustus – called the Prima Porta type – of which more than one hundred and seventy examples are known. Striking in its pose and overall composition, this multi-layered work shows a cuirassed emperor addressing an invisible audience. His pose harks back to Greek models such as Polykleitos's *Doryphoros* or that of the late Etruscan *Arringatore* Aulus Metullus. He is portrayed here as 'a great general, a powerful orator … with the body of a Greek athlete'. Augustus's face, hair and body are those of a youthful man, yet at the time the statue was created the emperor would have been in his early forties. Some art historians claim to see slight signs of ageing on the face of another portrait type of the emperor – the so-called Forbes or *Ara Pacis* type – that might post-date the Prima Porta type of portrait, but such claims remain unconvincing, with the known portrait types of Augustus that circulated throughout his reign and up to his death in 14 BC, at the age of forty-nine, all portraying him as an eternal youth or youthful adult.[73]

As for the emperor Trajan, he came late to power, at the age of forty-five in AD 98, and died in AD 117 at the age of sixty-four. Throughout his reign his portraits show him as the middle-aged man that he was when he first became emperor; he was 'the ageless adult'. Another conundrum regarding Trajan's life is revealed in the artworks adorning the Arch of Trajan at Benevento, a monument planned during the emperor's lifetime and started in the last three years of his life, being completed by his successor Hadrian in AD 118. Here the emperor, though childless, is portrayed in one scene almost as the father of the country, distributing *alimenta* or food relief to the impoverished children of Italy.[74]

Similarly, Pliny the Younger had earlier described in a panegyric[75] the forty-six-year-old emperor's triumphant entry into Rome in AD 99, in terms of his impressive physical appearance – his tall body – and how he drew crowds of small children, young people, old men, the infirm and particularly women who, he wrote, 'looked upon Trajan and rejoiced ... because they clearly saw for which ruler they bore citizens, for which military leader they bore soldiers'. As has been pointed out, 'here he becomes father to Roman children through the reconfiguration of relations between husbands and wives, adults and children.[76] And, in the process, he takes on the erotic character for the women of Rome that he seems not to have in relation to his own childless wife; he works like an aphrodisiac. In Pliny's construction of an imperial sexuality, Trajan is granted the power to transform all human relationships, to name them as he will.' In his portraits he assumed the power to stop or control time and to hold back the physical signs of ageing.

The third example of age confusion in Roman art is in this case related to an extraordinary trend among Roman matrons from the first century AD onwards into the second century to be portrayed in the guise of a nude Venus, with their realistic portrait heads being set atop the youthful naked bodies of the goddess.[77] These statues were set up in tombs and may have been influenced in their inception by an imperial tradition of representing female members of the imperial family as Venus, though not perhaps as nudes. A study of these artworks depicting nude matrons has concluded that while 'to a modern audience these portraits appear incongruous, the often stern features and lined faces of matrons oddly juxtaposed with the highly charged eroticism of figures that display a youthful anatomy and firm flesh ... the mythological conceit implied that these women rivalled Venus in beauty, charm, and the ability to bear healthy children'. Venus's nudity, it has been suggested, is in these instances 'worn as a costume that replaces rather than reveals the body of the deceased' mature or elderly woman.[78]

The gravity, modesty, or self-restraint conveyed by the portrait heads of these mature women, probably all freedwomen, acted perhaps as a visual manifestation of their identification with those mature and elderly elite matrons who were praised by historians and eulogists for their dignified bearing and achievements in domestic and civic spheres. 'If the portrait head conveys the dignity and authority of the matron, then the replacement of the ageing body by the immortal physique of Venus suggests a belief in the resilience of the maternal body ... the rejuvenating nude portrait with its Venus imagery was appropriate for matrons whose bodies were renewed and whose social horizons were extended through several marriages.'[79] The commissioning of such portraits may also have been a visual counterblast to the cacophonous din of contemporary misogynistic satirists such as Martial, who publicly and popularly stereotyped older women for their 'foul smelling cavernous genitals, ugly breasts, and animalistic sexual voracity'.[80]

It has been demonstrated by ancient historians that there was a fluidity in Roman society in defining the age at which an individual would be considered as being old, with physical and mental well-being being equally important signifiers as chronology alone. An examination of a number of visual images principally from Rome and Italy again suggests that physical age was a state that could be celebrated or analysed in art but also one that could be manipulated or inverted for personal or political ends. Emperors such as Augustus and Trajan could have themselves depicted as respectively an eternal youth and an ageless adult, while the fashion among freedwomen at one time to have themselves portrayed in tombs as having sloughed off their aged bodies and replaced them with younger versions suggests that manipulation of the signs of ageing was sometimes as much morally underpinned as it was politically. Just as Roman monumental inscriptions could be read according to differently constructed or perceived chronologies,[81] so can some Roman portraits also sometimes be read in ways which defy the passing of time sequentially. Raging against the dying of the light could be carved in stone as easily as set down in poetry upon the page.

Such a nuanced set of strategies for depicting and sometimes manipulating images of the elderly unfortunately cannot be seen to be reflected in artworks from Roman Britain, from where come only two possible sculptural depictions of aged citizens, both of which are semi-veristic in the approach taken by the artist to depict the passage of time on the sitters' faces. The first is a small, carved, finely grained white marble portrait head of an elderly man, from Blackheath, Essex.[82] His partially balding head is turned slightly to the left, helping to accentuate the heavy lining of his brow and neck and around his mouth. His lank, thinning hair is slightly waved. He has large ears, a very pronounced but flattened nose, a thick bottom lip, and a double chin. His neck is thick and trunk-like. The piece was originally thought to be Vespasianic but is now thought to date to the early third century, though the veristic elements of the portrait certainly hark back to the much earlier period at which the Otricoli Man was carved. As noted above, some doubts have been expressed about its provenance and it has been suggested that this could be a lost souvenir from the Grand Tour of more recent times. However, there is still the possibility that it could be a Romano-British piece, albeit imported, seeing as how it is carved of marble, from a genuine archaeological context. In that case its open and honest response to ageing is of considerable interest here.

A twice-life-size stone head of an elderly woman with an elaborate and fashionable Flavian period hairstyle was found at Walcot, Bath, Somerset in the eighteenth century, and probably derived from some kind of funerary monument. Though the woman could represent one of the women of the imperial court at the time, the find-spot of the head and the fact that it is carved in local Bath stone argues against this and for her identification as a local elite individual.[83] The face of the portrait is unfortunately now quite badly damaged, though it can be made out that the sitter was an older woman with a lined and here unidealised face. The hair is twisted into a chignon at the back and bunched at the nape of the neck. At the front the hair is bunched up into a crescentic mass of curls in what has been dubbed 'the sponge' style. As with the Blackheath man there is no attempt here to hide or apologise for the sitter's age.

False Oppositions

In a way this chapter has been structured around what was set up to be a false opposition, between the self and social self in Roman Britain and a shakily defined group of outsiders or others – comprising here black Africans, the disabled, and the elderly. By setting up this opposition there was immediately implied a tension in the very existence of these two entities together, yet their co-existence would appear to have been the case in Roman Britain. Perhaps the general absence of discussion of one or the other of this group of others – or of all three groups – in most works on Roman Britain has in a way made each group 'other' in our contemporary view of what Roman Britain was like.

There is not a great deal of evidence for black Africans being present in Roman Britain in any numbers at any time, and this is reflected in visual culture, where a substantial presence might perhaps have been expected to be mirrored in a large number of artworks. There are in fact few depictions of black Africans in Romano-British art. A young black African male appears in one artwork as a soldier and a number of black youths appear depicted in a way that suggests they might have been slaves and thus certainly outsiders. The other few depictions are more neutral in content and must otherwise be classed simply as genre pieces. The disabled and the elderly are likewise largely absent in artworks from the province, but osteological study and the analysis of burial evidence suggests that both separate groups were not generally in any way marginalised, or necessarily accorded more or less significant treatment than others in society at the time. They were certainly not other. In Britain today there is a groundswell or undercurrent of refashioning normal generational difference in an oppositional manner, through the castigation of the older generation for owning homes while the young do not, having too many unused rooms in those homes while the young do not, in having private pensions which the young might not get, and in enjoying free bus passes or other travel concessions which the young might claim to be subsidising. Of course, most of this is political and especially media rhetoric, but it does show how marginalisation of one particular sector of a society can easily come about.

NARRATIVES OF THE PAST

Monumentality and Empire

As has been demonstrated in the preceding chapters, some objects used in Roman Britain were produced specifically for the purposes of carrying symbolic meaning and other objects sometimes had symbolism thrust upon them, as it were. They were in some instances functional objects which were redefined by some use outside of their specific function. This redefinition took many disparate forms.

As an example of how this process might work I want to briefly consider the case of the humble, utilitarian iron nail, a ubiquitous find on sites of the Roman period in Britain, though numbers of nails found on any particular site of course vary, depending on the nature of the site itself. Although there are perhaps nine different types of iron nail found in Roman Britain, excluding hobnails, three of these types are relatively rare and were probably specialised upholstery nails, with the other six types representing structural or construction nails for carpentry, joinery, and general building work. Of these six types of structural nails by far the commonest type, known to archaeologists as the Manning Type 1 nail, has 'a square-sectioned, tapering stem with a rounded or rectangular head. They may be subdivided on their length and the form of the head'. These nails can be as long as thirty centimetres, but most commonly are between four and seven centimetres in length.[1]

At the legionary fortress of Inchtuthil, near Blairgowrie, Perth and Kinross, in Scotland a hoard of over eight hundred and seventy-five thousand iron nails, weighing around seven tonnes, was excavated in 1959, the largest single find of nails from any site in Roman Britain and probably in the western empire. All of these nails were Manning Type 1 nails, almost 90 per cent of them being between four and seven centimetres in length. These nails, along with a small number of other iron items, had been buried in a huge, twelve-feet-deep pit dug through the beaten earth floor of the fort's workshop building or *fabrica*. The iron in the pit had been capped and sealed at the base of the pit by six feet or so of gravel, with other spoil on top of that. The workshop building, like the rest of the fort's buildings and defences, had been slighted at the time of the abandonment of the fort and others in the region, probably between AD 87 and 90. Two main explanations have been advanced for the burial of the nails here at the time of the abandonment of the fort: that they were buried to prevent them falling into the hands of those local tribal peoples who might be expected to look over the site once the Roman army had moved out; or that they were buried as part of the general decommissioning of the site since they could not be transported away for use elsewhere. Of course, either of these explanations sounds feasible, given the circumstances of the military pull-out from Inchtuthil.[2]

However, there may well also have been a symbolic subtext to the burial of the cache of nails at Inchtuthil, related to the retaining of control over the cultural symbolism of the architectural difference between Roman and local tribal buildings and a need to ensure no loss of face in abandoning the fortress here. I have written elsewhere about the use of images of building types as one of a suite of artistic motifs to define, stress, and enforce the difference between Roman and German on scenes on the Column of Marcus Aurelius in Rome of around AD 192 and indeed this can also be demonstrated to have also occurred on the artworks on Trajan's Column in Rome some eighty years earlier in AD 113, this time stressing the difference between Romans and Dacians, at a time closer to the date of the Inchtuthil abandonment.[3]

On Marcus's Column the burning of German villages appears in a number of scenes, the depicted flimsy construction of these 'rude huts' being easily consumed by the fires set by Roman torches. These huts are round, as opposed to rectangular, something that archaeologically can be seen to mark out the difference between Roman and native in many provinces of the empire. They are small structures that would appear to have been constructed of wattle and daub or of bundled reeds. Defences at the villages appear to have been built simply of panels of hurdling, of intertwined branches and twigs. It is interesting the way in which the artists of the column frieze have used architecture as a signifier of the difference between Roman and non-Roman, thus between civilisation and barbarism. In scenes involving the Roman army crossing the Danube we can see that along the banks of the river, on the civilised side, there are depicted a number of buildings forming a small village or hamlet. The buildings are rectangular in plan and probably of two storeys, as there are windows or openings at second-floor level on all three houses. They all have pitched roofs. The largest building would appear to have been constructed of dressed stone, with a tiled roof and grand entrance. The building next to it would also appear to be of stone, though built of less monumentally sized blocks, and again has a tiled roof. It stands within a compound formed by a stout wooden fence and a solid wooden gate. The third building would appear to be of timber construction, with a thatched or shingle roof. Once more it stands within a fenced compound. Together these structures represent the variety of Romanised buildings that constitute a civilised urban centre.[4]

Further points are made about monumentality in the depiction of Roman military encampments on the column, their solidity further emphasising the materiality, the sheer physicality of the Roman presence. In one scene the Germans attempt to overcome the Romans by trying to turn around the Romans' architectural superiority, in the form of their impenetrable fort, by laying siege to the camp. Their construction of a siege tower marks an attempt to assault the very fabric, the very physicality of the Roman construction and thus challenge the superiority of Roman monumentality and thus its cultural values. Architecture and buildings were indeed expressions of Roman imperialism but more than this they played 'an often pivotal role in "materialising" imperial ideologies and coercion, as the most visible means through which to present the Roman state, a social construction, physically throughout the empire'.[5]

It is interesting to note in this context that the decorative scene on one of the legionary distance slabs from Hutcheson Hill, Bearsden, on the Antonine Wall in Scotland, set up by the Twentieth Legion in the AD 140s, also uses the motif of a classical-style building and a classical deity to provided contrast with the figures of defeated barbarians here. The scene on the slab contains an elaborately designed architectural setting, either a temple or a triumphal arch, with figures placed in the central arched space and in the pedimented spaces on either side. The central scene depicts Victory crowning a member of the triumphant Roman forces, in this case a standard-bearer, while looking on from the sides are two bound barbarian captives, the line of their gaze suggesting that they are viewers of the victory ceremony.[6]

It was not only the opposition of barbarity to civilisation that was indicated by the depiction of native huts on the column used as juxtaposed images to Romanised buildings. The organic nature of these huts, built of wood, wattle and daub, reeds or rushes, gave them an in-built obsolescence, a temporal limit, as opposed to the implied permanence of the more stout-looking Romanised structures. The Roman empire, this implied, would last. These barbarian cultures, while they might now be virile and a threat to Rome, would eventually decay like rotting wood.[7]

The burial of the nail cache at Inchtuthil could therefore have been something more than a tidying up exercise; it may have had symbolic value in itself and constitute the closing off of a temporal episode of Roman occupation here. The sealing of the nail cache under a thick gravel deposit in the pit again implies that the gravel was a formal closing deposit of some kind. It must also be remembered that there is even better evidence for the Roman army symbolically marking the end of a later period of occupation in Scotland, at the time of the decommissioning and abandonment of the Antonine Wall in the AD 160s. At that time the individually inscribed and decorated legionary distance slabs, which had formed a decorative and commemorative series set in the wall structure, were taken down and buried in pits away from the slighted defence system.[8]

The burial of the Inchtuthil nail cache is not necessarily the only instance where utilitarian items such as iron nails have been disposed of with far greater care than might have been expected for such common and apparently mundane items. I am certainly aware of an instance of the as-yet-unpublished excavation of a Romano-British inhumation burial in Leicestershire being accompanied by grave-goods in the form of a pot filled up with about two dozen or so iron nails and with no other grave-goods.[9] Without any details available to me on the skeletal remains from the burial, no further informed comment can really be made on this occurrence. Was the person buried here a carpenter or tradesman of some sort, or did the nails buried here carry some kind of symbolic value?

There is no doubt that iron as a material, or rather the working of iron to create objects and artefacts, is viewed in many cultures as highly symbolic, indeed as it was in the Greek and Roman worlds. Blacksmiths are often seen as figures with powers to create and oversee both symbolic and real transformations.[10] The Roman god Vulcan was a deity of destructive, devouring fire who came to be linked to blacksmiths and other craftsmen working with fire. Images of the god and of related blacksmith deities are certainly known from Roman Britain, as was discussed in Chapter 7.[11] This juxtaposition of destruction and creativity in the god's persona, and thus in iron objects themselves, perhaps might account for the creative disposal of iron objects in certain contexts in Roman Britain and the burial of certain iron items in pits, as at the Roman fort site of Newstead in Scotland and indeed at Inchtuthil, as discussed above. Some element of otherwordly significance may therefore on occasions have been accorded objects of iron in Roman society, some added symbolic value, that might make even the presence of the humble structural iron nail of significance in certain contexts.[12]

There are other situations in which the use of iron nails could perhaps have been viewed to be much more overtly symbolic than purely functional, indeed where the act of using and hammering in the nails was itself highly laden with meaning.[13] Classical sources attest to the ritual of hammering the *clavus annalis* – literally the annual nail – into a temple wall in Rome, though the exact significance of the rite remains uncertain. I would not be the first person to point out that in Roman Britain the building of a wooden coffin, using iron nails to hold it together, may have been considered as being more than a standard carpentry task. Or that the nailing of metal letters or metal leaves and feathers onto the inside walls of Romano-British temple buildings, where such *ex votos* and others were put on display, may have carried a ritual charge of its own. Indeed, were specially prepared or blessed iron nails used for such tasks, even though their form and appearance were otherwise utilitarian? Specially selected or prepared iron nails may have been hammered into inscribed lead curse tablets or *defixiones* in order to 'fix' the curse inscribed thereon, though equally probable is the use of bog-standard, ordinary structural nails for this purpose or copper alloy nails.[14]

In the case of the Inchtuthil iron nail cache, and to a greater extent of the Leicestershire pot full of iron nails, some degree of imagination is required to try and explain the context of the find, otherwise we could not proceed beyond reporting that a big pit was found containing hundreds of thousands of nails or that a pot was found containing only nails. That application of imagination can almost be construed as being akin to creating a fictional narrative or alternative narratives around the find, the value of which I will now turn briefly to consider.

Objects in Fictional Worlds

As this study comes towards its end, it seems appropriate to return to the theme of consumers and consumption which opened the book, but to engage with this topic from an altogether different perspective from that adopted in Chapter 1. I must confess to a fascination with novels in which objects or material culture play a central role, not in terms of the lazy citing of product brand names to situate a particular character socially within today's western consumer society or to act as a kind of shorthand way of avoiding building a literary character. Rather my fascination is with fiction and novels where the mechanics and processes of consumption underpin a consideration of the role of objects in relation to the people who bought, used, and discarded them and thus indirectly allude to the broader society or culture in which these various transactions take place. A number of examples will be given here to help illustrate this point. In many ways fiction provided the only arena for the discussion of consumers and consumption and the illumination of the relationship between the two before academics in the Social Sciences turned their attention to the study of material culture and its attendant mechanisms from the 1950s onwards.

The first work to be considered here is not a novel as such, rather it is the ancient Irish mythological saga, the *Táin Bó Cuailnge* or *The Cattle Raid of Cooley*, part of a cycle of works that has been said to provide 'a window on the Iron Age'.[15] My particular focus here is on that part of the saga dubbed 'the pillowtalk' in the most accessible of the modern translations of the story. Lying in bed together, King Ailill and Queen Medb of Connacht fall into conversation about their relative levels of wealth, thus of their individual status, and what each of them has therefore brought to their marriage in terms of material goods and, by extension, of prestige. So heated does this conversation become that a decision is made to conduct a census of the possessions of each, and these are duly paraded before the sparring couple.

> ... the lowliest of their possessions were brought out, to see who had more property and jewels and precious things; their buckets and tubs and iron pots, jugs and wash-pails and vessels with handles. Then their finger-rings, bracelets, thumb-rings and gold treasures were brought out, and their cloth of purple, blue, black, green and yellow, plain grey and many-coloured, yellow-brown, checked and striped.[16]

Duly listed by the storyteller, the goods were compared like with like until the process reached its end, with both Ailill and Medb equal in goods owned and thus in prestige possessed. All their beasts from the fields far and near were now collected, brought in, counted and compared; flocks of sheep, teams and herds of horses, their pigs, herds of cattle and so on. Again those of the queen matched those of the king animal by animal. That was until the king produced his final animal, the champion stud bull *Finnbennach* – 'the White Horned'. At this point the queen admitted defeat, albeit temporarily, for she had no equivalent creature to match with Finnbennach. Thus was set in train the bloody cattle raid which forms the main narrative of the story, as Queen Medb dispatches forces to Ulster to steal *Donn Cuailnge* – 'the Brown Bull of Cuailnge', a bull that will be more than a match for her husband's one.

Moving many centuries forward in time, the solid and ubiquitous material culture of Victorian Britain, a society so perfectly described by Henry James as 'the Empire of Things', can be evoked no better than through the writings of Dickens, Thackeray, or indeed James himself. In his book *The Spoils of Poynton*,[17] James recounts a story centred, rather like the *Táin*, on the battle between two individuals over material goods, in this case between the widowed Mrs Gereth and her son Owen, over the contents of the stately home of Poynton Park, the family home that Owen had inherited on the death of his father. To Mrs Gereth, now no longer the chatelaine of the house, the things in it 'were ... the sum of the world'.[18] For her 'the old golds and brasses, old ivories and bronzes, the fresh old tapestries and deep old damasks threw out a radiance in which [she] saw in solution all her old loves and patiences, all her old tricks and triumphs'.[19] The contents of the house were not merely an assemblage of artefacts but were rather to Mrs Gereth 'the record of a life ... written in great syllables of colour and form, the tongues of other countries and the hands of rare artists';[20] for their very essence could not be captured or tamed in an inventory for it was rather embodied in 'a presence, a perfume, a touch'.[21] Mrs Gereth's younger companion Fleda shares her love of the house's contents for themselves rather than for their undoubted monetary value. However, to Owen Gereth and his fiancée the house's contents hold no such memories and triggered no such nostalgia; they were just valuable items and nothing more. Not recognising Mrs Gereth's emotional attachment to some items she has taken from Poynton to furnish her new home, Mona, the fiancée, demands and gets their return to Poynton. There all the contents of the house are later consumed in an accidental fire, along with Poynton itself.

A different approach to the material world can be seen in my third and final fictional example of consumers interacting with material goods. Georges Perec's novel *Les Choses*, translated as *Things: A Story of the Sixties*,[22] is an experimental novel in which the book's protagonists, Jerome and Sylvie, are realised and their characters defined almost entirely through an examination of their relationship with material culture. Their elevation from a bohemian student existence to the world of work was marked by an accompanying change in material circumstances and lifestyle: 'they ... burned what they had previously worshipped: the witches' mirrors, the chopping-blocks, those stupid little mobiles, the radiometers, the multi-coloured pebbles, the Hessian panels adorned with expressive squiggles'[23] and they moved on to acquiring objects 'which only the taste of the day decreed to be beautiful: imitation Epinal pseudo-naive cartoons, English-style etchings, agates, spun-glass tumblers, neo-primitive paste jewellery, para-scientific apparatus'.[24] Later in the novel, out of work, they leave France and take up teaching posts in Tunisia. While still surrounded by their possessions, the material paraphernalia that had previously given their lives meaning now seemed curiously alienating in a new environment and though it still 'exuded a little warmth' it was more of a barrier than a bridge between cultures. Their host culture did not entice them and they bought nothing 'because they did not feel drawn to these things'. In essence 'it was wanting that had been all their existence'.[25] Perec's plot, which at times reads rather like a psychological case study rather than a novel, particularly owes something to the then-fashionable work of anthropologists, sociologists, and consumer researchers, whose approaches to material culture through personal observation and interview provide a dimension alien to the kind of object-led study to which many archaeologists are by necessity restricted.

In each of the three fictional works discussed here there are quite marked differences in the ways in which the characters in the stories relate to material culture and how these relationships vary between individuals. In the *Táin*, goods equal status, power, and prestige, with an interesting gendered dimension to the competition for material supremacy. In *The Spoils of Poynton*, the value placed on the same goods by members of different generations in the same family differ significantly, demonstrating that relationships with material culture are not static or fixed, or indeed necessarily predictable. Value here is either emotionally defined or in financial terms, though once more the theme of power through possession is pursued. Perec attempts, in *Les Choses*, to show that what was central to his characters in terms of material possessions and what was incidental end up being more or less reversed. His investigation of the object as cultural sign or signifier was then a new phenomenon in fiction, though perhaps the best examples of an almost obsessive search into the ramifications of the object as symbol are to be found earlier, in the works of Franz Kafka, though these will not be considered here. Some writers use objects to create a stage setting in an unashamedly nostalgic manner which triggers, when successful, recognition and response in the reader. Perec uses objects in quite the opposite way; to make readers question their relationship with what are in the end just 'things' but 'things' that are so often imbued by us or by society with such power, status, or emotion that their acquisition and use open a window onto our souls.

A Fictional Object?

It would appear that fact and fiction have become inextricably merged in the various narratives surrounding the curious case of the Shepton Mallet silver Chi Rho amulet, found during excavations just outside the small Somerset town in the summer of 1990 (Plate 76). I must confess here to having some personal interest in the site, as I directed the archaeological field evaluation of the site in February–March 1990 and visited the site a number of times during the subsequent area excavation campaign of the summer, directed by my then-colleague Peter Leach. The amulet was discovered by excavator Quentin Hutchinson in an undisturbed Romano-British grave, according to one of the narratives. This grave had been identified during my evaluation but was not excavated at that stage. According to another narrative, the grave excavated by Quentin was not undisturbed, as he believed and still believes, but rather had been disturbed shortly before its excavation by him by the planting of the silver amulet in the grave by person or persons unknown. This second narrative was created retrospectively, in a piecemeal fashion over time, by a number of authorities. At the time of its excavation the find was in fact hailed as a spectacular discovery, unique in Roman Britain and indeed in the western empire. Here was an overtly Christian object buried with a middle-aged male, according to the specialist analysis of the skeleton from the grave, marking him out as a Christian figure, perhaps a priest, living and serving in a small late Roman community on the fringes of the empire. The date of the object was determined as being late Roman, perhaps as late as the fifth century, both on stylistic grounds and through the analysis of the site's archaeological sequence and a radiocarbon dating of bones from the skeleton from the burial. The finding of the amulet provided narrative ammunition for a small group of local protesters who had been opposed to the development on the site and understandably attracted the interest of the media and of the local churches. Indeed, so celebrated was this find that a replica was made of the amulet as a gift to George Carey when he left his post as Bishop of Bath and Wells to become Archbishop of Canterbury. Lord Carey wore the replica pendant around his neck at his inauguration at Westminster Abbey in 1991, thus stressing the Christian narrative relating to the find.

Doubts about the find were first raised on stylistic grounds, principally that the design of the Shepton pendant was remarkably similar, too similar it was said, in certain respects to a silver brooch from Sussex bought by the British Museum in the 1950s and without any detailed provenance. This might be thought to have been an unusual turnaround in archaeological reasoning, that an unprovenanced find was given primacy of place over an excavated find in an argument over authenticity. However, a preliminary analysis of the metal from which the Shepton amulet was made added to the confusion, as the silver was found to be 92.6 per cent pure, that is very close in composition to modern sterling silver. When a monograph detailing the results of the 1990 Shepton Mallet excavation was published in 2001,[26] the exemplary specialist report on the silver pendant by Catherine Johns was couched in careful terms that allowed the reader to appreciate the uniqueness of the object 'on the assumption that the amulet is late Roman' but at the same time to realise that there were doubts about the object. 'If it were a stray find, there would certainly be serious doubts about its antiquity, but in view of the archaeological context, it seems wise to keep an open mind, and hope that future discoveries may produce evidence which will resolve the apparent contradiction.'[27] The media soon became alerted to the question of the authenticity of the amulet and, aided by some unfortunate off-the-cuff and probably out-of-context comments from one archaeological authority, declared it to be a fake. The tone of some of the reporting was highly distressing for Quentin Hutchinson, the original finder of the amulet. His personal narrative of triumphant discovery and professional endeavour was now usurped by one in which he felt he was being linked to an elaborate, very clever hoax.

Despite the fact that neither the scientific analysis nor the stylistic parallels proved that the amulet was a fake and that the published report on the find could not have been more even-handed in the care taken to present the find, it was true to say that the Shepton amulet was now viewed as a discredited object. An old analysis of the silver content of the large silver plate known as the Corbridge *lanx* showed that this too consisted of 92.6 per cent silver and that the Shepton amulet therefore was not the only piece of late Roman silver from Britain that resembled sterling silver.[28]

However, the authenticity of the Corbridge *lanx*, probably part of a hoard found in the Tyne at Corbridge, has never been called into question.

A second, more detailed scientific investigation of the Shepton Mallet amulet took place in 2008 at Liverpool University, and showed that the Shepton amulet silver 'had a far greater correlation with modern, 19th century or later, refined silver' than with samples of Roman silver, making it '99%' certain that the Shepton amulet is a modern conceit planted as a hoax.[29] Again, the press release of this information created another flurry of media hoax narratives and heaped further distress on Quentin Hutchinson. Since then all has gone silent on this enigmatic object. It no longer has pride of place on display in Taunton Museum. It is never mentioned in the archaeological literature on Roman finds. Yet that 1 per cent of remaining doubt hopefully gives some solace to Quentin Hutchinson, whose archaeological professionalism should never have been called into doubt and subsumed into a quasi-fictional narrative about this find of someone else's creation.

Final Thoughts

Reflections on the role of material culture and identity in our lives and in past lives are important. Material goods can testify sometimes to instances of the bodying forth of order out of chaos. The very solidity of things, their physicality, can appeal to us beyond the purely sentimental, in as much as they embody time and on occasions they can be personally, socially, or culturally symbolic in some way or they can be made to be.

When this survey was first envisaged it was hoped that the study and discussion of certain types of finds from Roman Britain and of various ideas linked to certain finds would contribute towards a better understanding of life in the province, though in some instances the more we try to understand some aspects of life in Roman Britain perhaps the less we do. I have deliberately eschewed a typological approach to the finds discussed in this book, for this was never intended to be a catalogue of any kind. I have also avoided trying to discuss every category of find that comes from Roman Britain, which would have made for a considerably longer book, and I have also quite deliberately not created a single, overarching narrative of daily life, for instance, around which discussion of finds can be fitted. Rather, the structure of the book has evolved over a number of years in tandem with my archaeological career and interests; an interest in material culture and consumer behaviour led on to an interest in how objects and ideas often circulated in tandem, in the past as in today. The study of finds and artworks in general from religious sites in turn led on to a particular interest in anatomical *ex votos* and that in turn led me to think about fragmentation of objects. Trying to understand ancient perceptions of the body led me to consider the definition of self in the past, both in terms of an individual's self-definition and that of society more broadly, and that interest also grew out of my fascination with the Romans' depiction of barbarian peoples and their views of those who were viewed as other or somehow marginal.

The relationship between consumers and the goods they consumed in Roman Britain is a subject that is about so much more than trade and economics, and discussion of this theme above has centred on the processes that might have led to the acquisition of new goods and the possible motives behind that acquisition, as well as on the patterns behind the way new goods were taken up within Romano-British society. The consumption of goods in the Roman world was linked to complex systems in place there for interpreting visual information, mainly religious signs and symbols, encoded in some objects, and mnemonic systems for accessing such information have also been discussed.

Another major theme of the book has been the way in which religious sites in Roman Britain functioned as centres for the management of fear in that society at certain times; fear of illness or death, fear of infertility, fear of theft and crime, fear of social exclusion, fear of the gods, and fear of not finding the favour of the gods. These themes were pursued through discussion of the artefacts found at two excavated temple sites in Roman Britain at West Hill, Uley, Gloucestershire and Orton's Pasture, Rocester, Staffordshire and by the analysis of the small number of medical or anatomical *ex votos* found at Romano-British temple sites. The discussion of the significance of prehistoric flint and stone tools reused in Romano-British ritual and religious contexts, and especially of those found at Ivy Chimneys, Witham, Essex, centred on the way in which the past and the ancestors may have been evoked by the deposition of such items at temple sites. Fear of dislocation from the ancestors may well have led to such attempts to conflate past and present by ritual action.

The role played by Romano-British urban centres in the creation and dissemination of written and visual culture, and of the arts and ideas more generally, was discussed at some length above. Urban art and Roman imperial ideology were inextricably linked, and the large towns and cities of Roman Britain acted as centres for the dissemination of ideas that underpinned the empire. Social memory, culture, and ideology met and overlapped here, and male display perhaps linked ideas of masculinity with those of power and empire. The apparent lack, though, of benevolent individuals sponsoring the upkeep of the towns of Roman Britain raises the issue of whether personal aggrandisement or the celebration of the individual in this way were anathema to the upper echelons of Romano-British society. Following on from this, an examination was made of partial objects and images from Roman Britain and what this might again tell us about how individuals viewed themselves and their bodies in that society. The significance of the fragmented image or artefact was also discussed in its broader geographical, chronological, and cultural context in the Roman world, indicating considerable differences between the centre and the periphery. Ideas of the self and of the other in Roman Britain were discussed with regard to what objects can tell us about self-definition at this time and about the possible marginalisation of certain groups in society, including black Africans, the elderly, and the disabled, though it has been shown that insisting on the marginalisation of such groups in

Roman Britain might simply be a reflection of a modern ambivalence towards their academic study. The book has concluded with a return to the consideration of ideas around concepts of consumers and consumption and how objects and ideas have been shown to interact in the world of goods that was Roman Britain.

There are some themes just touched upon in this book which surely merit more in-depth researching by someone in the future. I have barely been able to do anything other than skim the surface of these topics above, and each would surely merit a book in their own right. These topics include: an exploration of the special position of the sick in Romano-British society, a temporary or permanent state which placed them on society's margins as other; an examination of the way in which self was defined in parts of the province and how this related to views on the body, on personal hygiene, and on grooming; an exploration of how a sense of writing and portraying the self helped focus on those who were perceived perhaps as being other in Roman Britain; and, finally, an examination of the creation, manipulation, and maintenance of male identity through the demonstration of individual affinity with hyper-masculine figures such as the gladiator and the god Hercules and by the use of phallic symbolism.

To return once more, though, to the writings of James Deetz in *In Small Things Forgotten*, from which I quoted towards the very start of this book, his words on artefacts in America could just as well apply to those from Roman Britain:

> Material culture may be the most objective source of information we have concerning America's past. It certainly is the most immediate. When an archaeologist carefully removes the earth from the jumbled artefacts at the bottom of a trash pit, he or she is the first person to confront those objects since they were placed there centuries before. When we stand in the chamber of a seventeenth-century house that has not been restored, we are placing ourselves in the same architectural environment occupied by those who lived there in the past. The arrangement of gravestones in a cemetery and the designs on their tops create a *Gestalt* not of our making but of the community whose dead lie beneath the ground. If we bring to this world, so reflective of the past, a sensitivity to the meaning of the patterns we see in it, the artifact becomes a primary source of great objectivity and subtlety.[30]

This present book has tried to demonstrate how close readings of the contexts of certain types of small finds from archaeological excavations, archaeological surveys, and sometimes metal-detector surveys can enable certain aspects of the past history and use of objects in Roman Britain to be reconstructed in terms of writing biographies of those objects. Recognising that some types of objects had an emotional currency in the past, as they do today, allows us to do more than just locate them as props in the quotidian routine of a past, dead society. Rather, forging an understanding of the ways in which the circulation of objects and ideas in the province took place and how they were inextricably interrelated allows some sense to be made of the nature of this world of goods.

ACADEMIC NOTES

Preface

1. Deetz original edition 1977, expanded and revised edition 1996.
2. Deetz 1996, pp. 259–60.
3. Colchester: Crummy 1983; South Shields: Allason-Jones and Miket 1984; York: Cool *et al.* 1995; Aldborough: Bishop 1996; and Castleford: Cool and Philo 1998.
4. Crummy 1983.
5. Cool *et al.* 1995.
6. Shepton Mallet: Leach 2001; Castleford: Cool and Philo 1998; and Binchester: Ferris 2010.
7. Shepton Mallet: Leach 2001; Orton's Pasture, Rocester: Ferris *et al.* 2000; and Binchester: Ferris 2010. Other useful studies on spatial analysis of Roman finds are Allison 2008 and Hoffman 1995.
8. Iron objects: Manning 1976 and 1985; earrings: Allason-Jones 1989b; jet: Allason-Jones 1996; toilet implements: Eckardt and Crummy 2008; cosmetic grinders: Jackson 2010; brooches: Mackreth 2011; *intaglios*: Henig 1974 and 1978; and jewellery: Johns 1996. The general books are de la Bédoyère 1989 and Allason-Jones 2011.
9. The literature on material culture studies, use-life, and biographies of objects is vast and only a small selection of references can be given here. See, for example: Allison 1999; Appadurai 1986, especially Kopytoff 1986; Baudrillard 1968; Beaudry 2009; Clarke *et al.* 1985; Connor 2010; Csikszentmihalyi and Rochberg-Halton 1981: Deetz 1996; Douglas and Isherwood 1978; Fine 2002; Gosden and Marshall 1999; Heckler 1989; Hodder 1989; Hoskins 1998 and 2006; Karklins 2000; Lubar and Kingery 1993; MacGregor 2010; Mack 2007; Miller 1995; Myers 2001; Tilley 1991 and 1999; and Tilley *et al.* 2006.
10. MacGregor 2010; de Waal 2010.
11. Bonnichsen 1973.
12. On finds and daily life see Liversidge 1968. For thematic studies see de la Bédoyère 1989 and Allason-Jones 2011. The volume Hingley and Willis 2007 takes a more wide-ranging and theoretical approach to the study of Roman finds.

Chapter 1: A World of Goods

1. On consumption see Preface Note 9 above, but particularly Csikszentmihalyi and Rochberg-Halton 1981 and Douglas and Isherwood 1978. On historical consumption, particularly in the early modern period see, for instance: Berg 2004; Breen 1986; Brewer and Porter 1994; Casimiro 2011; Cocks 1989; Courtney 1996; Deetz 1996; Vickery 1994; and Weatherill 1986 and 1996. On consumers, consumer choice, and consumption in Roman Britain specifically see Ferris 1995 and Martins 2005.
2. Douglas and Isherwood 1978, p. 57.
3. Douglas and Isherwood 1978, p. 60.
4. Csikszentmihalyi and Rochberg-Halton 1981, p. 43.
5. Weatherill 1996.
6. On the contents of Pompeian households see Allison 2004 and 2009 and Berry 1997. On reconstructing household inventories in Ancient Greece see Cahill 2010. The quotation is from Berry 1997, p. 195.

7.   Weatherill 1996, p. 3.
8.   Weatherill 1996, p. 3.
9.   Millett 1990a, p. 98–9 on Samian in Britain in general and Griffiths 1989 on Northamptonshire specifically.
10. Griffiths 1989.
11. Henig 1998.
12. Evans 1988 and Chapter 5, pp. 102–103.
13. Weatherill 1996, p. 45.
14. Weatherill 1996, p. 67.
15. Higham 1989, p. 153.
16. Millett 1990b.
17. Blagg 1980 and Evans 1988, pp. 331–3.
18. Bennett 1983, p. 217.
19. Higham 1989, p. 169.
20. Higham 1989, p. 160.
21. Allason-Jones 1991, p. 3.
22. Hingley 1989, pp. 145–7.
23. Lewis 1959.
24. Reece 1990, p. 32.
25. On Maidenbrook see Ferris 1993 and on Whitley Grange see Gaffney and White 2007, pp. 95–142.
26. Leech 1982.
27. Gaffney and White 2007, p. 139.
28. Fanon 1961, p. 179.
29. Boon 1986, p. 240.
30. Quintilian *Institutio Oratoria* 4.223.
31. Spence 1984, 3. Also on Ricci see Laven 2011.
32. Spence 1984, p. 9–10.
33. Bourdieu 1972, p. 88.
34. Hutchinson 1986a and 1986b.
35. March 1998, p. 136.
36. Hutchinson 1986a and 1986b.
37. Hutchinson 1986a, p. 6.
38. Hutchinson 1986a catalogue entries: Ge-151, p. 514 (Wroxeter *intaglio*); Me pp. 99–101, pp. 306–7 (London spoons); Me 75, pp. 274–5 (Walker mount); Ge-141, p. 510 (Corbridge *intaglio*); and Ge-142, p. 510 (Caister by Yarmouth *intaglio*).
39. Hutchinson 1986a, p. 14.
40. Ferris *et al.* 2000 and Chapter 2, pp. 44–58.
41. Hutchinson 1986a, pp. 96–101.
42. Hutchinson 1986a, pp. 112–3.
43. Barrett 1993, p. 237.
44. Connerton 1986, p. 19.
45. Le Goff 1992.
46. Purcell 1990, p. 13.
47. Purcell 1990, p. 21.
48. Woolf 1994.

Chapter 2: A World of Gods

1.   On dedication and the vow in Roman religion see, for instance, Derks 1995 and Webster 1986.
2.   On the Fossdyke Mars see, for instance: Henig 1984, p. 51 and 54 and 1995, 126–7; Lindgren 1980, pp. 107–8; and Toynbee 1962, p. 131 and 1964, p. 66.
3.   RIB 274.
4.   Colchester: RIB 2432.8; Caister-on-Sea: RIB 2432.2; and Brancaster: RIB 2432.5.
5.   On *lararia* in Britain see Boon 1983. On Pompeian *lararia* see, for instance, Orr 1978 and 1988.

6.   Woodward 1992, p. 66–7.
7.   Tomlin 2002, pp. 170–1.
8.   Whitehouse 1996.
9.   Wait 1985.
10.   Woodward 1992, pp. 66–7.
11.   See principally Green 1975 and Kiernan 2009.
12.   Walker, D. R., *The Roman Coins in Cunliffe* (1988), pp. 281–358, especially pp. 295–7.
13.   On brooches and religion in general see principally: Johns 1995; Mackreth 2011, pp. 241–2; and Simpson and Blance 1998.
14.   Mackreth 2011, Plate 30 No. 9995.
15.   Johns 1995 and 1996, pp. 170–80; Mackreth 2011, pp. 154–88; and Simpson and Blance 1998, pp. 275–7.
16.   Crummy 2007.
17.   Crummy 2007, p. 225.
18.   Ferris 1986. But also on horse-and-rider brooches see: Fillery-Travis Forthcoming; Johns 1995, pp. 104–5 and 1996, p. 174; Mackreth 2011, pp. 181–2; and Simpson and Blance 1998, p. 275.
19.   For the two principal types see Ferris 1986; Fillery-Travis Forthcoming suggests many more sub-types; Mackreth 2011, pp. 181–3 recognises five types.
20.   Ferris 1986, pp. 2–4.
21.   Fillery-Travis: Forthcoming.
22.   The distribution map was drawn by Ruth Fillery-Travis and will appear in Fillery-Travis: Forthcoming.
23.   Fillery-Travis: Forthcoming.
24.   Ferris 1986, pp. 7–8 and Mackreth 2011, pp. 181–2.
25.   On Samian ware see Henig 1998; on Nene Valley hunt cups see Perring 1977, pp. 262–3 Fig. 10.6 a and c; on Colchester products see Perring 1977, p. 262, p. 265 Fig. 10.8 c, p. 266 Fig. 10.9 a and c; and on the Bath relief see Toynbee 1964, p. 143 and Plate XXXVIIIa.
26.   On the Wint Hill bowl see: Henig 1995, p. 143, p. 145 Plate 87; and Toynbee 1962, pp. 185–6 No. 142 and Plate 161.
27.   On the Scargill Moor shrine see Richmond and Wright 1949 and RIB 732, 733, and 737; other altar fragments RIB 735, 736, and 738.
28.   Greenfield 1963; Henig 1984, p. 51; and Taylor 1963.
29.   Martlesham-Ambrose and Henig 1980 and Henig 1984, p. 51; Willingham Fen: Henig 1984, pp. 51–3, Taylor 1963 and Toynbee 1964, p. 119; Brough: Johns 1990a; Bourne: Johns 1990a; Westwood Bridge: Toynbee 1964, p. 119; Stow Cum Quy: PAS SF-99E3E4 *Britannia* XXXVIII, pp. 328–30; and Lincolnshire: PAS YORYM-C2A231. Stragglethorpe: Ambrose and Henig 1980 and Henig 1984, pp. 51–3.
30.   Hargrave 2009.
31.   Ferris 1994, pp. 24–5 and Ferris 2000, pp. 155–60.
32.   The origins of this motif are discussed in Bergmann 1990 and Ferris 2000, p. 159 and sources listed in p. 197 Notes 29–31. Subsequent to this see Dimitrova 2002.
33.   Chapter 5, pp. 109–113.
34.   RIB 3172.
35.   The account of the excavations at West Hill, Uley is based on Woodward and Leach 1993, supplemented in places by information from Woodward 1992 and, to a lesser extent, Smith 2001, pp. 107–16. The account of the excavations at Orton's Pasture, Rocester is based on Ferris *et al.* 2001.
36.   Tomlin 2002, p. 174.
37.   Woodward and Leach 1993, pp. 327–31.
38.   Esmonde Cleary and Ferris 1996.
39.   J. Cooper in Esmonde Cleary and Ferris 1996, pp. 134–6. See also Bevan 1999.
40.   Wheeler and Wheeler 1936, pp. 190–3, pp. 200–2.
41.   Wheeler and Wheeler 1936, pp. 118–20.
42.   Monaghan 1997, pp. 858–9.
43.   Wedlake 1982, pp. 244–5.
44.   Isserlin 1994.
45.   Dorrington and Legge 1985, pp. 122–34.

46. Murphy *et al.* 2000.
47. On Newstead see: Curle 1911; Clarke 1994, 1997, and 1999; and Clarke and Jones 1994. On Castleford see Cool and Philo 1998.
48. Clarke and Jones 1994, p. 119.
49. Cool and Philo 1998, p. 362.
50. Wilmott 1991.
51. Merrifield 1987.
52. Merrifield 1987, pp. 38–40. On the Piercebridge ritual ploughman see Mann 1975, p. 23.
53. Drury 1986, pp. 62–4 and Fig. 3.7.
54. Derks 1998, pp. 150–2.
55. Henig 1984, pp. 33–4.
56. Uley: Woodward and Leach 1993, pp. 241–9; Henley Wood: Watts and Leach 1996, pp. 120–6.
57. Henig 1986, pp. 93–5.
58. Scargill Moor: see Chapter 2 Note 27 above; Bollihope Common: RIB 1041.
59. Derks 1998, pp. 134–44.
60. Hutchinson 1986a, p. 23 and Chapter 1, pp. 25–29.
61. Hutchinson 1986a, p. 26.
62. Parallels for the environmental data from Orton's Pasture, provided in the report by A. Monckton, were up to date to 2000.
63. The Llys Awel material is presently unpublished and in the National Museums of Wales collections, Cardiff.
64. For a discussion on the iconography of images of dogs in Roman Britain and the Roman world more widely, and a bibliography on the subject, see Ferris In Press.

Chapter 3: The Comfort of Strangers

1. Jackson 1988, p. 138.
2. RIB 1028; Hooppell 1891, pp. 28–9 and Ferris 2011b, p. 35.
3. Wait 1985.
4. Bradley 1990.
5. Wait 1985, p. 186.
6. Green 1975.
7. Van Straten 1981.
8. Van Straten 1981, p. 105.
9. Ferris 1999a.
10. See, for instance, Potter 1985 and Blagg 1985 and 1986.
11. Henig in Cunliffe 1988, p. 8.
12. Bath: Henig in Cunliffe 1988, p. 8 Nos. 4–5, Fig. 4 Nos. 4–5; Lamyatt Beacon: Leech 1986, pl. XXXIV B; West Hill, Uley: Woodward and Leach 1993, p. 100 Nos. 7–9, p. 101 Fig. 88 Nos. 7–9, p. 107 No. 1, p. 108 Fig. 94 No. 1; Lydney: Wheeler and Wheeler 1932, p. 87 No. 105, Fig. 21 No. 105, p. 89 Nos. 121 and 122, Plate XXVI Nos. 121 and 122; Wroxeter: Painter 1971 and Barker *et al.* 1997; Springhead: Penn 1964, Fig. 10 No. 5, pl. 1B, and pl. 1A; and Verulamium: Hazel Simons personal communication.
13. Muntham Court: Bedwin 1980, p. 192; Woodeaton, plaque: Kirk 1949, p. 38, Fig. 8 No. 7; child's foot: Bagnall Smith 1995, p. 181; Winchester: P. Barker personal communication; Harlow: Britannia 1991, p. 262; and Segontium: Casey and Davies 1993, p. 210 No. 512.
14. The Arbeia plaster eyes are unpublished. Details were kindly provided by Alex Croom. West Wight head: Bagnall Smith *et al.* 2003; Caistor St Edmund eye: PAS NMS835; Market Lavington eye: PAS WILT-1F1EB2; North Kesteven finger: PAS LIN-A80353; Hambleden arm and hand: PAS LON-B3AB11; South Cambridgeshire foot: PAS CAM-6C84E2; Berkshire foot sole: PAS BERK-98EFC8. The discounted PAS finds are respectively as follows: an ear from Brompton on Swale, Yorkshire: PAS YORYM-08CBC4; a foot from Wallington, Hertfordshire: PAS BH-F35CB3; a foot and leg from Barnetby Le Wold, Lincolnshire: PAS NLM120; a lower leg from Broadland, Norfolk: NMS-3CECC3; a foot, leg and calf from Whittington, Northumberland: PAS NCL-BD0923; a leg and foot from Fulford, Yorkshire:

PAS SWYOR-7714D4; a foot from Coddenham, Suffolk: PAS SF-CDD3E6; a foot and ankle from Colerne, Wiltshire: PAS WILT-1A26D5; an arm and hand from Aldborough, Yorkshire: PAS LUPL-E01531; an arm from Packenham, Suffolk: PAS SF6092; a hand from Wenhaston with Mells, Suffolk: PAS SF11000; and a finger tip from Offenham, Worcestershire: PAS WMID4313.

15. Allason-Jones and McKay 1985 Nos. 35–7.
16. Toynbee 1964, pp. 63–4 No. 4.
17. Allason-Jones and McKay 1985, p. 37.
18. Webster 1983, pp. 16–20.
19. Webster 1983, p. 15.
20. Merrifield 1977 and 1987, pp. 96–106.
21. Frere 1972, p. 144 Nos. 156 and 157.
22. Evans 2000, pp. 300–2.
23. Deyts 1994, p. 15.
24. Potter 1985.
25. Sigerist 1977, pp. 390–1.
26. Allason-Jones 1989a, p. 157.
27. Henig in Cunliffe 1988, p. 8.
28. Henig in Cunliffe 1988, p. 29.
29. Wheeler and Wheeler 1932, p. 89.
30. Bathurst 1879, Plate XXI No. 3.
31. Toynbee 1964, p. 361–2.
32. L. Bevan in Leach 1998, pp. 88–90. On the hair/hairpin dedication L. Bevan personal communication.
33. Britannia XL 2009, pp. 353–4.
34. RIB II.3, 2423.1 and *Britannia* 1996, p. 27, p. 443 No. 10.
35. Bath: Tomlin in Cunliffe 1988, No. 97; Lydney: Wheeler and Wheeler 1932, p. 100; and London: RIB 7.
36. Tomlin in Cunliffe 1988, p. 62.
37. Henig in Woodward and Leach 1993.
38. Barker *et al.* 1997.
39. Painter 1971.
40. Wacher 1974, p. 298.
41. MacMullen 1981, p. 49.
42. Gancel 2001.
43. Bush and Zvelebil 1991, p. 5.
44. Webster 1986, p. 58.
45. Tomlin in Cunliffe 1988.
46. Landy 1977, p. 388.
47. Durkheim 1961.
48. Scheff 1979, p. 128.
49. Corbrier 1991, p. 170.
50. Van Straten 1981, p. 112.
51. Sigerist 1977, p. 389.
52. Van Straten 1981, pp. 112–3.
53. Van Straten 1981, p. 115.
54. Van Straten 1981, p. 122.
55. Van Straten 1981, pp. 124–5.
56. MacMullen 1981, pp. 59–60.
57. Van Straten 1981, p. 144 and MacMullen 1981, p. 159 No. 79.
58. Van Straten 1981, pp. 144–5.
59. Van Straten 1981, p. 99 and Blagg 1986a, p. 218 No. 7.
60. Van Straten 1981, p. 96.
61. Van Straten 1981, p. 115.
62. Webster 1986, p. 60.
63. On Ponte di Nona see Potter 1985 and on Nemi see Blagg 1985 and 1986 and Nottingham Museums 1983.
64. Martin 1965 and Deyts 1983 and 1985.

65. See Merrifield 1987, pp. 88–90 for British examples, de Beauvoir 1965, p. 573 for more contemporary usage in Brazil, and Johns 1982, p. 24 for examples of wax votive phalluses from eighteenth-century Naples.
66. Van Straten 1981, p. 75.
67. Merrifield 1987, pp. 88–90.
68. Henig 1978, p. 110.
69. Scott 1991.
70. Croxford 2003.
71. *Contra* Merleau: Ponty, as quoted in Meskell 2000, p. 16.
72. Pacteau 1994, p. 61.

Chapter 4: Discovered Under Other Skies

1. For the history of the debate about the contexts of prehistoric tools found on Romano-British sites see, in chronological order: Adkins and Adkins 1985; Bradley 1986 (*contra* Adkins and Adkins); Merrifield 1987 (*pro* Adkins and Adkins); Ferris and Smith 1985; and Eckardt 2004, pp. 41–2.
2. Turner and Wymer 1987, pp. 48–52 and Turner 1999, p. 107.
3. Turner and Wymer 1987, p. 49.
4. Turner 1999, p. 107.
5. Turner and Wymer 1987, p. 54.
6. Turner 1999, p. 107.
7. M. J. Green in Turner 1999, p. 257.
8. Turner 1999, p. 107, p. 244.
9. F. Healey in Turner 1999, pp. 107–10.
10. Turner 1999, p. 89 No. 69, Figure 62.
11. Turner 1999, p. 90 No. 70, Plate XXI and Figure 62.
12. Turner 1999, p. 90 No. 72, Plate XXI and Figure 62.
13. G. Webster in Turner 1999, pp. 112–5, Plate XXIV and Figure 78.
14. Turner 1999, p. 193 No. 8, Figure 125.
15. R-M. Luff in Turner 1999, p. 223.
16. Rodwell 1988, p. 55.
17. Rodwell 1988, p. 55, p. 136.
18. King and Soffe 1998, p. 41.
19. Lynne Bevan personal communication.
20. Adkins and Adkins 1985.
21. Bradley 1986.
22. Evans *et al.* 2000.
23. L. Bevan in Evans *et al.* 2000, pp. 66–7, Figure 44.
24. Adkins and Adkins 1985.
25. Philpott 1991.
26. Philpott 1991, pp. 163–4.
27. Meaney 1981.
28. Britannia 1981.
29. Britannia 1988.
30. Philpott 1991, p. 164 and Field 1965.
31. Green 1976, p. 192, p. 301 Plate XX and Cunliffe and Fulford 1982, pp. 37–8 No. 137 and Plate 35 No. 137.
32. Horne and King 1980.
33. Turner 1999, p. 107.
34. Horne and King 1980.
35. As with Eckhardt 2004, p. 41.
36. Hingley 2009.
37. R. Hingley personal communication.
38. Hingley 2009, p. 143.
39. Stead 1998 and Hingley 2009, p. 150.

40. Foster 1986 and Hingley 2009, pp. 154–5.
41. Hayling Island: Hingley 2009, p. 156; Ashwell: Hingley 2009, p. 149, p. 159 Note 19; Sheepen: The Colchester Archaeologist 1999 No. 12, pp. 8–9; and Harlow: n.d. East of England Archaeological Research Framework online The Roman Period, p. 60.
42. Kiernan 2010, p. 146 and Merrifield 1987, p. 15.
43. Robinson 1995 and Kiernan 2010, pp. 118–9.
44. Hingley 2009, p. 159 Note 14.
45. Kiernan 2010, p. 119.
46. Kiernan 2010, p. 143, pp. 145–8. Kiernan (2010, p. 145 Note 90) misrepresents the balance of evidence for occurrence of prehistoric stone tools at British and Gallic sites. The phenomenon is still more clearly pronounced in Gaul on present evidence when context is primary.
47. On Jupiter and thunderstones and on elfshot see, for instance Henig 1984, pp. 188–9, Merrifield 1987, pp. 10–16, and Kiernan 2010, pp. 146–8.
48. Pliny the Elder *Naturalis Historia* 37, pp. 134–5.
49. Courlander 1960.
50. Courlander 1960, p. 21.
51. Paine 2004, p. 88. See also Gollán 1977 on amulets.
52. Paine 2004, p. 88.
53. Pomian 1990, p. 22. On collecting see also, for instance, Blom 2002 and Forrester 1998.
54. Pomian 1990.
55. Pomian 1990, p. 5.
56. Baudrillard 1968, p. 49.
57. Turner and Wymer 1987, p. 54.
58. Turner and Wymer 1987, pp. 54–5.
59. Davies 1937, Sunter and Woodward 1987, and Martingell 2003, p. 93.
60. C. Conneller in Garrow *et al.* 2006, pp. 129–30.
61. Martingell 2003.
62. C. Conneller in Garrow *et al.* 2006, p. 130.
63. Young and Humphrey 1999 and Humphrey and Young 2003. *Contra* Saville 1981.
64. Cool n.d.
65. Cool *et al.* 1995, Miles 1977, and Pollard and Baker 1999.
66. Clarke *et al.* 1985.
67. Bradley 1987. The literature on archaeology and memory and archaeologies of memory is vast and ever-growing. See also, for instance: Alcock 2001 and 2002; Alcock and Van Dyke 2003; Baroin 2010; Barrett 1993; Boardman 2002; Bradley 2002; Bradley and Williams 1998; Caple 2006; Connerton 1989; Damgaard Andersen 1993; Dasen 2010; Dasen and Späth 2010; Dupont 1987; Eckardt 2004; Farrell 1997; Flower 1996; Forcey 1998; Fulford 2001; Gehrke 2001 and 2010; Giuliani 2010; Hallam and Hockey 2001; Harrison 2003; Haskell 1993; Haug 2001; Hingley 2011; Le Goff 1992; Lucas 2005; Rowlands 1993; Roymans 1995; Schnapp 1996; Small 1997; Small and Tatum 1995; Spence 1985; Van Dyke and Alcock 2003; Williams 1998a, 1998b, 2003 and 2004; Woodward 1993; and Yegüul 2000.
68. Mayor 2000.
69. Mayor 2000, p. 140.
70. Mayor 2000, p. 143.
71. Poulton and Scott 1993, p. 122.
72. Poulton and Scott 1993, p. 129.
73. Millett 1994.
74. Dark 1993.
75. Sanjuan *et al.* 2007.
76. Woodward 1992, pp. 22–30. See also Smith 2001, p. 163.
77. Smith 2001, pp. 150–1.
78. Eckardt 2009, pp. 83–4.
79. Hutton 2011.
80. Williams 1998a, p. 72.
81. Niblett 1999, p. 63.
82. Forcey 1998, p. 87.
83. Forcey 1998, p. 93 quoting Crummy 1997, pp. 27–8, pp. 102–7.

84. Hughes *et al.* 1995.
85. Chapman 2000 and Chapman and Gaydarska 2007.
86. White 1988.
87. Ferris 2010 and 2011b.
88. These stones came from excavations directed by the author at the former Owen Owen department store in central Shrewsbury, Shropshire in 1990 and 1991 and were found in deposits with later Anglo-Saxon pottery. Sadly the excavations are unpublished.
89. Williams 1998a, p. 78.
90. Tomlin 1995 and Chapter 5, pp. 106–107.
91. Eckardt 2004.

Chapter 5: Cities of Ideas

1. Wacher 1974 and 1995 and Burnham and Wacher 1990.
2. Greep 1993; Rogers 2011; Schofield and Leech 1987; and Todd 1989.
3. Burnham and Wacher 1990.
4. Brewer 1986; Coulston and Phillips 1988; Cunliffe and Fulford 1982; Henig 1993 and 2004; Huskinson 1994; Keppie and Arnold 1984; Phillips 1977; and Tufi 1983.
5. Merrifield 1977 and Henig 1978 and 2000.
6. Toynbee 1986.
7. Henig 1999.
8. Phillips 1976a.
9. Blagg 1989; Henig 1995; and Toynbee 1962 and 1964.
10. Smith 1969 and 1984 and Cosh 1998.
11. Henig 1995, p. 111.
12. Henig 1995, pp. 113–6.
13. Henig 1995, pp. 116–7 and Phillips 1976a.
14. Aitchison 1999.
15. Boatwright 2000b; Brogiolo and Ward Perkins 1999; Cornell and Lomas 1995; Favro 1996; Haussler 1999; Jones 1987; Jouffroy 1986; Laurence *et al.* 2011; Lomas 1995, 1997 and 1998; Mackie 1990; Parkins 1997; Revell 1999; Woolf 1995; Yegül 2000; and Zanker 1988 and 2000.
16. Whittaker 1997, p. 145.
17. Mackreth 1987 and Millett 1990a, p. 106.
18. Henig 1993, p. 24.
19. Mackreth 1987, p. 134.
20. Isserlin 1998, pp. 126–7.
21. Isserlin 1998, p. 132.
22. Bauchhenss and Noelke 1981.
23. Henig 1993, pp. 8–9 and Phillips 1976b.
24. Hutchinson 1986a and 1986b.
25. Derks 1998, pp. 105–9.
26. Derks 1998, p. 107.
27. Derks 1998, p. 107 Note 131.
28. Drury 1984.
29. MacMullen 1982.
30. Barrett 1993.
31. On the viewer in Roman art see, for instance, Elsner 1995.
32. Barrett 1993, pp. 236–7 and Ferris 1999b.
33. Henig 1984 and 1995.
34. Henig 1999.
35. Blagg 1990.
36. Haynes 2000, p. 91.
37. Esmonde Cleary 1987.
38. Smith 1984 and Neal 1981.
39. Davey and Ling 1981.

40. Ellis 1991 and Scott 1993 and 1995.
41. RIB 311.
42. Blagg 1990.
43. Millett 1977.
44. Millett 1977, pp. 292–3 Appendix 1.
45. Millett 1990a, p. 117, based on the work of Lindgren 1980.
46. Blagg 1983 and Hill *et al.* 1980.
47. Blagg 1983, p. 130.
48. London: Blagg 1983; Chester: Clay 2004.
49. Blagg 1983, p. 130.
50. Alchermes 1994.
51. Blagg 1983, p. 130.
52. Blagg 1983, p. 130.
53. Biro 1975.
54. RIB 311.
55. Blagg 1990.
56. Collingwood 1937.
57. Evans 1987.
58. Funari 1993.
59. London *graffito*: RIB 2503.100; Caerleon *graffito*: Wheeler and Wheeler 1928, p. 188 Plate XXXIII.4; Blackwardine *graffito*: RIB 2417.4; and Binchester *graffito*: Ferris 2010, p. 245 No. 14 and Fig. 71.14.
60. Leicester *graffito*: RIB 2447.28a-d; Alresford *graffito*: RIB 2447.1a; London *graffito*: RIB 2450.3; Silchester *graffito*: RIB 2447.39; Farmingham *graffito*: RIB 2491.79; and Colchester *graffito*: RIB 2491.157.
61. Willis 2005.
62. Willis 2005, pp. 103–7.
63. Hanson and Conolly 2002.
64. Andrews 2010 and Holmes 1995.
65. Bushe-Fox 1916, pp. 27–30.
66. Derks 1998, pp. 226–30.
67. Andrews 2010.
68. Holmes 1995.
69. Furger *et al.* 2009.
70. Derks and Roymans 2002 and 2006.
71. As Chapter 5 Note 63 above.
72. Tomlin 1995.
73. Barrett 1978.
74. James and Millett 2001, p. 2.
75. Millett 2001, p. 64.
76. See papers by Favro and Kellum in Bergmann and Kondoleon 1999.
77. Isserlin 1998.
78. D'Ambra 1993 and Kampen 1991a, 1991b, and 1994.
79. Eger 2007.
80. Kampen 2002, p. 7.
81. R. White unpublished manuscript report.
82. On gladiators in Britain see, for example, Jackson 2000 and Wilmott 2008. On the Latin sexual vocabulary see Adams 1987 and Richlin 1992a and b.
83. R. Ling in Crummy 1984, pp. 146–53 and Henig 1995, pp. 118–9.
84. Bignor mosaic, Eccles mosaic, and Brading mosaic: Henig 1995, p. 121 and p. 160; London figurines: Toynbee 1964, pp. 118–19; Lexden figurine: Jackson 2000, p. 4; London ceramic lamp: H. Eckardt in Allason-Jones 2011, p. 186; Corbridge clasp knife handle: PAS NCL-393023; Piddington clasp knife handle: Friendship-Taylor and Jackson 2001; South Shields ivory handle: Allason-Jones and Miket 1984, No. 6.2. Glass cups from London, Colchester, Wroxeter, Dorchester and Leicester: RIB 2419.22–4, pp. 26–8, pp. 31–5; and Vindolanda glass bowl: Wilmott 2008, Plate 28; Chester relief: Jackson 2000, pp. 2–3 and Wilmott 2008, p. 94; and Colchester plaque: Wilmott 2008, p. 101.
85. On the image of Herakles/Hercules in the ancient world see, for example, Uhlenbrock 1986.

86.   From the northern military zone; High Rochester: RIB 1284; Corbridge relief: Henig 1984, pp. 92–3; Rudchester statue: Toynbee 1964, p. 75; Housesteads altar: Toynbee 1964, p. 159; Housesteads figure: Toynbee 1964, p. 75; Netherby statue: Toynbee 1964, pp. 75–6; Chester gravestone: Henig 1995, p. 48; Birdoswald statuette: Henig 1984, pp. 210–1 and Toynbee 1964, p. 74; two South Shields figurines, Piercebridge figurine and unprovenanced figurine: Toynbee 1964, p. 74, Note 4; York figurine: Toynbee 1964, p. 75 Note 7 and Henig 1984, p. 201; Traprain Law bowl: Henig 1995, p. 163; and Capheaton skillet: Toynbee 1964, pp. 304–6 and Henig 1984, pp. 117–8. From the civilian parts of the province: Sibson statue: Toynbee 1964, p. 76 Note 1; Bath carving: Toynbee 1964, p. 153; Compton Dando carving: Toynbee 1964, p. 158 Note 4; Colerne carving: Toynbee 1964, p. 159; London bronze: Henig 1995, pp. 81–2; Ford Green figurine: Toynbee 1964, p. 73 Note 2; Bruton figurine: Toynbee 1964, pp. 74–5; East Anglian figurines from Ely, Sutton near Ely, Icklingham, and Colchester: Toynbee 1964, pp. 73–4 Notes 3–5; metal detector find from Suffolk: PAS ESS-B4CEF5; Verulamium figurines: Toynbee 1964, p. 75 Note 7; Bedfordshire figurine: PAS-BH-2259B6; Bramdean mosaic: Henig 1984, p. 177; Mildenhall dish: Toynbee 1964, p. 309 and G. Boon in Zienkiewicz 1986, pp. 157–66; Welshpool jug: Toynbee 1964, pp. 324–5; Caerleon strigil: Henig 1984, p. 179; Eccles ivory knife handle: Henig 1984, p. 179; Lincolnshire handle: PAS LIN-15BB58; Hertfordshire knife handle: PAS BH-A5EBE7; Reculver strigil handle: Henig 1984, p. 179; Hertfordshire head: PAS BH-C53040; small-scale representations of the club at Thetford, London, and Birdoswald: Henig 1984, p. 187; Ashstead, Kent: Henig 1995, p. 91; Nene Valley pottery: Henig 1995, p. 102, Toynbee 1964, p. 414, Welney: Toynbee 1964, pp. 414–5, Verulamium: Toynbee 1964, p. 415; Stibbington-cum-Sibson mould: Toynbee 1964, p. 402; and pipeclay figurine from child's grave at Colchester: Henig 1984, p. 201.
87.   Bedon *et al.* 1988; Drinkwater 1985; Kleiner 1998; and Woolf 1998 and 2000.
88.   Esperandieu 1907–66.
89.   Nicassio 1991.
90.   Rykwert 1975, p. 24.
91.   Metzler *et al.* 1995.
92.   Florida 2004, 2005a, 2005b, and 2008.
93.   See various sections of Gramsci 1971.
94.   Hannestad 1988 and Ferris 2000.
95.   Ferris 1995.

Chapter 6: *An Empire in Pieces*

1.   Forrester 1994, p. 227.
2.   Dubois 1996 and 1998 and Ellis 2000.
3.   Chapman 2000 and Chapman and Gaydarska 2007.
4.   See, for example: Brown 1988; Bynum 1992; Hallett and Skinner 1997; Halperin *et al.* 1990; Kampen 1996; Kampen *et al.* 2002; Koloski-Ostrow and Lyons 1997; Meskell 1998 and 2000; Montserrat 1998 and 2000; Rautman 2000; Rouselle 1988; and Wyke 1998.
5.   For example: Burrus 2000; Kampen *et al.* 2002; Kuefler 2001; and Walters 1997.
6.   Richlin 1992a and 1997, pp. 27–8.
7.   Dubois 1996 and 1998.
8.   Kristeva 1998.
9.   On the fragment in art history see Nochlin 1994, though also see Elsen 1969 and 1969–70 and Pingeot 1990. On Schwitters see Elderfield 1985.
10.   Dasen 1993; Dupont 1987; Flower 1996; and Rambaud 1978.
11.   On masks in the home see Dwyer 1982, and in funeral processions see Bodel 1999.
12.   Barr-Sharrar 1987.
13.   Beard and Henderson 2001, pp. 227–32; Flower 1996; Gazda 1973; Huskinson 2000; Nodelman 1975; and Walker 1985 and 1995.
14.   Stella *et al.* 1998, p. 71.
15.   Doxiadis 1995.
16.   Koortbojian 1996.
17.   Della Porta 1999, pp. 124–9.

18. Braithwaite 1984.
19. Chapter 3, pp. 66–67.
20. Arce *et al.* 1997, p. 408.
21. Stella *et al.* 1998, p. 48.
22. www.arch.cam.ac.uk/keros.
23. As Chapter 3 Note 22.
24. Ferris 1994, 1997, 2000, 2001, 2003a, and 2011a; Zanker 1998 and 2000a.
25. Ferris 1994 and 2000, pp. 114–5.
26. Ferris 2000, pp. 8–81.
27. Pollitt 1986, pp. 118–9.
28. On the games see Barton 1989 and 1993 and on judicial punishment see Coleman 1990 and MacMullen 1986.
29. Govi and Vitali 1988, p. 344.
30. MacMullen 1986, pp. 209–12.
31. Kinney 1997, Nylander 1998, and Varner 2000.
32. Pliny Panegyric 52.4.
33. Besançon 2001 and Sauer 2003.
34. Croxford 2003.
35. Woodward and Leach 1993, pp. 71–2.
36. Padgett 2001, pp. 92–3 and p. 251.
37. Kleiner 1992, p. 67.
38. Arce *et al.* 1997, p. 370.
39. Gregory 1994, p. 96.
40. Pollini 1993, p. 426.
41. See principally: Bronzi Dorati 1987; de Marinis 2002; de Marinis and Quiri 1999; Gattai and Poma 1987; Kleiner 1990; Luni 1988; Pollini 1993; and Stucchi 1960, 1987 and 1988.
42. On the equestrian statue of Marcus Aurelius see Knauer 1990, Torelli 1989, and Sommella 1990. On the Horses of San Marco see Pallottino *et al.* 1979, especially the chapter by Vlad *et al.* On the imperial portrait heads from Brescia see Stella 1998, p. 38.
43. Oddy *et al.* 1979, p. 182.
44. Pollini 1993, p. 425 and *contra* Pollini see Calvani 2002.
45. Pollini 1993.
46. Stucchi 1988, Fig. 102 and Pollini 1993, p. 424 Fig. 1. On the fifth figure see Pollini 1993, p. 431.
47. Pollini 1993, pp. 426–39.
48. On refuting imperial identifications see Pollini 1993, pp. 426–31 and de Marinis 2002, p. 42. On local aristocratic families see Coarelli 1998. On the Ahenobarbi see Pollini 1993, pp. 440–4. On Cicero see Böhn 2000 and *contra* Böhn see de Marinis 2002, p. 43.
49. Pollini 1993, p. 425.
50. Croxford 2003 and Ferris 2003b and 2005.
51. Sommella 1990, pp. 16–25. On the equestrian Augustus on coins see Brilliant 1963, p. 55. On equestrian images in general on coins see Hill 1989, pp. 66–71.
52. Wood 1999, p. 90 and Calvani 2002, p. 59.
53. Pollini 1993, pp. 438–9 Figs 17 and 18 and Liverani 2002, pp. 139–41.
54. Boatwright 1991, pp. 260–1 and pp. 268–9 Note 48 and Kleiner 1996.
55. On elite women and power see, for instance: Crook 1986; Lefkowitz 1983, p. 57; Saller 1994; and Van Bremen 1983 pp. 235–6. On Tettia Casta see MacMullen 1980, p. 164.
56. Vermeule 1968, p. 489; Van Bremen 1983, p. 236 and 1996; Boatwright 1991, 1993 and 2000, pp. 64–6; Newby 2003, pp. 200–1; and Rodgers 2003, p. 75.
57. Clay 2004.
58. Clay 2004, pp. 11–3.
59. Musgrave 1990, Bruni 2000, and Damgaard Andersen 1993.
60. Woodward 1993.
61. Biddle 1986; Brown 1981; Butler and Morris 1986; and Rollason 1986 and 1989.
62. Blom 2002.
63. Buvelot 2004.
64. Philpott 1991, pp. 77–89.
65. M. Atkinson conference presentation on Elms Farm, Heybridge.

66. Isserlin 1997.
67. Lloyd 1973, pp. 75–90.
68. Dunbabin 1986.
69. On the rite in general see Graham 2009 and 2011, and on the Lincoln burial see Graham *et al.* n.d.
70. Graham *et al.* n.d., p. 4.
71. Johns 1982 and Turnbull 1978.
72. Kellum 1996.
73. Bevan 1994 and Clarke 1996 and 1998.
74. Richlin 1997, p. 33.
75. Ling 1990.
76. British Museum collections online database PRB.P.1978.1.2 (Inv. No. 2210).
77. RIB 3358.
78. Johns 1982.
79. For example, Winter 1996.
80. Johns 1982, pp. 72–5.
81. Arce *et al.* 1997, p. 414.
82. Johns 1982, p. 68, Plate 51.
83. Bevan 1994, p. 42.
84. Chapter 7, p. 152.
85. Chapter 4, pp. 78–79.
86. Chapter 7, p. 152.
87. See, for instance, examples in Bevan 1994; Plouviez 2005; Turnbull 1978; and Webster 1989.
88. Brooch: Mackreth 2011, p. 182 and Plate 124 No. 7942; pin: Hall and Wardle 2005, pp. 174–5 and p. 178 Fig. 6; rings: Johns 1996, p. 12 Figure 1.3, p. 62; pendants and amulets: Green 1976, Plates XXV and XXVI, Green 1978, Plates 139–44, and Plouviez 2005. On East Anglia see Plouviez 2005.
89. On hand-and-phallus items in general see Greep 1983. On Catterick see Wilson 2002 Part II, p. 68 No. 244 and p. 70 Fig. 260.
90. Keppie and Arnold 1984, p. 37 Nos. 97–9 and Plate 28 Nos. 97–9. No. 97 is mainly discussed.
91. Plouviez 2005, pp. 159–60 and p. 158 Fig. 1 No. 8.
92. RIB 3172.
93. Henig 2004, p. 55 No. 168 and Plate 46.
94. Bevan 1994, p. 44, Turnbull 1978, and Webster 1989, p. 22.
95. Ferris 2000, p. 6.
96. Brisson 2002, pp. 8–22.
97. Deonna 1925 and Brisson 2002, pp. 18–21.
98. Kampen *et al.* 2002, p. 73.
99. Most 1992, especially pp. 395–6 and pp. 400–8. In addition, on Stoic stances see Sedley 1982.
100. Wilfong 1998, p. 116.
101. Adams 1987, Parker 1992, and Richlin 1992a.
102. Funari 1993, especially pp. 138–43.

Chapter 7: The Self and Others

1. As Chapter 5 Note 4 above.
2. RIB 558.
3. de Kind 2005.
4. Cunliffe and Fulford 1982, p. 5 No. 1 and Plate 1.
5. Huskinson 1994, pp. 14–5 No. 26 and Plate 13 No. 26.
6. Chapter 6.
7. Stewart 2003, pp. 174–9 and 2010.
8. Stewart 2010.
9. On tattoos in Roman society broadly see Jones, C. P. 1987. For Roman Britain, with reservations, see Carr 2005.

10. On cosmetic grinders see Jackson 2010. On toilet implements see Eckardt and Crummy 2006.
11. Eckardt and Crummy 2006.
12. Eckardt and Crummy 2006, pp. 21–4.
13. Eckardt and Crummy 2006, pp. 40–1.
14. Eckardt and Crummy 2006, pp. 65–8.
15. Philpott 1991, pp. 180–1 (combs), p. 182 (toilet implements), and pp. 182–3 (mirrors).
16. Derks and Wouter 2010.
17. Derks and Wouter 2010, Note 7.
18. Ferris 1995, 1997, 2000, 2001, 2002, 2003, 2006, 2009, and 2011.
19. Culham 1997.
20. Eckardt 2010.
21. Swan 1992, 1999, and 2009.
22. RIB 2042.
23. RIB 3445.
24. In 2004.
25. See, for instance, Hingley 2010 and Tollia-Kelly and Nesbitt 2009.
26. *Scriptores Historiae Augustae* 22.3–6.
27. RIB 1064.
28. See, for instance, Toynbee 1964, p. 119 and Plate XXXIIa where he is described as a barbarian.
29. Leicester steelyard weight: Toynbee 1964, p. 120, Plate XXXIIe; Wall statuette: Toynbee 1964, p. 356, Plate LXXXIc and Snowden 1976, p. 229, Plate 301; Bath statuette: Toynbee 1964, p. 356, Plate LXXXIb; Colchester amber head: Crummy 2010, p. 47 and p. 48 Fig. 9 No. 4; Bayford oil flask: British Museum 1964, p. 13 and p. 12 Fig. 5 No. 11 and Toynbee 1964, p. 327; London boxwood scoop: unpublished; and London ceramic lamp: Museum of London Acc. No. 1422.
30. Uttlesford, near Saffron Walden, Essex: PAS ESS-6F60D3 *Britannia* XXXVIII, pp. 331–2; South Oxfordshire: PAS BERK-34F754; Kings Sutton, Northamptonshire: PAS WMID-CFC578; and Bury, Greater Manchester: PAS LVPL114.
31. Caerleon: Toynbee 1964, pp. 379–80, Plate LXXXVIIb and c and Price 1974, p. 292; South Shields: Toynbee 1964, p. 379; London: Price 1974; Caersws and Camelon: J. Price personal communication.
32. Havari 2004.
33. London: British Museum online catalogue M.1073; Cirencester: McWhirr *et al.* 1982 Microfiche C12 D1437; Piercebridge: Cool and Mason 2008 Digital File Chapter 9 Page 9.108 Fig. D9.1. No. 1; Newstead: Curle 1911 No. 69, p. 219 and p. 217 Fig. 15; Inveresk: Richmond 1980 Microfiche 1: A13 2.40 (21).
34. On Saartjie Baartman – the Hottentot Venus – see Crais and Scully 2009.
35. See, for instance: Beardsley 1929; Eckardt Forthcoming; Ferris 2000, pp. 163–5; Gruen 2011, pp. 197–220; Snowden 1970, 1976, 1983, and 1997; and Thompson 1989. For a later period see, for instance, Boime 1990 and Stacey 1999.
36. Clarke 2003.
37. Clarke 1996.
38. Clarke 2003, p. 242.
39. Balsdon 1979; Ferris 2000, pp. 162–5; Isaac 2004; and Sherwin White 1967.
40. RIB 946.
41. *Brittunculi*: Ferris 2000, p. 198 Note 44; Carlisle inscription: RIB 946; and Corbridge altar: RIB 1142.
42. Taylor 1993.
43. C. Duhig in Taylor 1993, pp. 201–2.
44. M. J. Green in Taylor 1993, pp. 194–201.
45. Garland 1995.
46. Southwell-Wright 2010 and on-going PhD research.
47. Southwell-Wright 2010, p. 53.
48. PAS LIN-1213A7.
49. Toynbee 1962, p. 191 and Plate 186.
50. Garland 1995, p. 104.
51. Keisby relief: Henig 1995, p. 113 and p. 114 (74); Duns Tew relief: Toynbee 1964, p. 153; Catterick statuette: Wilson 2002, pp. 115–6 Fig. 285, Plate 97 and Henig 1995, p. 128 and

p. 129 Plate 78; Richborough statuette: Henig 1995, p. 81 and p. 82 (50); North Bradley statuette: Henig 1995, p. 39; gold rings, Newark: PAS DENO-C7EA54 and Brant Braughton: Henig 1995, p. 128; Wroxeter pot: Toynbee 1964, p. 389; Vulcan motif on Samian: F. Wild personal communication; Corbridge mould: Toynbee 1964, pp. 401–4; Barkway and Stony Stratford plaques: Toynbee 1964, p. 329; Old Carlisle altar: RIB 899; and Chesterholm/ Vindolanda altar: RIB 1700.

52. Pakenham herm: Johns 1990b and Johns and Henig 1991; Haxey herm: Henig and Leahy 1995; Thorrington statuette: PAS ESS-E6F9E3 *Britannia* XLII, p. 425 and p. 426 Fig. 21; Ingham bronze: PAS SF-177545; Telford lead figure: UK Detector Finds Database online UKDFD Ref. No. 20854; Helmsley figurine: UKDFD Ref. No. 6469; Birrens slab: RIB 2106; and Binchester relief: Ferris 2011b, p. 24.

53. Plouviez 2005.

54. Chapter 5, pp. 109–113.

55. Harlow and Laurence 2002, p. 117.

56. Harlow and Laurence 2002, p. 118.

57. Harlow and Laurence 2002, p. 118–9.

58. On Romano-British tombstones see, for instance, Adams and Tobler 2007, Hope 1997, and Raybould 1999.

59. RIB I 1965 Collingwood and Wright and RIB III 2009 Tomlin, Wright and Hassall.

60. Clarke 1979.

61. Farwell and Molleson 1987.

62. RIB 221.

63. Kleiner 1992, p. 38 Plate 16.

64. Kleiner 1992, p. 63–7 and p. 66 Plate 42.

65. Kleiner 1992, p. 208.

66. Kleiner 1992, p. 36–7 and p. 36 Plate 13.

67. Kleiner 1992, p. 37.

68. Kleiner 1992, p. 38 Plate 16.

69. Kleiner 1992, p. 40 and p. 39 Plate 18.

70. Pollitt 1986, p. 144 Plate 155.

71. Pollitt 1986, p. 142.

72. Kleiner 1992, pp. 63–7, p. 208.

73. Kleiner 1992, pp. 68–9.

74. Kleiner 1992, p. 226 Plate 190.

75. Pliny *Panegyricus* 28.5.

76. Currie 1996, pp. 167–73.

77. D'Ambra 1996.

78. D'Ambra 1996, pp. 219–21.

79. D'Ambra 1996, p. 229.

80. Martial *Epigrams* 3.93, 11.21, 11.99.

81. Barrett 1993.

82. Cunliffe and Fulford 1982, p. 5 No. 1 and Plate 1.

83. Huskinson 1994, pp. 14–5 No. 26 and Plate 13 No. 26.

Chapter 8: Narratives of the Past

1. Manning 1985, pp. 133–7.

2. Angus *et al.* 1962, Manning 1985, pp. 134–5, and Pitts and St Joseph 1985.

3. Ferris 2000, pp. 65–6 and 2009, pp. 153–7.

4. Ferris, 2009, pp. 153–5.

5. Ferris 2009, pp. 157.

6. Ferris 2000, p. 117 and Keppie and Arnold 1984, pp. 53–4 No. 149 and Plate 37 No. 149.

7. Ferris 2009, p. 157.

8. Ferris 1994, pp. 25–6 and pp. 29–30 and Keppie 1975.

9. Leicestershire pot, provenance unknown: unpublished but seen *c.* 2002.

10. On blacksmithing symbolism see, for instance Bevan 2006, pp. 79–83, especially pp. 81–3 and accompanying notes and references re: metalworking, gender and sexuality.
11. Chapter 7, pp. 151–2.
12. See, for instance, Hingley 2006.
13. Dungworth 1998
14. Dungworth 1998, pp. 153–6.
15. The edition I have used here is Kinsella, T. (trans.), *The Tain* (Oxford University Press, 1970).
16. *The Tain*, as Note 15, pp. 54–5.
17. Henry James 1897. The edition I have used here is James, H., *The Spoils of Poynton* (Harmondsworth: Penguin Classic: 1978).
18. James 1897, as Note 17, p. 20.
19. James 1897, as Note 17, p. 43.
20. James 1897, as Note 17, pp. 18–9.
21. James 1897, as Note 17, p. 18.
22. Georges Perec 1965. The edition I have used here is Perec, G. and Bellos, D. (trans.), *Things: A Story of the Sixties* (London: Harvill, 1991).
23. Perec 1965, as Note 22, pp. 33–4.
24. Perec 1965, as Note 22, p. 33.
25. Perec 1965, as Note 22, p. 119.
26. Leach 2001.
27. C. Johns in Leach 2001, pp. 257–60.
28. Strong 1966, p. 216. This analysis though is some years old and therefore probably not up to modern standards.
29. S. Minnitt 2008, *The Shepton Mallet Amulet CBA South-West Journal* 22 http://britarch. ac.uk/cbasw/
30. Deetz 1996, p. 259.

BIBLIOGRAPHY

Adams, J. N., 1987: *The Latin Sexual Vocabulary* (London: Duckworth).

Adams, G. W. and Tobler, R., 2007: 'Romano-British Tombstones Between the 1st and 3rd Centuries: Epigraphy, Gender and Familial Relations', *British Archaeological Reports British Series* 437 (Oxford: Archaeopress).

Adkins, L. and Adkins, R., 1985: 'Neolithic Axes from Roman Sites in Britain', *Oxford Journal of Archaeology* 4(1), pp. 69–75.

Aitchison, K., 1999: 'Monumental Architecture and Becoming Roman in the First Centuries BC and AD' in Barker, P. *et al.* (eds), pp. 26–35.

Aitchison, N. B., 1988: 'Roman Wealth, Native Ritual: Coin Hoards Within and Beyond Roman Britain', *World Archaeology* 20(2), pp. 270–283.

Alchermes, J., 1994: 'Spolia in Roman Cities of the Late Empire: Legislative Rationales and Architectural Sense', *Dumbarton Oaks Papers* 48, pp. 167–178.

Alcock, S. E., 2001: 'The Reconfiguration of Memory in the Eastern Roman Empire' in Alcock, S. E., D'Altroy, T. N., Morrison, K. D. and Sinopoli, C. M. (eds), *Empires: Perspectives from Archaeology and History* (Cambridge University Press), pp. 323–350.

Alcock, S. E., 2002: *Archaeologies of the Greek Past: Landscapes, Monuments, and Memories* (Cambridge University Press).

Alcock, S. E. and R. Van Dyke (eds), 2003: *The Archaeology of Memory* (Oxford: Blackwell).

Aldrete, G. S., 1999: *Gestures and Acclamations in Ancient Rome* (Baltimore: Johns Hopkins University Press).

Allason-Jones, L., 1989a: *Women in Roman Britain* (London: British Museum Press).

Allason-Jones, L., 1989b: 'Ear-Rings in Roman Britain', *British Archaeological Reports British Series* 201 (Oxford).

Allason-Jones, L., 1991: 'Roman and Native Interaction in Northumberland' in Maxfield, V. A. and Dobson, M. J. (eds), *Roman Frontier Studies: Proceedings of the XVth International Congress of Roman Frontier Studies*, pp. 1–5.

Allason-Jones, L., 1995: '"Sexing" Small Finds' in Rush, P. (ed.), pp. 22–32.

Allason-Jones, L., 1996: *Roman Jet in the Yorkshire Museum* (Yorkshire Museum).

Allason-Jones, L., 1999: *Health Care in the Roman North*, Britannia XXX, pp. 133–145.

Allason-Jones, L. (ed.), 2011: *Artefacts in Roman Britain: Their Purpose and Use* (Cambridge University Press).

Allason-Jones, L. and McKay, B., 1985: *Coventina's Well: A Shrine on Hadrian's Wall* (Hexham: Chesters Museum).

Allason-Jones, L. and Miket, R., 1984: 'The Catalogue of Small Finds from South Shields Roman Fort', *The Society of Antiquaries of Newcastle Upon Tyne Monograph Series* 2 (Newcastle).

Allison, P. M., 1997: 'Why Do Excavation Reports Have Finds Catalogues?' in Cumberpatch, C. G. and Blinkhorn, P. W. (eds), *Not So Much a Pot, More a Way of Life: Current Approaches to Artefact Analysis in Archaeology*, Oxbow Monograph 83 (Oxford: Oxbow Books), pp. 77–84.

Allison, P. M. (ed.), 1999: *The Archaeology of Household Activities* (London: Routledge).

Allison, P. M., 2004: 'Pompeian Households: An Analysis of the Material Culture', *The Cotsen Institute of Archaeology*, Monograph 42 (University of California).

Allison, P. M., 2008: 'The Women and Children Inside 1st and 2nd-Century Forts: Comparing the Archaeological Evidence' in Brandl, U. (ed.), *Frauen und Römisches Militär: British Archaeological Reports International Series*, 1759 (Oxford: Archaeopress). pp. 120–139.

Allison, P. M., 2009: 'Understanding Pompeian Households Practices Through Their Material Culture', *Facta* 3, pp. 11–33.

Alston, R., 1998: 'Arms and the Man: Soldiers, Masculinity and Power in Republican and Imperial Rome' in Foxhall, L. and Salmon, J. B. (eds), pp. 205–223.

Ambrose, T. and Henig, M., 1980: 'A New Rider-Relief from Stragglethorpe, Lincolnshire', *Britannia* XI, pp. 135–138.

Andrews, C. J., 2010: *Roman Seal-Boxes in Britain*, PhD Thesis (Milton Keynes, Open University).

Angus, N. S., Brown, G. T. and Cleere, H. F., 1962: 'The Iron Nails from the Roman Legionary Fortress at Inchtuthil, Perthshire', *Journal of the Iron and Steel Institute* 200, pp. 956–968.

Appadurai, A. (ed.), 1986: *The Social Life of Things: Commodities in Cultural Perspectives* (Cambridge University Press).

Arce, J., Ensoli, S. and La Rocca, E. (eds), 1997: *Hispania Romana: Da Terra di Conquita a Provincia dell'Impero* (Milan: Electa).

Bagnall Smith, J., 1995: 'Interim Report on the Votive Material from Romano-Celtic Temple Sites in Oxfordshire', *Oxoniensia* LX, pp. 177–203.

Bagnall Smith, J., Henig, M., and Trott, K., 2003: 'A Votive Head from West Wight', *Britannia* XXXIV, pp. 265–268.

Balsdon, J. P. V. D., 1979: *Romans and Aliens* (London: Duckworth).

Barker, P., White, R. H., Pretty, K. B., Bird, H. and Corbishley, M., 1997: 'Excavations on the Site of the Baths Basilica, Wroxeter 1966–1990', *English Heritage Archaeological Reports* 8 (London).

Barker, P. and White, P., 2000: *Wroxeter: Life and Death of a Roman City* (Stroud: Tempus).

Barker, P., Forcey, C., Jundi, S. and Witcher, R. (eds), 1999: *TRAC 98: Proceedings of the Eighth Theoretical Roman Archaeology Conference, Leicester 1998* (Oxford: Oxbow).

Baroin, C., 2010: 'Remembering One's Ancestors, Following in Their Footsteps, Being Like Them: the Role and Forms of Family Memory in the Building of Identity' in Dasen, V. and Späth, T. (eds), pp. 19–48.

Barr-Sharrar, B., 1987: *The Hellenistic and Early Imperial Decorative Bust* (Mainz: Verlag Philipp Von Zabern).

Barrett, A. A., 1978: 'Knowledge of the Literary Classics in Roman Britain', *Britannia* IX, pp. 307–313.

Barrett, J. C., 1993: 'Chronologies of Remembrance: the Interpretation of Some Roman Inscriptions' *World Archaeology* 25(2): *Conceptions of Time and Ancient Society*, pp. 236–247.

Barrett, J. C., Fitzpatrick, A. P., and MacInnes, L. (eds), 1989: 'Barbarians and Romans in North-West Europe from the Late Republic to Late Antiquity', *British Archaeological Reports International Series* 471 (Oxford).

Barton, C. A., 1989: 'The Scandal of the Arena', *Representations* 27, pp. 1–36.

Barton, C. A., 1993: *The Sorrows of the Ancient Romans: The Gladiator and the Monster* (Princeton University Press).

Bathurst, W. H., 1879: *Roman Antiquities at Lydney Park, Gloucestershire* (London: Longmans).

Bauchhenss, B. and Noelke, P., 1981: 'Die Jupitersaulen in der Germanischen Provinzen', *Bonner Jahrbucher Beiheft* 41 (Bonn).

Baudrillard, J., 1968: 'Subjective Discourse or the Non-Functional System of Objects', reprinted in Foss, P. and Pefanis, J. (trans. and eds), *Revenge of the Crystal: Selected Writings on the Modern Object and its Destiny, 1968–1983* (London: Pluto Press).

Beard, M. and Henderson, J., 2001: *Classical Art: From Greece to Rome* (Oxford University Press).

Beardsley, G., 1929: *The Negro in Greek and Roman Civilization: a Study of the Ethiopian Type* (Baltimore: John Hopkins University Press).

Beaudry, M., 2009: 'Bodkin Biographies' in White, C. L. (ed.), *The Materiality of Individuality: Archaeological Studies of Individual Lives* (New York: Springer), pp. 95–108.

de Beauvoir, S. and Howard, R. (trans.), 1965: *Force of Circumstance* (Harmondsworth: Penguin).

Bedwin, O., 1980: 'Excavations at Chanctonbury Ring, Wiston, West Sussex 1977', *Britannia* XI, pp. 173–222.

Besançon, A., 2001: *The Forbidden Image; an Intellectual History of Iconoclasm* (University of Chicago Press).

Bedon, R., Chevallier, R. and Pinon, P., 1988: *Architecture et Urbanisme en Gaule Romaine* (Paris).

de la Bédoyère, G., 1989: *The Finds of Roman Britain* (London: Batsford).

Bennett, J., 1983: 'The End of Roman Settlement in North England' in Chapman, J. C. and Mytum, H. C. (eds), *Settlement in North Britain, 1000BC–AD1000: British Archaeological Reports British Series* 118, pp. 205–232.

Berg, M., 2004: 'In Pursuit of Luxury: Global History and British Consumer Goods in the Eighteenth Century', *Past and Present* 182, pp. 85–142.

Bergemann, J., 1990: *Römische Reiterstatuen: Ehrendenkmäler im öffentlichen Bereich* (Mainz: Ehrendenkmäler im Öffentlichen Bereich).

Bergmann, B. and Kondoleon, C. (eds), 1999: *The Art of Ancient Spectacle* (National Gallery of Art, Yale University Press).

Berry, J., 1990: 'Household Artefacts: Towards a Re-Interpretation of Roman Domestic Space' in Laurence, R. and Wallace-Hadrill, A. (eds), *Domestic Space in the Roman World: Pompeii and Beyond: Journal of Roman Archaeology Supplementary Series*, No. 22, pp. 183–195.

Bevan, L., 1994: 'Powerful Pudenda: the Penis in Prehistory', *Journal of Theoretical Archaeology* 3/4, pp. 41–57.

Bevan, L., 1999: 'Ecstatic Celebrants: Bacchic Metalwork from the Roman Midlands', *Transactions of the Staffordshire Archaeological and Historical Society* 38, pp. 6–11.

Bevan, L. (ed.), 2001: *Indecent Exposure: Sexuality, Society and the Archaeological Record* (Glasgow: Cruithne Press).

Bevan, L., 2006: 'Worshippers and Warriors. Reconstructing Gender Relations in the Prehistoric Rock Art of Naquane National Park, Valcamonica, Brescia, Northern Italy', *British Archaeological Reports International Series* 1485 (Oxford: Archaeopress).

Biddle, M., 1986: 'Archaeology, Architecture, and the Cult of Saints' in Butler, L. A. S. and Morris, R. K. (eds), pp. 1–31.

Bird, J., Chapman, H. and Clark, J. (eds), 1978: 'Collectanea Londiniensia: Studies Presented to Ralph Merrifield', *London and Middlesex Archaeological Society*, Special Paper No. 2.

Biro, M., 1965: 'The Inscriptions of Roman Britain', *Acta Archaeologica Scientarum Hungaricae* 27, pp. 13–57.

Bishop, M. C., 1996: 'Finds from Roman Aldborough: A Catalogue of Small Finds from the Romano-British Town of Isurium Brigantum', *Oxbow Monograph* 65 (Oxford: Oxbow Books).

Black, E. W., 1986: 'Romano-British Burial Customs and Religious Beliefs in South-East England', *Archaeological Journal* 143, pp. 201–239.

Blagg, T. F. C., 1980: 'Roman Civil and Military Architecture in the Province of Britain: Aspects of Patronage, Influence and Craft Organisation', *World Archaeology* 12(1), pp. 25–42.

Blagg, T. F. C., 1983: 'The Reuse of Monumental Masonry in Late Roman Defensive Walls' in Maloney, J. and Hobley, B. (eds), pp. 96–117.

Blagg, T. F. C., 1985: 'Cult and Practice and its Social Context in the Religious Sanctuaries of Latium and Southern Etruria' in Malone, C. and Stoddart, S. (eds), *Papers in Italian Archaeology IV: British Archaeological Reports International Series* 246 (Oxford) pp. 33–50.

Blagg, T. F. C., 1986a: 'The Cult and Sanctuary of Diana Nemorensis' in Henig, M. and King, A. (eds), pp. 211–220.

Blagg, T., 1986b: 'Roman Religious Sites in the British Landscape', *Landscape History* 8, pp. 15–26.

Blagg, T. F. C., 1989: 'Art and Architecture' in Todd, M. (ed.), pp. 203–217.

Blagg, T. F. C., 1990: 'Architectural Munificence in Britain: the Evidence of Inscriptions', *Britannia* XXI, pp. 13–31.

Blagg, T. and Millett, M. (eds), 1990: *The Early Roman Empire in the West* (Oxford: Oxbow Books).

Blom, P., 2002: *To Have and to Hold: an Intimate History of Collectors and Collecting* (Harmondsworth: Allen Lane).

Boardman, J., 2002: *The Archaeology of Nostalgia: How the Greeks Re-Created Their Mythical Past* (London: Thames & Hudson).

Boatwright, M. T., 1991: 'Plancia Magna of Perge: Women's Roles and Status in Roman Asia Minor' in Pomeroy, S. B. (ed.), pp. 249–272.

Boatwright, M. T., 1993: 'The City Gate of Plancia Magna in Perge' in D'Ambra, E. (ed.), *Roman Art in Context: An Anthology* (New Jersey: Prentice Hall), pp. 189–207.

Boatwright, M. T., 2000a: 'Just Window Dressing? Imperial Women as Architectural Sculpture' in Kleiner, D. E. E. and Matheson, S. B. (eds), *I Claudia II* (University of Texas Press), pp. 61–75.

Boatwright, M. T., 2000b: *Hadrian and the Cities of the Roman Empire* (Princeton University Press).

Bodel, J., 1999: 'Death on Display: Looking at Roman Funerals' in Bergmann, B. and Kondoleon, C. (eds), pp. 259–82.

Böhn, V. H., 2000: 'Herkunft Geklärt? Die Bronzen von Cartoceto und die Exedra der Ciceronen auf Samos', *Antike Welt* 2000, pp. 9–22.

Boime, A., 1990: *The Art of Exclusion Representing Blacks in the Nineteenth Century* (London: Thames & Hudson)

Bonnichsen, R., 1973: 'Millie's Camp: an Experiment in Archaeology', *World Archaeology* 4(3), pp. 277–91.

Boon, G., 1983: 'Some Romano-British Domestic Shrines and Their Inhabitants' in Hartley, B. and Wacher, J. (eds), *Rome and Her Northern Provinces* (Gloucester: Alan Sutton) pp. 33–55.

Bourdieu, P., 1977: *Outline of a Theory of Practice* (Cambridge University Press).

Bourke, J., 1999: *Dismembering the Male: Men's Bodies, Britain and the Great War* (London: Reaktion Books).

Bradley, R., 1986: 'Neolithic Axes in Roman Britain: an Exercise in Archaeological Source Criticism', *Oxford Journal of Archaeology* 5(1), pp. 119–120.

Bradley, R., 1987: 'Time Regained: the Creation of Continuity', *Journal of the British Archaeological Association* 140, pp. 1–17.

Bradley, R., 1990: *The Passage of Arms: An Archaeological Analysis of Prehistoric Hoards and Votive Deposits* (Cambridge University Press).

Bradley, R., 2002: *The Past in Prehistoric Societies* (London: Routledge).

Bradley, R. and Williams, H. (eds), 1998: 'The Past in the Past', *World Archaeology* 30 (1).

Braithwaite, G., 1984: 'Romano-British Face Pots and Head Pots', *Britannia* XV, pp. 99–131.

Breen, T. H., 1986: 'An Empire of Goods: the Anglicization of Colonial America, 1690–1776', *Journal of British Studies* 25(4), pp. 467–499.

Brewer, J. and Porter, R. (eds), 1994: *Consumption and the World of Goods* (London: Routledge).

Brewer, R. J., 1986: *Corpus Signorum Imperii Romani, Great Britain, Volume 1, Fascicule 5: Wales* (Oxford University Press).

Brilliant, R., 1963: 'Gesture and Rank in Roman Art: The Use of Gestures to Denote Status in Roman
    Sculpture and Coinage', *Memoirs of the Connecticut Academy of Arts and Sciences* XI (New
    Haven).
Brisson, L., 2002: *Sexual Ambivalence: Androgyny and Hermaphroditism in Graeco–Roman Antiquity*
    (University of California Press).
British Museum, 1964: *Guide to the Antiquities of Roman Britain*. (British Museum).
Brogiolo, G. P. and Ward-Perkins, B. (eds), 1999: 'The Idea and Ideal of the Town Between Late
    Antiquity and the Early Middle Ages', *European Science Foundation, Transformation of the Roman
    World* 4.
Bronzi Dorati, 1987: *Bronzi Dorati da Cartoceto: Un Restauro* (Florence).
Brown, P., 1981: *The Cult of the Saints: Its Rise and Function in Latin Christianity* (Chicago: Student
    Christian Movement).
Brown, P., 1988: *The Body and Society: Men, Women and Sexual Renunciation in Early Christianity*
    (New York: Columbia University Press).
Bruni, S., 2000: 'Sculpture' in Torelli, M. (ed.), *The Etruscans* (London: Thames & Hudson), pp.
    365–91.
Burnham, B. and Wacher, J., 1990: *The Small Towns of Roman Britain* (London: Batsford).
Burrus, V., 2000: *Begotten, Not Made: Conceiving Manhood in Late Antiquity* (Stanford University
    Press).
Bush, H. and Zvelebil, M., 1991: 'Pathology and Health in Past Societies: an Introduction' in Bush,
    H. and Zvelebil, M. (eds), *Health in Past Societies: Biocultural Interpretations of Human Skeletal
    Remains in Archaeological Contexts: British Archaeological Reports International Series* 567
    (Oxford), pp. 3–9.
Bushe-Fox, J. P., 1913: 'Excavations on the Site of the Roman Town at Wroxeter, Shropshire in 1912',
    Society of Antiquaries of London Research Report 1 (London).
Butler, L. A. S. and Morris, R. K. (eds), 1986: 'The Anglo-Saxon Church: Papers on History,
    Architecture and Archaeology in Honour of Dr H. M. Taylor', *Council for British Archaeology
    Research Report* 60 (London).
Buvelot, Q. (ed.), 2004: *Albert Eckhout: a Dutch Artist in Brazil*, Exhibition Catalogue. (Waanders:
    Zwolle).
Bynum, C. W., 1992: *Fragmentation and Redemption: Essays on Gender and the Human Body in
    Medieval Religion* (New York: Zone Books).
Cahill, N., 2010: 'Functional Analyses of Ancient House Inventories' in *Städtisches Wohnen in
    Östlichen Mittelmeerraum 4. Jh.v. Chr.-1.Jh. n. Chr.* (Österreichische Akademie der Wissenschaften),
    pp. 477–494.
Calvani, M. M., 2002: 'Un'Origine Cispadana per i Bronzi di Cartoceto' in de Marinis, G. Rinaldi Tufi,
    S. and Baldelli, G. (eds), pp. 57–60.
Camuset-Le Porzou, F., 1985: *Figurines Gallo-Romains en Terre Cuite* (Paris).
Caple, C., 2006: *Objects: Reluctant Witnesses to the Past* (London: Routledge).
Carr, G., 2005: 'Woad, Tattooing and Identity in Later Iron Age and Early Roman Britain', *Oxford
    Journal of Archaeology* 24(3), pp. 273–292.
Carr, G., 2006: 'Creolised Bodies and Hybrid Identities: Examining the Later Iron Age and Early
    Roman Periods of Essex and Hertfordshire', *British Archaeological Reports British Series* 418
    (Oxford: Archaeopress).
Cartledge, P., 1998: 'The Machismo of the Athenian Empire – Or the Reign of the Phaulus' in Foxhall,
    L. and Salmon, J. B. (eds), pp. 54–65.
Casey, P. J. and Davies, J. L., 1993: 'Excavations at Segontium (Caernarfon) Roman Fort, 1975–1979',
    Council for British Archaeology Research Report 90 (York).
Casimiro, T. M., 2011: 'Portuguese Faience in England and Ireland', *British Archaeological Reports
    International Series* 2301 (Oxford: Archaeopress).
Cèbe, J. P., 1966: *La Caricature et la Parodie dans le Monde Romain Antique, des Origines à Juvenal*
    (Paris: E. de Boccard).
Chapman, J., 2000: *Fragmentation in Archaeology: People, Places and Broken Objects in the Prehistory
    of South Eastern Europe* (London: Routledge).
Chapman, J. and Gaydarska, B., 2007: *Parts and Wholes: Fragmentation in Prehistoric Context*
    (Oxford: Oxbow Books).
Clarke, D. V., Cowie, T. G. and Foxon, A., 1985: 'Symbols of Power at the Time of Stonehenge',
    National Museum of Antiquities of Scotland (Edinburgh: Her Majesty's Stationery Office).
Clarke, G. N., 1979: *Pre-Roman and Roman Winchester, Part 2: the Roman Cemetery at Lankhills*
    (Oxford University Press).
Clarke, J. R., 1996: 'Hypersexual Black Men in Augustan Baths: Ideal Somatypes and Apotropaic
    Magic' in Kampen, N. B. (ed.), pp. 184–98.
Clarke, J. R., 1998: *Looking at Lovemaking: Constructions of Sexuality in Roman Art 100 BC–AD
    250* (University of California Press).

Clarke, J. R., 2003: *Art in the Lives of Ordinary Romans: Visual Representation and Non-Elite Viewers in Italy, 100 BC–AD 315* (University of California Press).

Clarke, J. R., 2007: *Looking at Laughter: Humor, Power, and Transgression in Roman Visual Culture, 100 BC–AD 250* (University of California Press).

Clarke, S., 1994: 'A Quantitative Analysis of the Finds from the Roman Fort of Newstead' in Cottam, S. *et al.* (eds), pp. 72–82.

Clarke, S., 1997: 'Abandonment, Rubbish Disposal and Special Deposits' in Meadows, K. *et al.* (eds), pp. 73–81.

Clarke, S., 1999: 'In Search of a Different Roman Period: the Finds Assemblage at the Newstead Military Complex' in Fincham, G. *et al.* (eds), pp. 22–29.

Clarke, S. and Jones, R. F. J., 1994: 'The Newstead Pits', *Journal of Roman Military Equipment Studies* 5, pp. 109–124.

Clay, C., 2004: 'Iconoclasm in Roman Chester: the Significance of the Mutilated Tombstones from the North Wall', *Journal of the British Archaeological Association* 157, pp. 1–16.

Coarelli, F., 1998: 'I Bronzi di Cartoceto. Un'Ipotesi' in Luni, M. and Motta, F. G. (eds), *I Bronzi Dorati di Pergola: Un Enigma?* (Urbino), pp. 81–95.

Cocks, A. S., 1989: 'The Nonfunctional Use of Ceramics in the English Country House During the Eighteenth Century', in Jackson-Stops, G., Schochet, G. J., Orlin, L. C. and MacDougall, E. B. (eds), *The Fashioning and Functioning of the British Country House: Studies in the History of Art 25* (Center for Advanced Study in the Visual Arts: Symposium Papers X), pp. 195–215.

Coleman, K. M., 1990: 'Fatal Charades: Roman Executions Staged as Mythological Enactments', *Journal of Roman Studies* 80, pp. 44–73.

Collins, R. and Allason-Jones, L. (eds), 2010: 'Finds from the Frontier: Material Culture in the 4th–5th Centuries', *Council for British Archaeology Research Report* 162 (York).

Conneller, C., 2006: 'The Roman Flintworking' in Garrow, D. *et al.*, pp. 129–130.

Connerton, P., 1989: *How Societies Remember* (Cambridge University Press).

Connor, S., 2010: *Paraphernalia: the Curious Lives of Magical Things* (London: Profile).

Cool, H. E. M., 2010: 'Finding the Foreigners' in Eckardt, H. (ed.), pp. 27–44.

Cool, H. E. M., *Roman Struck Flint and Glass* (www.barbicanra.co.uk/shopimages/Documents/Roman_flint_glass.doc)

Cool, H. E. M., Lloyd-Mŏrgan, G. and Hooey, A. D., 1995: 'Finds from the Fortress', *The Archaeology of York: The Small Finds* 17/10 (York Archaeological Trust and the Council for British Archaeology).

Cool, H. E. M. and Philo, C., 1998: *Roman Castleford Excavations 1974–85. Volume 1: The Small Finds* (Wakefield: West Yorkshire Archaeology Service).

Cool, H. E. M. and Mason, D. J. P., 2008: 'Roman Piercebridge: Excavations by D. W. Harding and Peter Scott 1969–1981', *The Architectural and Archaeological Society of Durham and Northumberland Research Report* 7 (Durham).

Cooley, A. E. (ed.), 2002: 'Becoming Roman, Writing Latin? Literacy and Epigraphy in the Roman West', *Journal of Roman Archaeology Supplementary Series* 48.

Cooper, N. J., 1997: 'Searching for the Blank Generation: Consumer Choice in Roman and Post-Roman Britain' in Webster, J. and Cooper, N. J. (eds), pp. 85–98.

Cooper, N. J., 2007: 'Promoting the Study of Finds in Roman Britain: Democracy, Integration and Dissemination. Practice and Methodologies for the Future' in Hingley, R. and Willis, S. (eds), pp. 35–52.

Corbeill, A., 2004: *Nature Embodied: Gesture in Ancient Rome* (Princeton University Press).

Corbrier, M., 1991: 'Family Behaviour of the Roman Aristocracy, Second Century BC–Third Century AD' in Pomeroy, S. B. (ed.), pp. 173–196.

Cornell, T. J. and Lomas, K. (eds), 1995: *Urban Society in Roman Italy* (UCL Press).

Cosh, S. R., 1998: 'Mosaic Schools, Officinae and Groups in Fourth Century Britain', *Mosaic* 25, pp. 9–14.

Cottam, S., Dungworth, D., Scott, S. and Taylor, J. (eds), 1994: *TRAC 94: Proceedings of the Fourth Annual Theoretical Roman Archaeology Conference, Durham 1994* (Oxford: Oxbow Books).

Cotton, J., 1996: 'A Miniature Chalk Head from the Thames at Battersea and the "Cult of the Head" in Roman London' in Bird, J., Hassall, M. and Sheldon, H. (eds), *Interpreting Roman London* (Oxford: Oxbow Books), pp. 85–96.

Coulston, J. C. and Phillips, E. J., 1988: *Corpus Signorum Imperii Romani, Great Britain Volume 1 Fascicule 6: Hadrian's Wall West of the North Tyne, and Carlisle* (Oxford University Press).

Courlander, H., 1960: *The Drum and the Hoe: Life and Lore of the Haitian People* (Berkeley: University of California Press).

Courtney, P., 1996: 'In Small Things Forgotten: the Georgian World View, Material Culture and the Consumer Revolution', *Rural History* 7(1), pp. 87–95.

Crais, C. and Scully, P., 2009: *Sara Baartman and the Hottentot Venus: a Ghost Story and a Biography* (Princeton University Press).

Crook, J. A., 1986: 'Women in Roman Succession' in Rawson, B. (ed.), *The Family in Ancient Rome: New Perspectives* (Ithaca: Cornell University Press) pp. 58–82.

Croom, A. T., 2000: *Roman Clothing and Fashion* (Stroud: Tempus).

Croxford, B., 2003: 'Iconoclasm in Roman Britain?', *Britannia* XXXIV, pp. 81–95.

Crummy, N., 1983: 'The Roman Small Finds from Excavations in Colchester 1971–9', *Colchester Archaeological Reports* 2 (Colchester).

Crummy, N. (ed.), 2005: *Image, Craft and the Classical World: Essays in Honour of Donald Bailey and Catherine John*, Instrumentum M1–29.

Crummy, N., 2007: 'Brooches and the Cult of Mercury', *Britannia* XXXVIII, pp. 225–230.

Crummy, P., 1984: 'Excavations at Lion Walk, Balkerne Lane, and Middleborough, Colchester, Essex', *Colchester Archaeological Report* 3 (Colchester).

Crummy, P., 1997: *City of Victory: the Story of Colchester – Britain's First Roman Town* (Colchester Archaeological Trust).

Csikszentmihalyi, M. and Rochberg-Halton, E., 1981: *The Meaning of Things: Domestic Symbols and the Self* (London: Routledge).

Culham, P., 1997: 'Did Roman Women Have an Empire?' in Golden, M. and Toohey, P. (eds), *Inventing Ancient Culture: Historicism, Periodization, and the Ancient World* (London: Routledge), pp. 192–204.

Cunliffe, B. W. (ed.), 1988: 'The Temple of Sulis Minerva at Bath, Volume 2: The Finds from the Sacred Spring' *Oxford University Committee for Archaeology*, Monograph 16 (Oxford).

Cunliffe, B. W. and Fulford, M. G., 1982: *Corpus Signorum Imperii Romani, Great Britain Volume 1 Fascicule 2: Bath and the Rest of Wessex* (Oxford University Press).

Curle, J., 1911: *A Roman Frontier Post and its People: The Fort of Newstead in the Parish of Melrose* (Glasgow: James Maclehose & Sons).

Currie, S., 1996: 'The Empire of Adults: the Representation of Children on Trajan's Arch at Beneventum' in Elsner, J. (ed.), *Art and Text in Roman Culture* (Cambridge University Press), pp. 153–181.

D'Ambra, E., 1993: *Private Lives, Imperial Virtues: The Frieze of the Forum Transitorium in Rome* (New Jersey: Princeton University Press).

D'Ambra, E., 1996: 'The Calculus of Venus: Nude Portraits of Roman Matrons' in Kampen, N. B. (ed.), pp. 219–232.

Damgaard Andersen, H., 1993: 'The Etruscan Ancestor Cult – its Origin and Development and the Importance of Anthropomorphization', *Analecta Romana Instituti Danici* 21, pp. 7–66.

Dark, K. R., 1993: 'Roman Period Activity at Prehistoric Ritual Monuments in Britain and in the Armorican Peninsula' in Scott, E. (ed.), 'Theoretical Roman Archaeology Conference: First Conference a Proceedings', *Worldwide Archaeology Series* 4 (Aldershot: Avebury), pp. 133–146.

Dasen, V., 1993: 'Dwarfs in Ancient Egypt and Greece', *Oxford Monographs on Classical Archaeology* (Oxford University).

Dasen, V., 2010: 'Wax and Plaster Memories: Children in Elite and Non-Elite Strategies' in Dasen, V. and Späth, T. (eds), pp. 109–146.

Dasen, V. and Späth, T. (eds), 2010: *Children, Memory, and Family Identity in Roman Culture* (Oxford University Press).

Davey, N. and Ling, R., 1981: 'Wall-Painting in Roman Britain', *Britannia Monograph Series* 3 (London: Society for the Promotion of Roman Studies).

Davies, H. F., 1937: 'The Shale Industries at Kimmeridge, Dorset', *Archaeological Journal* 93, pp. 200–219.

Deetz, J., 1996: *In Small Things Forgotten: an Archaeology of Early American Life* (2nd ed.) (New York: Anchor Books Doubleday).

Della Portella, I., 1999: *Subterranean Rome* (Cologne: Konemann).

de Marinis, G., 2002: 'I Bronzi Dorati da Cartoceto: Il Punto Sulle Conoscenze' in de Marinis, G. Rinaldi Tufi, S. and Baldelli, G. (eds), pp. 37–43.

de Marinis, G. and Quiri, P., 1999: *I Bronzi Dorati da Cartoceto di Pergola nel Museo Archeologico Nazionale delle Marche* (Ancona).

de Marinis, G., Rinaldi Tufi, S. and Baldelli, G. (eds), 2002: *Bronzi e Marmi della Flaminia: Sculture Romane a Confronto* (Provincia di Pesaro e Urbino).

Deonna, W., 1925: 'Orphée et l'Oracle à la Tête Coupé', *Revue des Études Grecques* 28, pp. 44–69.

Derks, T., 1995: 'The Ritual of the Vow in Gallo-Roman Religion' in Metzler, J., Millett, M., Roymans, N. and Slofstra, J. (eds), 'Integration in the Early Roman West: The Role of Culture and Ideology', *Dossiers d'Archéologie du Musée National d'Histoire et d'Art* 4 (Paris).

Derks, T., 1998: *Gods, Temples and Ritual Practices: The Transformation of Religious Ideas and Values in Roman Gaul* (Amsterdam University Press).

Derks, T. and Wouter, V., 2010: 'Wooden Combs from the Roman Fort at Vechten: the Bodily Appearance of Soldiers', *Journal of Archaeology in the Low Countries* 2-2, pp. 53–77. www.jalc.nl.

Derks, T. and Roymans, N., 2002: 'Seal Boxes and the Spread of Latin Literacy in the Rhine Delta' in Cooley, A. E. (ed.), pp. 87–134.

Derks, T. and Roymans, N., 2006: 'Returning Auxiliary Veterans: Some Methodological Considerations', *Journal of Roman Archaeology* 19, pp. 121–135.

Deyts, S., 1983: 'Les Bois Sculptes des Source of the Seine', *Gallia* 42.

Deyts, S., 1985: *Le Sanctuaire des Source of the Seine* (Paris).

Deyts, S., 1994: 'Un Peuple de Pelerins: Offrandes de Pierre et de Bronze des Sources de la Seine', *Revue Archeologique de l'Est et du Centre-Est* (Dijon: Treizieme Supplement).

Dimitrova, N., 2002: 'Inscriptions and Iconography in the Monuments of the Thracian Rider', *Hesperia* 71, pp. 209–229.

Dixon, S., 1983: 'A Family Business: Women's Role in Patronage and Politics at Rome 80–44 BC', *Classica et Medievalia* 34, pp. 91–112.

Dorrington, E. and Legge, A., 1985: 'The Animal Bone' in France, N. E. and Gobel, B. M., 'The Romano-British Temple at Harlow, Essex', *West Essex Archaeological Group Monograph*, pp. 122–134.

Dougherty, C., 1992: 'When Rain Falls from the Clear Blue Sky: Riddles and Colonization Oracles', *Classical Antiquity* 11(1), pp. 28–44.

Douglas, M. and Isherwood, B., 1978: *The World of Goods: Towards an Anthropology of Consumption* (New York: Basic Books).

Doxiadis, E., 1995: *The Mysterious Fayum Portraits: Faces from Ancient Egypt* (London: Thames & Hudson).

Driel-Murray, C. van, 1987: 'Roman Footwear: a Mirror of Fashion and Society' in Friendship-Taylor, R., Swann, J. M. and Thomas, S. (eds), 'Recent Research in Archaeological Footwear', *Association of Archaeological Illustrators and Surveyors* Technical Paper 8, pp. 32–42.

Driel-Murray, C. van, 1995: 'Nailing Roman Shoes', *Archaeological Leather Group Newsletter* 1, pp. 6–7.

Driel-Murray, C. van, 1995: 'Gender in Question' in Rush, P. (ed.), pp. 3–21.

Driel-Murray, C. van, 1998: 'The Leatherwork from the Fort' in Cool, H. E. M. and Philo, C., pp. 285–334.

Driel-Murray, C. van, 1999: 'And Did Those Feet in Ancient Time … Feet and Shoes as a Material Projection of the Self' in Baker, P. *et al.* (eds), pp. 131–140.

Driel-Murray, C. van, 2002: 'Regarding the Stars' in Carruthers, M., Driel-Murray, C. van, Gardner, A., Lucas, J., Revell, L. and Swift, E. (eds), *TRAC 2001 Proceedings of the Eleventh Theoretical Roman Archaeology Conference Glasgow 2001* (Oxford: Oxbow Books) pp. 96–103.

Drinkwater, J. F., 1985: 'Urbanization in the Three Gauls: Some Observations' in Grew, F. and Hobley, B. (eds), pp. 49–55.

Drury, P. J. 1980: 'Non-Classical Religious Buildings in Iron Age and Roman Britain' in Rodwell, W. (ed.), pp. 45–78.

Drury, P. J., 1984: 'The Temple of Claudius at Colchester Reconsidered', *Britannia* XV, pp. 7–50.

Dubois, P., 1996: 'Archaic Bodies in Pieces' in Kampen, N. B. (ed.), pp. 55–64.

Dubois, P., 1998: *Sowing the Body: Psychoanalysis and Ancient Representations of Women* (University of Chicago Press).

Dunbabin, K., 1986: 'Sic erimus cuncti … the Skeleton in Graeco-Roman Art', *Jahrbuch des Deutschen Archäologischen Instituts* 101, pp. 185–255.

Dundes, A. (ed.), 1981: *The Evil Eye: a Casebook* (Madison: University of Wisconsin Press).

Dungworth, D., 1998: 'Mystifying Roman Nails: clavus annalis, defixiones and minkisi' in Forcey, C. *et al.* (eds), pp. 148–159.

Dupont, F., 1987: 'Les morts et la mémoire: le masque funèbre' in Hinard, F. (ed.), *La mort, les morts et l'au-delà dans le monde Romain* (Actes du Colloque de Caen), pp. 167–72.

Durkheim, E., 1961: *The Elementary Forms of the Religious Life* (London: Allen & Unwin).

Dwyer, E., 1982: *Pompeian Domestic Structures: a Study of Five Pompeian Houses and Their Contents* (Rome).

Eckardt, H., 1999: 'The Colchester "Child's Grave"', *Britannia* XXX, pp. 57–89.

Eckardt, H., 2004: 'Remembering and Forgetting in the Roman Provinces' in Croxford, B., Eckardt, H., Meade, J. and Weekes, J. (eds), *TRAC 2003: Proceedings of the Thirteenth Annual Theoretical Roman Archaeology Conference, Leicester 2003* (Oxford: Oxbow Books), pp. 36–50.

Eckardt, H., 2005: 'The Social Distribution of Roman Artefacts: the Case of Nail-Cleaners and Brooches in Britain', *Journal of Roman Archaeology* 18, pp. 139–160.

Eckardt, H., 2009: 'Roman Barrows and Their Landscape Context: a GIS Case Study at Bartlow, Cambridgeshire', *Britannia* XL, pp. 65–98.

Eckardt, H., 2010: 'Introduction' in Eckardt (ed.), pp. 7–12.

Eckardt, H., (ed.) 2010: 'Roman Diasporas: Archaeological Approaches to Mobility and Diversity in the Roman Empire', *Journal of Roman Archaeology Supplementary Series* 78.

Eckardt, H., Forthcoming: *Objects and Identities and Roman Britain and the North-West Provinces*.

Eckardt, H., Chenery, C., Leach, S., Lewis, M., Müldner, G. and Nimmo, E., 2010: 'A Long Way From Home: Diaspora Communities in Roman Britain' in Eckardt, H. (ed.), pp. 99–130.

Eckardt, H. and Crummy, N., 2006: '"Roman" or "Native" Bodies in Britain: the Evidence of Late Roman Nail-Cleaner Strap-Ends', *Oxford Journal of Archaeology* 25(1), pp. 83–103.

Eckardt, H. and Crummy, N., 2008: 'Styling the Body in Late Iron Age and Roman Britain: A Contextual Approach to Toilet Implements', *Monographies Instrumentum* 36 (Montagnac: Éditions Monique Mergoil).

Eger, A. A., 2007: 'Age and Male Sexuality: "Queer Space" in the Roman Bath House' in Harlow, M. and Laurence, R. (eds), 'Age and Ageing in the Roman Empire', *Journal of Roman Archaeology Supplementary Series* 65, pp. 131–151.

Elderfield, J., 1985: *Kurt Schwitters* (London: Thames & Hudson).

Ellis, P., 2000: 'Sexual Metaphors in the Neolithic' in Bevan, L. (ed.), pp. 56–63.

Ellis, S., 1991: 'Power, Architecture, and Décor: How the Late Roman Aristocrat Appeared to His Guests' in Gazda, E. K. (ed.), pp. 117–134.

Elsen, A. E., 1969: 'Notes on the Partial Figure' *Artforum* 8, pp. 58–63.

Elsen, A. E., 1969: *The Partial Figure in Modern Sculpture: from Rodin to 1969* (Baltimore Museum of Art).

Elsner, J., 1995: *Art and the Roman Viewer: The Transformation of Art from the Pagan World to Christianity* (Cambridge University Press).

Emerson, R. W., 1941: 'The Poet' in Haight, G. S. (ed.) *The Best of Ralph Waldo Emerson* (New York: Van Nostrand).

Esmonde Cleary, A. S., 1987: 'Extra-Mural Areas of Romano-British Towns', *British Archaeological Reports British Series* 169 (Oxford).

Esmonde Cleary, A. S. and Ferris, I. M., 1996: 'Excavations at the New Cemetery, Rocester, Staffordshire, 1985–1987', *Staffordshire Archaeological and Historical Society Transactions* XXXV.

Espérandieu, E., 1966: *Recueil Général des Bas-Reliefs de la Gaule Romaine et Pre-Romaine* (Paris: Ernest Leroux).

Evans, C., 1989: 'Digging with the Pen: Novel Archaeologies and Literary Traditions', *Archaeological Review from Cambridge* 8(2), pp. 185–211.

Evans, C. J., Jones, L. and Ellis, P., 2000: 'Severn Valley Ware Production at Newland Hopfields. Excavation of a Romano-British Kiln Site at North End Farm, Great Malvern, Worcestershire in 1992 and 1994', *British Archaeological Reports British Series* 313 (Oxford: Archaeopress).

Evans, E., 2000: 'The Caerleon Canabae: Excavations in the Civil Settlement 1984–1990', *Britannia Monograph Series* 16 (London: Society for the Promotion of Roman Studies).

Evans, J., 1987: 'Graffiti and the Evidence of Literacy and Pottery Use in Roman Britain', *Archaeological Journal* 144, pp. 191–204.

Fanon, F. and Farrington, C. (trans.), 1961: *The Wretched of the Earth* (Harmondsworth: Penguin).

Fantham, E., 1995: 'Aemilia Pudentilla: or the Wealthy Widow's Choice' in Hawley, R. and Levick, B. (eds), *Women in Antiquity; New Assessments* (London) pp. 220–232.

Farioli Campanati, R. (ed.), 1984: *Terzo Colloquio Internazionale Sul Mosaico Antico* (Ravenna).

Farrell, J., 1997: 'The Phenomenology of Memory in Roman Culture', *Classical Journal* 92, pp. 373–383.

Farwell, D. E. and Molleson, T. I., 1987: *Excavations at Poundbury, Dorchester, Dorset, 1966–1982 Volume 2: The Cemeteries* (Dorset Natural History and Archaeological Society).

Favro, D., 1996: *The Urban Image of Augustan Rome* (Cambridge University Press).

Favro, D., 1999: 'The City is a Living Thing: the Performative Role of an Urban Site in Ancient Rome, the Vallis Murcia' in Bergmann, B. and Kolodeon, C. (eds), pp. 205–220.

Fentress, E., (ed.), 2000: 'Romanization and the City: Creation, Transformations, and Failures', *Journal of Roman Archaeology Supplementary Series* 38.

Ferris, I. M., 1986: 'Horse-and-Rider Brooches in Britain: a New Example from Rocester, Staffordshire', *Transactions of the South Staffordshire Archaeological and Historical Society* XXVI, pp. 1–10.

Ferris, I. M., 1990: 'The Lion Motif in Romano-British Art', *Transactions of the South Staffordshire Archaeological & Historical Society* XXX, pp. 1–17.

Ferris, I. M., 1993: 'Excavations at Maidenbrook Farm, Cheddon Fitzpaine, 1990', *Proceedings of the Somerset Archaeological and Natural History Society* 137, pp. 1–40.

Ferris, I. M., 1994: 'Insignificant Others; Images of Barbarians on Military Art from Roman Britain' in Cottam, S. *et al.* (eds), pp. 24–31.

Ferris, I. M., 1995: 'Shoppers Paradise: Consumers in Roman Britain' in Rush, P. (ed.), pp. 132–140.

Ferris, I. M., 1997: 'The Enemy Without, the Enemy Within: More Thoughts on Images of Barbarians in Greek and Roman art' in Meadows, K. *et al.* (eds), pp. 22–8.

Ferris, I. M., 1999a: 'Alchemy of Suffering. Hope and Faith Beyond the Healing Arts in Roman Britain' in Leslie, A. (ed.), *Theoretical Roman Archaeology and Architecture, The Third Conference Proceedings* (Glasgow: Cruithne Press) pp. 1–13.

Ferris, I. M., 1999b: 'Invisible Architecture: Inside the Roman Memory Palace' in Leslie, A. (ed.), *Theoretical Roman Archaeology and Architecture, The Third Conference Proceedings* (Glasgow: Cruithne Press) pp. 191–199.

Ferris, I. M., 2000: *Enemies of Rome: Barbarians Through Roman Eyes* (Stroud: Sutton Publishing).

Ferris, I. M., 2001: 'The Body Politic: the Sexuality of Barbarians in Augustan Art' in Bevan, L. (ed.), pp. 100–9.

Ferris, I. M., 2003a: 'The Hanged Men Dance: Barbarians in Trajanic Art' in Scott, S. and Webster, J. (eds), pp. 53–68.

Ferris, I. M., 2003b: 'An Empire in Pieces: Roman Archaeology and the Fragment' in Carr, G., Swift, E. and Weekes, J. (eds), *TRAC 2002: Proceedings of the Twelfth Theoretical Roman Archaeology Conference, Canterbury* (Oxford: Oxbow Books) pp. 14–28.

Ferris, I. M., 2003c: 'Collage and Spectacle: Urban Art in Roman Britain' in Wilson, P. (ed.), *The Archaeology of Roman Towns: Studies in Honour of John. S. Wacher* (Oxford: Oxbow Books) pp. 86–94.

Ferris, I. M., 2005: 'A Severed Head. Prologomena to a Study of the Fragmented Body in Roman Archaeology and Art' in Hingley, R. and Willis, S. (eds), pp. 115–126.

Ferris, I. M., 2009: *Hate and War: The Column of Marcus Aurelius* (Stroud: The History Press).

Ferris, I. M., 2010: *The Beautiful Rooms Are Empty: Excavations at Binchester Roman Fort, County Durham 1976–1981 and 1986–1991* (Durham County Council)

Ferris, I. M., 2011a: 'The Pity of War: Representations of Gauls and Germans in Roman Art' in Gruen, E. S. (ed.), *Cultural Identity in the Ancient Mediterranean* (Los Angeles: Getty Research Institute) pp. 185–201.

Ferris, I. M., 2011b: *Vinovia: The Buried Roman City of Binchester in Northern England* (Stroud: Amberley).

Ferris, I. M., In Press: 'A Roman Carved Jet Dog from Binchester Roman Fort, County Durham', *Durham Archaeological Journal*.

Ferris, I. M., Forthcoming: 'Roman Religious Sites in the West Midlands' in White, R. (ed.), 'Research Issues in the Roman Period in the West Midlands: LPRIA to Sub-Roman', *West Midlands Regional Research Framework for Archaeology* (Oxford: Oxbow Books).

Ferris, I. M., Forthcoming: *The Arch of Constantine in Rome: Inspired by the Divine* (Stroud: Amberley).

Ferris, I. M., Bevan, L. and Cuttler, R., 2000: 'The Excavation of a Romano-British Shrine at Orton's Pasture, Rocester, Staffordshire', *British Archaeological Reports British Series* 314 (Oxford: Archaeopress).

Ferris, I. M. and Smith, J., 1998: 'Discovered Under Other Skies. Prehistoric Stone Tools in Romano-British and Gallo-Roman Ritual and Religious Contexts', *Journal of Theoretical Archaeology* 5/6, pp. 175–186.

Field, N. H., 1965: 'Fossil Sea-Urchins from a Romano-British Site', *Antiquity* 39, p. 298.

Fitzpatrick, A. P., 1984: 'The Deposition of La Tène Iron Age Metalwork in Watery Contexts in Southern England' in Cunliffe, B. and Miles, D. (eds), 'Aspects of the Iron Age in Central Southern Britain', *Oxford Monograph* 2, pp. 178–188.

Fine, B., 2002: *The World of Consumption: the Material and Cultural Revisited* (London: Routledge).

Florida, R., 2004: *The Rise of the Creative Class; and How It's Transforming Work, Leisure, Community and Everyday Life* (New York: Basic Books).

Florida, R., 2005a: *The Flight of the Creative Class: the New Global Competition for Talent* (New York: HarperBusiness).

Florida, R., 2005b: *Cities and the Creative Class* (London: Routledge).

Florida, R., 2008: *Who's Your City: How the Creative Economy is Making Where to Live the Most Important Decision of Your Life* (New York: Basic Books).

Flower, H. I., 1996: *Ancestor Masks and Aristocratic Power in Roman Culture* (Oxford: Clarendon Press).

Forcey, C., 1998: 'Whatever Happened to the Heroes? Ancestral Cults and the Enigma of Romano-Celtic Temples' in Forcey, C. *et al.* (eds), pp. 87–98.

Forcey, C., Hawthorne, J. and Witcher, R. (eds), 1998: *TRAC 97: Proceedings of the Seventh Annual Theoretical Roman Archaeology Conference, Nottingham 1997* (Oxford: Oxbow Books).

Forrester, J., 1994: 'Freud and Collecting' in Elsner, J. and Cardinal, R. (eds), *The Cultures of Collecting* (London: Reaktion Books), pp. 224–251.

Foster, J., 1986: 'The Lexden Tumulus: A Reappraisal of an Iron Age Burial from Colchester, Essex', *British Archaeological Reports British Series* 156 (Oxford).

Foster, J., 1993: 'The Identification of Male and Female Graves Using grave-goods' in Struck, M. (ed.), *Römerzeitliche Gräber als Quellen zur Religion, Bevölkerungsstruktur und Sozialgeschicte* (Mainz: Johannes Gutenberg Institut für Vor-und Frühgeschicte), pp. 207–213.

Foxhall, L. (ed.), 1998: *Thinking Men: Masculinity and its Self-Representation in the Classical Tradition* (London: Routledge).

Foxhall, L., Gehrke, H-J. and Luraghi, N. (eds), 2010: *Intentional History: Spinning Time in Ancient Greece* (Stuttgart: Franz Steiner Verlag).

Foxhall, L. and Salmon, J. B. (eds), 1998: *When Men Were Men: Masculinity, Power and Identity in Classical Archaeology* (London: Routledge).

Francis, D. (ed.), 2007: *Faith and Transformation: Votive Offerings and Amulets from the Alexander Girard Collection, Museum of International Folk Art* (Santa Fe: Museum of New Mexico Press).

Fredrick, D., 2002: 'Mapping Penetrability in Late Republican and Early Imperial Rome' in Fredrick, D. (ed.), pp. 236–264.

Fredrick, D. (ed.), 2002: *The Roman Gaze: Vision, Power, and the Body* (Baltimore: Johns Hopkins University Press)

Frere, S. S., 1972: 'Verulamium Excavations Volume 1', *Society of Antiquaries Research Report* 28 (London).

Friendship-Taylor, R. and Jackson, R., 2001: 'A New Roman Gladiator Find from Piddington, Northamptonshire', *Antiquity* 75, pp. 27–28.

Fulford, M., 2001: 'Links with the Past: Pervasive "Ritual" Behaviour in Roman Britain', *Britannia* XXXII, pp. 199–218.

Fulford, M., 2010: 'Roman Britain: Immigration and Material Culture' in Eckardt, H. (ed.), pp. 67–78.

Funari, P. P. A., 1993: 'Graphic Caricature and the Ethos of Ordinary People at Pompeii', *Journal of European Archaeology* 1:2, pp. 133–50.

Furger, A. R., Wartmann, M. and Riha, E., 2009: 'Die Römischen Siegelkapseln Aus Augusta Raurica', *Furschungen in Augst* 44.

Gaffney, V. L. and White, R. H., 2007: 'Wroxeter, the Cornovii, and the Urban Process: Final Report on the Wroxeter Hinterland Project 1994–1997, Volume 1: Researching the Hinterland', *Journal of Roman Archaeology Supplementary Series* 68.

Gager, J. G. (ed.), 1992: *Curse Tablets and Binding Spells from the Ancient World* (Oxford University Press).

Galliou, P., 1989: 'Les Tombes Romaines d'Armorique: Essai de Sociologie et d'Economie de la Mort', *Documents d'Archéologie Française* 17 (Paris).

Gancel, H., 2001: *Les Saints qui Guérissent en Bretagne* (Luçon: Éditions Ouest-France).

Garland, R., 1995: *The Eye of the Beholder: Deformity and Disability in the Graeco-Roman World* (Ithaca: Cornell University Press).

Garrow, D., Lucy, S. and Gibson, D., 2006: 'Excavations at Kilverstone, Norfolk: an Episodic Landscape History', *East Anglian Archaeology* 113.

Garwood, P., Jennings, D., Skeates, R. and Toms, J. (eds), 1991: 'Sacred and Profane: Proceedings of a Conference on Archaeology, Ritual, and Religion: Oxford 1989', *Oxford University Committee for Archaeology Monograph* 32 (Oxford).

Gattai, R. and Poma, R., 1987: *I Bronzi di Cartoceto* (Florence).

Gazda, E. K., 1973: 'Etruscan Influence in the Funerary Reliefs of Late Republican Rome: a Study of Vernacular Portraiture', *Aufstieg und Niedergang der Römischen Welt* 1(4), pp. 855–70.

Gazda, E. K. (ed.), 1991: *Roman Art in the Private Sphere: New Perspectives on the Architecture and Décor of the Domus, Villa, and Insula* (University of Michigan Press).

Gehrke, H-J., 2001: 'Myth, History, and Collective Identity: Uses of the Past in Ancient Greece and Beyond' in Luraghi, N. (ed.), *The Historian's Craft in the Age of Herodotus* (Oxford University Press) pp. 286–313.

Gehrke, H-J., 2010: 'Representations of the Past in Greek Culture' in Foxhall, L., Gehrke, H-J. and Luraghi, N. (eds), pp. 15–34.

Giuliani, L., 2010: 'Myth as Past? On the Temporal Aspect of Greek Depictions of Legend', in Foxhall, L., Gehrke, H-J. and Luraghi, N. (eds), pp. 35–56.

Gollán, A. Z., 1977: *Supersticiones y Amuletos* (Argentina).

Gosden, C. and Marshall, Y., 1999: 'The Cultural Biography of Objects', *World Archaeology* 31(2), pp. 167–178.

Govi, C. M. and Vitali, D., 1988: *Il Museo Civico Archeologico di Bologna* (Bologna, University Press).

Graf, F., 1997: *Magic in the Ancient World* (Harvard University Press).

Graham, E-J., 2009: 'Becoming Persons, Becoming Ancestors: Personhood, Memory and the Corpse in Roman Rituals of Social Remembrance', *Archaeological Dialogues* 16(1), pp. 51–74.

Graham, E-J., 2011: 'From Fragments to Ancestors: Re-Defining the Role of Os Resectum in Rituals of Purification and Commemoration in Republican Rome' in Carroll, M. and Rempel, J. (eds), 'Living Through the Dead: Burial and Commemoration in the Classical World', *Studies in Funerary Archaeology* 5 (Oxford: Oxbow Books), pp. 91–109.

Graham, E-J., Sulosky, C. L., and Chamberlain, A. T., Forthcoming: *A Probable Case of Os Resectum in a Romano-British Cremation Burial from Lincoln.*

Gramsci, A., Hoare, Q. and Nowell, G. (eds, trans), 1971: *Selections from the Prison Notebooks of Antonio Gramsci.* (London: Lawrence & Wishart).

Green, M. J., 1975: 'Romano-British Non-Ceramic Model Objects in South-East Britain', *Archaeological Journal* 132, pp. 54–70.

Green, M. J., 1976: 'The Religions of Civilian Roman Britain. A Corpus of Religious Material from the Civilian Areas of Roman Britain', *British Archaeological Reports British Series* 24 (Oxford).

Green, M. J., 1978: 'Small Cult Objects from the Military Areas of Roman Britain', *British Archaeological Reports British Series* 52 (Oxford).

Green, M. J., 1991: 'Triplism and Plurality: Intensity and Symbolism in Celtic Religious Expression' in Garwood, P. *et al.* (eds), pp. 100–108.

Greenfield, E., 1963: 'The Romano-British Shrines at Brigstock, Northamptonshire', *Antiquaries Journal* 43, pp. 228–263.

Greep, S. J., 1983: 'Hand-and-Phallus Pendants' in Crummy, N., pp. 139–140.

Greep, S. J. (ed.), 1993: 'Roman Towns: The Wheeler Inheritance', *Council for British Archaeology Research Report* 93 (York).

Gregory, A. P., 1994: '"Powerful Images": Responses to Portraits and the Political Uses of Images in Rome', *Journal of Roman Archaeology* 7, pp. 80–99.

Grew, F. and Hobley, B. (eds), 1985: 'Roman Urban Topography in Britain and the Western Empire', *Council for British Archaeology Research Report* 59 (London).

Griffiths, K. E., 1989: 'Marketing of Roman Pottery in Second-Century Northamptonshire and the Milton Keynes Area', *Journal of Roman Pottery Studies* 2, pp. 67–76.

Gruen, E. S., 2011: *Rethinking the Other in Antiquity* (Princeton University Press).

Guido, M., 1978: 'The Glass Beads of the Prehistoric and Roman Periods in Britain and Ireland', *Society of Antiquaries of London Research Report* 35 (London).

Hall, J. and Wardle, A., 2005: 'Dedicated Followers of Fashion? Decorative Bone Hairpins from Roman London' in Crummy, N. (ed.), pp. 173–179.

Hallam, E. and Hockey, J., 2001: *Death, Memory and Material Culture* (Oxford: Berg).

Hallett, J. P. and Skinner, M. B. (eds), 1997: *Roman Sexualities* (Princeton University Press).

Halperin, D., Winkler, J., and Zeitlin, F., 1990: *Before Sexuality: the Construction of the Erotic Experience in the Ancient Greek World* (Princeton University Press).

Hamp, E. P., 1975: 'Social Gradience and British Spoken Latin', *Britannia* VI, pp. 150–162.

Hannestad, N., 1988: *Roman Art and Imperial Policy* (Aarhus University Press).

Hanson, W. S. and Conolly, R., 2002: 'Language and Literacy in Roman Britain: Some Archaeological Considerations' in Cooley, A. (ed.), pp. 151–164.

Hargrave, F., 2009: 'The Hallaton Treasure: Evidence of a New Kind of Shrine?', *Current Archaeology* 236, pp. 36–41.

Harlow, M. and Laurence, R., 2002: *Growing Up and Growing Old in Ancient Rome: A Life Course Approach* (London: Routledge).

Harrison, R. P., 2003: *The Dominion of the Dead* (University of Chicago Press).

Haskell, F. 1993: *History and its Images: Art and the Interpretation of the Past* (New Haven: Yale University Press).

Haug, A., 2001: 'Constituting the Past-Forming the Present. The Role of Material Culture in the Augustan Period', *Journal of the History of Collections* 13.2, pp. 111–124.

Haussler, R., 1999: 'The Role of State Architecture in the Roman Empire' in Barker, P. *et al.* (eds), pp. 1–13.

Havari, M., 2004: 'A Short History of Pygmies in Greece and Italy' in Lomas, K. (ed.), 'Greek Identity in the Western Mediterranean', *Mnemosyne Supplement* 246 (Leiden: Brill), pp. 163–190.

Haynes, I., 2000: 'Religion in Roman London' in Haynes, I., Sheldon, H. and Hannigan, L. (eds), pp. 85–101.

Haynes, I., Sheldon, H. and Hannigan, L. (eds), 2000: *London Under Ground: The Archaeology of a City* (Oxford: Oxbow).

Heckler, I. (ed.) 1989: *The Meaning of Things: Material Culture and Symbolic Expression* (London: Unwin Hyman).

Henig, M., 1974 & 1978: 'A Corpus of Roman Engraved Gemstones from British Sites', *British Archaeological Reports British Series* 8 (Oxford).

Henig, M., 1978: 'Some Reflections of Greek Sculpture and Painting in Roman Art From London' in Bird, J., Chapman, H. and Clark, J. (eds), pp. 109–123.

Henig, M., 1980: 'Art and Cult in the Temples of Roman Britain' in Rodwell, W. J. (ed.), pp. 91–113.

Henig, M., 1984: *Religion in Roman Britain* (London: Batsford).

Henig, M., 1985: 'Graeco-Roman Art and Romano-British Imagination', *Journal of the British Archaeological Association* CXXXVIII, pp. 1–22.

Henig, M., 1995: 'Ita Intellexit Numine Inductus Tuo: Some Personal Interpretations of Deity in Roman Religion' in Henig, M., and King, A. (eds), pp. 159–169.

Henig, M., (ed.), 1990: 'Architecture and Architectural Sculpture in the Roman Empire', *Oxford University Committee for Archaeology Monograph* 29 (Oxford).

Henig, M., 1993: *Corpus Signorum Imperii Romani, Great Britain Volume 1 Fascicule 7: Roman Sculpture from the Cotswold Region with Devon and Cornwall* (Oxford University Press).

Henig, M., 1995: *The Art of Roman Britain* (London: Batsford).

Henig, M., 1998: 'Romano-British Art and Gallo-Roman Samian' in Bird, J. (ed.), *Form and Fabric: Studies in Rome's Material Past in Honour of Brian Hartley* (Oxford: Oxbow Books), pp. 59–67.

Henig, M., 1999: 'A New Star Shining Over Bath', *Oxford Journal of Archaeology* 18(4), pp. 419–425.

Henig, M., 2000: 'Art in Roman London' in Haynes, I., Sheldon, H. and Hannigan, L. (eds), pp. 62–84.

Henig, M., 2004: *Corpus Signorum Imperii Romani, Great Britain Volume 1 Fascicule 9: Roman Sculpture from the North West Midlands* (Oxford University Press).

Henig, M., and King, A., (eds), 1986: 'Pagan Gods and Shrines of the Roman Empire', *Oxford University Committee for Archaeology Monograph* 8 (Oxford).

Henig, M., and Leahy, K., 1995: 'A Herm of Priapus from Haxey, Lincolnshire', *Journal of the British Archaeological Association* 148, pp. 169–170.

Higham, N. J., 1989: 'Roman and Native in England North of the Tees: Acculturation and Its Limitations' in Barrett, J. *et al.* (eds), pp. 153–174.

Hill, P. V., 1989: *The Monuments of Ancient Rome as Coin Types* (London: Seaby).

Hill, C., Millett, M. and Blagg, T., 1980: 'The Roman Riverside Wall and Monumental Arch in London: Excavations at Baynard's Castle, Upper Thames Street, London 1974–76', *London and Middlesex Archaeological Society Special Paper* 3.

Hingley, R., 1989: *Rural Settlement in Roman Britain* (London: Seaby).

Hingley, R., 2006: 'The Deposition of Iron Objects in Britain During the Later Prehistoric and Roman Periods: Contextual Analysis and the Significance of Iron', *Britannia* XXXVII, pp. 213–257.

Hingley, R., 2009: 'Esoteric Knowledge? Ancient Bronze Artefacts from Iron Age Contexts', *Proceedings of the Prehistoric Society* 75, pp. 143–165.

Hingley, R., 2010: 'Tales of the Frontier: Diasporas on Hadrian's Wall' in Eckardt, H. (ed.), pp. 227–243.

Hingley, R., 2011: 'Iron Age Knowledge: Pre-Roman Peoples and Myths of Origin' in Moore, T. and Armada, X-L. (eds), *Atlantic Europe in the First Millennium BC: Crossing the Divide* (Oxford University Press), pp. 617–637.

Hingley, R. and Willis, S. (eds), 2005: *Roman Finds: Context and Theory* (Oxford: Oxbow Books).

Hodder, I. (ed.), 1989: 'The Meanings of Things: Material Culture and Symbolic Expression', *One World Archaeology* 6 (London: Harper Collins Academic).

Hoffman, B., 1995: 'The Quarters of Legionary Centurions of the Principate', *Britannia* XXVI, pp. 107–151.

Holbrook, P. and Haynes, I. (eds), 1996: 'Architecture in Roman Britain', *Council for British Archaeology Research Report* 94 (York).

Holmes, S., 1995: 'Roman Seal Boxes: a Classification of the Seal Boxes from Roman London', *London Archaeologist* 7.15, pp. 391–395.

Hooppell, R. E., 1891: *Vinovia: A Buried Roman City in the County of Durham* (London: Whiting & Co.).

Hope, V., 1997: 'Words and Pictures: the Interpretation of Romano-British Tombstones', *Britannia* XXVIII, pp. 245–258.

Horne, P. D. and King, A. C., 1980: 'Romano-Celtic Temples in Continental Europe: a Gazetteer of Those with Known Plans' in Rodwell, W. J. (ed.), pp. 369–555.

Hoskins, J., 1998: *Biographical Objects: How Things Tell the Stories of Peoples' Lives* (London: Routledge).

Hoskins, J., 2006: 'Agency, Biography and Objects' in Tilley, C. *et al.* (eds), pp. 74–84.

Hughes, G., Leach, P. and Stanford, S. C., 1995: 'Excavations at Bromfield, Shropshire 1981–91', *Transactions of the Shropshire Archaeological and Historical Society* 70, pp. 23–94.

Humphrey, J. and Young, R., 2003: 'Flint Use in Later Bronze Age and Iron Age England? Some Criteria for Future Research' in Moloney, N. and Shott, M. J. (eds), *Lithic Analysis at the Millennium* (Institute of Archaeology, University College London) pp. 79–89.

Huskinson, J., 1994: *Corpus Signorum Imperii Romani, Great Britain Volume 1 Fascicule 8: Roman Sculpture from Eastern England* (Oxford University Press).

Huskinson, J., 1996: *Roman Children's Sarcophagi: Their Decoration and its Social Significance* (Oxford: Clarendon Press).

Huskinson, J., 2000: 'Portraits' in Ling, R. (ed.), *Making Classical Art: Process and Practice* (Stroud: Tempus), pp. 155–68.

Hutchinson, V., 1986a: 'Bacchus in Roman Britain: the Evidence of His Cult', *British Archaeological Reports British Series* 151 (Oxford).

Hutchinson, V., 1986b: 'The Cult of Bacchus in Roman Britain' in Henig, M., and King, A. (eds), 'Pagan Gods and Shrines of the Roman Empire', *Oxford University Committee for Archaeology Monograph* 8 (Oxford), pp. 135–146.

Hutton, R., 2011: 'Romano-British Reuse of Prehistoric Ritual Sites', *Britannia* XLII, pp. 1–22.

Isaac, B., 2004: *The Invention of Racism in Classical Antiquity* (Princeton University Press).

Isserlin, R. M. J., 1994: 'An Archaeology of Brief Time: Monuments and Seasonality in Roman Britain' in Cottam, S. *et al.* (eds), pp. 45–56.

Isserlin, R. M. J., 1997: 'Thinking the Unthinkable: Human Sacrifice in Roman Britain?' in Meadows, K. *et al.* (eds), pp. 91–100.

Isserlin, R., 1998: 'A Spirit of Improvement? Marble and the Culture of Roman Britain' in Laurence, R. and Berry, J. (eds), pp. 125–156.

Jackson, R., 1988: *Doctors and Diseases in the Roman Empire* (British Museum).

Jackson, R., 2000: 'Gladiators in Roman Britain', *British Museum Magazine* 38, pp. 16–21.

Jackson, R., 2010: *Cosmetic Sets of Late Iron Age and Roman Britain* (British Museum Press).

James, N., 1963: *The Spoils of Poynton* (Harmondsworth: Penguin Classics).

James, S. and Millett, M. (eds), 2001: 'Britons and Romans: Advancing an Archaeological Agenda', *Council for British Archaeology Research Report* 125 (York).

Jenkins, F., 1959: 'The Cult of the "Pseudo-Venus" in Kent', *Archaeologia Cantiana* 72, pp. 60–76.

Jenkins, F., 1977: *Clay Statuettes of the Roman Western Provinces*, Unpublished PhD thesis, (University of Kent).

Johns, C., 1982: *Sex or Symbol: Erotic Images of Greece and Rome* (British Museum Publications).

Johns, C., 1990a: 'A Romano-British Statuette of a Mounted Warrior God', *Antiquaries Journal* 70, pp. 446–452.

Johns, C., 1990b: 'A Romano-British Priapus', *Minerva* 1.9, p. 47.

Johns, C., 1995: 'Mounted Men and Sitting Ducks: the Iconography of Romano-British Plate-Brooches' in Raftery, B., Megaw, V. and Rigby, V. (eds), *Sites and Sights of the Iron Age: Essays on Fieldwork and Museum Research Presented to Ian Mathieson Stead* (Oxford: Oxbow Books), pp. 103–109.

Johns, C., 1996: *The Jewellery of Roman Britain: Celtic and Classical Traditions* (UCL Press).

Johns, C. and Henig, M., 1991: 'A Statuette of a Herm of Priapus from Pakenham, Suffolk', *Antiquaries Journal* 71, pp. 236–239.

Johnston, D. E., 1994: 'Some Possible North African Influences in Romano-British Mosaics' in Johnson, P., Ling, R. and Smith, D. J. (eds), 'Fifth International Colloquium on Ancient Mosaics Bath, 1987', *Journal of Roman Archaeology Supplementary Series* 91, pp. 295–306.

Jones, C. P., 1987: 'Stigma: Tattooing and Branding in Gallo-Roman Antiquity', *Journal of Roman Studies* 77, pp. 139–155.

Jones, R. F. J., 1987: 'A False Start? The Roman Urbanization of Western Europe', *World Archaeology* 19(1), pp. 47–57.

Jope, E. M., 1973: 'The Transmission of New Ideas: Archaeological Evidence for Impact and Dispersal', *World Archaeology* 4(3), pp. 368–373.

Jouffroy, H., 1986: 'La Construction Publique en Italie et dans L'Afrique Romaine', *Études et Travaux Groupe de Recherche d'Histoire Romaine de l'Université de Sciences Humaines de Strasbourg* (Strasbourg).

Jundi, S. and Hill, J. D., 1998: 'Brooches and Identities in First Century AD Britain: More Than Meets the Eye?' in Forcey, C. *et al.* (eds), pp. 125–137.

Kampen, N. B., 1991a: 'Between Public and Private; Women as Historical Subjects in Roman Art' in Pomeroy, S. B. (ed.), pp. 218–248.

Kampen, N. B., 1991b: 'Reliefs of the Basilica Aemilia', *Klio (Beitrage zur Alten Geschichte)* 73, pp. 448–458.

Kampen, N. B. 1994: 'Material Girl: Feminist Confrontations with Roman Art', *Arethusa* 27/1, pp. 111–149.

Kampen, N. B. (ed.), 1996: *Sexuality in Ancient Art* (Cambridge University Press).

Kampen, N. B., Marlowe, E., and Molholt, R. M., 2002: *What is a Man? Changing Images of Masculinity in Late Antique Art* (Douglas F. Cooley Memorial Art Gallery, Reed College, Portland).

Karklins, K. (ed.), 2000: 'Studies in Material Culture Research', *The Society for Historical Archaeology* (University of Pennsylvania).

Keegan, P., 2001: *Text, Artifact, Context: the Interaction of Literature, Material Culture and Mentality in the Ancient World* (University of New England Press).

Keegan, P., 2010: 'Blogging Rome: Graffiti as Speech, Act and Cultural Discourse' in Baird, J. A. and Taylor, C. (eds), *Ancient Graffiti in Context* (London: Routledge), pp. 165–190.

Kellum, B., 1996: 'The Phallus as Signifier: the Forum of Augustus and Rituals of Masculinity' in Kampen, N. B. (ed.), pp. 170–83.

Kellum, B., 1999: 'The Spectacle of the Street' in Bergmann, B. and Kolodeon, C. (eds), pp. 283–300.

Keppie, L. J. F., 1975: 'The Distance Slabs from the Antonine Wall: Some Problems', *Scottish Archaeological Forum* 7, pp. 57–65.

Keppie, L. J. F. and Arnold, B. J., 1984: *Corpus Signorum Imperii Romani, Great Britain Volume 1 Fascicule 4: Scotland* (Oxford University Press).

Kiernan, P., 2009: *Miniature Votive Offerings in the Roman North-West* (Mainz und Ruhpolding: Verlag Franz Philipp Rutzen).

de Kind, R., 2005: 'The Roman Portraits from the Villa of Lullingstone: Pertinax and His Father, P. Helvius Successus' in Ganschow, T. and Steinhart, M. (eds), *Otium: Festscrift für Volker Michael Strocka* (Remshalden), pp. 47–53.

King, A. and Soffe, G., 1998: 'Internal Organisation and Deposition at the Iron Age Temple on Hayling Island', *Proceedings of the Hampshire Field Club and Archaeological Society* 53, pp. 35–47.

King, J. C. H., 1982: *Thunderbird and Lightning: Indian Life in Northeastern North America 1600–1900* (British Museum).

Kinney, D., 1997: 'Spolia: Damnatio and Renovatio Memoriae', *Memoirs of the American Academy in Rome* 42, pp. 117–48.

Kirk, J. R., 1949: 'Bronzes from Woodeaton, Oxfordshire', *Oxoniensia* 14, pp. 1–45.

Kislev, M. E., 1988: 'Pinus Pinea in Agriculture, Culture and Cult', in Kuster, H-J., 'Der Prahistorisch Mensch und Seine Umwelt', *Forschungen und Berichte zur vor und Fruhgeshichte in Baden-Wurttenburg* 31, pp. 73–79.

Kleiner, D. E. E., 1992: *Roman Sculpture* (New Haven: Yale University Press).

Kleiner, D. E. E., 1977: *Roman Group Portraiture: The Funerary Reliefs of the Late Republic and Early Empire* (New York: Garland Publishing).

Kleiner, D. E. E. 1996: 'Imperial Women as Patrons of the Arts in the Early Empire' in Kleiner, D. E. E. and Matheson, S. B. (eds), *I Claudia: Women in Ancient Rome* (University of Texas Press), pp. 28–41.

Kleiner, D. E. E., 2000: 'Now You See Them, Now You Don't: The Presence and Absence of Women in Roman Art' in Varner, E. R. (ed.), pp. 45–57.

Kleiner, F. S. and Stucchi, S., 1988: 'Il gruppo bronzeo tiberiano da Cartoceto', *American Journal of Archaeology* 94, pp. 514–515.

Kleiner, F. S., 1998: 'The Roman Arches of Gallia Narbonensis', *Journal of Roman Archaeology* 11, pp. 610–612.

Knauer, E. R., 1990: 'Multa Egit Cum Regibus et Pacem Confirmavit: The Date of the Equestrian Statue of Marcus Aurelius', *Mitteilungen des Deutschen Archäologischen Instituts, Römische Abteilung* 97, pp. 277–305.

Koloski-Ostrow, A. O. and Lyons, C. L. (eds), 1997: *Naked Truths: Women, Sexuality and Gender in Classical Art and Archaeology* (London: Routledge).

Koortbojian, M., 1996: 'In Commemorationem Mortuorum: Text and Image Along the "Streets of Tombs"' in Elsner, J. (ed.), *Art and Text in Roman Culture* (Cambridge University Press), pp. 210–234.

Kopytoff, I., 1986: 'The Cultural Biography of Things: Commoditization as Process' in Appadurai, A. (ed.), *The Social Life of Things: Commodities in Cultural Perspectives* (Cambridge University Press), pp. 64–91.

Kristeva, J., 1998: *Visions Capitales* (Paris: Reunion des Musées Nationaux).

Kuefler, M., 2001: *The Manly Eunuch: Masculinity, Gender Ambiguity, and Christian Ideology in Late Antiquity* (University of Chicago Press).

Lacan, J., Sheridan, A. and Norton, W. W. (trans.), 1977: 'The Signification of the Phallus' in *Écrits* (New York) pp. 281–291.

Landy, D., 1977: 'Role Adaption: Traditional Curers Under the Impact of Western Medicine' originally published 1974, reprinted in Landy, D. (ed.) *Culture, Disease and Healing: Studies in Medical Anthropology* (London: MacMillan), pp. 468–480.

Laurence, R. and Berry, J. (eds), 1998: *Cultural Identity in the Roman Empire* (London: Routledge).

Laurence, R., Esmonde Cleary, A. S. and Sears, G., 2011: *The City in the Roman West c. 250 BC to AD 250* (Cambridge University Press).

Laven, M., 2011: *Mission to China: Matteo Ricci and the Jesuit Encounter with the East* (London: Faber & Faber).

Leach, P., 1998: 'Great Witcombe Roman Villa, Gloucestershire: A Report on Excavations by Ernest Greenfield 1960–1973', *British Archaeological Reports British Series* 266 (Oxford: Archaeopress).

Leach, P., 2001: 'Fosse Lane, Shepton Mallet: Excavation of a Romano-British Roadside Settlement in Somerset', *Britannia Monograph* 18 (London: Society for the Promotion of Roman Studies).

Lee, R., 2009: 'The Production, Use and Disposal of Romano-British Pewter Tableware', *British Archaeological Reports British Series* 478 (Oxford: Archaeopress).

Leech, R., 1982: 'The Roman Interlude in the South West' in Miles, D. (ed.), 'The Romano-British Countryside: Studies in Rural Settlement and Economy', *British Archaeological Reports British Series* 103 (Oxford), pp. 209–267.

Leech, R., 1986: 'The Excavation of a Romano-Celtic Temple and a Later Cemetery on Lamyatt Beacon, Somerset', *Britannia* XVII, pp. 259–328.

Lefkowitz, M. R., 1983: 'Influential Women' in Cameron, A. and Kuhrt, A. (eds), *Images of Women in Antiquity* (London: Routledge) pp. 49–64.

Le Goff, J., Rendall, S. and Claman, E. (trans.), 1992: *History and Memory* (New York: Columbia University Press).

Levi, D., 1941: 'The Evil Eye and the Lucky Hunchback' in Stillwell, R. (ed.), *Antioch-on-the-Orontes* (Princeton University Press).

Lewis, M. J. T., 1965: *Temples in Roman Britain* (Cambridge University Press).

Lewis, O., 1959: *Five Families: Mexican Case Studies in the Culture of Poverty* (New York: Basic Books).

Lindgren, C., 1980: *Classical Art Forms and Celtic Mutations: Figural Art in Roman Britain* (New Jersey: Park Ridge).

Ling, R., 1990: 'Street Plaques at Pompeii' in Henig, M., (ed.) 'Architecture and Architectural Sculpture in the Roman Empire', *Oxford University Committee for Archaeology Monograph* 29 (Oxford), pp. 51–66.

Liverani, P., 2002: 'Scheda 26: Busto Feminile' in de Marinis, G., Rinaldi Tufi, S. and Baldelli, G. (eds), pp. 139–141.

Liversidge, J., 1968: *Britain in the Roman Empire* (London: Routledge & Kegan Paul).

Lloyd, G. R., 1973: *Greek Science After Aristotle* (London: Chatto & Windus).

Lloyd-Morgan, G., 1983: 'Some Mirrors from Roman Canterbury', *Archaeologia Cantiana* 99, pp. 231–236.

Lloyd-Morgan, G., 1987: 'Report on Mirrors from Burials 3 and 15, Cranmer House, London Road, Canterbury' in Frere, S. S., Bennett, P., Rady, J. and Stow, S., *Canterbury Excavations: Intra- and Extra-Mural sites 1949–55 and 1980–84* (Canterbury Archaeological Trust), pp. 271–274.

Lloyd-Morgan, G., 1990: 'An Introduction to Roman Mirrors and their Literature', *Roman Finds Group Newsletter* 2, pp. 13–18.

Lomas, K., 1995: 'Urban Elites and Cultural Definition: Romanization in Southern Italy' in Cornell, T. J. and Lomas, K. (eds), pp. 107–120.

Lomas, K., 1997: 'The Idea of a City: Elite Ideology and the Evolution of Urban Form in Italy, 200 BC–AD 100' in Parkins, H. M. (ed.), pp. 21–41.

Lomas, K., 1998: 'Roman Imperialism and the City in Italy' in Laurence, R. and Berry, J. (eds), pp. 64–78.

Lubar, S. and Kingery, D. W. (eds), 1993: *History from Things: Essays on Material Culture* (Smithsonian Institute Press).

Lucas, G., 2005: *The Archaeology of Time* (London: Routledge).

Luni, M., 1988: 'Il Gruppo Bronzeo di Cartoceto e il Territorio del Rinvenimento in Età Romana' in *La Civiltà Picena nelle Marche* (Ancona), pp. 526–555.

MacGregor, N., 2010: *A History of the World in 100 Objects* (London: Allen Lane).

Mack, J., 2007: *The Art of Small Things* (British Museum Press).

Mackie, N., 1990: 'Urban Munificence and the Growth of Urban Consciousness in Roman Spain' in Blagg, T. F. C. and Millett, M. (eds), pp. 179–192.

Mackreth, D. F., 1987: 'Roman Public Buildings' in Schofield, J. and Leech, R. (eds), pp. 133–146.

Mackreth, D. F., 2011: *Brooches in Late Iron Age and Roman Britain* (Oxford: Oxbow Books).

MacMullen, R., 1980: 'Women in Public in the Roman Empire', *Historia* 29, pp. 208–218.

MacMullen, R., 1990: *Changes in the Roman Empire: Essays in the Ordinary* (Princeton University Press).

MacMullen, R., 1981: *Paganism in the Roman Empire* (New Haven: Yale University Press).

MacMullen, R., 1982: 'The Epigraphic Habit in the Roman Empire', *American Journal of Philology* 103, pp. 233–246.

MacMullen, R., 1986: *Judicial Savagery in the Roman Empire*. Reprinted in MacMullen, R., 1990: *Changes in the Roman Empire: Essays in the Ordinary* (Princeton University Press), pp. 204–217.

Maloney, J. and Hobley, B. (eds), 1983: 'Roman Urban Defences in the West', *Council for British Archaeology Research Report* 51 (York).

Mann, J., 1975: *The Romans in the North: Catalogue of the Exhibition* (Universities of Lancaster and Durham).

Manning, W. H., 1976: *Catalogue of Romano-British Ironwork in the Museum of Antiquities Newcastle Upon Tyne* (Department of Archaeology, University of Newcastle Upon Tyne).

Manning, W. H., 1985: *Catalogue of the Romano-British Iron Tools, Fittings and Weapons in the British Museum* (British Museum).

Manning, W. H., Price, J. and Webster, J., 1995: *Usk: The Roman Small Finds* (Cardiff: University of Wales Press).

March, J., 1998: *Dictionary of Classical Mythology* (London: Cassell).

Marshall, A. J., 1975: 'Roman Women and the Provinces', *Ancient Society* 6, pp. 124–125.

Martin, R., 1965: 'Wooden Figures from the Source of the Seine', *Antiquity* 39, pp. 247–252.

Martingell, H. E., 2003: 'Later Prehistoric and Historic Use of Flint in England' in Moloney, N. and Shott, M. J. (eds), *Lithic Analysis at the Millennium* (Institute of Archaeology, University College London), pp. 91–97.

Martins, C. B., 2005: 'Becoming Consumers: Looking Beyond Wealth as an Explanation for Villa Variability', *British Archaeological Reports British Series* 403 (Oxford: Archaeopress).

Massart, C., 2002: 'Au-Dejá du Bijou, le Pouvoir du Symbole: les Amulettes en Forme de Lunule et de Phallus' in Sas, K. and Thoen, H. (eds), *Schone Schijn: Romeinse Juweelkunst in West-Europa/ Brilliance et Prestige: la Joaillerie Romaine en Europe Occidentale* (Leuven: Peeters), pp. 101–104.

Mattingly, D. J. (ed.), 1997: 'Dialogues in Roman Imperialism. Power, Discourse, and Discrepant Experience in the Roman Empire', *Journal of Roman Archaeology Supplementary Series* 23.

Mawer, C. F., 1995: 'Evidence for Christianity in Roman Britain: The Small Finds', *British Archaeological Reports British Series* 243 (Oxford: Archaeopress).

Mayor, A., 2000: *The First Fossil Hunters: Paleontology in Greek and Roman Times* (Princeton University Press).

McWhirr, A., Viner, L., Wells, C. and Griffiths, N., 1982: *Romano-British Cemeteries at Cirencester: Cirencester Excavations II* (Cirencester Excavation Committee, Corinium Museum).

Meadows, K., Lemke, C., and Heron, J. (eds), 1997: *TRAC 96: Proceedings of the Sixth Annual Theoretical Roman Archaeology Conference, Sheffield 1996* (Oxford: Oxbow Books).

Meaney, A. L., 1981: 'Anglo-Saxon Amulets and Curing Stones', *British Archaeological Reports British Series* 96 (Oxford).

Merrifield, R., 1977: 'Art and Religion in Roman London – an Inquest on the Sculptures of Londinium' in Munby, J., and Henig, M. (eds), pp. 375–406.

Merrifield, R., 1987: *The Archaeology of Ritual and Magic* (London: Batsford).

Meskell, L. M., 1998: 'The Irresistible Body and the Seduction of Archaeology' in Montserrat, D. (ed.), pp. 139–61.

Meskell, L. M., 2000: 'Writing the Body in Archaeology' in Rautman, A. E. (ed.), *Reading the Body: Representations and Remains in the Archaeological Record* (University of Pennsylvania Press), pp. 13–21.

Metzler, J., Millett, M., Roymans, N. and Slofstra, J. (eds), 1995: 'Integration in the Early Roman West: The Role of Culture and Ideology', *Dossiers d'Archeologie du Musée National d'Histoire et d'Art* 4 (Luxembourg).

Miles, H., 1977: 'The Honeyditches Roman Villa, Seaton, Devon', *Britannia* VIII, pp. 107–148.

Miller, D., 1995: *Acknowledging Consumption: a Review of New Studies* (London: Routledge).

Millett, M., 1977: 'Art in the "Small Towns": "Celtic" or "Classical"' in Munby, J. and Henig, M. (eds), pp. 283–296.

Millett, M., 1990a: *The Romanization of Britain: an Essay in Archaeological Interpretation* (Cambridge University Press).

Millett, M., 1990b: 'Historical Issues and Archaeological Interpretations' in Blagg, T. F. C. and Millett M. (eds), pp. 35–41.

Millett, M., 1994: 'Treasure: Interpreting Roman Hoards' in Cottam, C. *et al.* (eds), pp. 99–106.

Millett, M., 2001: 'Approaches to Urban Societies' in James, S. and Millett, M. (eds), pp. 60–66.

Mitard, P-H., 1982: 'La Tête en Tôle de Bronze de Genainville (Val-d'Oise)', *Gallia* 40, pp. 1–33, pp. 287–291.

Monaghan, J., 1997: 'Roman Pottery from York', *The Archaeology of York, the Pottery* 16/8 (York Archaeological Trust).

Montserrat, D. (ed.), 1998: *Changing Bodies, Changing Meanings: Studies on the Human Body in Antiquity* (London: Routledge).

Montserrat, D., 2000: 'Reading Gender in the Roman World' in Huskinson, J. (ed.), *Experiencing Rome: Culture, Identity and Power in the Roman Empire* (London: Routledge), pp. 153–181.

Most, G., 1992: 'The Rhetoric of Dismemberment in Neronian Poetry' in Hexter, R. and Selden, D. (eds), *Innovations of Antiquity* (London: Routledge), pp. 391–419.

Munby, J. and Henig, M. (eds), 1977: 'Roman Life and Art in Britain: A Celebration in Honour of the Eightieth Birthday of Jocelyn Toynbee', *British Archaeological Reports British Series* 41 (Oxford).

Murphy. P., Albarella, U., Germany, M. and Locker, A., 2000: 'Production, Imports and Status: Biological Remains from a Late Roman Farm at Great Holts Farm, Boreham, Essex, UK', *Environmental Archaeology* 5, pp. 35–48.

Musgrave, J., 1990: 'Dust and Damn'd Oblivion: a Study of Cremation in Ancient Greece', *Annual of the British School at Athens* 85, pp. 271–99.

Myers, F., 2001: *The Empire of Things: Regimes of Value and Material Culture* (New Mexico: School of American Research Press).

Nead, L., 1992: *The Female Nude: Art, Obscenity and Sexuality* (London: Routledge).

Neal, D. S., 1981: 'Roman Mosaics in Britain', *Britannia Monograph* 1 (London: Society for the Promotion of Roman Studies).

Newby, Z., 2003: 'Art and Identity in Asia Minor' in Scott, S. and Webster, J. (eds), pp. 192–213.

Niblett, R., 1999: 'The Excavation of a Ceremonial Site at Folly Lane, Verulamium', *Britannia Monograph Series* 14 (London: Society for the Promotion of Roman Studies).

Nicassio, S. V., 1991: 'A Tale of Three Cities? Perceptions of Eighteenth-Century Modena', *Journal of Interdisciplinary History* 21(3), pp. 415–445.

Nochlin, L., 1994: *The Body in Pieces: The Fragment as a Metaphor of Modernity* (London: Thames & Hudson).

Nodelman, S., 1975: 'How to Read a Roman Portrait', *Art in America* 63, pp. 26–33. Reproduced with postscript in D'Ambra, E. (ed.), 1993: *Roman Art in Context: An Anthology*, pp. 10–26.

Nottingham Museums, 1983: *Mysteries of Diana: the Antiquities from Nemi in Nottingham Museums* (Nottingham Museum).

Noy, D., 2010: 'Epigraphic Evidence for Immigrants at Rome and in Roman Britain' in Eckardt, H. (ed.), pp. 13–26.

Nylander, C., 1998: 'The Mutilated Image. "We" and "They" in History and Prehistory?', *Kungl. Vitterhets Historie och Antikvitets Akademien Konferenser* 40 (Stockholm), pp. 235–51.

Oddy, W. A., 1982: 'Gold in Antiquity: Aspects of Gilding and of Assaying', *Journal of the Royal Society of Arts* 130[5315], pp. 730–743.

Oddy, W. A., 2002: 'The Technology and Conservation of Two Fragments of Life-Size Gilt Bronze Roman Statuary' in Mattusch, C., Brauer, A. and Knudsen, S. E. (eds), 'From the Parts to the Whole: Acta of the 13th International Bronze Congress', *Journal of Roman Archaeology Supplementary Series* 39, pp. 98–103.

Oddy, W. A., Vlad, L. B. and Meeks, N. D., 1979: 'The Gilding of Bronze Statues in the Greek and Roman World' in Pallottino, M. *et al.*, pp. 182–187.

Oddy, W. A., Crowell, M. R., Craddock, P. T. and Hook, D. R., 1991: 'The Gilding of Bronze Sculptures in the Classical World' in True, M. and Podany, J. (eds), *Small Bronze Sculpture from the Ancient World* (Oxford University Press), pp. 103–124.

Orr, D. G., 1978: 'Roman Domestic Religion: the Evidence of the Household Shrine', *Aufsteig und Nidergang der Römischen Welt II, Principat* 16.2, pp. 1557–1591.

Orr, D. G., 1988: 'Learning from Lararia: Notes on Household Shrines in Pompeii' in Curtius, R. I. (ed.), *Studia Pompeiana and Classica: In Honour of Wilhelmina F. Jashemski* (New York: Caratzas), pp. 293–303.

Osborne, R., 1998: 'Men Without Clothes: Heroic Nakedness and Greek Art' in Wyke, M. (ed.), pp. 80–104.

Pacteau, F., 1994: *The Symptom of Beauty* (London: Reaktion Books).

Padgett, J. M. (ed.), 2001: *Roman Sculpture in the Art Museum* (Princeton University Press).

Paine, S., 2004: *Amulets: A World of Secret Powers, Charms and Magic* (London: Thames & Hudson).

Painter, K. S., 1971: 'A Roman Gold Ex-Voto from Wroxeter, Shropshire', *Antiquaries Journal* 51, pp. 329–331.

Pallottino, M. *et al.*, 1979: *The Horses of San Marco, Venice* (London: Royal Academy of Arts).

Parker, H., 1992: 'Love's Body Anatomized: the Ancient Erotic Handbooks and the Rhetoric of Sexuality' in Richlin, A. (ed.), *Pornography and Representation in Greece and Rome* (Oxford University Press), pp. 90–111.

Parkin, T. G., 1997: 'Out of Sight, Out of Mind: Elderly Members of the Roman Family' in Rawson, B. and Weaver, P. (eds), *The Roman Family in Italy: Status, Sentiment and Space* (Oxford: Clarendon Press, Oxford), pp. 123–148.

Parkins, H. M., 1997: 'The "Consumer City" Domesticated? The Roman City in Elite Economic Strategies' in Parkins, H. M. (ed.), pp. 81–111.

Parkins, H. M. (ed.), 1997: *Roman Urbanism: Beyond the Consumer City* (London: Routledge).

Pearce, J., 1998: 'From Death to Deposition: the Sequence of Ritual in Cremation Burials of the Roman Period' in Forcey, C. *et al.* (eds), pp. 99–111.

Peirce, P., 1989: 'The Arch of Constantine: Propaganda and Ideology in Late Roman Art', *Art History* 12/4, pp. 387–418.

Penn, W. S., 1959: 'Springhead: the Temple Ditch Site', *Archaeologia Cantiana* 29, pp. 170–189.

Perec, G. and Bellos, D. (trans.), 1991: *Things: A Story of the Sixties* (London: Harvill).

Perring, D., 1977: 'Aspects of Art in Romano-British Pottery' in Munby, J. and Henig, M. (eds), pp. 253–282.

Pestilli, L., 2005: 'Disabled Bodies: The (Mis)Representation of the Lame in Antiquity and Their Reappearance in Early Christian and Medieval Art' in Hopkins, A. and Wyke, M. (eds), *Roman Bodies: Antiquity to the Eighteenth Century* (British School at Rome), pp. 85–99.

Phillips, E. J., 1976a: 'A Workshop of Roman Sculptors at Carlisle', *Britannia* VII, pp. 101–108.

Phillips, E. J., 1976b: 'A Roman Figured Capital in Cirencester', *Journal of the British Archaeological Association* CXXIX, pp. 35–41.

Phillips, E. J., 1977: *Corpus Signorum Imperii Romani, Great Britain Volume 1 Fascicule 1: Corbridge Hadrian's Wall East of the North Tyne* (Oxford University Press).

Philpott, R., 1991: 'Burial Practices in Roman Britain: A Survey of Grave Treatment and Furnishing AD 43–410', *British Archaeological Reports British Series* 219 (Oxford).

Pierson, S., 2007: *Collectors, Collections and Museums:The Field of Chinese Ceramics in Britain, 1560–1960* (Oxford: Peter Lang).

Pingeot, A. (ed.), 1990: *Le Corps en Morceaux* (Paris; Musée d'Orsay).

Pitts, L. F. and St Joseph, J. K., 1985: 'Inchtuthil: The Roman Legionary Fortress', *Britannia Monograph* 6 (London: Society for the Promotion of Roman Studies).

Pitts, M., 2010: 'Artefact Suites and Social Practice: an Integrated Approach to Roman Provincial Finds Assemblages', *Facta* 4, pp. 125–152.

Plouviez, J., 2005: 'Whose Good Luck? Roman Phallic Ornaments from Suffolk' in Crummy, N. (ed.), pp. 157–164.

Pollard, J. and Baker, P., 1999: 'Early Roman Activity at Keeley Lane, Wooton', *Bedfordshire Archaeology* 23, pp. 90–97.

Pollini, J., 1993: 'The Cartoceto Bronzes: Portraits of a Roman Aristocratic Family of the Late First
　　Century B.C', *American Journal of Archaeology* 97, pp. 423–446.
Pollitt, J. J., 1986: *Art in the Hellenistic Age* (Cambridge University Press).
Pomeroy, S. B. (ed.), 1991: *Women's History and Ancient History* (Chapel Hill, University of North
　　Carolina Press).
Pomian, K., 1990: *Collectors and Curiosities: Paris and Venice, 1500–1800* (Oxford: Polity Press in
　　association with Blackwell).
Potter, T., 1985: 'A Republican Healing Sanctuary at Ponte di Nona Near Rome and the Classical
　　Tradition of Votive Medicine', *Journal of the British Archaeological Association* 138, pp. 23–47.
Poulton, R. and Scott, E., 1993: 'The Hoarding, Deposition and Use of Pewter in Roman Britain'
　　in Scott, E. (ed.), *Theoretical Roman Archaeology Conference First Conference Proceedings*
　　(Aldershot: Avebury), pp. 115–132.
Price, J., 1974: 'A Roman Mould-Blown Negro-Head Glass Beaker from London', *Antiquaries Journal*
　　54, pp. 291–292.
Proust, M., Scott, C. K. and Kilmartin T. (trans.), 1922: *Cities of the Plain: In Remembrance of Things
　　Past Volume 3* (Harmondsworth: Penguin).
Pugsley, P., 2003: 'Roman Domestic Wood: Analysis of the Morphology, Manufacture and Use of
　　Selected Categories of Domestic Wooden Artefacts with Particular Reference to the Material from
　　Roman Britain', *British Archaeological Reports International Series* 1118 (Oxford).
Purcell, N., 1990: 'The Creation of Provincial Landscape. The Roman Impact on Cisalpine Gaul' in
　　Blagg, T. F. C. and Millett, M. (eds), pp. 7–29.
Rabinowitz, N. S. and Richlin, A. (eds), 1993: *Feminist Theory and the Classics* (London: Routledge).
Rambaud, M., 1978: 'Masques et Imagines: Essai sur Certains Usages Funéraires de l'Afrique Noire et
　　de la Rome Ancienne', *Les Études Classiques* 46, pp. 3–21.
Rautman, A. E., 2000: *Reading the Body: Representations and Remains in the Archaeological Record*
　　(University of Pennsylvania Press).
Raybould, M. E., 1999: 'A Study of Inscribed Material from Roman Britain: an Enquiry into Some
　　Aspects of Literacy in Romano-British Society', *British Archaeological Reports British Series* 281
　　(Oxford: Archaeopress).
Reece, R., 1990: 'Romanization: a Point of View' in Blagg, T. F. C. and Millett, M. (eds), pp. 30–34.
Rees, H., Crummy, N., Ottaway, P. J. and Dunn, G., 2008: *Artefacts and Society in Roman and
　　Medieval Winchester: Small Finds from the Suburbs and Defences, 1971–1986* (Winchester
　　Museums Service).
Revell, L., 1999: 'Roman Public Architecture and the Archaeology of Practice' in Barker, P. *et al.* (eds),
　　pp. 52–58.
Rey-Vodoz, V., 1991: 'Les Offrandes dans la Sanctuaires Gallo-Romains' in Brunaux, J. L. (ed.) *Les
　　Sanctuaires Celtiques et Leurs Rapport avec le Monde Méditerranéen: Dossiers de Protohistoire*
　　(Paris: Errance), pp. 215–220.
RIB I, 1965: *The Roman Inscriptions of Britain: Volume I Inscriptions on Stone*, R. G. Collingwood
　　and R. P. Wright (Oxford: Clarendon Press).
RIB II, 1991: *The Roman Inscriptions of Britain: Volume II Instrumentum Domesticum, Fascicules
　　1–8*, S. S. Frere and R. S. O. Tomlin (Gloucester: Alan Sutton).
RIB III, 2009: *The Roman Inscriptions of Britain: Volume III Inscriptions on Stone Found or Notified
　　Between 1 January 1955 and 31 December 2006*, R. S. O. Tomlin, R. P. Wright and M. W. C.
　　Hassall (Oxford: Oxbow Books).
Richlin, A., 1992a: *The Garden of Priapus: Sexuality and Aggression in Roman Humour* (2nd ed.)
　　(Oxford University Press).
Richlin, A. (ed.), 1992b: *Pornography and Representation in Greece and Rome* (Oxford University Press).
Richlin, A., 1997: 'Towards a History of Body History' in Golden, M. and Toohey, P. (eds), *Inventing
　　Ancient Culture: Historicism, Periodization, and the Ancient World* (London: Routledge), pp.
　　16–35.
Richmond, I. A., 1980: 'A Roman Fort at Inveresk, Midlothian', *Proceedings of the Society of
　　Antiquaries of Scotland* 110, pp. 286–304.
Richmond, I. A. and Wright, R. P., 1948: 'Two Roman Shrines to Vinotonus on Scargill Moor, near
　　Bowes', *Yorkshire Archaeological Journal* 37, pp. 107–116.
Rivet, A. L. F. (ed.), 1969: *The Roman Villa in Britain* (London: Routledge & Kegan Paul).
Robinson, P., 1995: 'Miniature Socketed Bronze Axes from Wiltshire', *Wiltshire Archaeological and
　　Natural History Magazine* 88, pp. 60–68.
Rodgers, R., 2003: 'Female Representation in Roman Art; Feminising the Provincial "Other"' in Scott,
　　S. and Webster, J. (eds), pp. 69–93.
Rodwell, K. A., 1988: 'The Prehistoric and Roman Settlement at Kelvedon, Essex', *Council for British
　　Archaeology Research Report* 63 (York).
Rodwell, W. J. (ed.), 1980: 'Temples, Churches and Religion in Roman Britain', *British Archaeological
　　Reports British Series* 77 (Oxford).

Rogers, A., 2011: *Late Roman Towns in Britain: Rethinking Change and Decline* (Cambridge University Press).

Rollason, D., 1986: 'The Shrines of the Saints in Later Anglo-Saxon England: Distribution and Significance' in Butler, L. A. S. and Morris, R. K. (eds), pp. 32–43.

Rollason, D., 1989: *Saints and Relics in Anglo-Saxon England* (Oxford: Blackwell).

Romeuf, A-M., 2000: *Les Ex-Voto Gallo-Romaine de Chamalières (Puy-de-Dôme): Les Bois Sculptés de la Source des Roches* (Paris).

Ross, A., 1980: 'A Pagan Celtic Shrine at Wall, Staffordshire', *Transactions of the South Staffordshire Archaeological and Historical Society* 11, pp. 3–11.

Ross, A. and Feachem, R., 1976: 'Ritual Rubbish? The Newstead Pits' in Megaw, J. V. S. (ed.), *To Illustrate the Monuments* (London: Thames & Hudson), pp. 230–237.

Rousselle, A., 1988: *Porneia: On Desire and the Body in Antiquity* (Oxford: Blackwell).

Rowlands, M., 1993: 'The Role of Memory in the Transmission of Culture', *World Archaeology* 25(2), pp. 141–151.

Royer, E. and Bigot, J., 2005: *Saints en Bretagne: Glanes de Légendes* (Jean-Paul Gisserot).

Roymans, N., 1995: 'The Cultural Biography of Urnfields and the Long-Term History of Mythical Landscapes', *Archaeological Dialogues* 2(1), pp. 2–25.

Rush, P. (ed.), 1995: 'Theoretical Roman Archaeology Second Conference Proceedings, Bradford 1994', *Worldwide Archaeology Series* 14 (Aldershot: Avebury).

Rykwert, J., 1976: *The Idea of a Town: The Anthropology of Urban Form in Rome, Italy and the Ancient World* (London: Faber & Faber).

Saller, R. P., 1994: *Patriarchy, Property and Death in the Roman Family* (Cambridge University Press).

Sanjuan, L. G., Gonzalez, P. G. and Gomez, F. L., 2008: 'The Use of Prehistoric Ritual and Funerary Sites in Roman Spain: Discussing Tradition, Memory and Identity' in Fenwick, C., Wiggins, M. and Wythe, D. (eds), *2007 TRAC 2007 Proceedings of the Seventeenth Annual Theoretical Roman Archaeology Conference: UCL London* (Oxford: Oxbow Book), pp. 1–13.

Sauer, E., 2003: *The Archaeology of Religious Hatred in the Roman and Early Medieval World* (Stroud: Tempus).

Saville, A., 1981: 'Iron Age Flint Working – Fact or Fiction?', *Lithics* 2, pp. 6–9.

Scheff, T. J., 1979: *Catharsis in Healing, Ritual and Drama* (University of California Press).

Schnapp, A., 1996: *The Discovery of the Past* (British Museum Press).

Schofield, J. and Leech, R. (eds), 1987: 'Urban Archaeology in Britain', *Council for British Archaeology Research Report* 61 (York).

Score, V., 2006: 'Rituals, Hoards and Helmets: a Ceremonial Meeting Place of the Corieltavi', *Transactions of the Leicestershire Archaeological and Historical Society* 80, pp. 197–207.

Scott, E., 1991: 'Animal and Infant Burials in Romano-British Villas: a Revitalization Movement?' in Garwood, P. *et al.* (eds), pp. 115–121.

Scott, S., 1993: 'A Theoretical Framework for the Study of Romano-British Villa Mosaics' in Scott, E. (ed.), pp. 103–114.

Scott, S., 1995: 'Symbols of Power and Nature: the Orpheus Mosaics of Fourth Century Britain and Their Architectural Contexts' in Rush, P. (ed.), pp. 105–123.

Scott, S. and Webster, J. (eds), 2003: *Roman Imperialism and Provincial Art* (Cambridge University Press).

Sebesta, J. L. and Bonfante, L. (eds), 1994: *The World of Roman Costume* (Wisconsin University Press).

Sedley, D., 1982: 'The Stoic Criterion of Identity', *Phronesis* 27, pp. 255–75.

Sherwin White, A. N., 1967: *Racial Prejudice in Imperial Rome* (Cambridge University Press).

Sigerist, H. E., 1960: 'The Special Position of the Sick'. Reprinted in Landy, D. (ed.), 1977: *Culture, Disease and Healing: Studies in Medical Anthropology* (London: MacMilland), pp. 388–394.

Simon, M. (ed.), 2011: *Identités Romaines: Conscience de Soi, et Représentations de l'Autre dans la Rome Antique* (Paris: Presses de l'ENS).

Simpson, G. and Blance, B., 1998: 'Do Brooches Have Ritual Associations?' in Bird, J. (ed.) 'Form and Fabric: Studies in Rome's Material Past in Honour of B. R. Hartley', *Oxbow Monograph* 80 (Oxford: Oxbow Books), pp. 267–279.

Small, J. P., 1997: *Wax Tablets of the Mind: Cognitive Studies of Memory and Literacy in Classical Antiquity* (London: Routledge).

Small, J. P. and Tatum, J., 1995: 'Memory and the Study of Classical Antiquity', *Helios* 22, pp. 149–177.

Smith, A., 2001: 'The Differential Use of Constructed Social Space in Southern Britain from the Late Iron Age to the 4th Century A.D', *British Archaeological Reports British Series* 318 (Oxford: Archaeopress).

Smith, D. J., 1969: 'The Mosaic Pavements' in Rivet, A. L. F. (ed.), pp. 71–125.

Smith, D. J. 1984: 'Roman Mosaics in Britain: a Synthesis' in Farioli Campanati, R., pp. 357–380.

Snowden, F. M., 1970: *Blacks in Antiquity: Ethiopians in the Greco-Roman Experience* (Harvard University Press).

Snowden, F. M., 1976: 'Iconographical Evidence on the Black Populations in Greco-Roman Antiquity' in Vercouter, J., *et al.* (eds), pp. 133–245.

Snowden, F. M., 1983: *Before Color Prejudice: The Ancient View of Blacks.* (Harvard University Press).

Snowden, F. M., 1997: 'Greeks and Ethiopians' in Coleman, J. E. And Walz, C. A. (eds) 'Greeks and Barbarians. Essays on the Interactions Between Greeks and Non-Greeks in Antiquity and the Consequences for Eurocentrism', *Occasional Publications of the Department of Near Eastern Studies and the Program of Jewish Studies, Cornell University* 4 (Maryland: CDL Press), pp. 103–126.

Sommella, A. M. (ed.), 1990: *The Equestrian Statue of Marcus Aurelius in Camidoglio* (Milan: Silvana Editoriale).

Southwell-Wright, W., 2010: *Approaching Disability in Roman Britain*, Unpublished MA thesis (UCL Institute of Archaeology).

Spence, J. D., 1985: *The Memory Palace of Matteo Ricci* (London: Faber & Faber).

Spender, S., 1951: *World Within Worlds* (London: Hamish Hamilton).

Stacey, M., 1999: *The Black Presence: The Representation of Black People in the Paintings of National Museums and Galleries on Merseyside* (Liverpool).

Stafford, B. M., 1993: 'Presuming Images and Consuming Words: the Visualization of Knowledge from the Enlightenment to Post-Modernism' in Brewer, J. and Porter, R. (eds), pp. 462–477.

Stead, I. M., 1998: *The Salisbury Hoard* (Stroud: Tempus).

Stella, C., 1998: *Brescia: L'Età Romana Santa Giulia Museo della Città* (Milan).

Stella, C., Valvo, A., and Morandini, F., 1998: *L'Età Romana, La Città, Le Iscrizioni: Bresica, Santa Giulia Museo della Città* (Milan: Electa).

Stewart, P., 2003: *Statues in Roman Society: Representation and Response* (Oxford University Press).

Stewart, P., 2010: 'Geographies of Provincialism in Roman Sculpture', *RIHA Journal* 0005 (http:www.riha-journal.org/articles/2010/stewart-geographies-of-provincialism. Accessed 7/1/2011).

van Straten, F. T., 1981: 'Gifts for the Gods' in Versnel, H. S. (ed.), *Faith, Hope and Worship: Aspects of Religious Mentality in the Ancient World* (Leiden: Brill), pp. 65–151.

Strong, D. E., 1966: *Greek and Roman Gold and Silver Plate* (London: Methuen & Co.).

Strong, D. E., 1973: 'Roman Museums' in Strong, D. E. (ed.), *Archaeological Theory and Practice: Essays Presented to Professor W. F. Grimes* (London: Seminar Press), pp. 247–264.

Stucchi, S., 1960: 'Gruppo Bronzeo di Cartoceto: Gli Elementi al Museo di Ancona', *Bolletino d'Arte* 45, pp. 7–44.

Stucchi, S., 1987: 'Interpretazione e Datazione dei Bronzi da Cartoceto' in del Francia, P. R. (ed.), *Bronzi Dorati da Cartoceto di Pergola* (Firenze), pp. 51–61.

Stucchi, S., 1988: *Il Gruppo Bronzeo Tiberiano da Cartoceto* (Rome).

Sunter, N. and Woodward, P., 1987: 'Romano-British Industries in Purbeck', *Dorset Natural History and Archaeological Society Monograph* 6 (Dorchester).

Swan, V. G., 1992: 'Legio VI and its Men: African Legionaries in Britain', *Journal of Roman Pottery Studies* 5, pp. 1–33.

Swan, V. G., 1999: 'The Twentieth Legion and the History of the Antonine Wall Reconsidered', *Proceedings of the Society of Antiquaries of Scotland* 129, pp. 399–480.

Swan, V. G., 2009: 'Ethnicity, Conquest and Recruitment: Two Case Studies from the Northern Military Provinces', *Journal of Roman Archaeology Supplement* 72.

Swift, E., 2009: *Style and Function in Roman Decoration: Living with Objects and Interiors* (Farnham: Ashgate).

Taylor, A., 1993: 'A Roman Lead Coffin With Pipeclay Figurines from Arrington, Cambridgeshire', *Britannia* XXIV, pp. 191–227.

Taylor, A., 1997: 'A Roman Child Burial with Animal Figurines and Pottery, from Godmanchester Cambridgeshire', *Britannia* XXVIII, pp. 386–393.

Taylor, M. V., 1963: 'Statuettes of Horsemen and Horses and Other Votive Objects from Brigstock, Northamptonshire', *Antiquaries Journal* XLIII, pp. 264–268.

Thomas, C., 1981: *Christianity in Roman Britain to AD500* (London: Batsford).

Thomas, G. D., 1988: 'Excavations at the Roman Civil Settlement at Inveresk 1976–1977', *Proceedings of the Society of Antiquaries of Scotland* 118.

Thompson, L. A., 1989: *Romans and Blacks* (University of Oklahoma Press).

Thomson de Grummond, N., 2011: 'A Barbarian Myth? The Case of the Talking Head' in Bonfante, L. (ed.), *The Barbarians of Ancient Europe: Realities and Interactions* (Cambridge University Press), pp. 313–347.

Tilley, C., 1991: *Material Culture and Text: the Art of Ambiguity* (London: Routledge).

Tilley, C., 1999: *Metaphor and Material Culture* (Oxford: Blackwell).

Tilley, C., Keane, W., Kuechler, S., Rowlands, M. and Spyer, P. (eds), 2006: *Sage Handbook of Material Culture* (London: Routledge).

Todd, M., 1989: 'The Early Cities' in Todd, M. (ed.), pp. 75–90.

Todd, M. (ed.), 1989: 'Research on Roman Britain 1960–1989', *Britannia Monograph* 11 (London: Society for the Promotion of Roman Studies).

Tollia-Kelly, D. P. and Nesbitt, C., 2009: *An Archaeology of Race: Exploring the Northern Frontier in Roman Britain* (Durham University).

Tomlin, R. S. O., 1995: 'A Five-Acre Wood in Roman Kent' in Bird, J., Hassall, M. and Sheldon, H. (eds), 'Interpreting Roman London: Papers in Memory of Hugh Chapman', *Oxbow Monograph* 58 (Oxford: Oxbow Books, Oxford), pp. 209–215.

Tomlin, R. S. O., 2002: 'Writing to the Gods in Britain' in Cooley, A. (ed.), pp. 165–179.

Torelli, M., 1987: 'Statue Equestris Inaurata Caesaris: Mos and Ius in the Statue of Marcus Aurelius', in Vaccaro, A. M. and Sommella, A. M. (eds), *Marcus Aurelius: History of a Monument and its Restoration* (Milan), pp. 83–102.

Toynbee, J. M. C., 1962: *Art in Roman Britain* (London: Phaidon).

Toynbee, J. M. C., 1964: *Art in Britain Under the Romans* (Oxford: Clarendon Press).

Toynbee, J. M. C., 1986: 'The Roman Art Treasures from the Temple of Mithras', *London and Middlesex Archaeological Society Special Paper 7*.

Tufi, S. R., 1983: *Corpus Signorum Imperii Romani, Great Britain Volume 1 Fascicule 3: Yorkshire* (Oxford University Press).

Turnbull, P., 1978: 'The Phallus in the Art of Roman Britain', *Bulletin of the Institute of Archaeology* 15, pp. 199–206.

Turner, R., 1999: 'Excavations of an Iron Age Settlement and Roman Religious Complex at Ivy Chimneys, Witham, Essex 1978–83', *East Anglian Archaeology Report 88*.

Turner, R. and Wymer, J. J., 1987: 'An Assemblage of Palaeolithic Hand-Axes from the Roman Religious Complex at Ivy Chimneys, Witham, Essex', *Antiquaries Journal* 117, pp. 43–60.

Uhlenbrock, J. P., 1986: *Herakles: Passage of the Hero Through 1000 Years of Classical Art* (New York: Aristide D. Caratzas).

Van Bremen, R., 1983: 'Women and Wealth' in Cameron, A. and Kuhrt, A. (eds), *Images of Women in Antiquity* (London: Routledge), pp. 223–242.

Van Bremen, R., 1996: *The Limits of Participation: Women and Civic Life in the Greek East in the Hellenistic and Roman Periods* (Amsterdam: J. C. Gieben).

Van Dyke, R. and Alcock, S., 2003: 'Archaeologies of Memory: an Introduction' in Van Dyke, R. and Alcock, S. (eds), *Archaeologies of Memory* (London: Routledge), pp. 1–13.

Varner, E. R., 2000: *From Caligula to Constantine: Tyranny and Transformation in Roman Portraiture* (Michael C. Carlos Museum, Emory University).

Varner, E., 2001: 'Portraits, Plots and Politics: Damnatio Memoriae and the Images of Imperial Women', *Memoirs of the American Academy in Rome* XLVI, pp. 41–93.

Varner, E. R., 2004: *Mutilation and Transformation: Damnatio Memoriae and Roman Imperial Portraiture* (Leiden: Brill).

Vercouter, J., Leclant, J., Snowden, F. M. and Desanges, J. (eds), 1976: *The Image of the Black in Western Art, Volume 1: From the Pharaohs to the Fall of the Roman Empire* (Harvard University Press).

Vermeule, C. C., 1968: *Roman Imperial Art in Greece and Asia Minor* (Harvard University Press).

Vermeule, C. C., 1981: *Greek and Roman Sculpture in America: Masterpieces in Public Collections in the United States and Canada* (University of California Press).

Versnel, H. S. (ed.), 1991: *Faith, Hope and Worship: Aspects of Religious Mentality in the Ancient World* (Leiden: Brill).

Vickery, A., 1994: 'Women and the World of Goods: a Lancashire Consumer and Her Possessions, 1751–81' in Brewer, J. and Porter, R. (eds), pp. 274–297.

Vikan, G., 2010: *Early Byzantine Pilgrimage Art: Revised edition* (Washington: Dumbarton Oaks).

Vlad, L. B., 1979: Fogolari, G. and Toniato, A. G., 'The Stylistic Problem of the Horses of San Marco' in Pallottino, M. *et al.*, pp. 15–44.

Vlahogiannis, N., 1998: 'Disabling Bodies' in Montserrat, D. (ed.), pp. 13–37.

Voisin, J-L., 2007: 'Têtes Coupées Antiques. Face à Face, Textes et Images', *Textes-Images: 4th Colloque Interdisciplinaire* (Musées d'Auxerre: Icône-Image).

Vout, C., 2007: *Power and Eroticism in Imperial Rome* (Cambridge University Press).

de Waal, E., 2010: *The Hare with Amber Eyes: a Hidden Inheritance* (London: Chatto & Windus).

Wace, A. J. B., 1949: 'The Greeks and Romans as Archaeologists', *Bulletin de la Société Royale d'Archaeologie d'Alexandrie* 38, pp. 21–35.

Wacher, J., 1974 and 1995: *The Towns of Roman Britain* (First and Second Editions) (London: Batsford).

Wait, G. A., 1985: 'Ritual and Religion in Iron Age Britain', *British Archaeological Reports British Series* 149 (Oxford).

Walker, S., 1985: *Memorials to the Roman Dead* (British Museum Press).

Walker, S., 1995: *Greek and Roman Portraits* (British Museum Press).

Walker, S., 2000: 'The Moral Museum: Augustus and the City of Rome' in Coulston, J. and Dodge, H. (eds), *Ancient Rome: The Archaeology of the Eternal City* (Oxford University School of Archaeology), pp. 61–75.

Wallace, C., 1995: 'Gallo-Roman Clay Figurines', *Roman Finds Group Newsletter* 10, pp. 2–5.
Walters, J., 1997: 'Invading the Roman Body: Manliness and Impenetrability in Roman Thought' in
    Hallett, J. P. and Skinner, M. B. (eds), pp. 29–43.
Walters, J., 1997: 'Manhood in the Graeco-Roman World' in Wyke, M. (ed.), pp. 191–193.
Watts, D., 1991: *Christians and Pagans in Roman Britain* (London: Routledge).
Watts, L. and Leach, P. J., 1996: 'Henley Wood, Temples and Cemetery Excavations 1962–1969 by the
    Late Ernest Greenfield', *Council for British Archaeology Research Report* 99 (York).
Weatherill, L., 1986: 'A Possession of One's Own: Women and Consumer Behavior in England, 1660–
    1740', *Journal of British Studies* 25(2), pp. 131–156.
Weatherill, L., 1996: *Consumer Behaviour and Material Culture in Britain 1660–1760* (2nd ed.)
    (London: Routledge).
Webster, G. 1983: 'The Function of Chedworth Roman "Villa"', *Transactions of the Bristol and
    Gloucestershire Archaeological Society* 101, pp. 5–20.
Webster, G., 1986: 'What the Britons Required from the Gods as Seen Through the Pairing of Roman and
    Celtic Deities and the Character of Votive Offerings' in Henig, M. and King, A. (eds), pp. 57–64.
Webster, G., 1989: 'Deities and Religious Scenes on Romano-British Pottery', *Journal of Roman Pottery
    Studies* 2, pp. 1–28.
Webster, G., 1991: 'Romano-British Scenes and Figures on Pottery' in Webster, G., *Archaeologist at
    Large* (London: Batsford), pp. 129–162.
Webster, J. and Cooper, N. (eds), 1996: 'Roman Imperialism: Post-Colonial Perspectives', *Leicester
    Archaeology Monographs* 3 (School of Archaeological Studies, University of Leicester).
Wedlake, W. J., 1982: 'The Excavation of the Shrine of Apollo at Nettleton, Wiltshire 1956–1971',
    Report of the Research Committee of the Society of Antiquaries of London 15 (London).
Wellcome Collection, 2011: *Charmed Life: The Solace of Objects, An Exhibition by Felicity Powell*
    (London: Wellcome Collection).
Wheeler, R. E. M. and Wheeler, T. V., 1932: 'Report on the Excavation of the Prehistoric, Roman,
    and Post-Roman Site in Lydney Park, Gloucestershire', *Society of Antiquaries of London Research
    Reports* 9 (London).
Wheeler, R. E. M. and Wheeler, T. V., 1936: 'Verulamium: A Belgic and Two Roman Cities', *Society of
    Antiquaries of London Research Reports* 11 (London).
White, R., 1988: 'Roman and Celtic Objects from Anglo-Saxon Graves: A Catalogue and Interpretation
    of Their Use', *British Archaeological Reports British Series* 191 (Oxford).
Whitehouse, R. D. 1996: 'Ritual Objects: Archaeological Joke or Neglected Evidence?' in Wilkins, J. B.
    (ed.), *Approaches to the Study of Ritual: Italy and the Ancient Mediterranean* (London: Accordia
    Research Centre), pp. 9–30.
Whittaker, C. R., 1997: 'Imperialism and Culture: the Roman Initiative' in Mattingly, D. J. (ed.), pp.
    143–164.
Wild, J. P., 1968: 'Clothing in the North-West Provinces of the Roman Empire', *Bonner Jahrbücher*
    168, pp. 166–240.
Wilfong, T., 1998: 'Reading the Disjointed Body in Coptic: from Physical Modification to Textual
    Fragmentation' in Montserrat, D. (ed.), pp. 116–38.
Williams, H. M. R., 1998a: 'The Ancient Monument in Romano-British Ritual Practices' in Forcey, C.
    et al. (eds), pp. 71–86.
Williams, H. M. R., 1998b: 'Monuments and the Past in Early Anglo-Saxon England', *World
    Archaeology* 30, pp. 90–108.
Williams, H. M. R. (ed.), 2003: *Archaeologies of Remembrance: Death and Memory in Past Societies*
    (New York: Plenum).
Williams, H. M. R., 2004: 'Ephemeral Monuments and Social Memory in Early Roman Britain',
    in Croxford, B., Eckardt, H., Meade, J. and Weekes, J. (eds), *TRAC 2003: Proceedings of the
    Thirteenth Annual Theoretical Roman Archaeology Conference, Leicester 2003* (Oxford: Oxbow
    Books), pp. 51–61.
Willis, S., 2006: 'The Context of Writing and Written Records in Ink: the Archaeology of Samian
    Inkwells in Roman Britain', *Archaeological Journal* 162, pp. 96–145.
Wilmott, A., 1991: 'Excavations in the Middle Walbrook Valley, City of London, 1927–1960', *London
    and Middlesex Archaeological Society Special Papers* 13.
Wilmott, A., 2008: *The Roman Amphitheatre in Britain* (Stroud: Tempus).
Wilson, P. R., 2002: 'Cataractonium, Roman Catterick and its Hinterland: Excavations and Research
    1958–1997', *Council for British Archaeology Research Report* 128 (York).
Wilson, R. J. A., 2003: 'The Rudston Venus Mosaic Revisited: a Spear-Bearing Lion', *Britannia* XXXIV,
    pp. 288–291.
Wilson, R. J. A., 2006: 'Aspects of Iconography in Romano-British Mosaics: the Rudston "Aquatic"
    Scene and the Brading Astronomer Revisited', *Britannia* XXXVII, pp. 295–336.
Winter, I., 1996: 'Sex, Rhetoric, and the Public Monument: the Alluring Body of Naram-Sîn of Agade'
    in Kampen, N. B. (ed.), pp. 11–26.

Wood, S. E., 1998: *Imperial Women: A Study in Public Images, 40 BC–AD 68* (Leiden: Brill).
Woodward, A., 1992: *Shrines and Sacrifice* (London: Batsford).
Woodward, A., 1993: 'The Cult of Relics in Prehistoric Britain' in Carver, M. O. H. (ed.), *In Search of Cult: Archaeological Investigations in Honour of Philip Rahtz* (Woodbridge: The Boydell Press), pp. 1–7.
Woodward, A. and Leach, P. J., 1993: *The Uley Shrines: Excavation of a Ritual Complex on West Hill, Uley, Gloucestershire 1977–1979* (London: English Heritage).
Woolf, G., 1992: 'The Unity and Diversity of Romanisation', *Journal of Roman Archaeology* 5, pp. 349–352.
Woolf, G., 1995: 'Romans as Civilizers: The Ideological Pre-Conditions of Romanization' in Metzler, J. *et al.* (eds), pp. 9–18.
Woolf, G., 1998: *Becoming Roman: The Origins of Provincial Civilisation in Gaul* (Cambridge University Press).
Woolf, G., 2000: 'Urbanization and its Discontents in Early Roman Gaul' in Fentress, E. (ed.), pp. 115–132.
Wyke, M. (ed.), 1998: *Gender and the Body in the Ancient Mediterranean* (Oxford: Blackwell).
Yegül, F. K., 2000: 'Memory, Metaphor and Meaning in the Cities of Asia Minor' in Fentress, E. (ed.) pp. 133–153.
Young, R. and Humphrey, J., 1999: 'Flint Use in Britain After the Bronze Age: Time for a Re-evaluation', *Proceedings of the Prehistoric Society* 65, pp. 231–242.
Zanker, P., 1988: *The Power of Images in the Age of Augustus* (University of Michigan Press).
Zanker, P., 1998: *Die Barbaren, der Kaiser und die Arena: Bilder der Gewalt in der Römischen Kunst.* Reprinted in translation as 2002: *I barbari, l'imperatore e l'arena: immagini di violenza nell'arte Romana* in Zanker, P., pp. 38–62.
Zanker, P., 2000a: *Die Frauen und Kinder der Barbaren auf der Markussäule.* Reprinted in translation as 2002: *Le donne e i bambini sui rilievi della colonna Aureliana* in Zanker, P., pp. 63–78.
Zanker, P., 2000b: 'Rome and the Creation of an Urban Image' in Fentress, E. (ed.), pp. 25–41.
Zanker, P., 2002: *Un'arte per l'impero: Funzione e intenzione delle immagini nel mondo Romano* (Milan: Electa).
Zienkiewicz, J. D., 1986: *The Legionary Fortress Baths at Caerleon, Volume 2: The Finds* (Cardiff: Cadw).

LIST OF IMAGES

Figures (embedded in text)

1.   A sherd of Samian pottery from Binchester Roman fort, County Durham decorated with an arena bull-leaping scene. (Drawn by Sandy Morris. From Ferris 2010, Fig. 63 No. 27)
2.   Distribution map of horse and rider brooches in Britain. (Drawn by Ruth Fillery-Travis. From Fillery-Travis Forthcoming, Fig. 2)
3.   The spatial distribution of votive objects at the temple site of West Hill, Uley, Gloucestershire. (From Woodward and Leach 1993, Fig. 225)
4.   Reconstruction drawing of the cult statue of Mercury from the temple site of West Hill, Uley, Gloucestershire. (Drawn by Joanna Richards. From Woodward and Leach 1993, Fig. 76)
5.   Layout of the enclosures at Orton's Pasture, Rocester, Staffordshire. (Drawn by Mark Breedon. From Ferris *et al.* 2000, Fig. 4)
6.   Spatial distribution of finds at Orton's Pasture, Rocester, Staffordshire. (Drawn by Mark Breedon. From Ferris *et al.* 2000, Fig. 34)
7.   A carved jet dog, possibly a knife handle, from Binchester, County Durham. (Drawn by Sandy Morris)
8.   Some cast lead model legs from West Hill, Uley temple site, Gloucestershire. (From Woodward and Leach 1993, Fig. 88)
9.   A copper alloy leg and arm from Verulamium, Hertfordshire. (From Frere 1972, Fig. 49)
10. Roman glass beads from Binchester Roman fort, County Durham. Nos 372, 378, and 398 were reused in an Anglo-Saxon necklace and placed in a burial of the mid-sixth century here. (Drawn by Mark Breedon, John Halstead *et al.* In Ferris 2010, Fig. 86)
11. *Graffiti* caricatures from 1. London, 2. Blackwardine, Herefordshire and 3. Binchester, County Durham. (Compiled from RIB II 2503.100, RIB II 2417.4, and Ferris 2010, Fig. 71 No. 14)
12. Broken Pseudo-Venus pipeclay figurines from Mill Street site in Caerleon, Gwent, Wales. (From Evans 2000, Fig. 72)
13. A selection of phallic objects from Suffolk. (Drawn by Donna Wreathall. Copyright Suffolk County Council. From Plouviez 2005, Fig. 1)
14. Copper alloy hand and phallus amulets from Catterick, North Yorkshire. (Drawn by Eddie Lyons. Copyright English Heritage. From Wilson 2002, Fig. 260)
15. A copper alloy figurine of a sleeping black African youth from near Saffron Walden, Essex. (PAS-ESS-6F60D3. Drawn by I. Bell: Copyright Essex County Council and Portable Antiquities Scheme)

Plates (in separate section at pp. 96–97)

1.   Giovanni Bellini and Titian *The Feast of the Gods* 1514. (National Gallery of Art, Washington)
2.   The Indian triumph of Bacchus portrayed on a two-handled ceramic vessel from the Roman necropolis of Lugone, Salò, Lombardy, Italy. (Photo: Civic Archaeological Museum of Valle Sabbia, Gavardo)
3.   Bacchic and marine scenes on the great silver dish from the Mildenhall Treasure from Suffolk. (Photo: Copyright Trustees of the British Museum)
4.   Marble statuette of Bacchus and feline companion from a grave near Spoonley Wood villa, Gloucestershire. (Photo: Copyright Trustees of the British Museum)
5.   A Bacchic motif on a copper alloy jug handle from the New Cemetery site, Rocester, Staffordshire. (Photo: Graham Norrie)
6.   Head of a Bacchic Medusa on the central medallion of a copper alloy *patera* from Faversham, Kent. (Photo: Copyright Trustees of the British Museum)
7.   Bacchus on the handle of a copper alloy *patera* from Brompton, Shropshire. (Photo: Graham Norrie)

INDEX

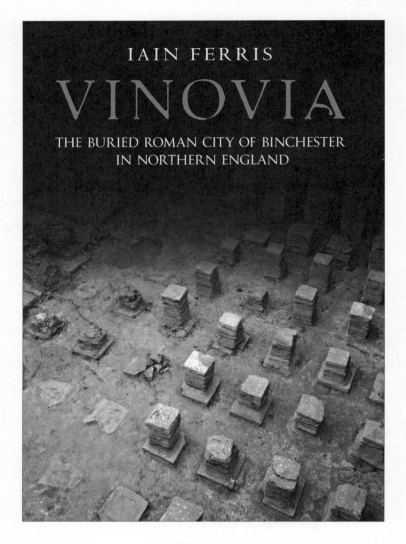

IAIN FERRIS

VINOVIA

THE BURIED ROMAN CITY OF BINCHESTER
IN NORTHERN ENGLAND